SAKURA TAISEN

Vol. 4

Story by
Ohji Hiroi

Art by
Ikku Masa

Characters by
Kosuke Fujishima

HAMBURG // LONDON // LOS ANGELES // TOKYO

Sakura Taisen Vol.4
Story by Ohji Hiroi
Art by Ikku Masa
Characters by Kosuke Fujishima

Translation - Yuko Fukami
Rewriter - Lillian Diaz-Przybyl
Retouch and Lettering - Nancy Star
Production Artist - Kimie Kim
Graphic Designer - James Lee

Editor - Katherine Schilling
Digital Imaging Manager - Chris Buford
Pre-Production Supervisor - Erika Terriquez
Art Director - Anne Marie Horne
Production Manager - Elisabeth Brizzi
VP of Production - Ron Klamert
Editor-in-Chief - Rob Tokar
Publisher - Mike Kiley
President and C.O.O. - John Parker
C.E.O. and Chief Creative Officer - Stuart Levy

A  Manga

TOKYOPOP Inc.
5900 Wilshire Blvd. Suite 2000
Los Angeles, CA 90036

E-mail: info@TOKYOPOP.com
Come visit us online at www.TOKYOPOP.com

ISBN: 1-59816-800-2

First TOKYOPOP printing: December 2006
10 9 8 7 6 5 4 3 2 1
Printed in the USA

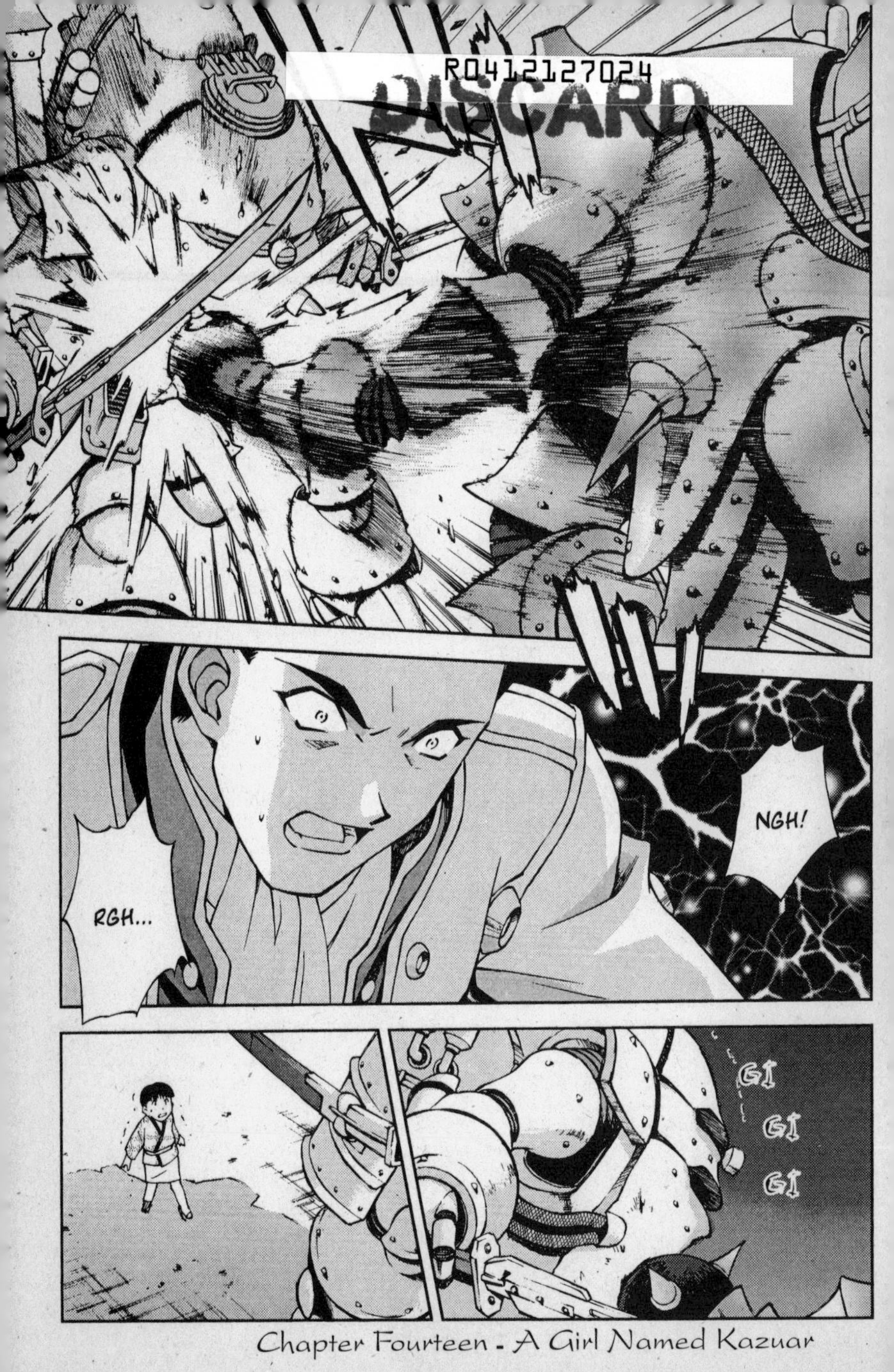
NGH!
RGH...
GI
GI
GI

Chapter Fourteen - A Girl Named Kazuar

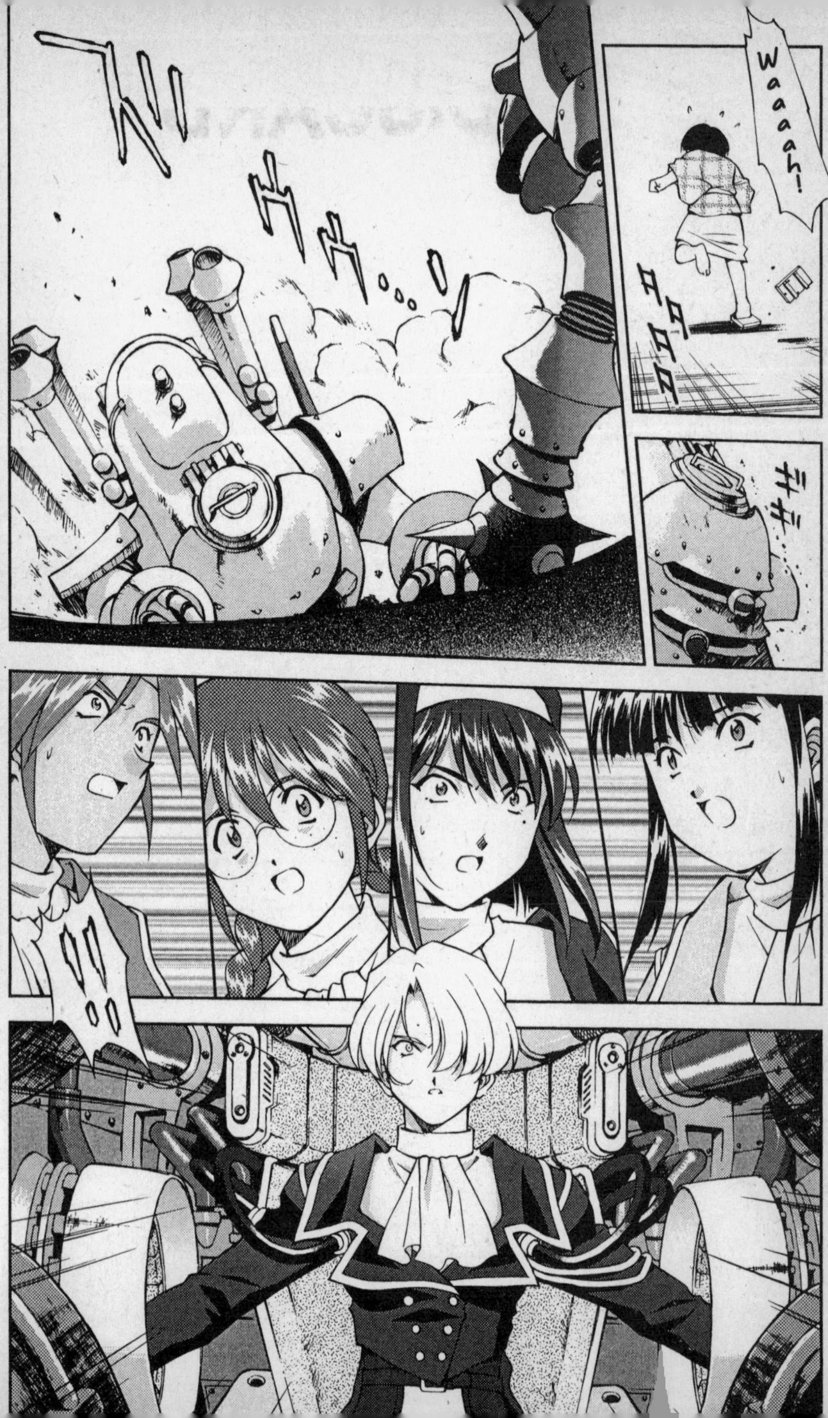
Waaaah!
ギギ

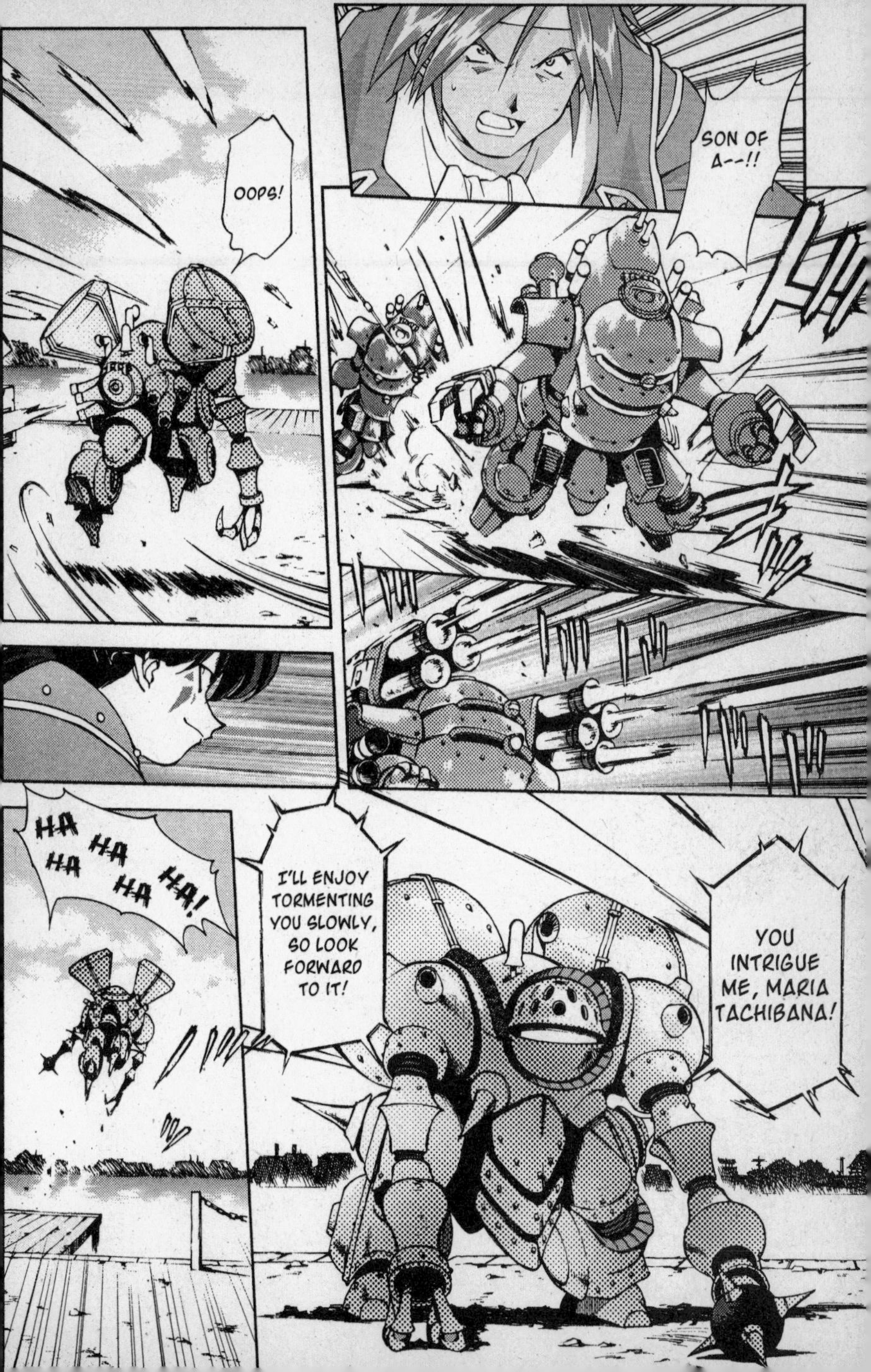
SON OF A--!!
OOPS!
YOU INTRIGUE ME, MARIA TACHIBANA!
I'LL ENJOY TORMENTING YOU SLOWLY, SO LOOK FORWARD TO IT!
HA HA HA HA HA!

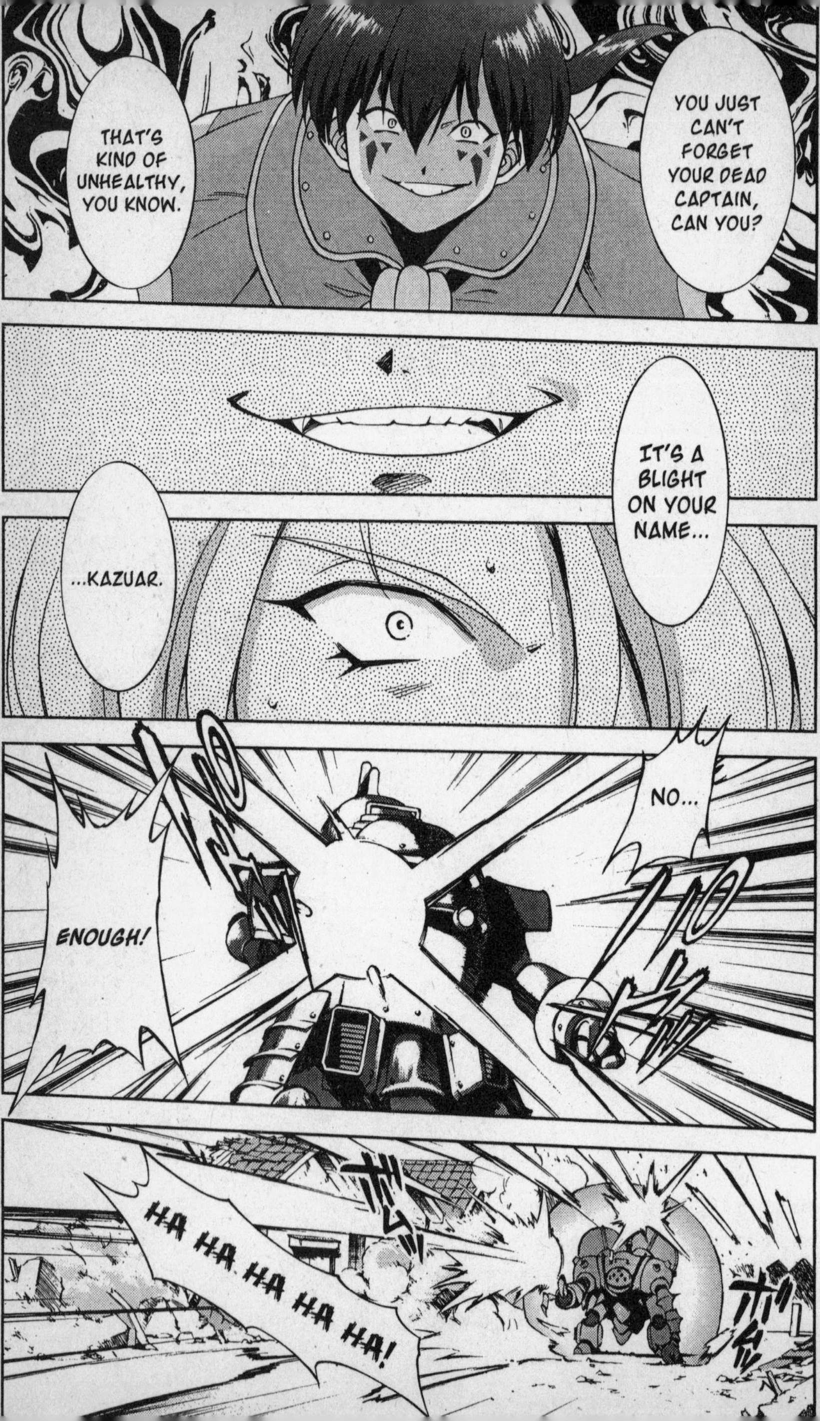
YOU JUST CAN'T FORGET YOUR DEAD CAPTAIN, CAN YOU?
THAT'S KIND OF UNHEALTHY, YOU KNOW.
IT'S A BLIGHT ON YOUR NAME...
...KAZUAR.
NO...
ENOUGH!
HA HA HA HA HA HA!

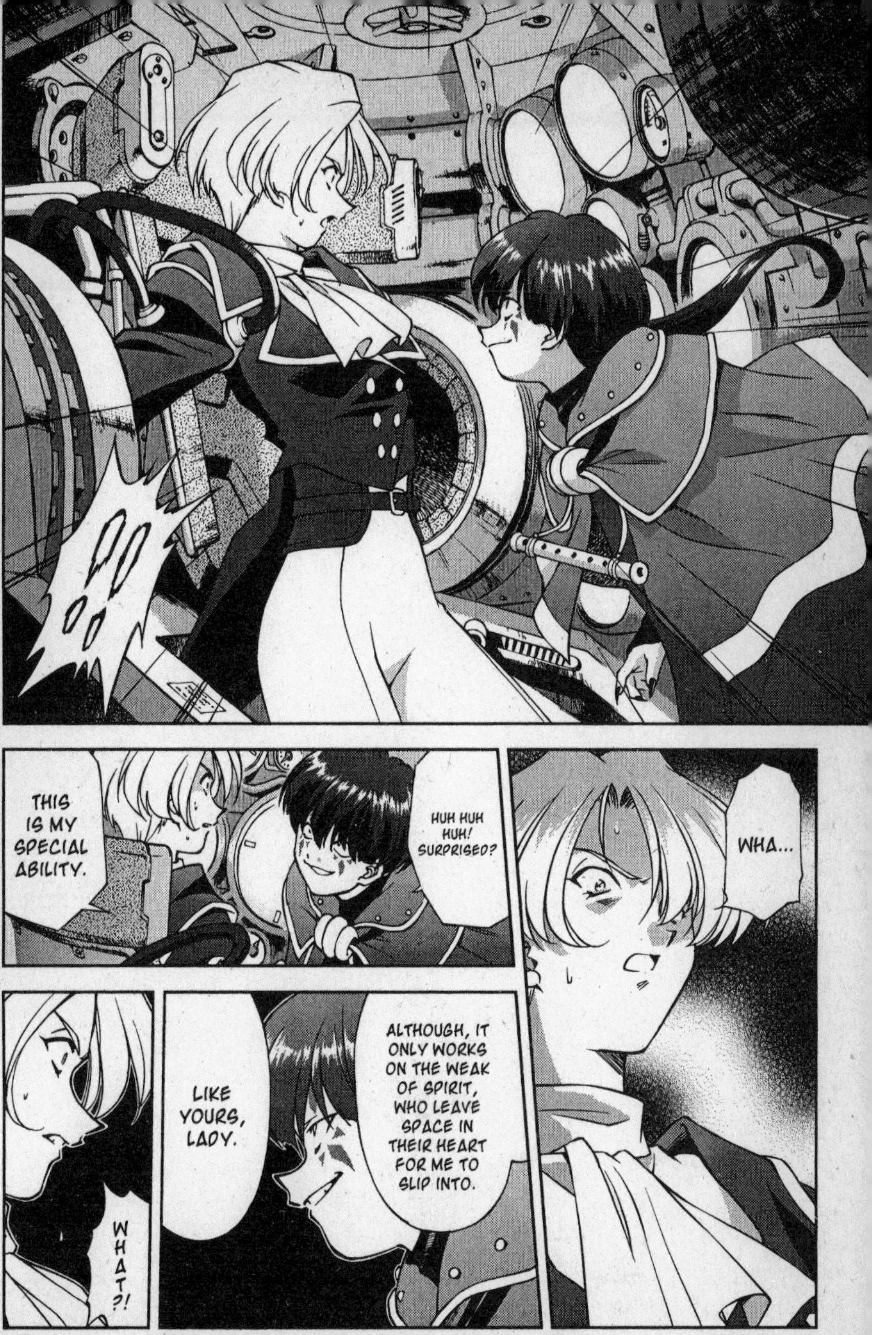
WHA...
HUH HUH HUH! SURPRISED?
THIS IS MY SPECIAL ABILITY.
ALTHOUGH, IT ONLY WORKS ON THE WEAK OF SPIRIT, WHO LEAVE SPACE IN THEIR HEART FOR ME TO SLIP INTO.
LIKE YOURS, LADY.
WHAT?!

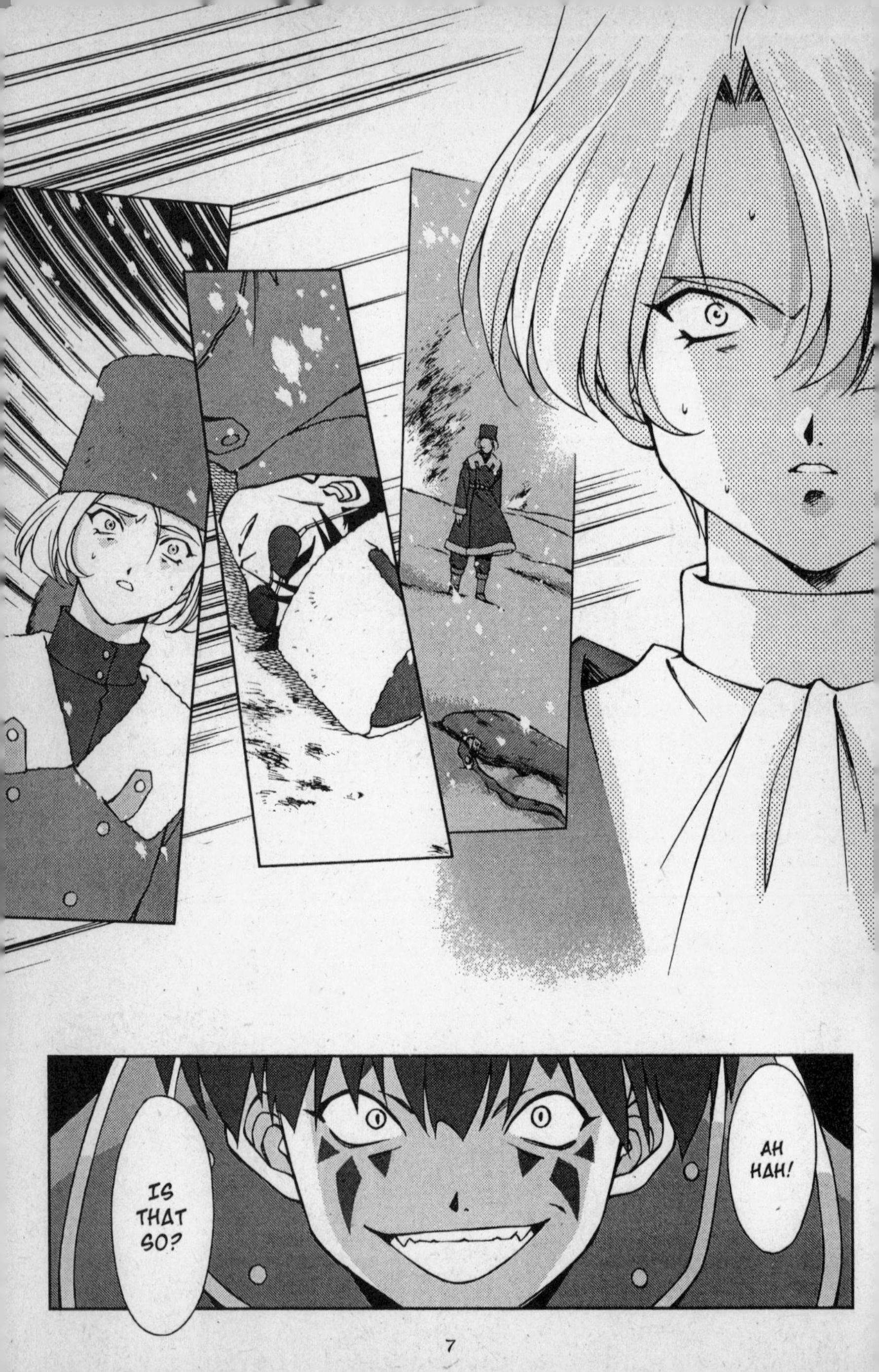
AH HAH!
IS THAT SO?

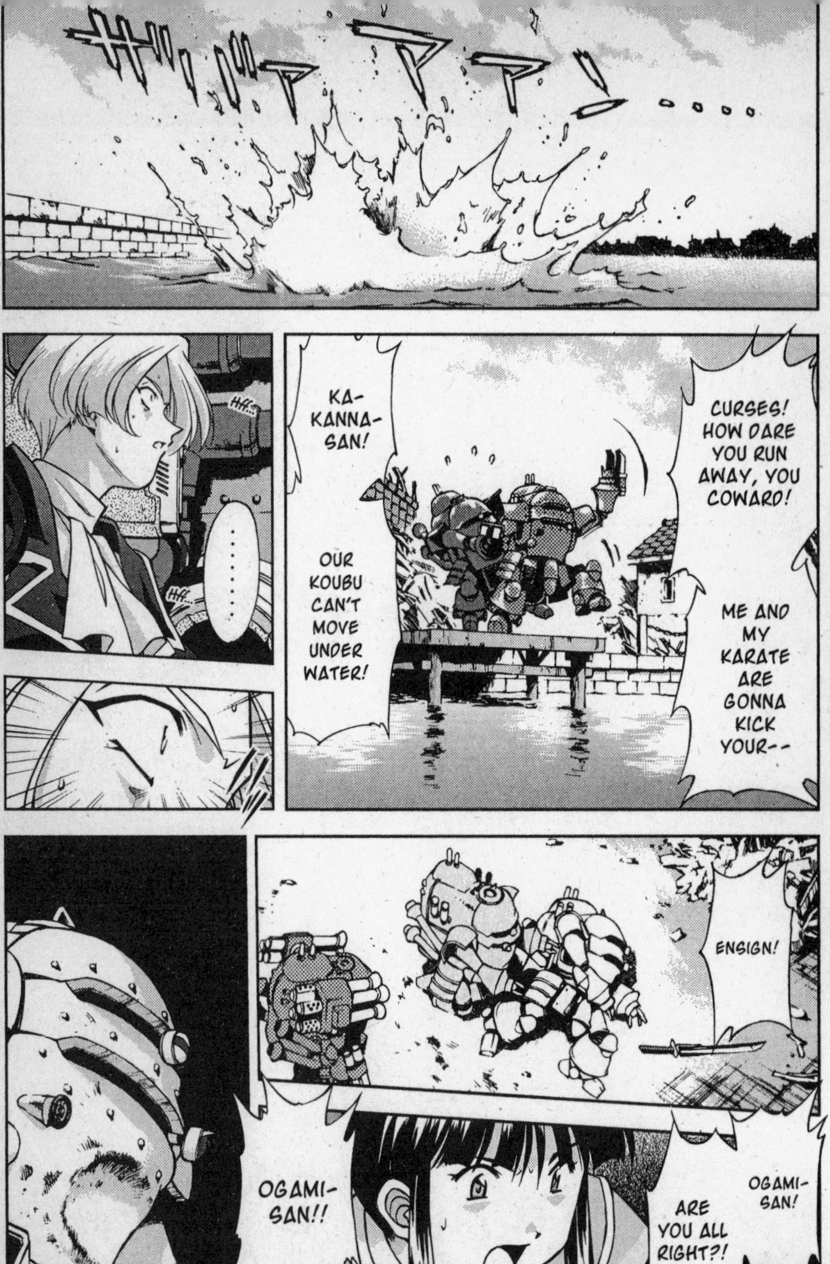
CURSES! HOW DARE YOU RUN AWAY, YOU COWARD!
ME AND MY KARATE ARE GONNA KICK YOUR--
KA-KANNA-SAN!
OUR KOUBU CAN'T MOVE UNDER WATER!
......
ENSIGN!
OGAMI-SAN!
ARE YOU ALL RIGHT?!
OGAMI-SAN!!

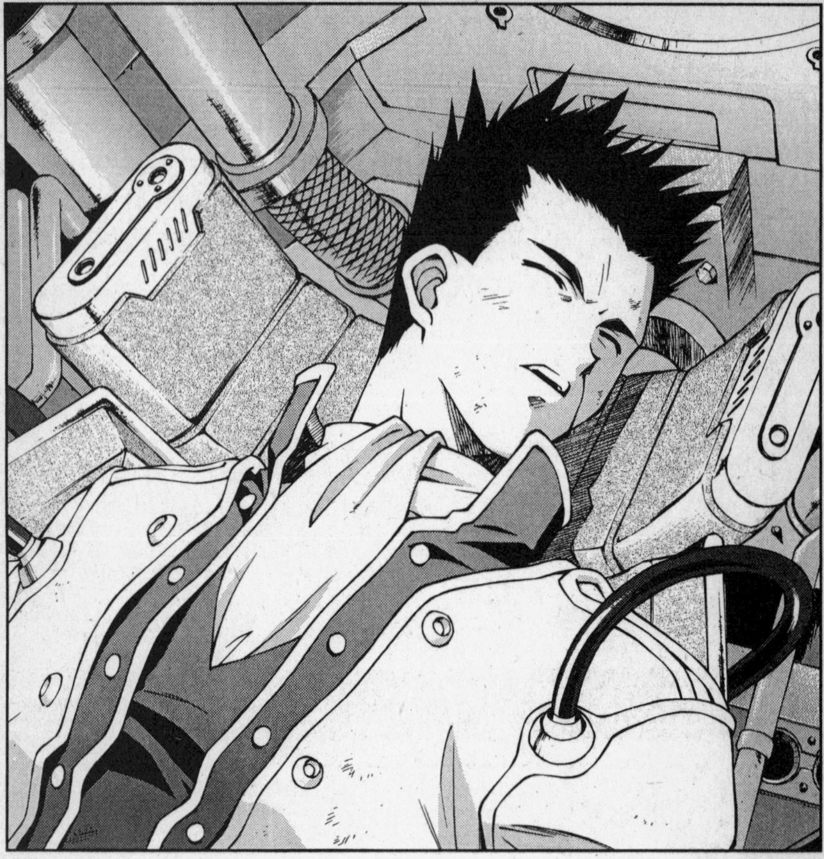

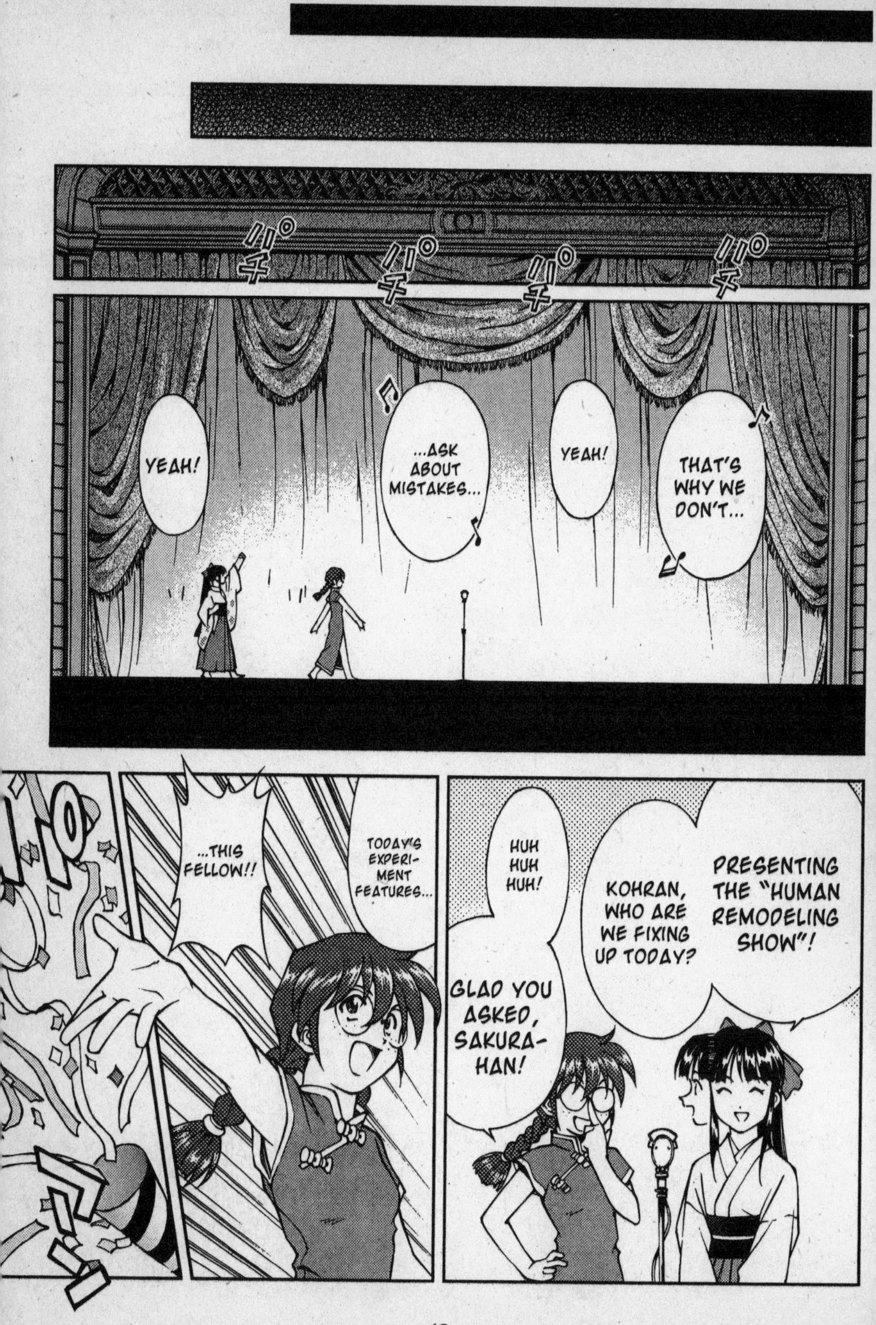
パチ
パチ
パチ
パチ
THAT'S WHY WE DON'T...
YEAH!
...ASK ABOUT MISTAKES...
YEAH!
PRESENTING THE "HUMAN REMODELING SHOW"!
KOHRAN, WHO ARE WE FIXING UP TODAY?
HUH HUH HUH!
GLAD YOU ASKED, SAKURA-HAN!
TODAY'S EXPERIMENT FEATURES...
...THIS FELLOW!!

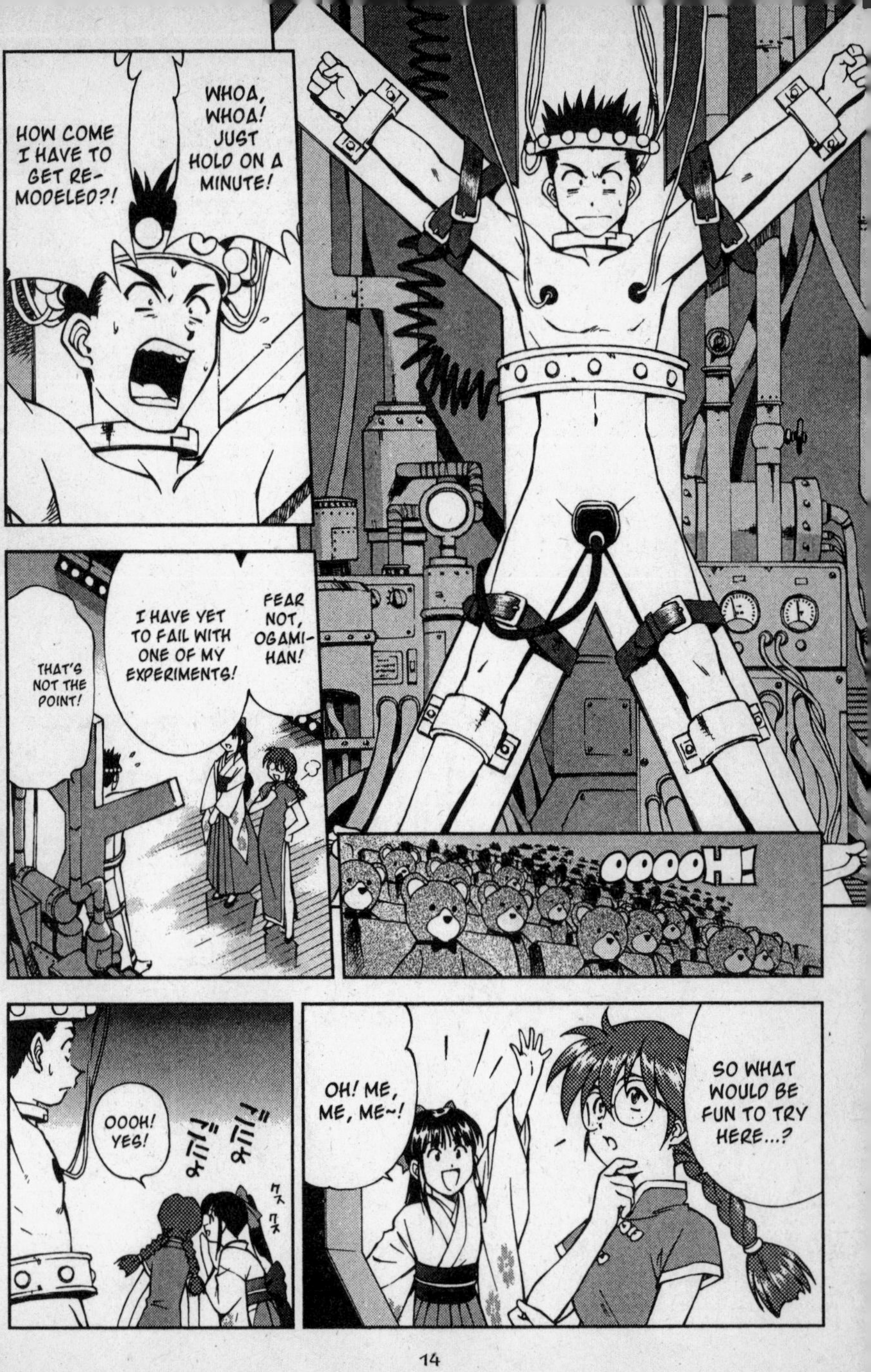
WHOA, WHOA! JUST HOLD ON A MINUTE!
HOW COME I HAVE TO GET RE-MODELED?!
FEAR NOT, OGAMI-HAN!
I HAVE YET TO FAIL WITH ONE OF MY EXPERIMENTS!
THAT'S NOT THE POINT!
OOOOH!
SO WHAT WOULD BE FUN TO TRY HERE...?
OH! ME, ME, ME~!
OOOH! YES!
ゴニョゴニョ
クスクス

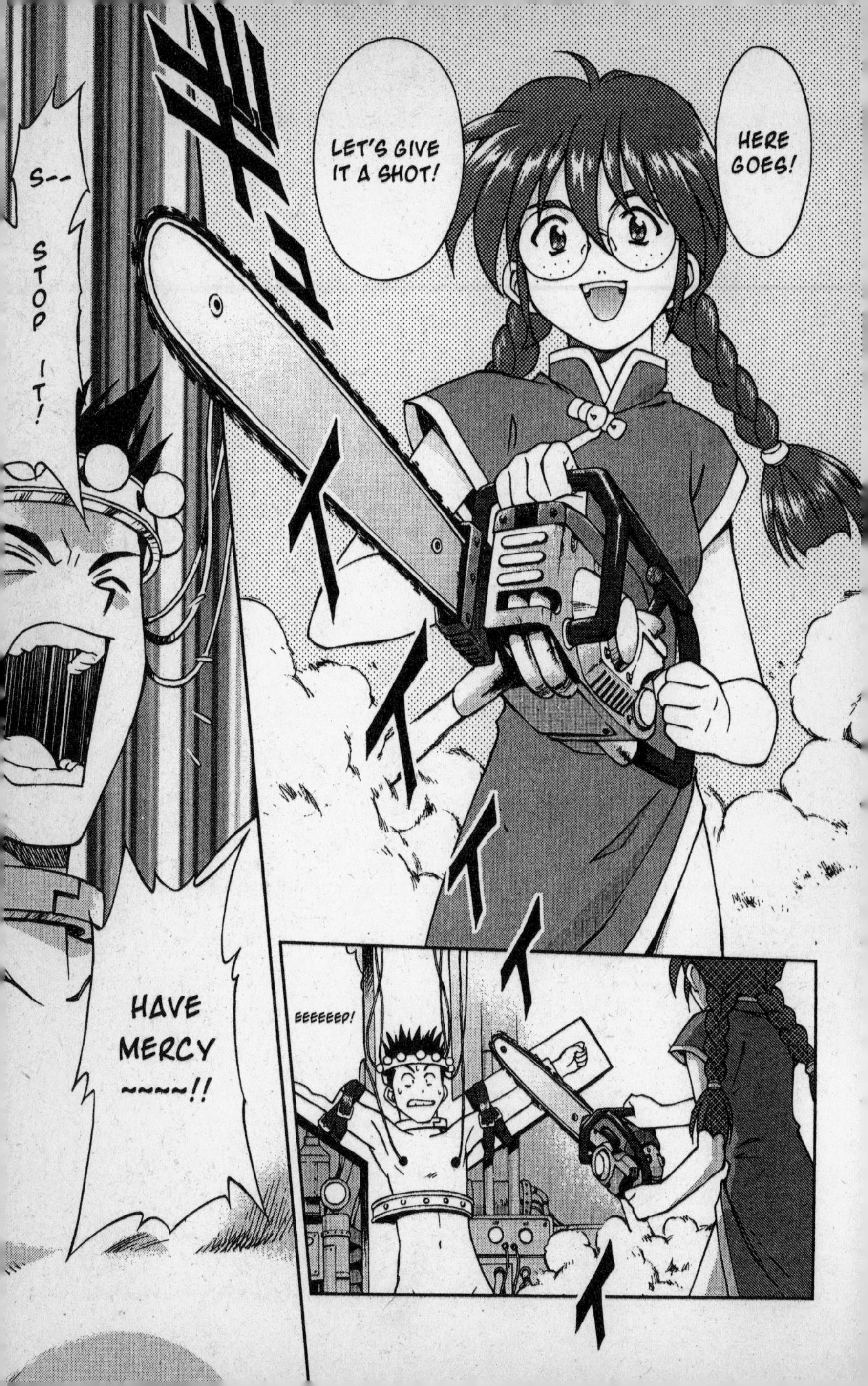
HERE GOES!
LET'S GIVE IT A SHOT!
EEEEEEP!
S-- STOP IT!
HAVE MERCY ~~~~~!!

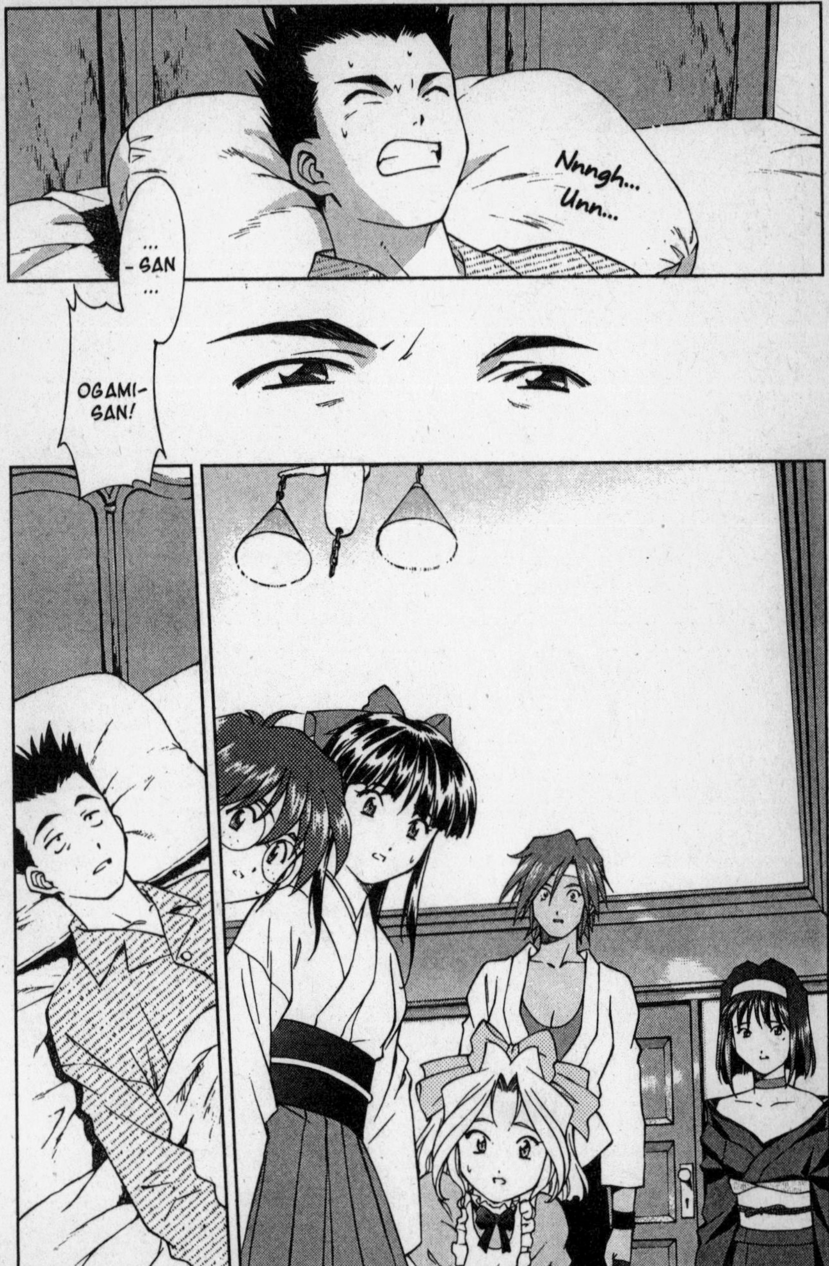
Nnngh...
Unn...
... - SAN ...
OGAMI-SAN!

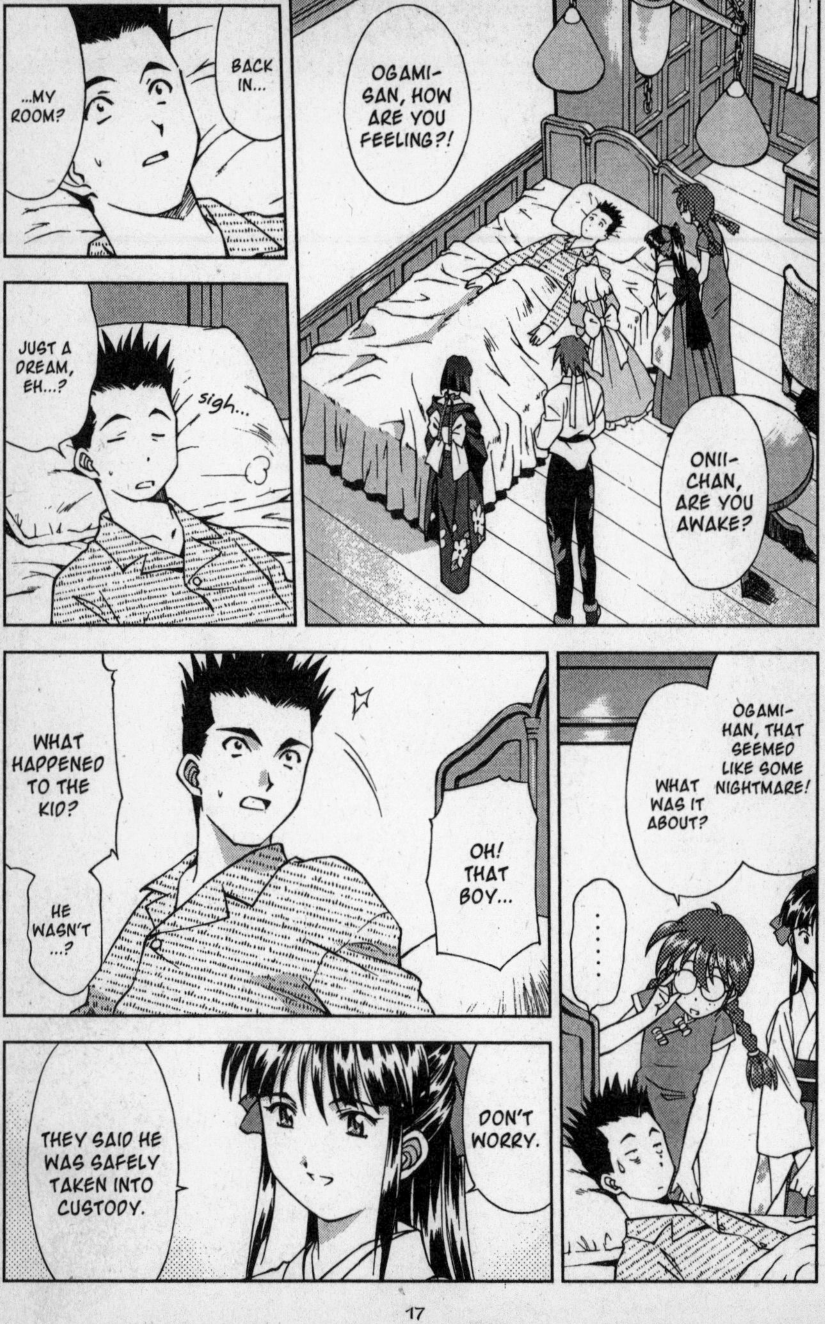
OGAMI-SAN, HOW ARE YOU FEELING?!
ONII-CHAN, ARE YOU AWAKE?
BACK IN...
...MY ROOM?
JUST A DREAM, EH...?
sigh...
OGAMI-HAN, THAT SEEMED LIKE SOME NIGHTMARE!
WHAT WAS IT ABOUT?
......
WHAT HAPPENED TO THE KID?
OH! THAT BOY...
HE WASN'T ...?
DON'T WORRY.
THEY SAID HE WAS SAFELY TAKEN INTO CUSTODY.

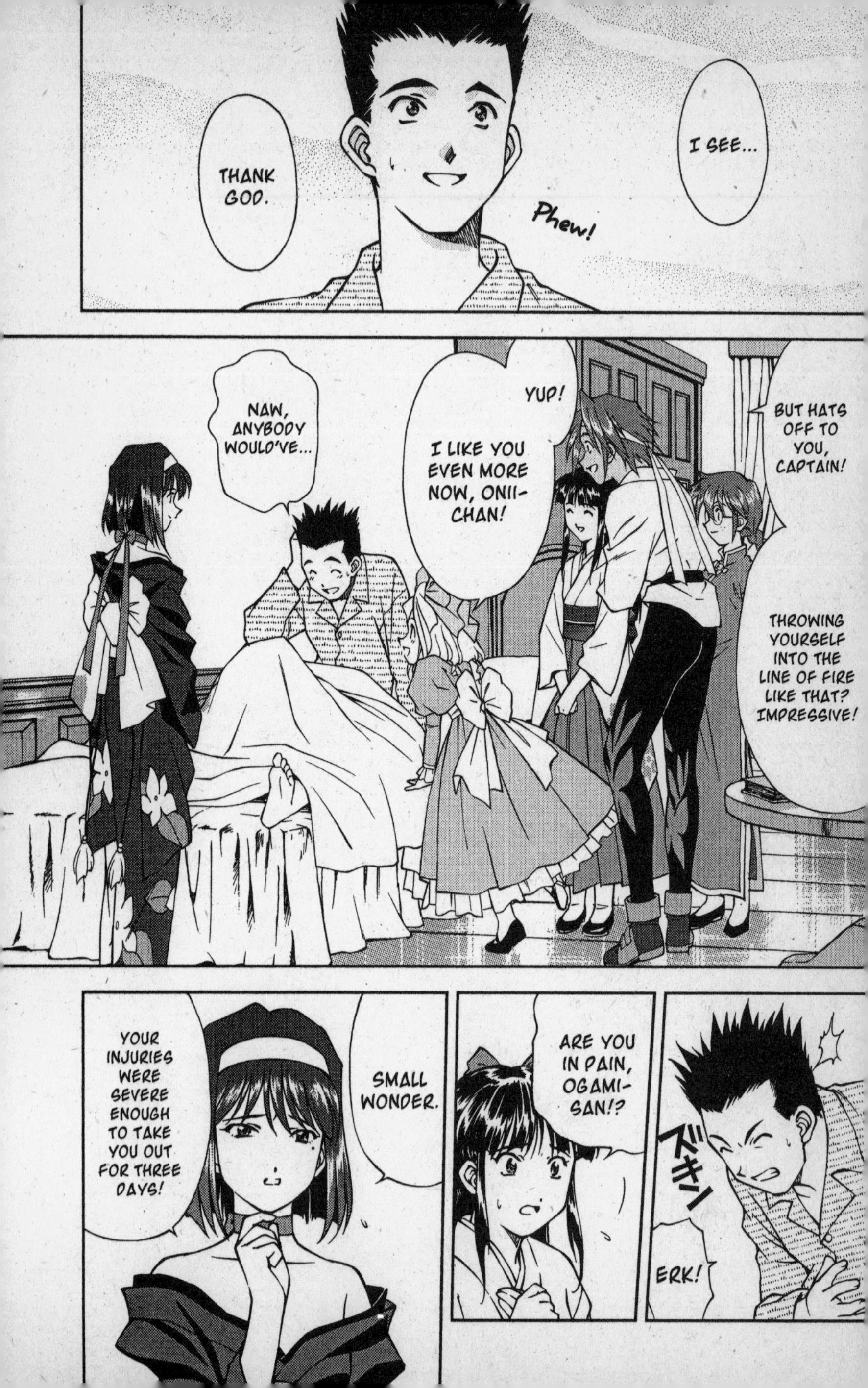
I SEE...
Phew!
THANK GOD.
BUT HATS OFF TO YOU, CAPTAIN!
THROWING YOURSELF INTO THE LINE OF FIRE LIKE THAT? IMPRESSIVE!
YUP!
I LIKE YOU EVEN MORE NOW, ONII-CHAN!
NAW, ANYBODY WOULD'VE...
ズキン
ERK!
ARE YOU IN PAIN, OGAMI-SAN!?
SMALL WONDER.
YOUR INJURIES WERE SEVERE ENOUGH TO TAKE YOU OUT FOR THREE DAYS!

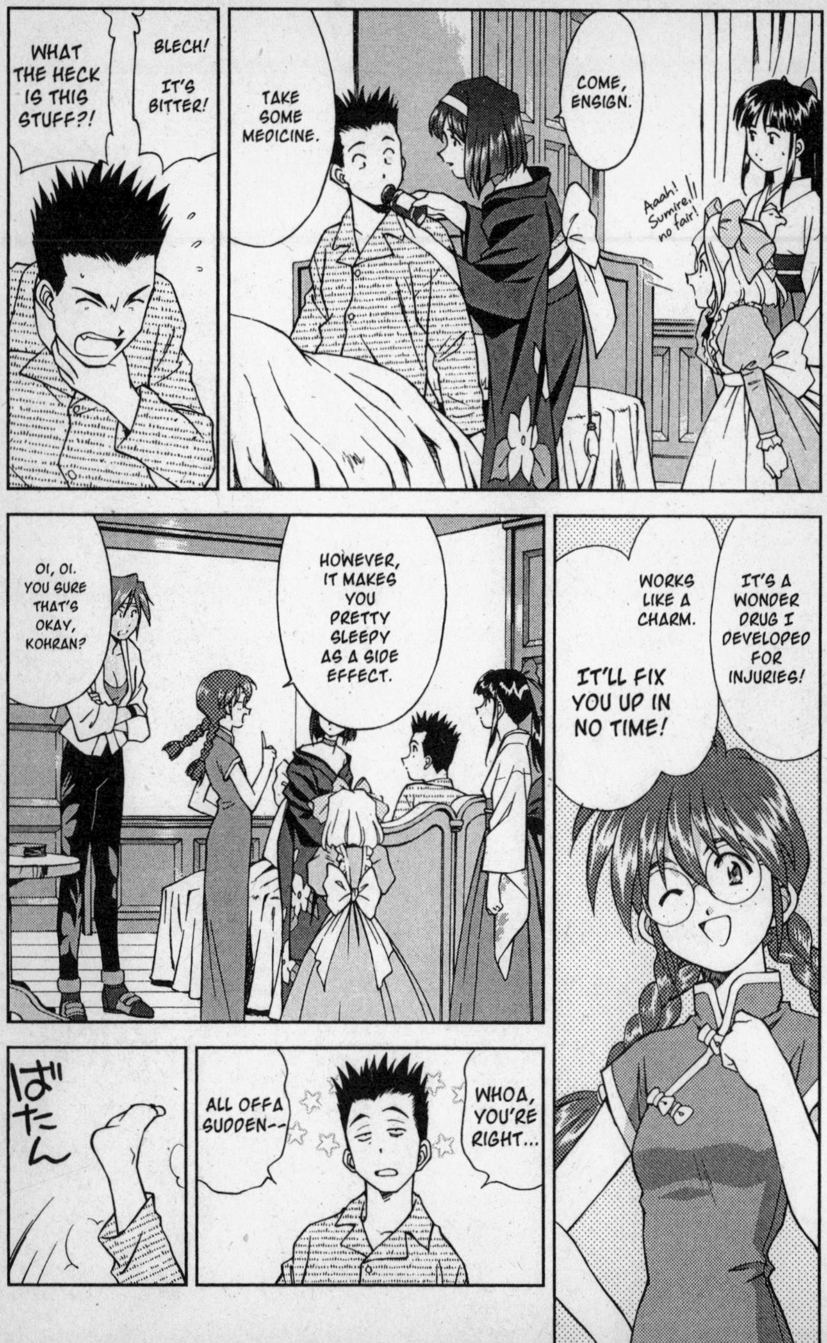
COME, ENSIGN.
TAKE SOME MEDICINE.
Aaah! Sumire, no fair!
BLECH! IT'S BITTER!
WHAT THE HECK IS THIS STUFF?!
IT'S A WONDER DRUG I DEVELOPED FOR INJURIES!
WORKS LIKE A CHARM.
IT'LL FIX YOU UP IN NO TIME!
HOWEVER, IT MAKES YOU PRETTY SLEEPY AS A SIDE EFFECT.
OI, OI. YOU SURE THAT'S OKAY, KOHRAN?
WHOA, YOU'RE RIGHT...
ALL OFFA SUDDEN--
ばたん

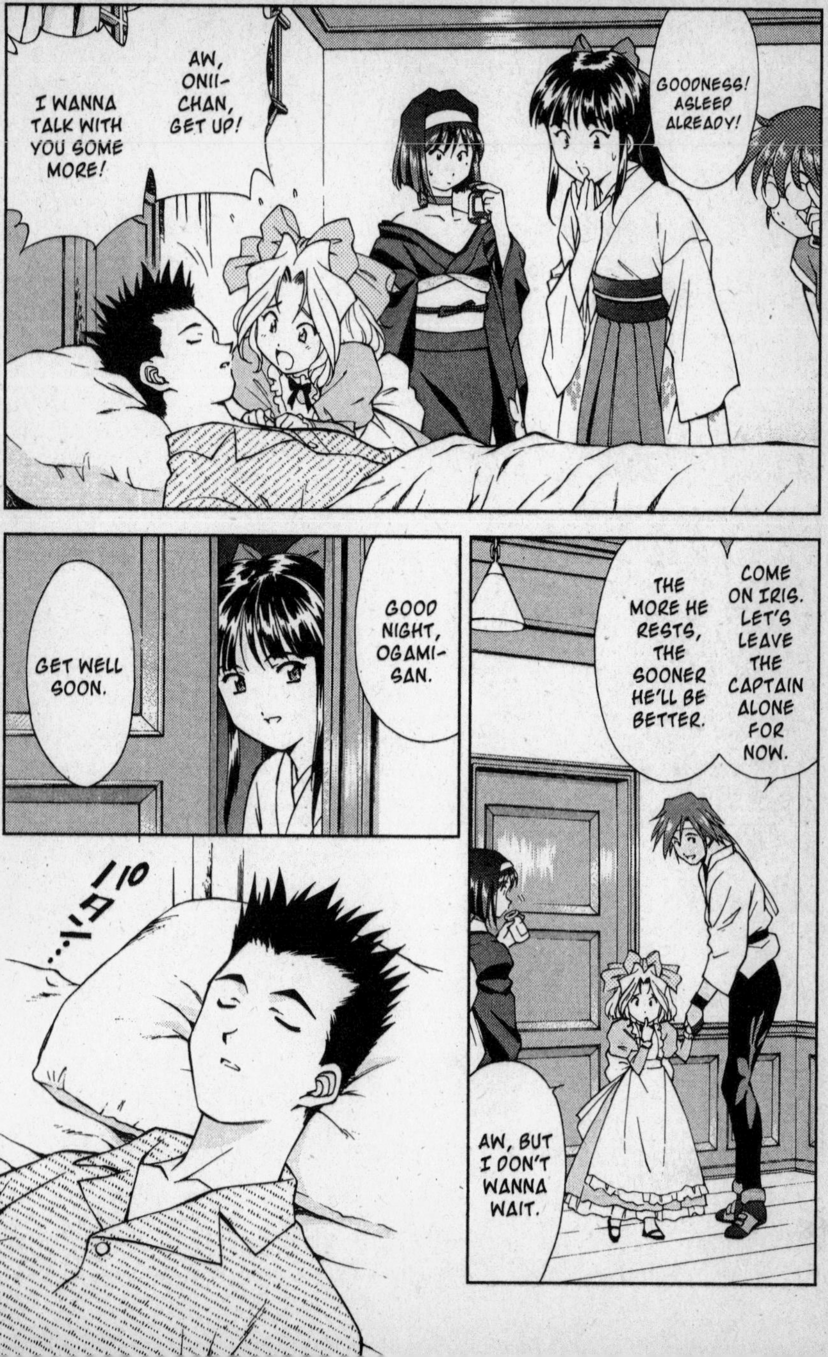
GOODNESS! ASLEEP ALREADY!
AW, ONII-CHAN, GET UP!
I WANNA TALK WITH YOU SOME MORE!
COME ON IRIS. LET'S LEAVE THE CAPTAIN ALONE FOR NOW.
THE MORE HE RESTS, THE SOONER HE'LL BE BETTER.
AW, BUT I DON'T WANNA WAIT.
GOOD NIGHT, OGAMI-SAN.
GET WELL SOON.
パタン…

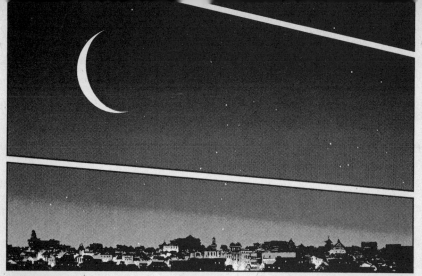

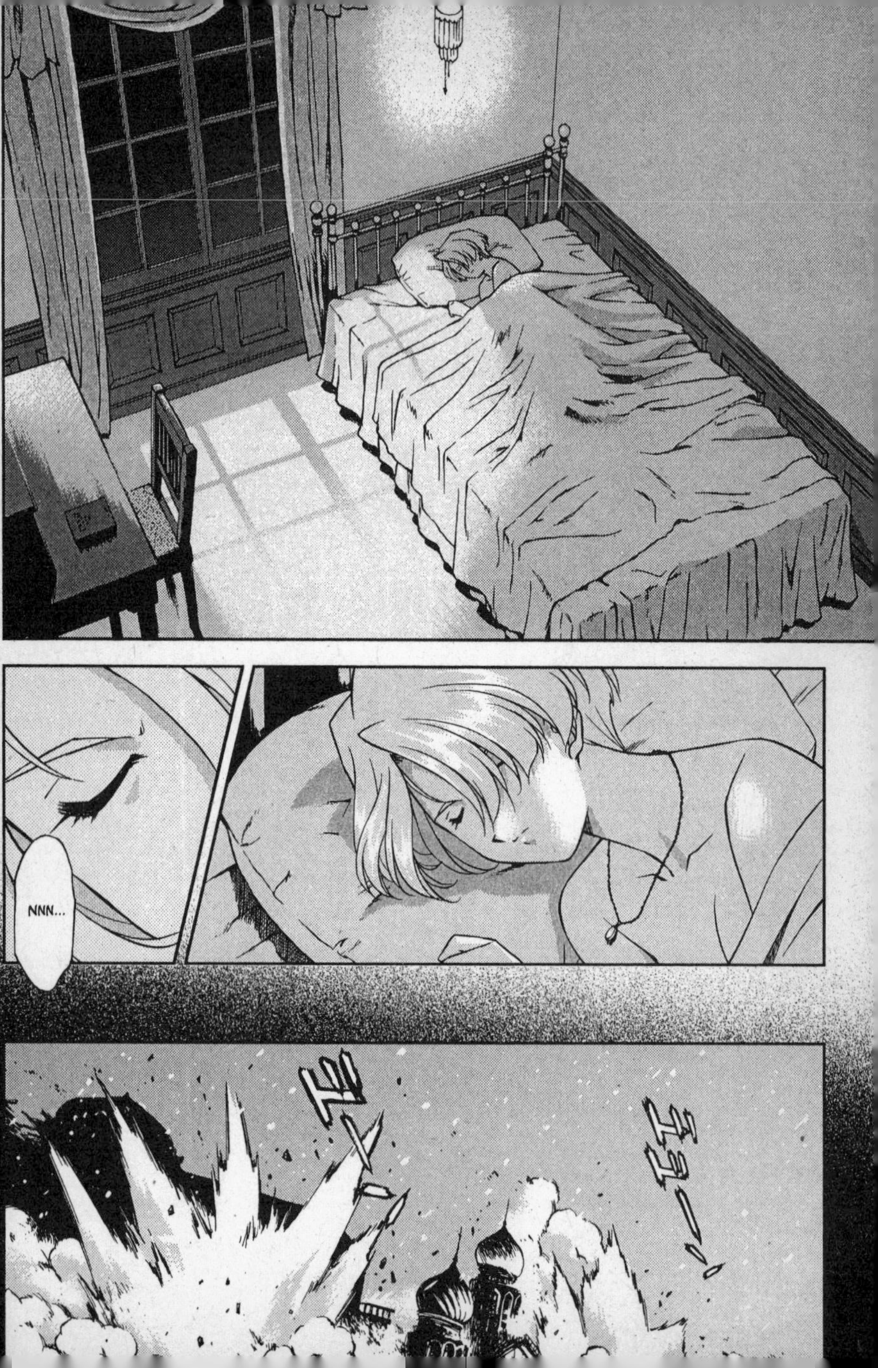
NNN...

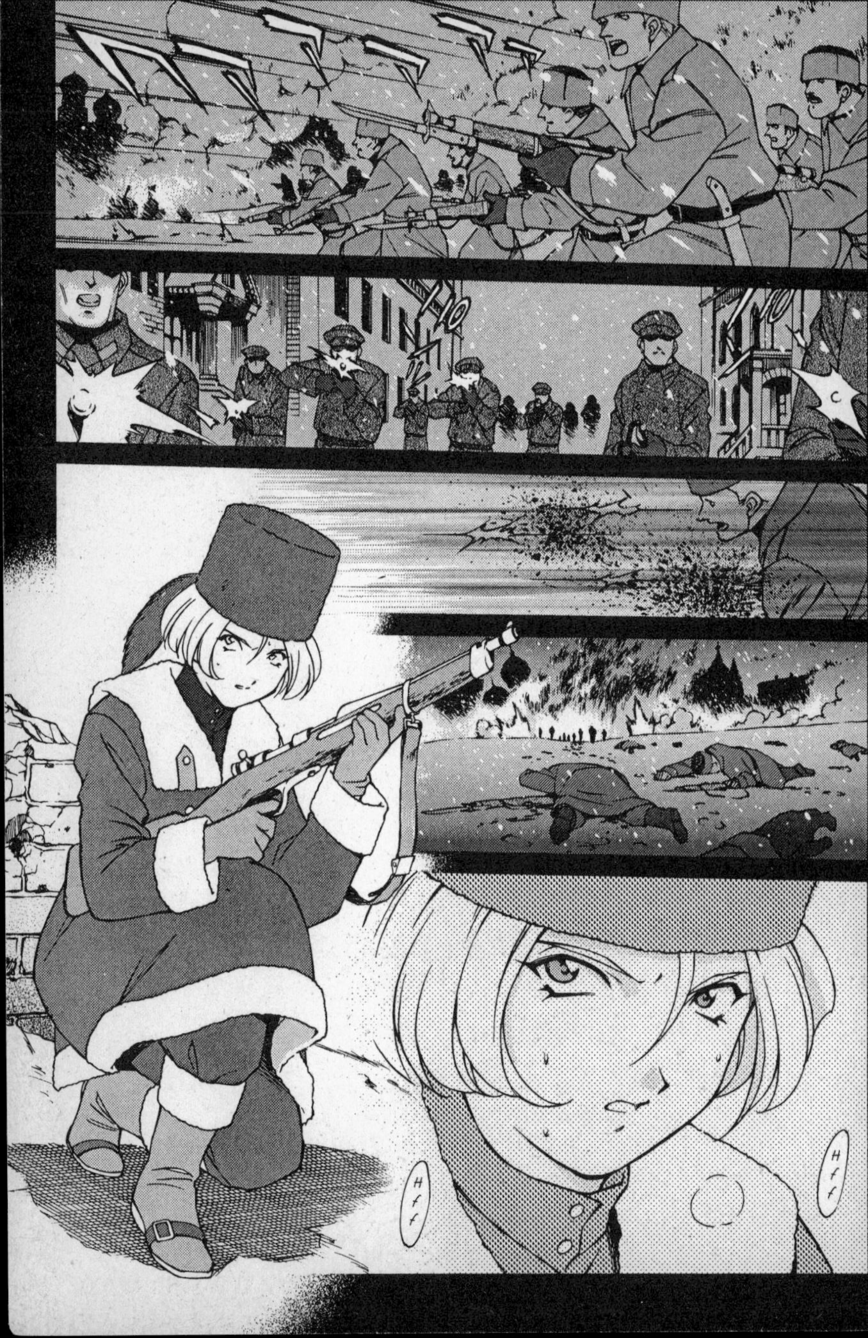
Hff
Hff

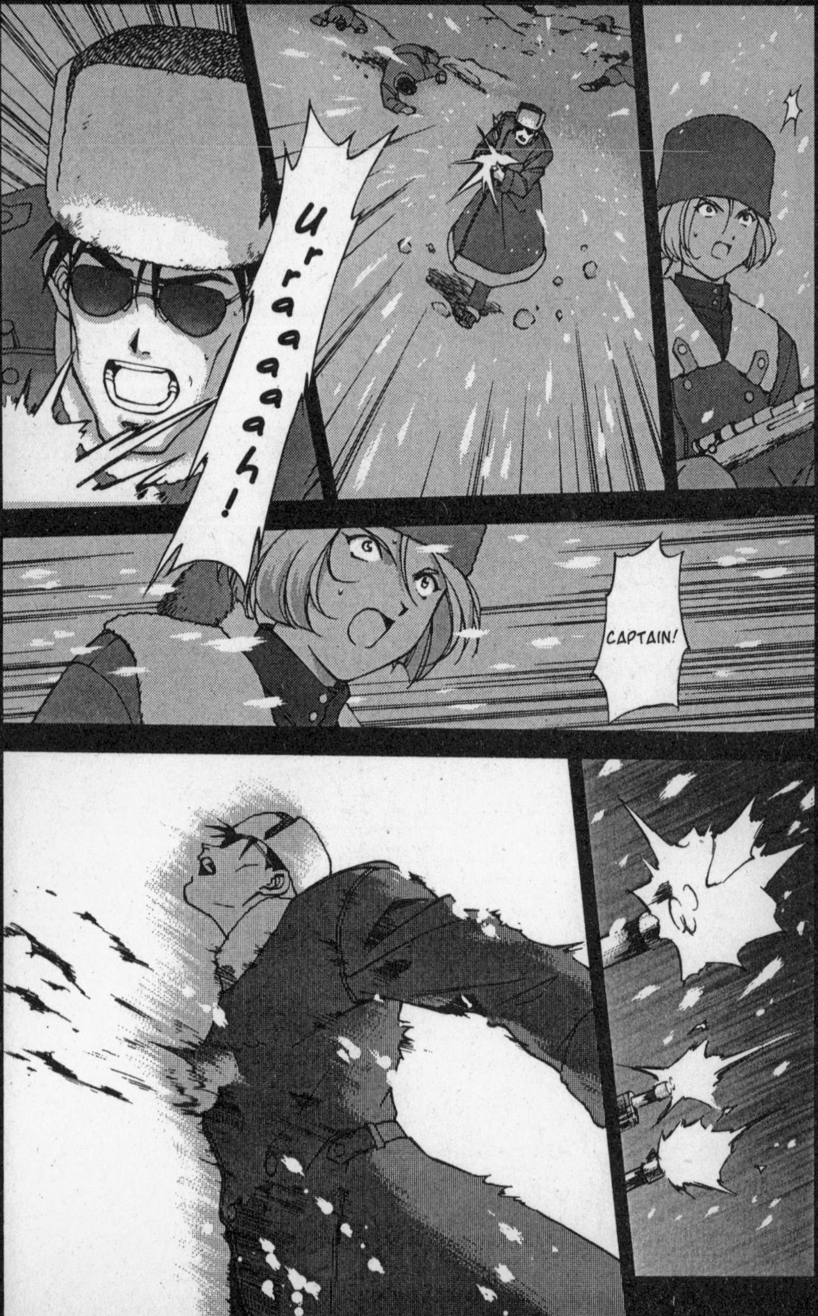
Urraaaaaah!
CAPTAIN!

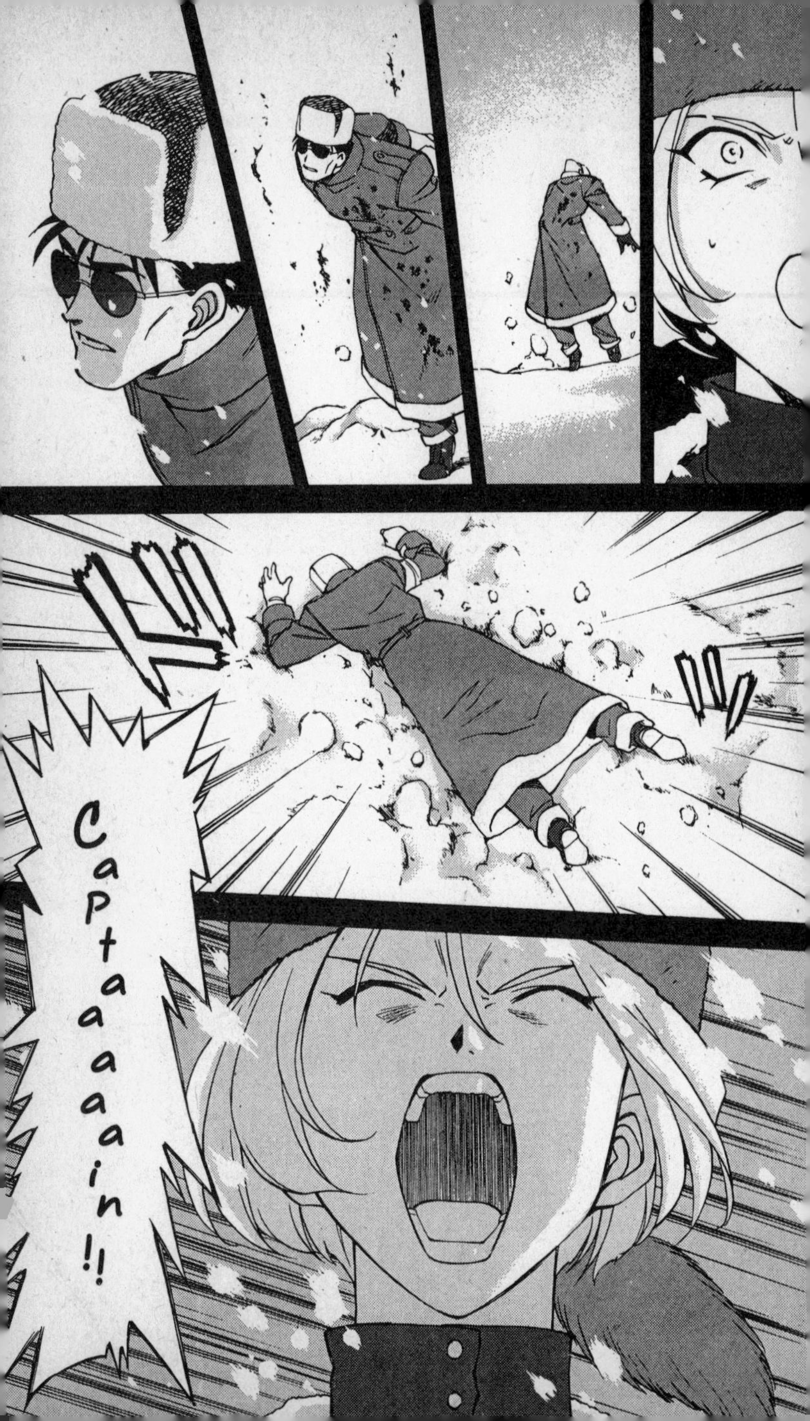
Captaaaaain!!

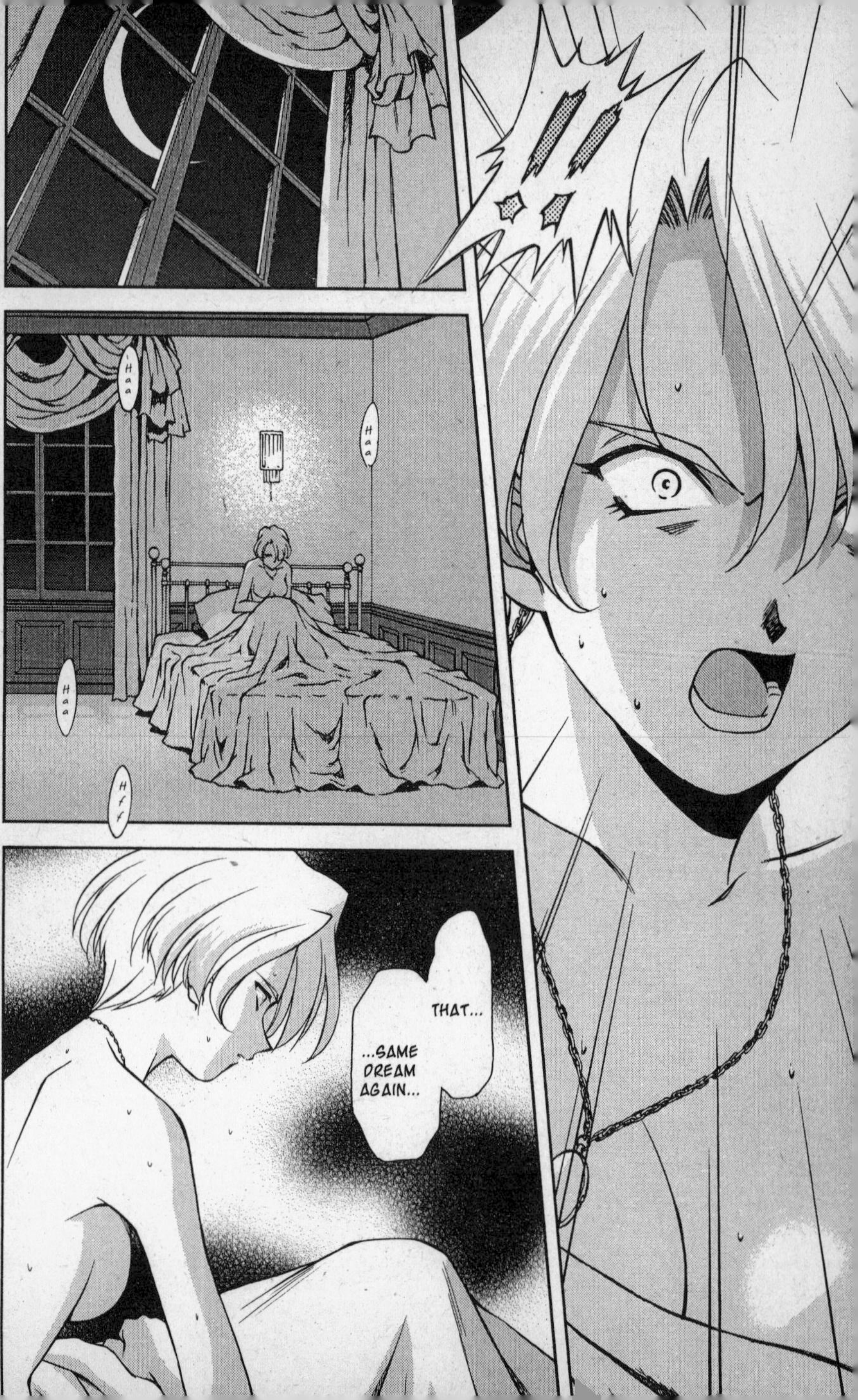
!!
Haa
Haa
Haa
Hff
THAT...
...SAME DREAM AGAIN...

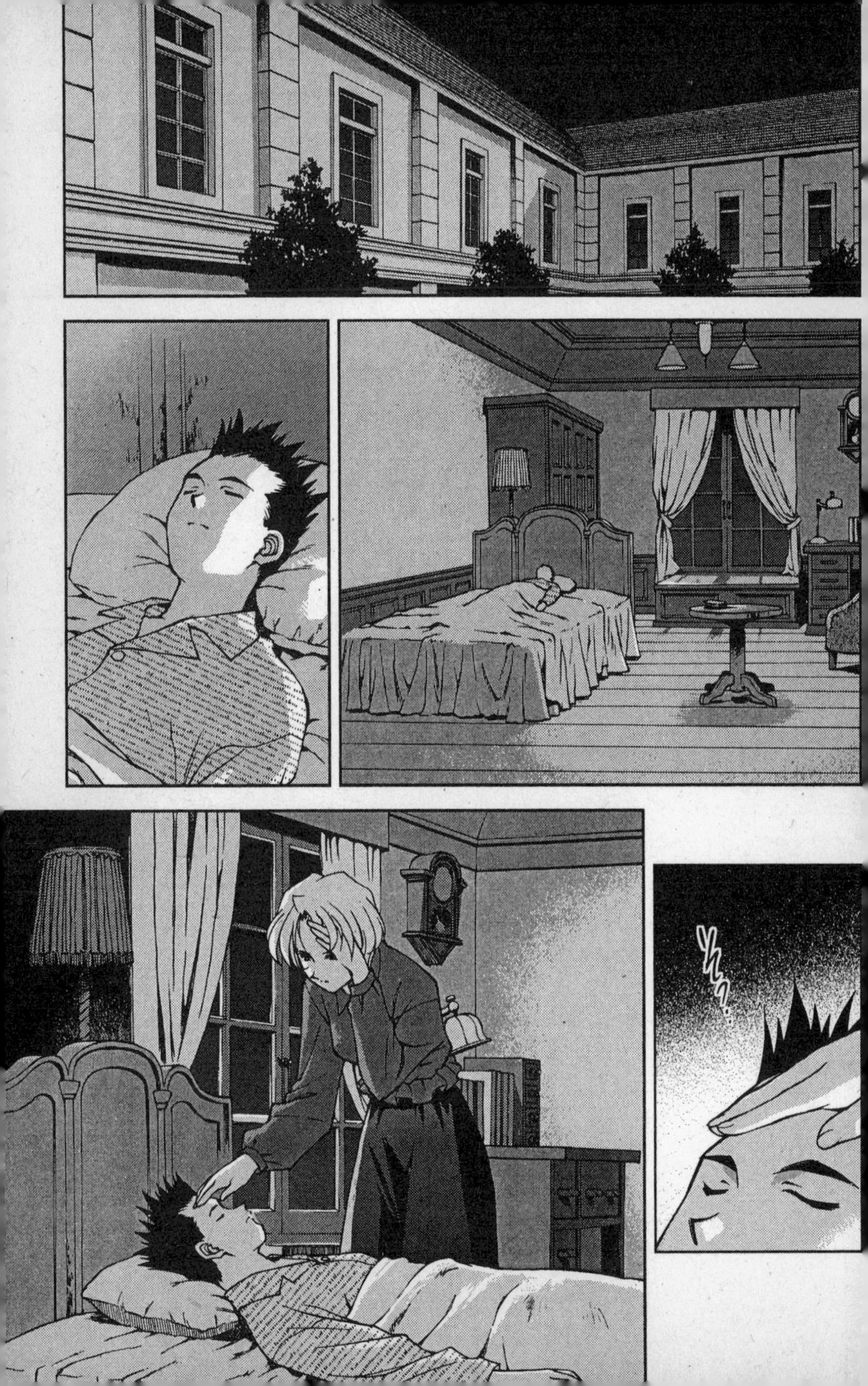
んん‥

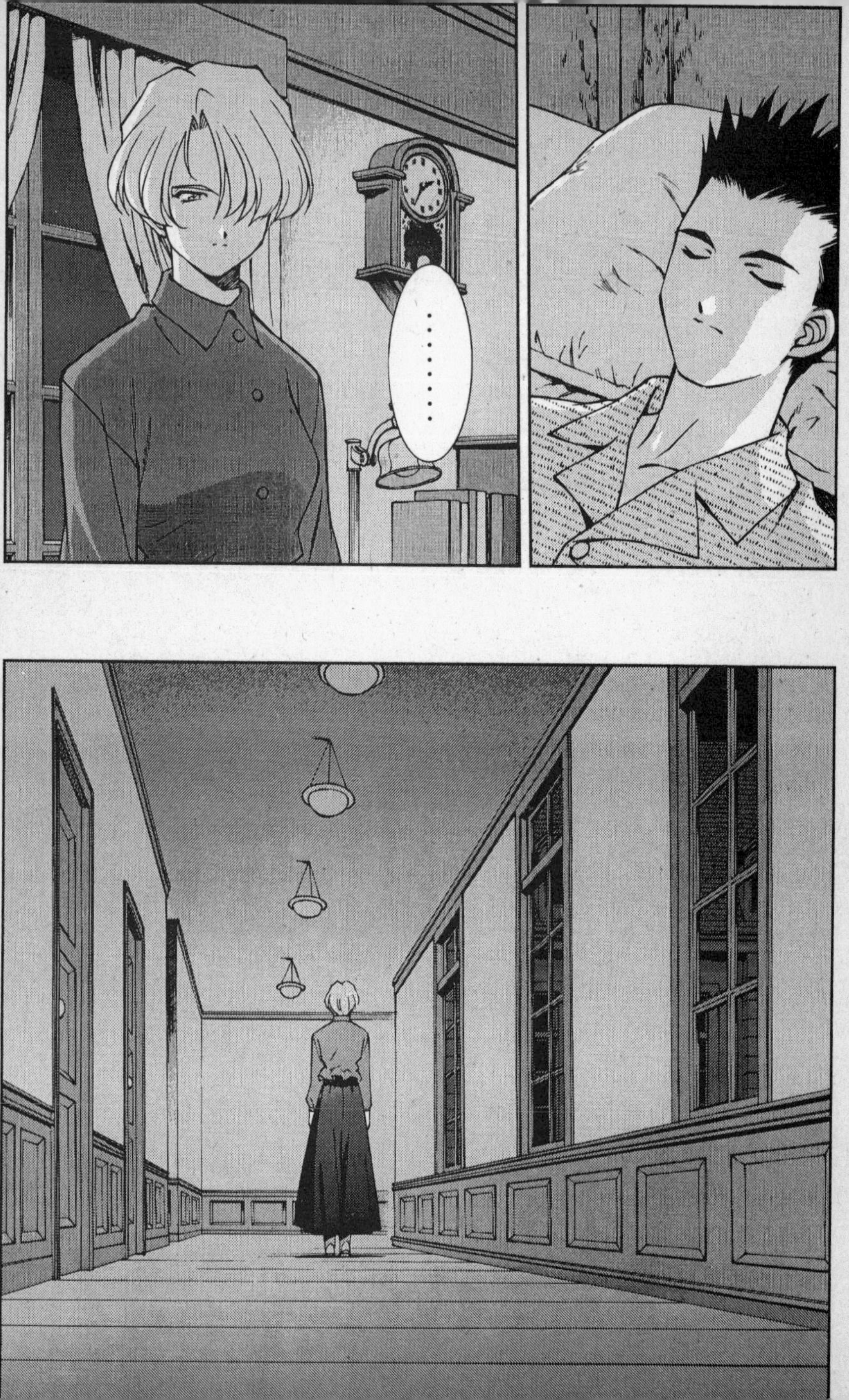
………

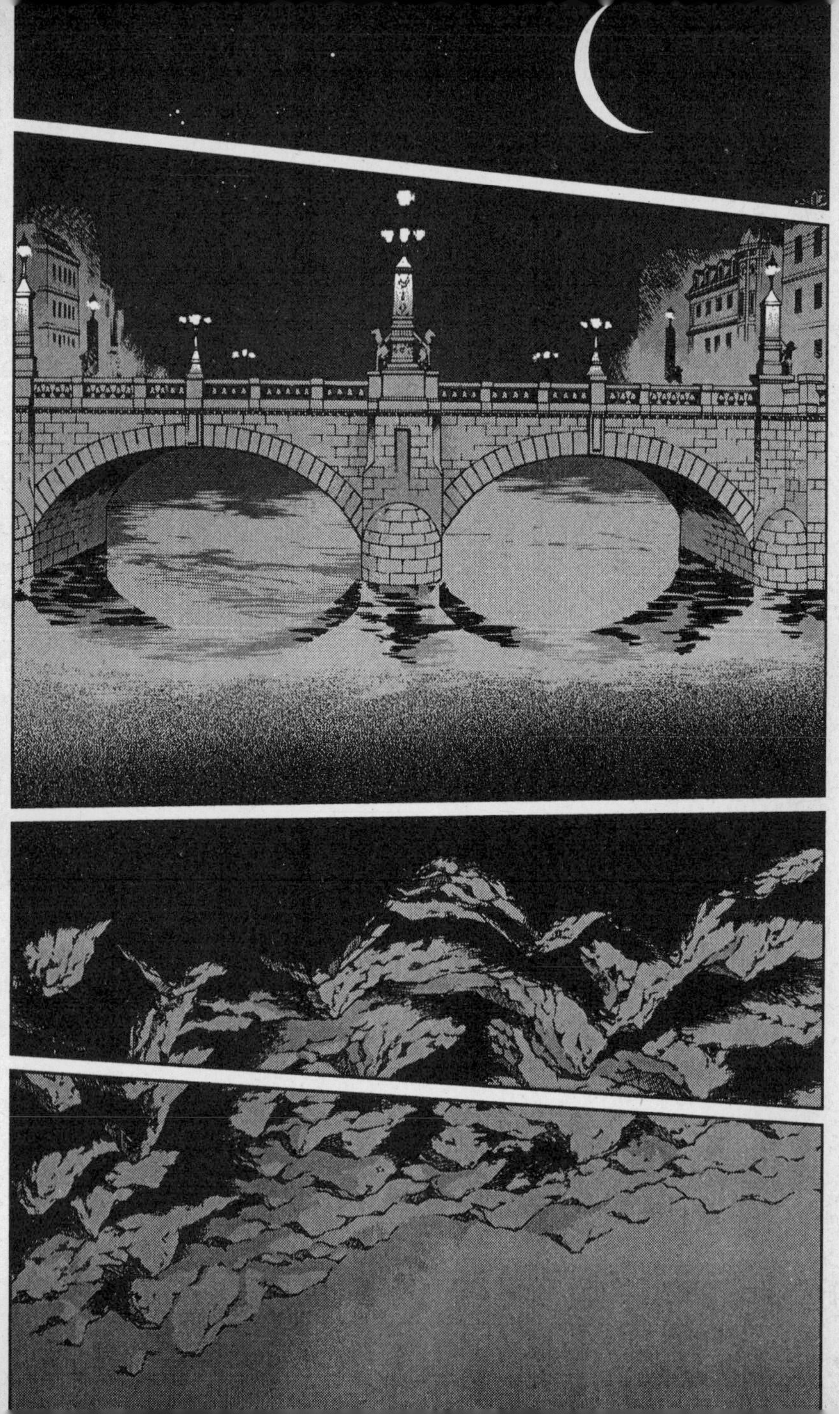

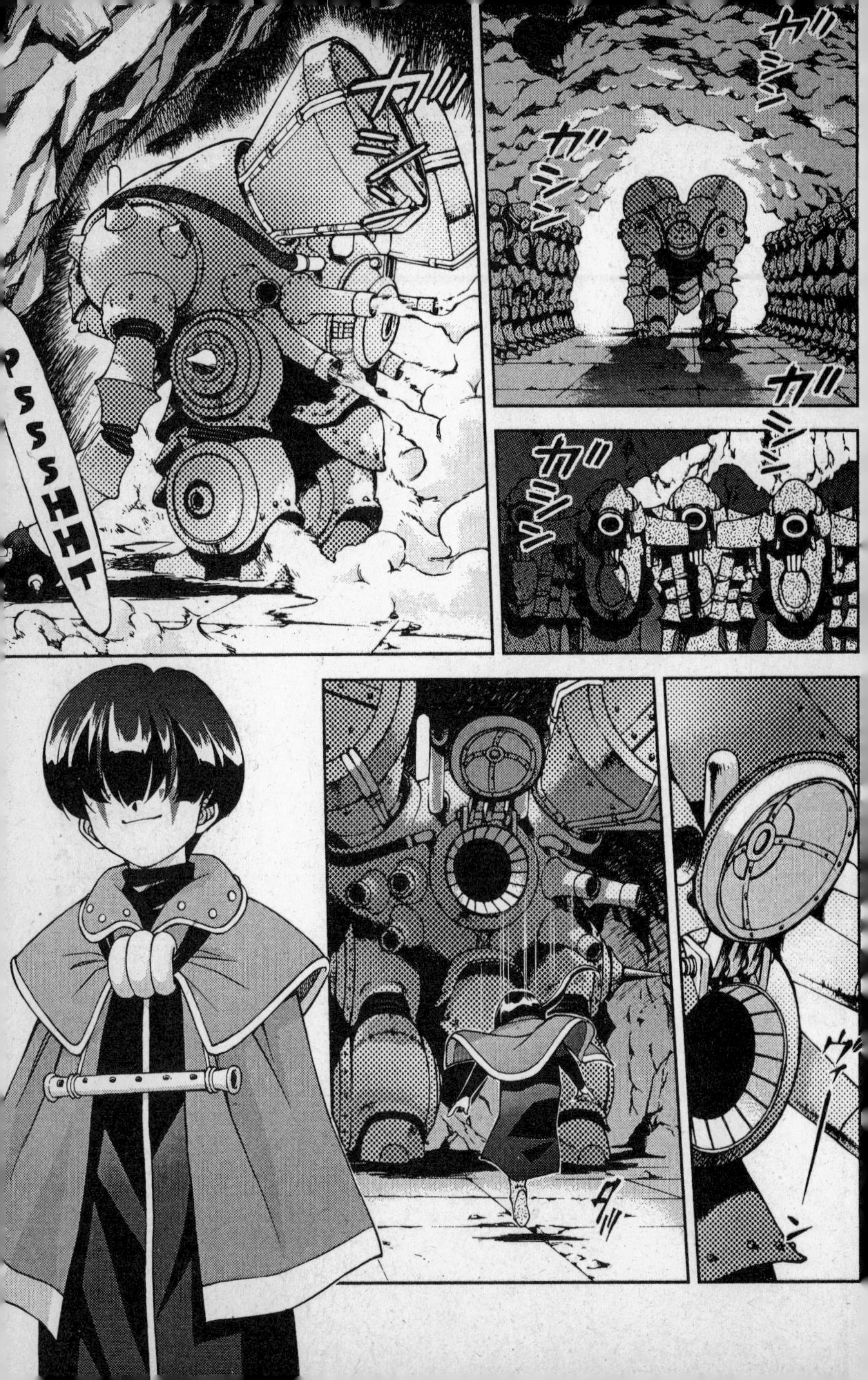
ガシャン
ガシャン
ガシャン
ガシャン
ガシャン
PSSSHHHT
ヴィーン
ダッ

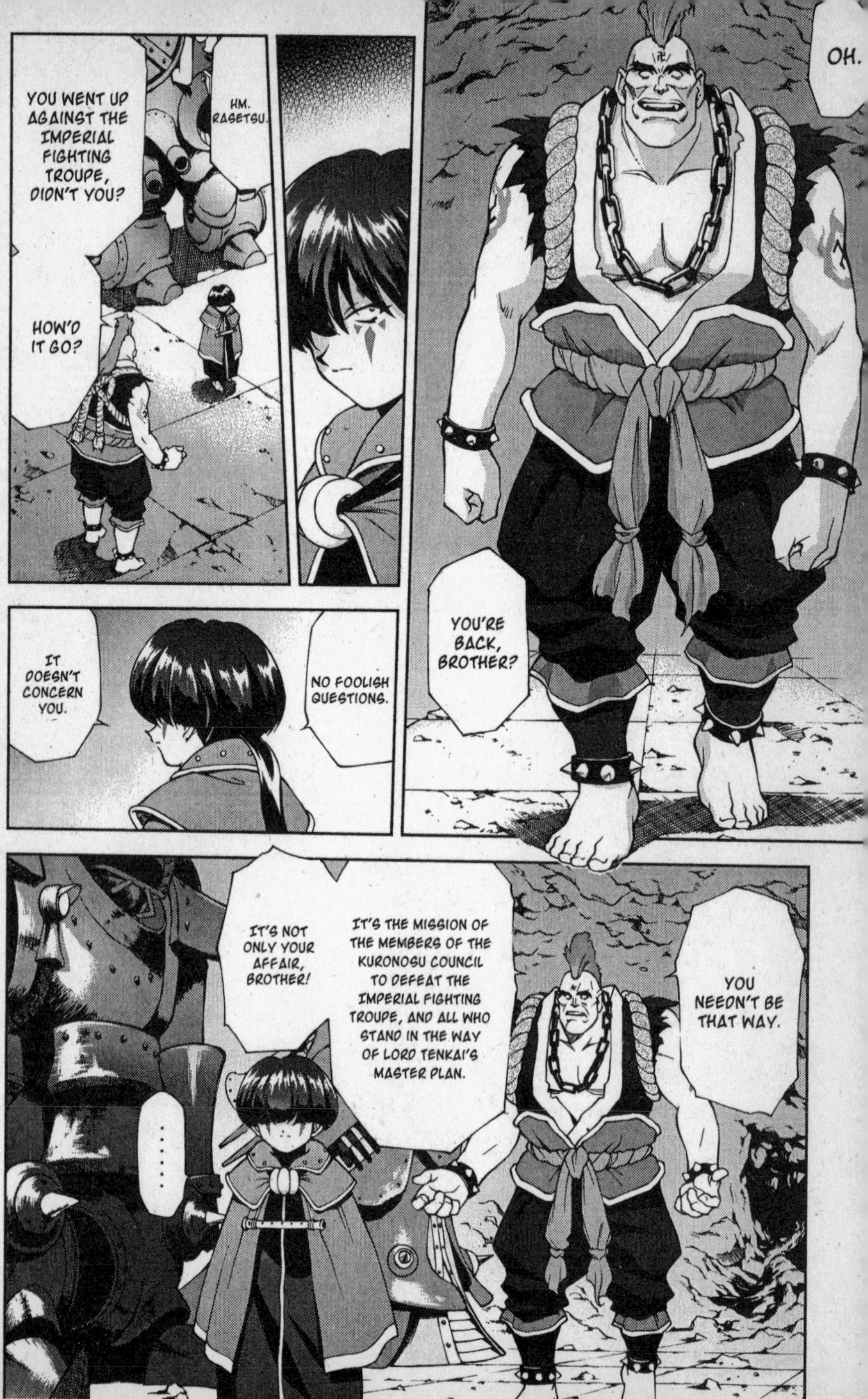
OH.
YOU'RE BACK, BROTHER?
HM. RASETSU.
YOU WENT UP AGAINST THE IMPERIAL FIGHTING TROUPE, DIDN'T YOU?
HOW'D IT GO?
NO FOOLISH QUESTIONS.
IT DOESN'T CONCERN YOU.
YOU NEEDN'T BE THAT WAY.
IT'S THE MISSION OF THE MEMBERS OF THE KURONOSU COUNCIL TO DEFEAT THE IMPERIAL FIGHTING TROUPE, AND ALL WHO STAND IN THE WAY OF LORD TENKAI'S MASTER PLAN.
IT'S NOT ONLY YOUR AFFAIR, BROTHER!
......

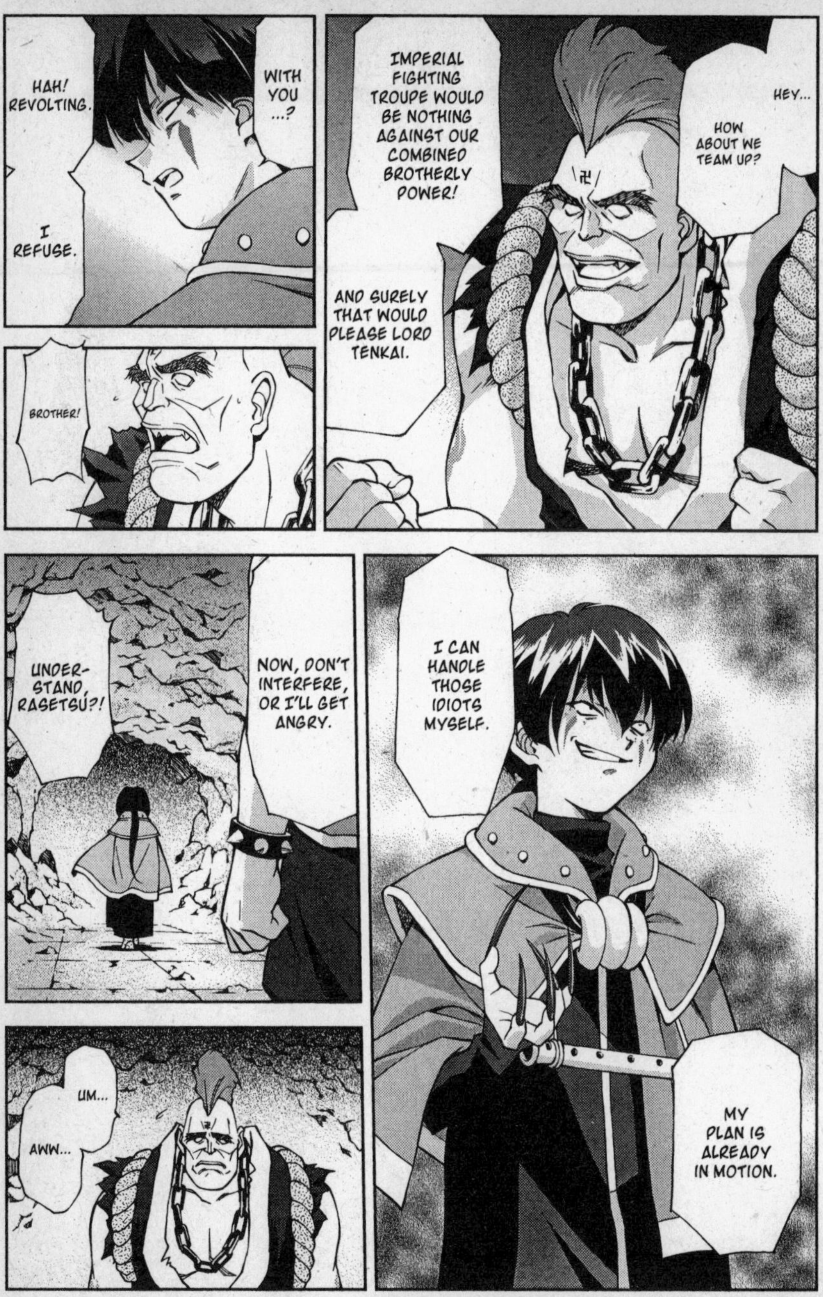
HEY...
HOW ABOUT WE TEAM UP?
IMPERIAL FIGHTING TROUPE WOULD BE NOTHING AGAINST OUR COMBINED BROTHERLY POWER!
AND SURELY THAT WOULD PLEASE LORD TENKAI.
WITH YOU ...?
HAH! REVOLTING.
I REFUSE.
BROTHER!
I CAN HANDLE THOSE IDIOTS MYSELF.
MY PLAN IS ALREADY IN MOTION.
NOW, DON'T INTERFERE, OR I'LL GET ANGRY.
UNDER-STAND, RASETSU?!
UM...
AWW...

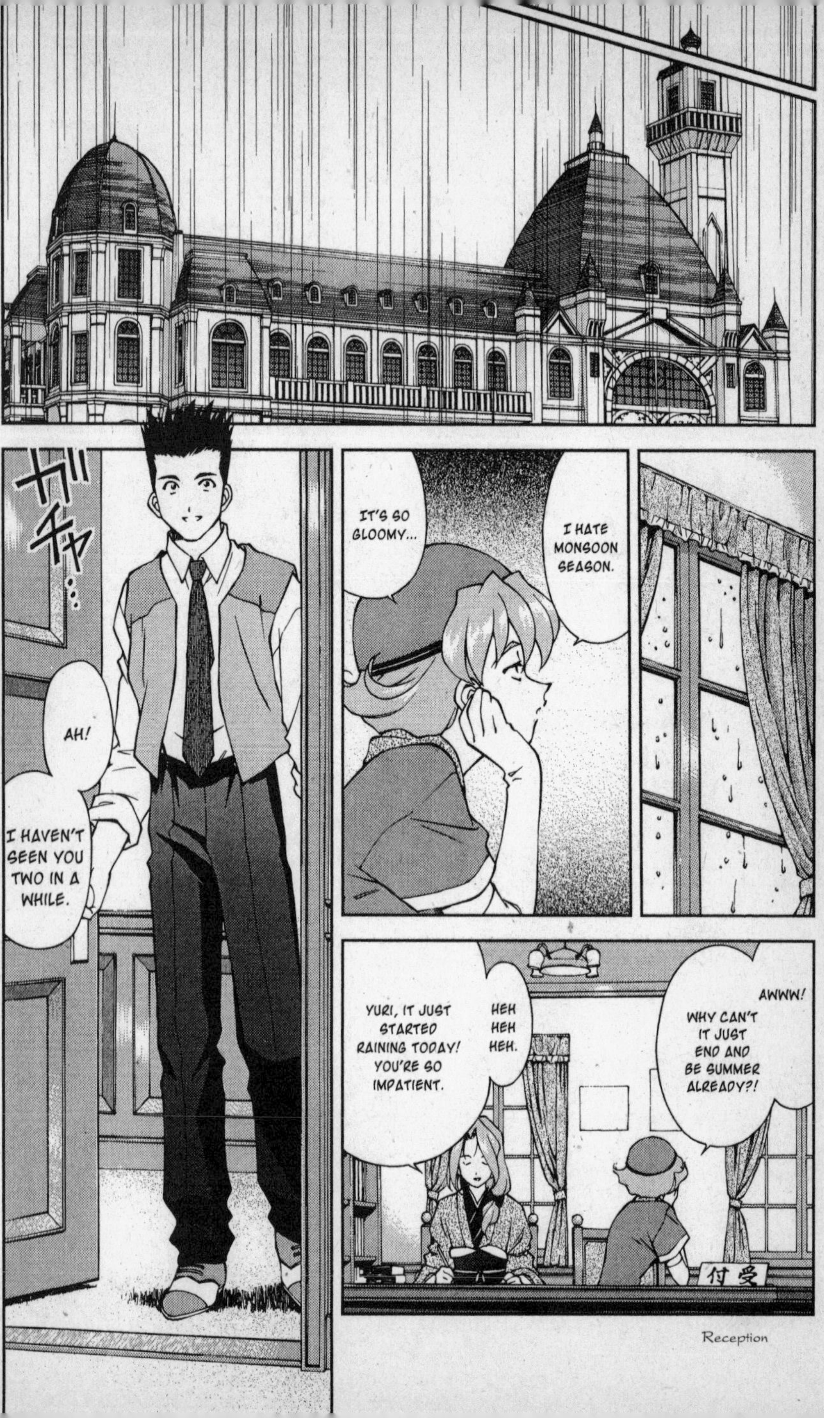
I HATE MONSOON SEASON.
IT'S SO GLOOMY...
AWWW! WHY CAN'T IT JUST END AND BE SUMMER ALREADY?!
HEH HEH HEH.
YURI, IT JUST STARTED RAINING TODAY! YOU'RE SO IMPATIENT.
付受
Reception
ガチャ...
AH!
I HAVEN'T SEEN YOU TWO IN A WHILE.

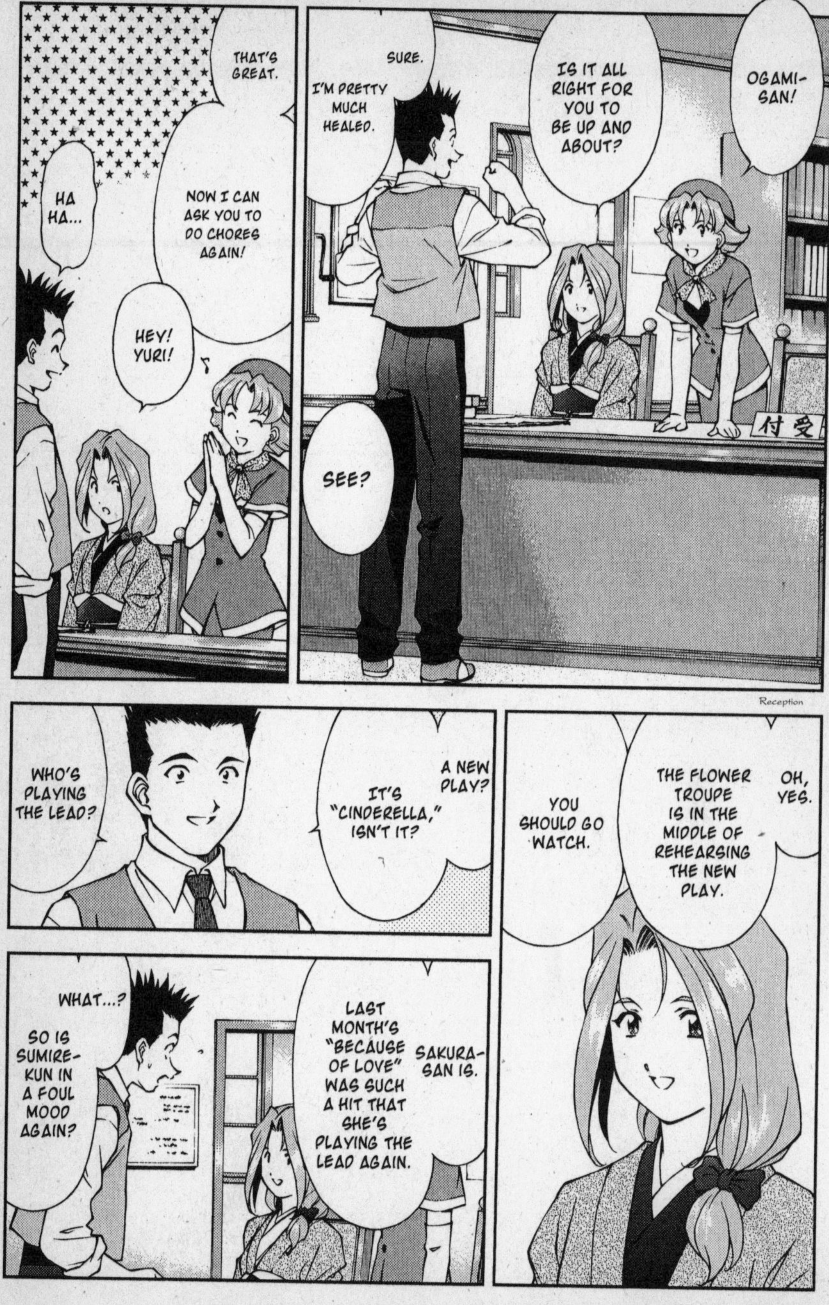
OGAMI-SAN!
IS IT ALL RIGHT FOR YOU TO BE UP AND ABOUT?
SURE.
I'M PRETTY MUCH HEALED.
SEE?
THAT'S GREAT.
NOW I CAN ASK YOU TO DO CHORES AGAIN!
HA HA...
HEY! YURI!
付受
OH, YES.
THE FLOWER TROUPE IS IN THE MIDDLE OF REHEARSING THE NEW PLAY.
YOU SHOULD GO WATCH.
A NEW PLAY?
IT'S "CINDERELLA," ISN'T IT?
WHO'S PLAYING THE LEAD?
SAKURA-SAN IS.
LAST MONTH'S "BECAUSE OF LOVE" WAS SUCH A HIT THAT SHE'S PLAYING THE LEAD AGAIN.
WHAT...?
SO IS SUMIRE-KUN IN A FOUL MOOD AGAIN?

Reception

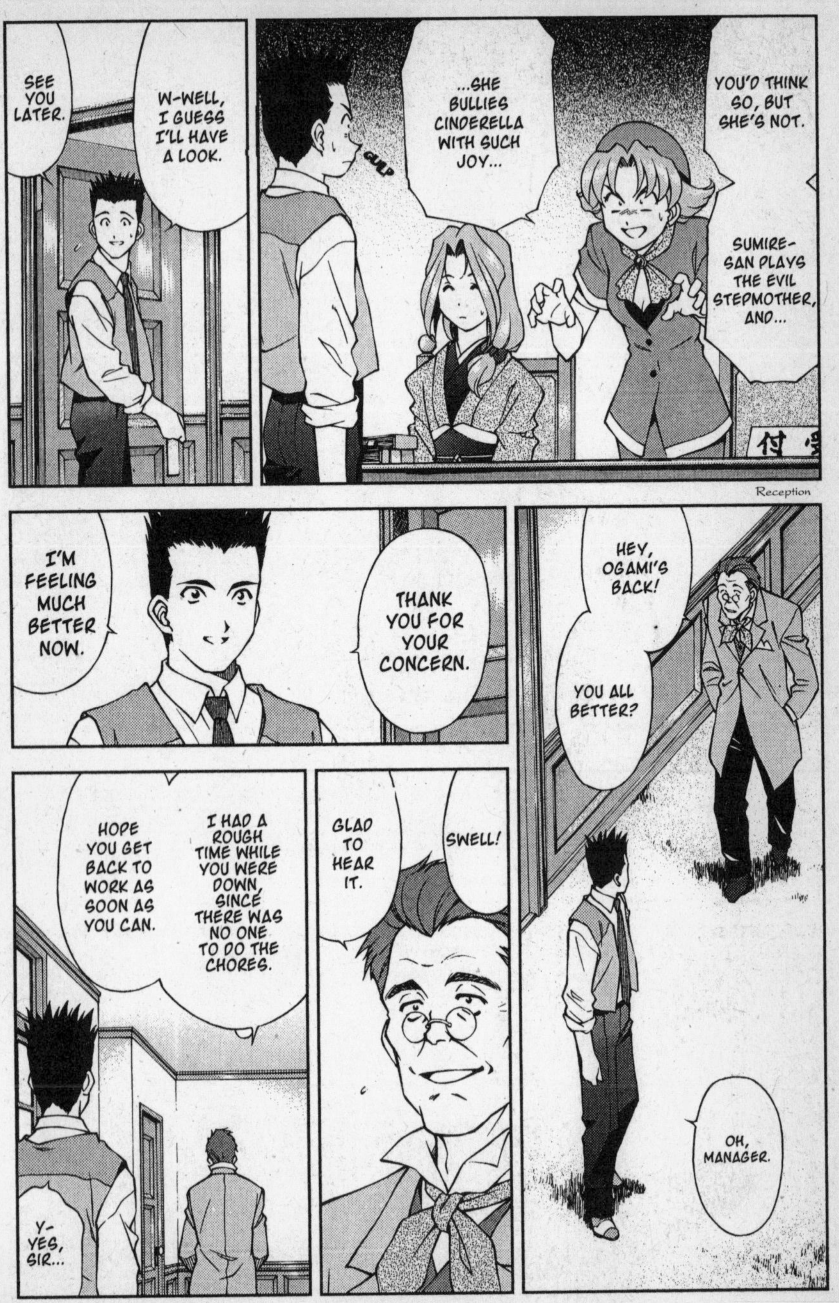
YOU'D THINK SO, BUT SHE'S NOT.
SUMIRE-SAN PLAYS THE EVIL STEPMOTHER, AND...
...SHE BULLIES CINDERELLA WITH SUCH JOY...
GULP
W-WELL, I GUESS I'LL HAVE A LOOK.
SEE YOU LATER.
HEY, OGAMI'S BACK!
YOU ALL BETTER?
OH, MANAGER.
I'M FEELING MUCH BETTER NOW.
THANK YOU FOR YOUR CONCERN.
SWELL!
GLAD TO HEAR IT.
I HAD A ROUGH TIME WHILE YOU WERE DOWN, SINCE THERE WAS NO ONE TO DO THE CHORES.
HOPE YOU GET BACK TO WORK AS SOON AS YOU CAN.
Y-YES, SIR...
Reception

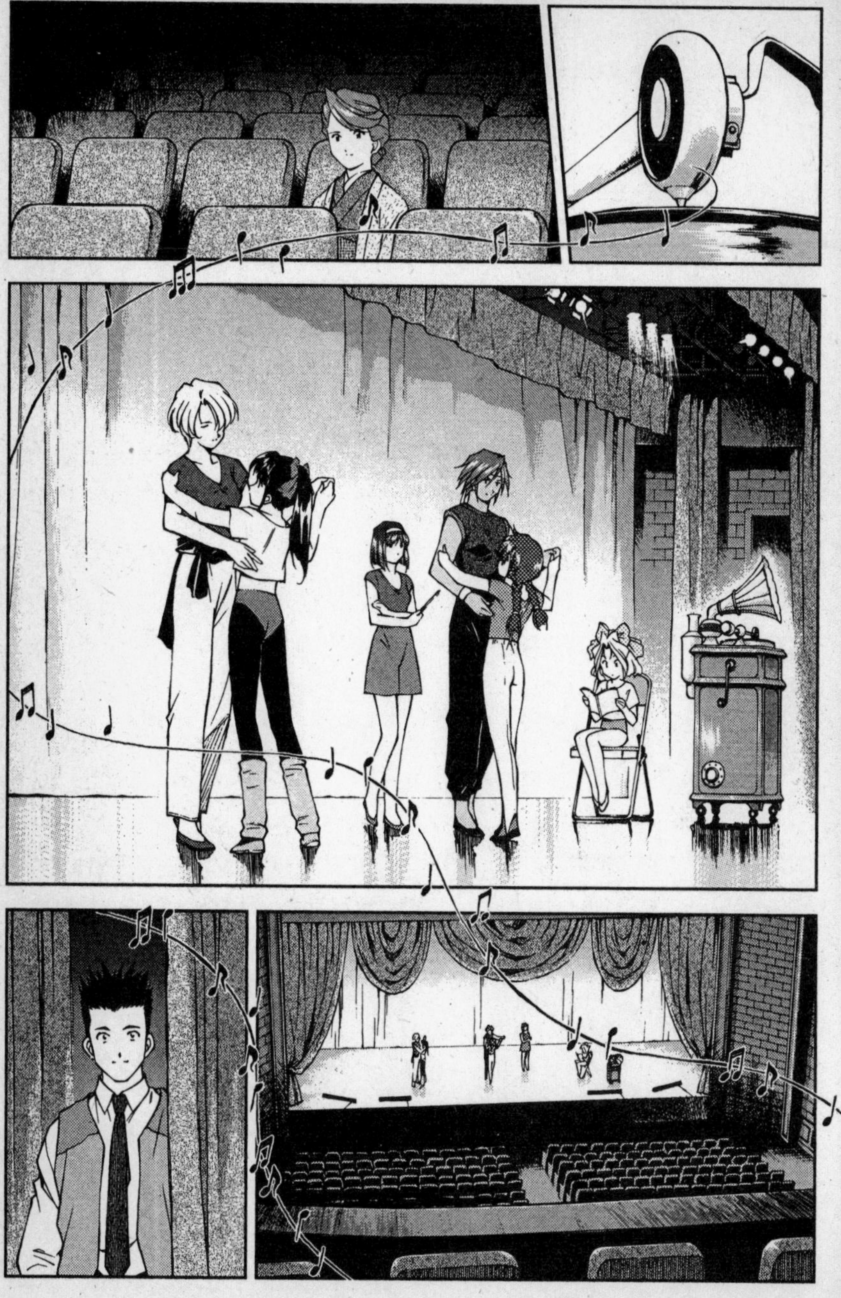

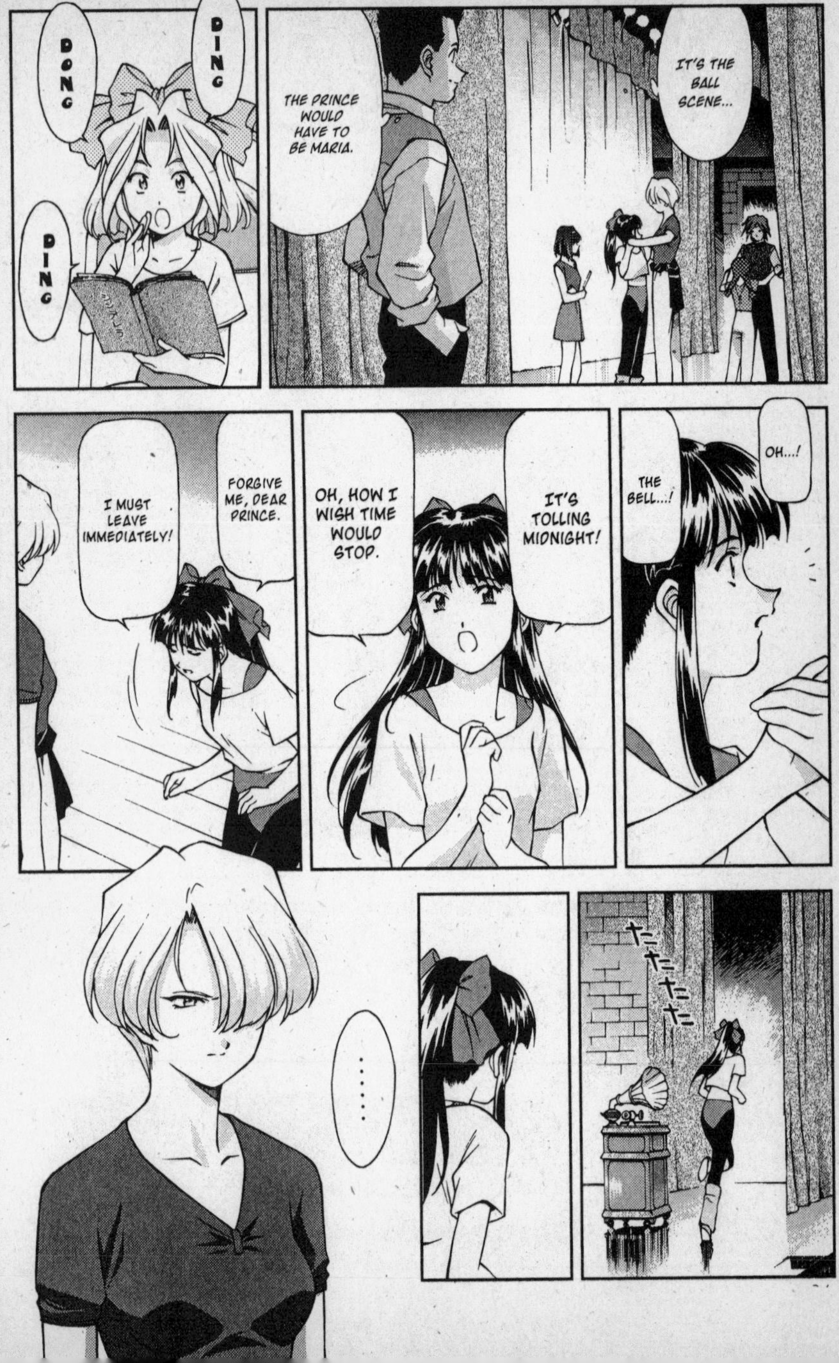
IT'S THE BALL SCENE...
THE PRINCE WOULD HAVE TO BE MARIA.
DING
DONG
DING
OH...!
THE BELL...!
IT'S TOLLING MIDNIGHT!
OH, HOW I WISH TIME WOULD STOP.
FORGIVE ME, DEAR PRINCE.
I MUST LEAVE IMMEDIATELY!
たたたた
......

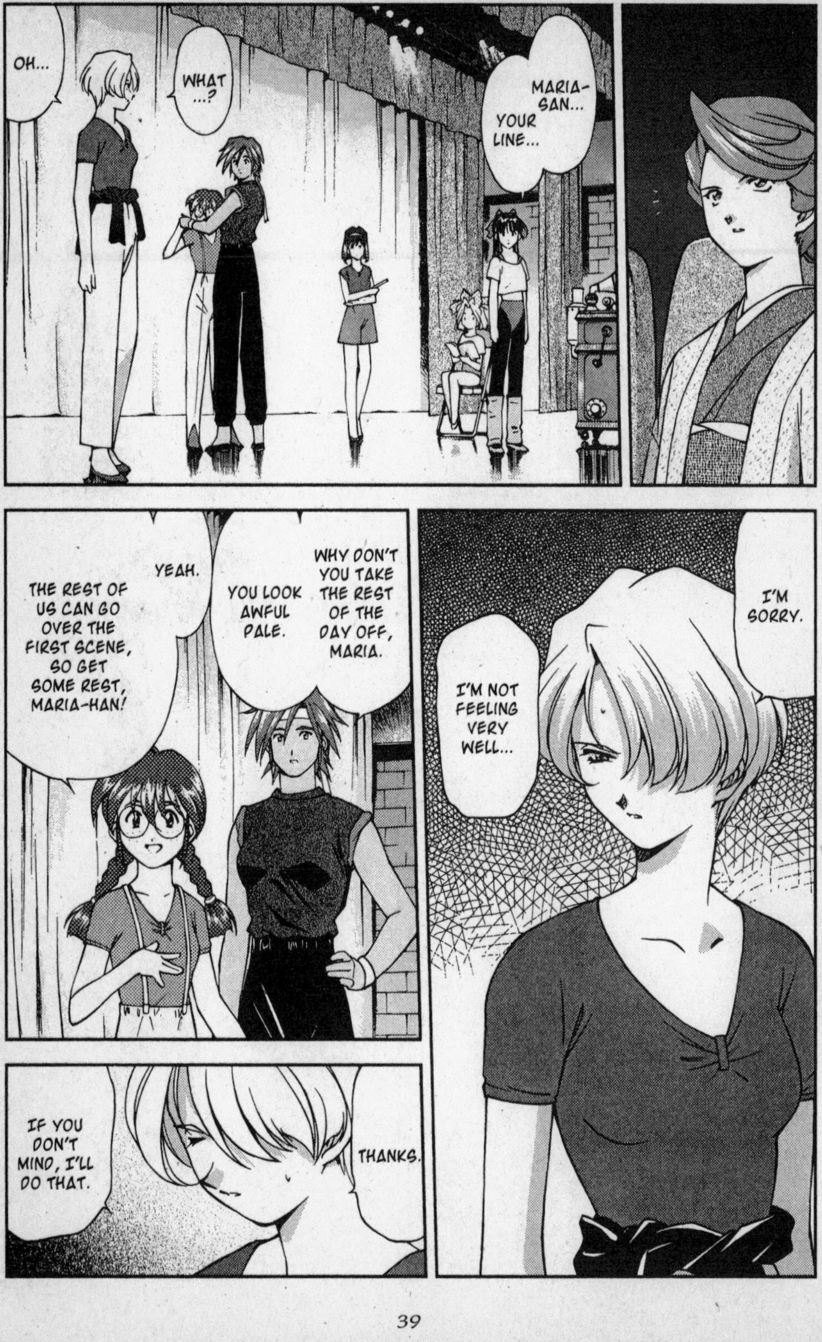
MARIA-SAN... YOUR LINE...
WHAT ...?
OH...
I'M SORRY.
I'M NOT FEELING VERY WELL...
WHY DON'T YOU TAKE THE REST OF THE DAY OFF, MARIA.
YOU LOOK AWFUL PALE.
YEAH.
THE REST OF US CAN GO OVER THE FIRST SCENE, SO GET SOME REST, MARIA-HAN!
THANKS.
IF YOU DON'T MIND, I'LL DO THAT.

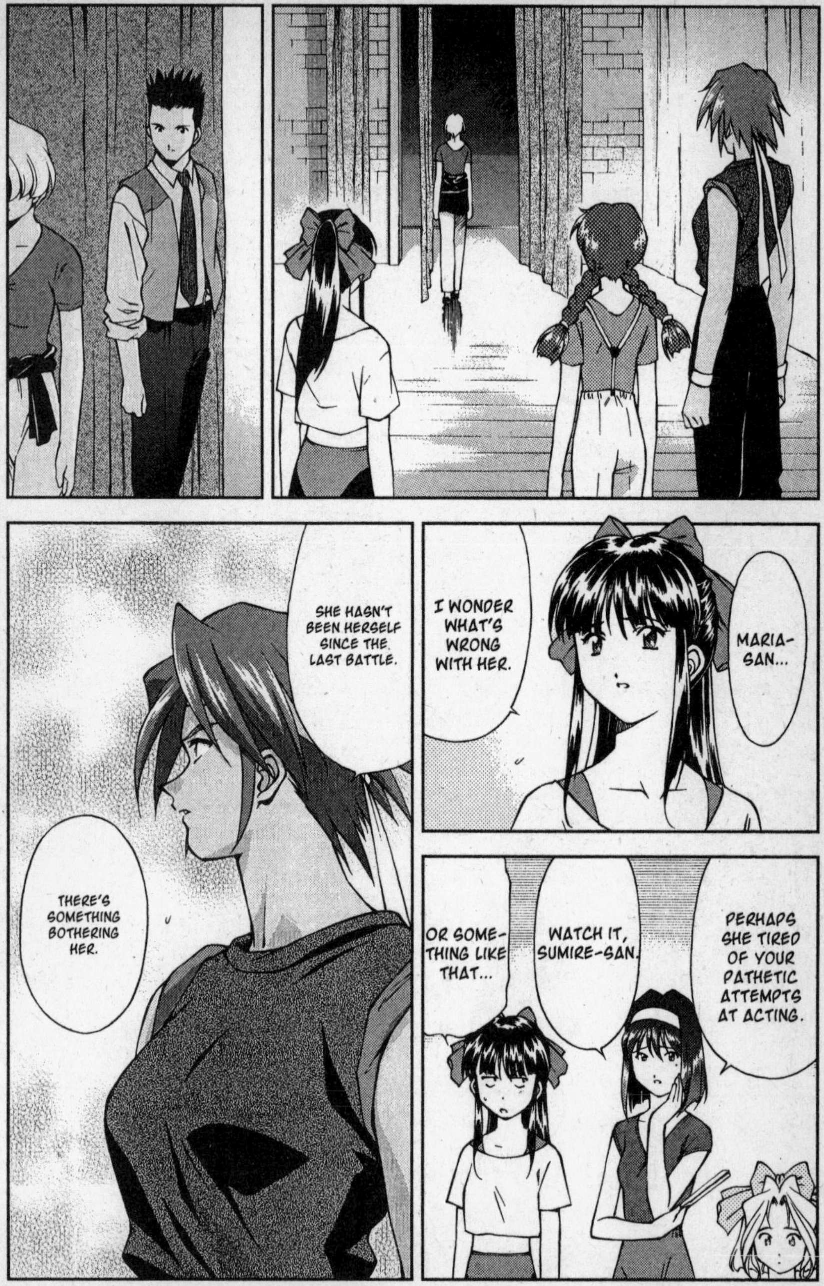
MARIA-SAN...
I WONDER WHAT'S WRONG WITH HER.
PERHAPS SHE TIRED OF YOUR PATHETIC ATTEMPTS AT ACTING.
WATCH IT, SUMIRE-SAN.
OR SOMETHING LIKE THAT...
SHE HASN'T BEEN HERSELF SINCE THE LAST BATTLE.
THERE'S SOMETHING BOTHERING HER.

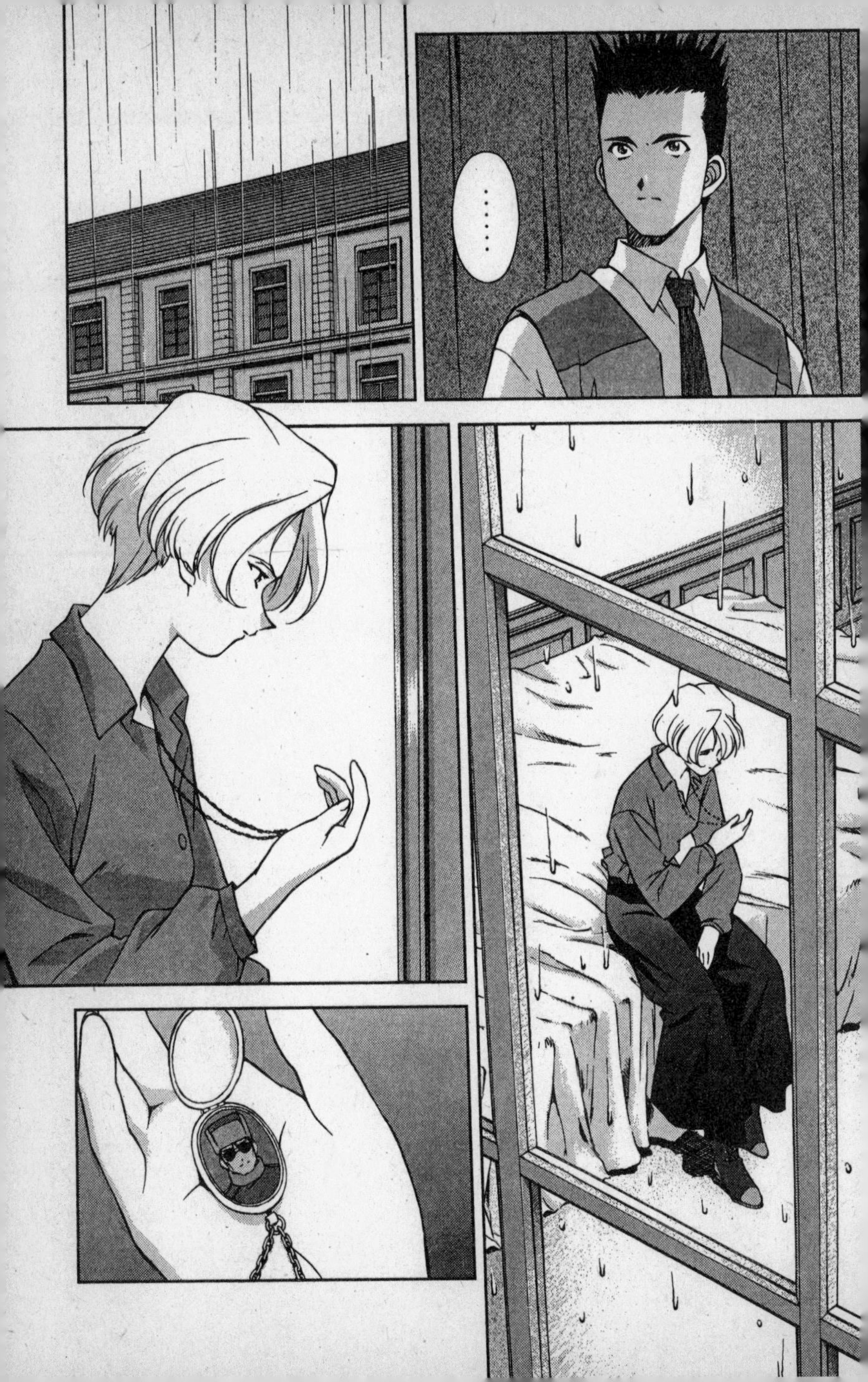
......

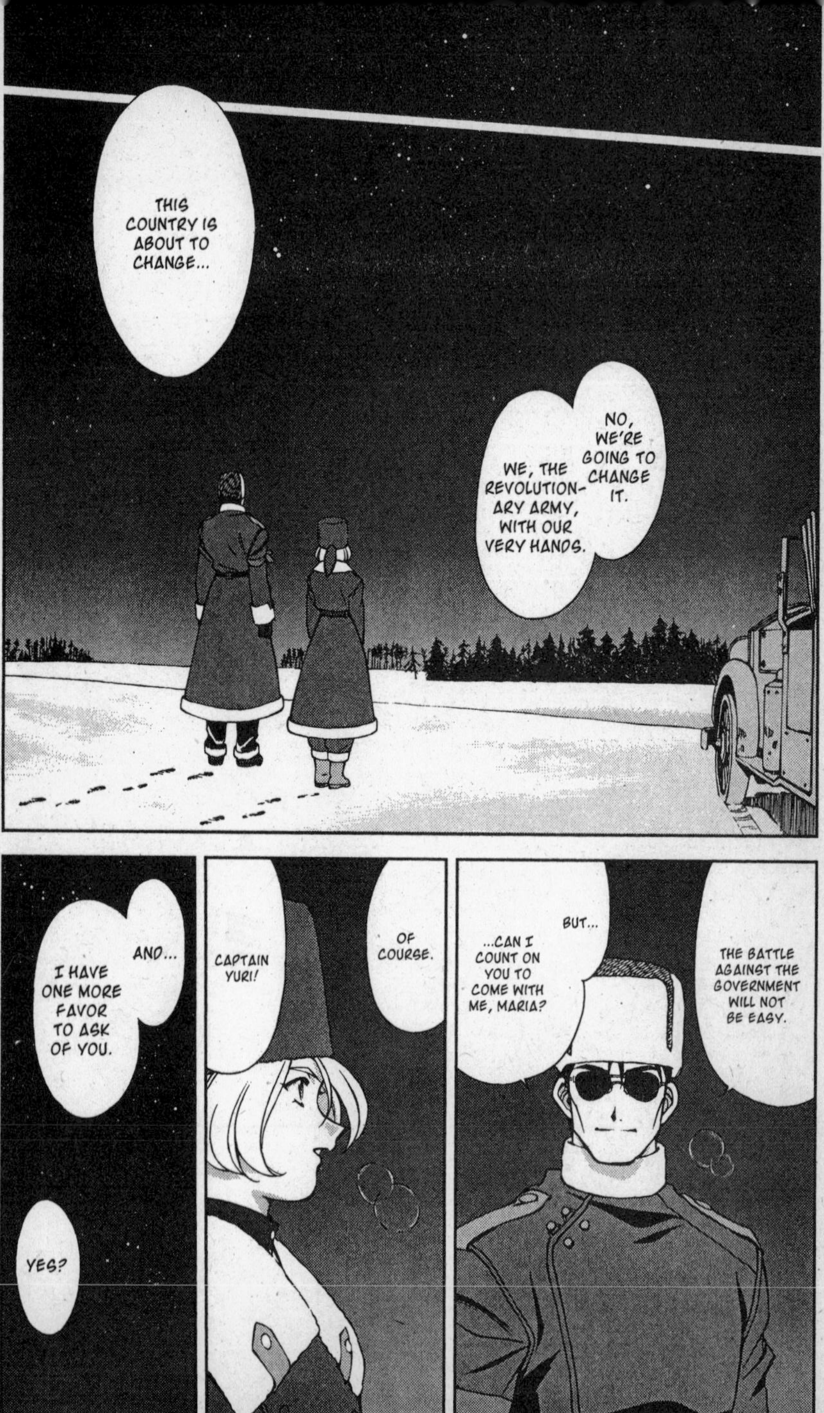
THIS COUNTRY IS ABOUT TO CHANGE...
NO, WE'RE GOING TO CHANGE IT.
WE, THE REVOLUTION-ARY ARMY, WITH OUR VERY HANDS.
THE BATTLE AGAINST THE GOVERNMENT WILL NOT BE EASY.
BUT...
...CAN I COUNT ON YOU TO COME WITH ME, MARIA?
OF COURSE.
CAPTAIN YURI!
AND...
I HAVE ONE MORE FAVOR TO ASK OF YOU.
YES?

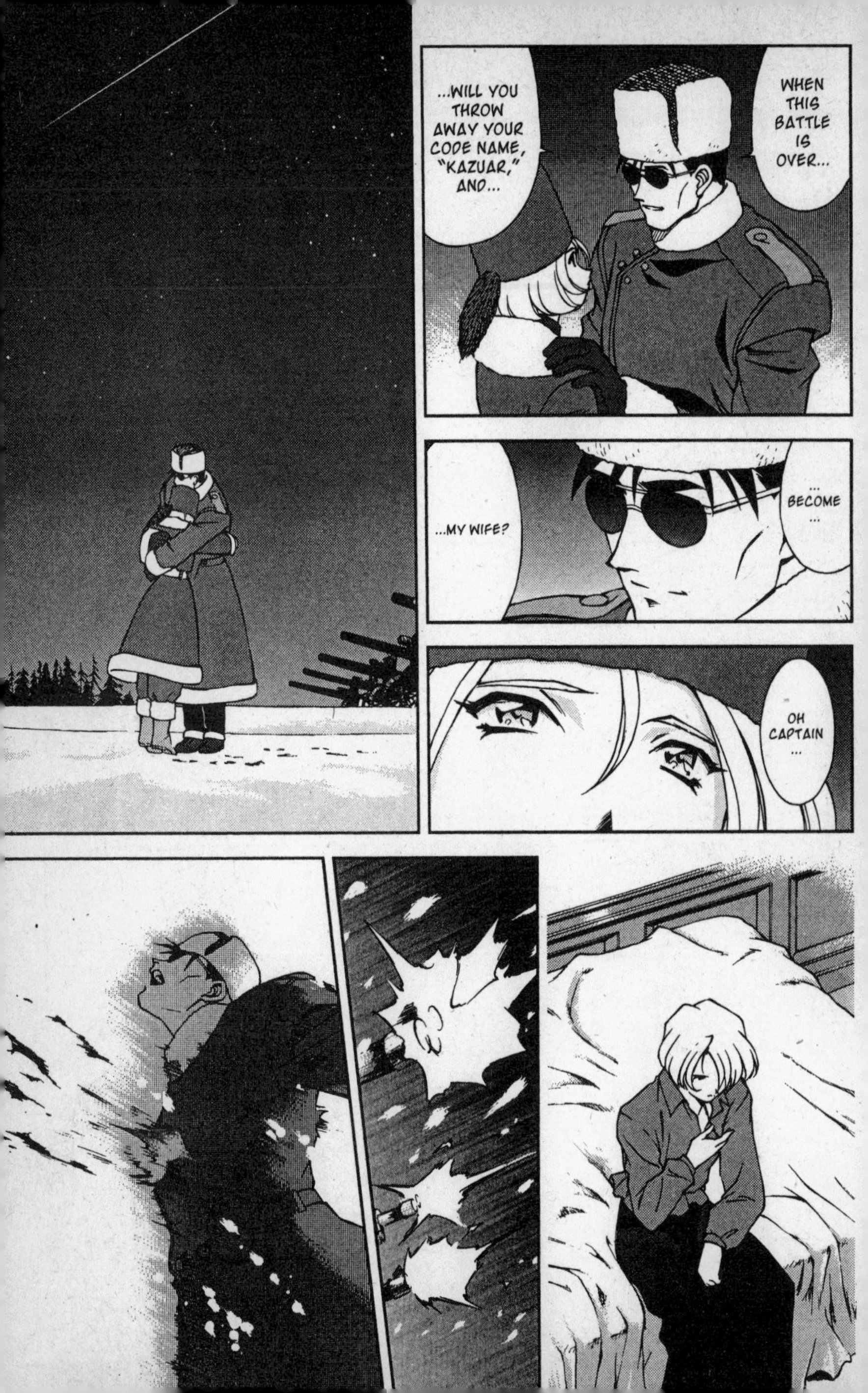
WHEN THIS BATTLE IS OVER...
...WILL YOU THROW AWAY YOUR CODE NAME, "KAZUAR," AND...
... BECOME ...
...MY WIFE?
OH CAPTAIN ...

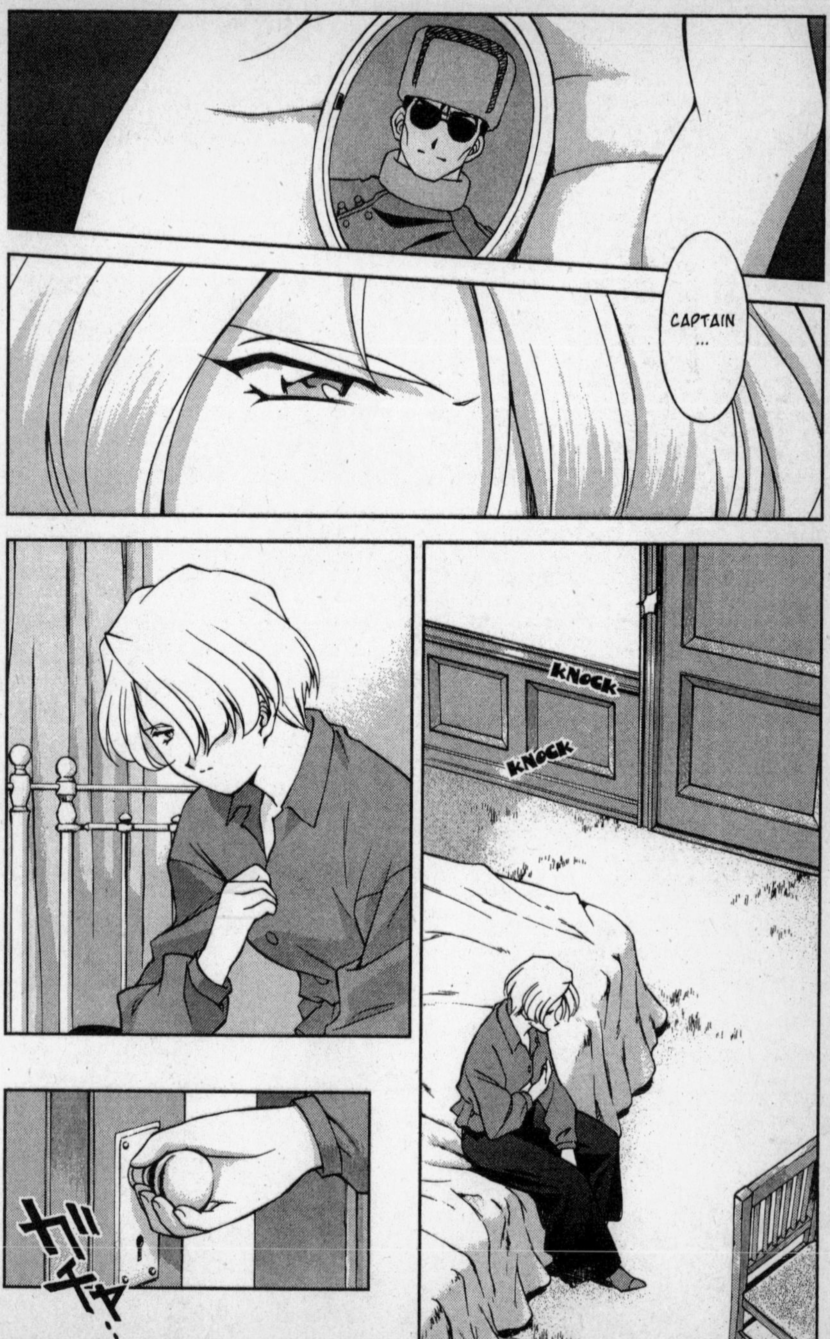
CAPTAIN ...
KNOCK
KNOCK
ガチャ‥

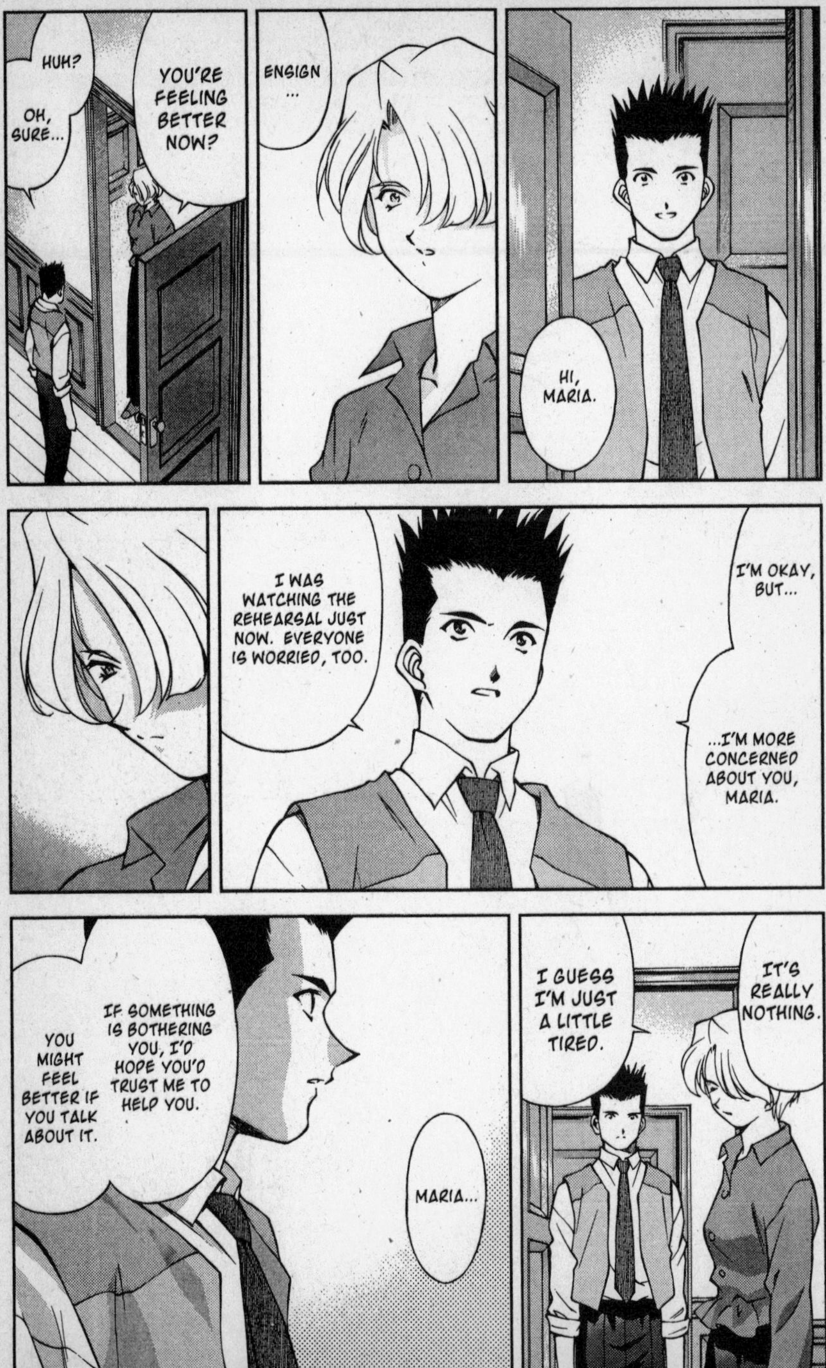
HI, MARIA.
ENSIGN ...
YOU'RE FEELING BETTER NOW?
HUH?
OH, SURE...
I'M OKAY, BUT...
I WAS WATCHING THE REHEARSAL JUST NOW. EVERYONE IS WORRIED, TOO.
...I'M MORE CONCERNED ABOUT YOU, MARIA.
IT'S REALLY NOTHING.
I GUESS I'M JUST A LITTLE TIRED.
IF SOMETHING IS BOTHERING YOU, I'D HOPE YOU'D TRUST ME TO HELP YOU.
YOU MIGHT FEEL BETTER IF YOU TALK ABOUT IT.
MARIA...

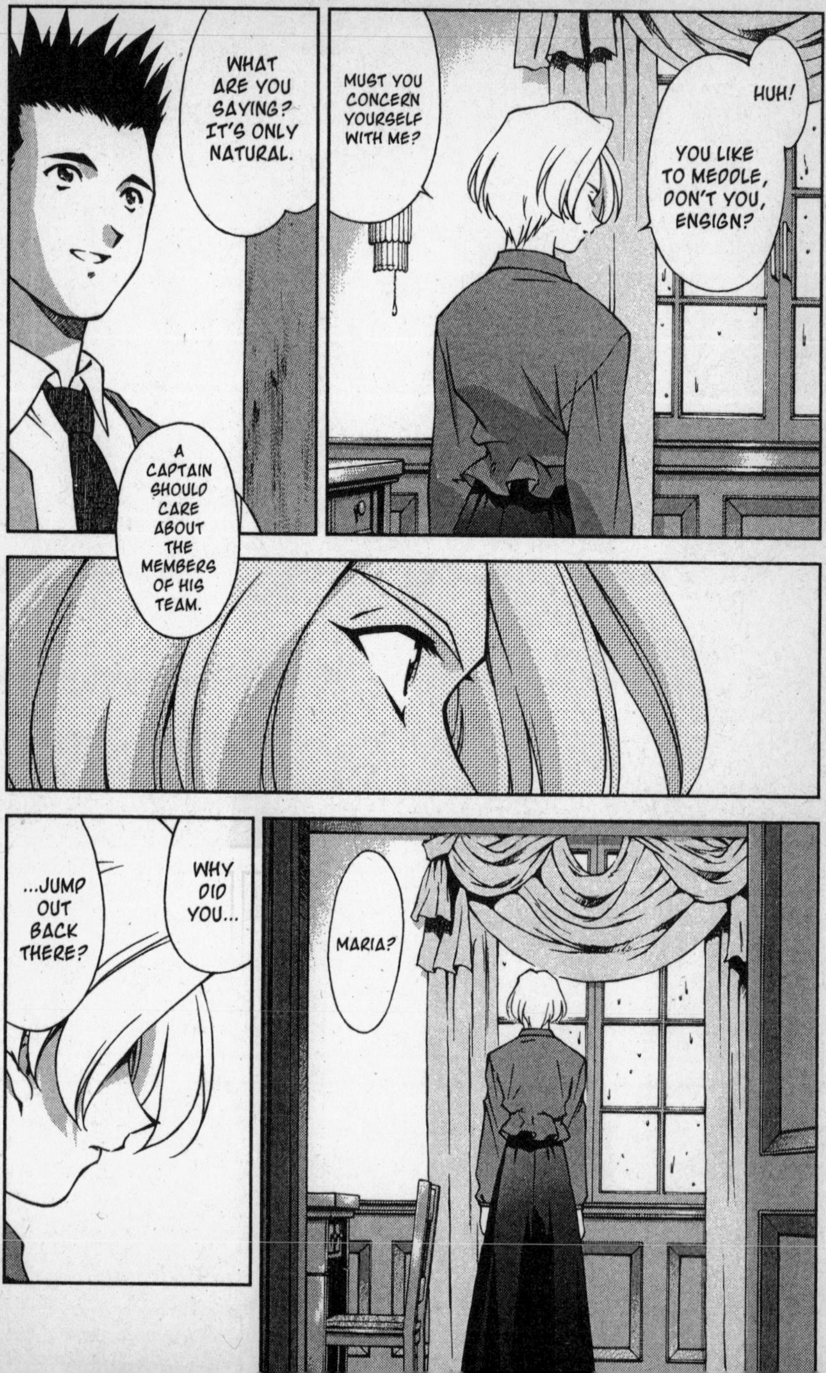
HUH!
YOU LIKE TO MEDDLE, DON'T YOU, ENSIGN?
MUST YOU CONCERN YOURSELF WITH ME?
WHAT ARE YOU SAYING? IT'S ONLY NATURAL.
A CAPTAIN SHOULD CARE ABOUT THE MEMBERS OF HIS TEAM.
MARIA?
WHY DID YOU...
...JUMP OUT BACK THERE?

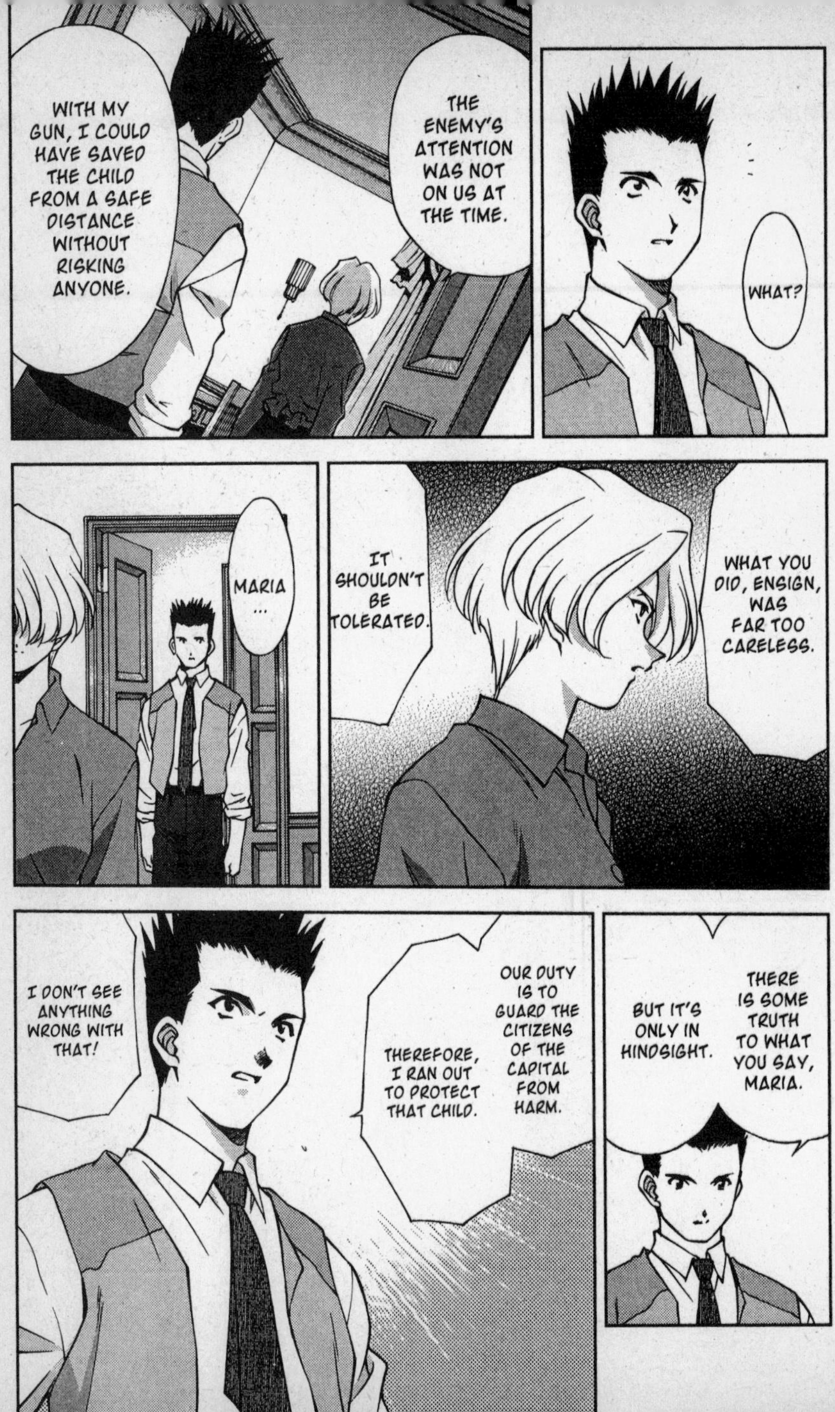
WHAT?
THE ENEMY'S ATTENTION WAS NOT ON US AT THE TIME.
WITH MY GUN, I COULD HAVE SAVED THE CHILD FROM A SAFE DISTANCE WITHOUT RISKING ANYONE.
WHAT YOU DID, ENSIGN, WAS FAR TOO CARELESS.
IT SHOULDN'T BE TOLERATED.
MARIA ...
THERE IS SOME TRUTH TO WHAT YOU SAY, MARIA.
BUT IT'S ONLY IN HINDSIGHT.
OUR DUTY IS TO GUARD THE CITIZENS OF THE CAPITAL FROM HARM.
THEREFORE, I RAN OUT TO PROTECT THAT CHILD.
I DON'T SEE ANYTHING WRONG WITH THAT!

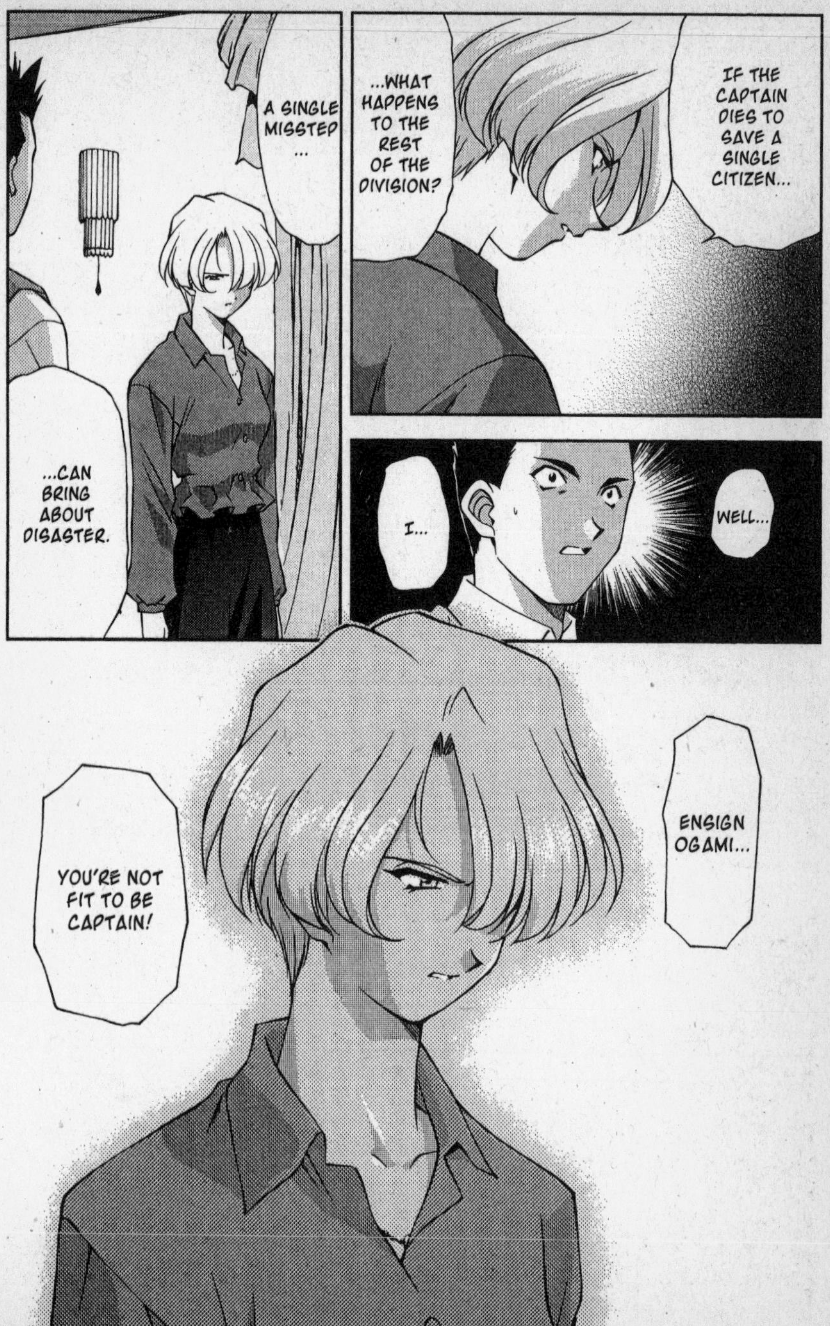
IF THE CAPTAIN DIES TO SAVE A SINGLE CITIZEN...
...WHAT HAPPENS TO THE REST OF THE DIVISION?
WELL...
I...
A SINGLE MISSTEP ...
...CAN BRING ABOUT DISASTER.
ENSIGN OGAMI...
YOU'RE NOT FIT TO BE CAPTAIN!

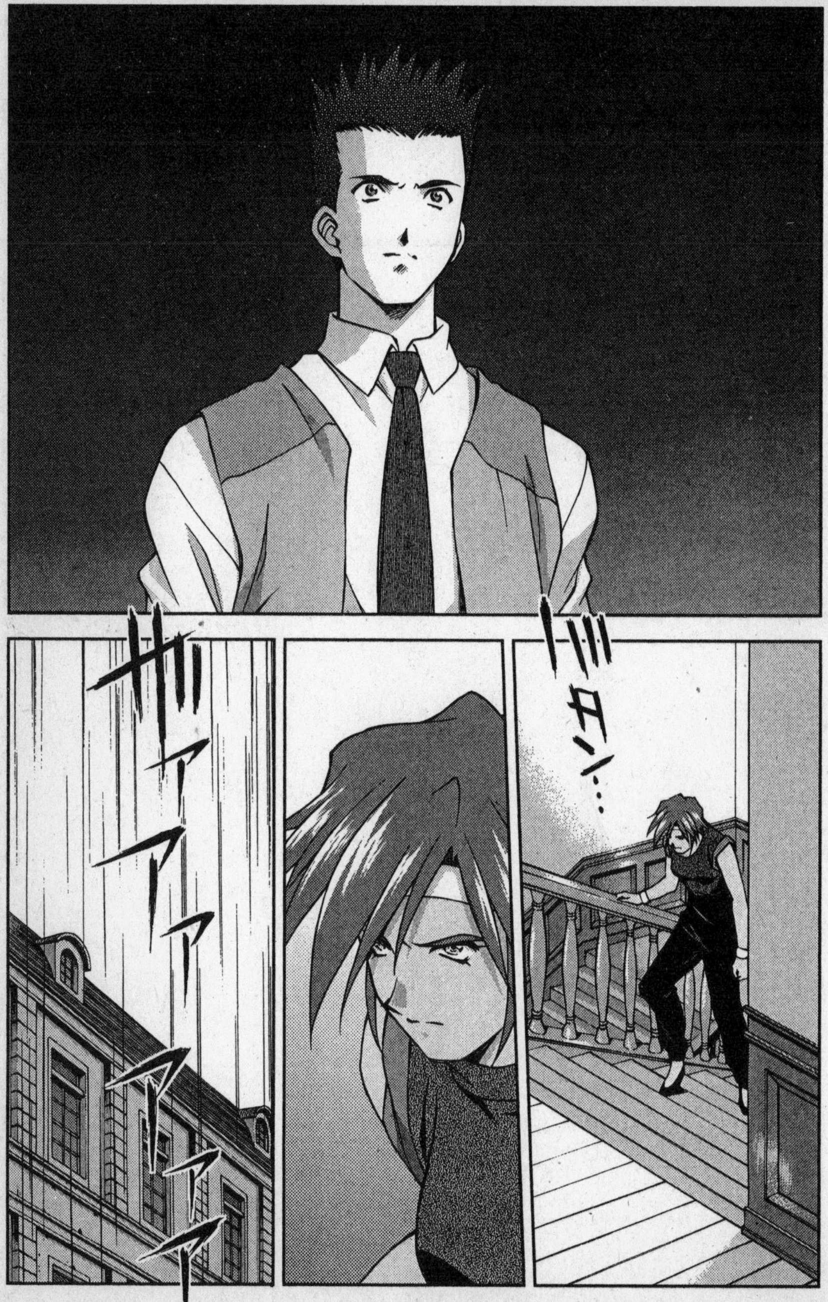
バタン…
ザァアァアァァ

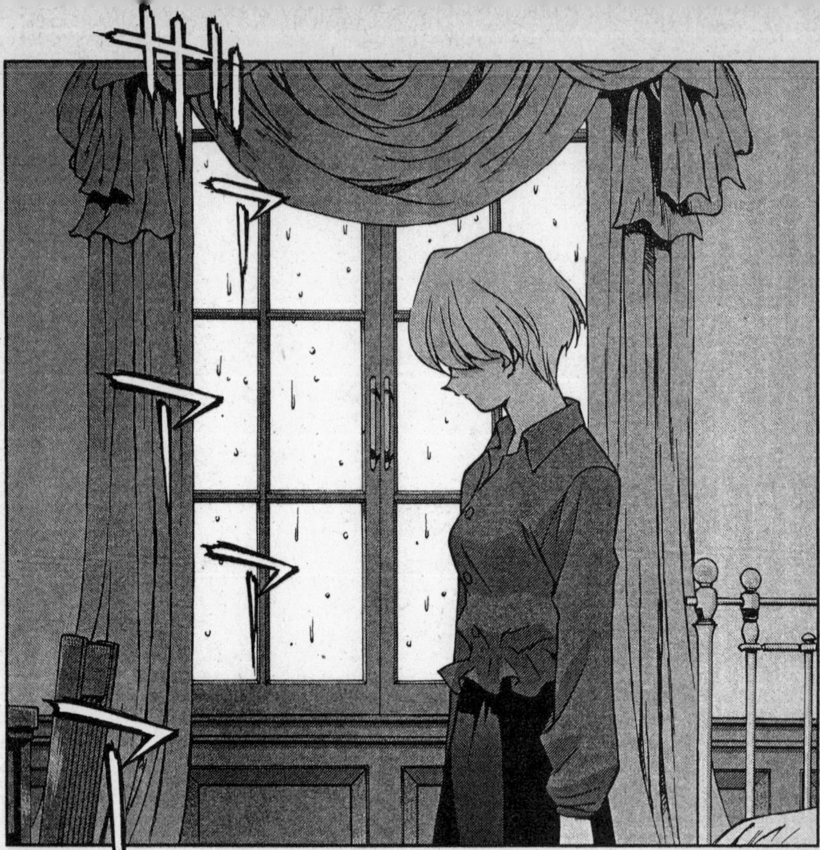
ザァァァァ
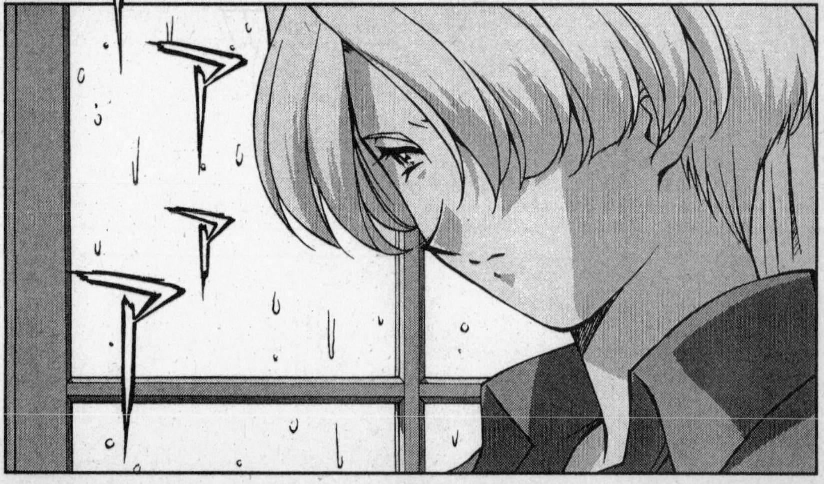
ァァァ

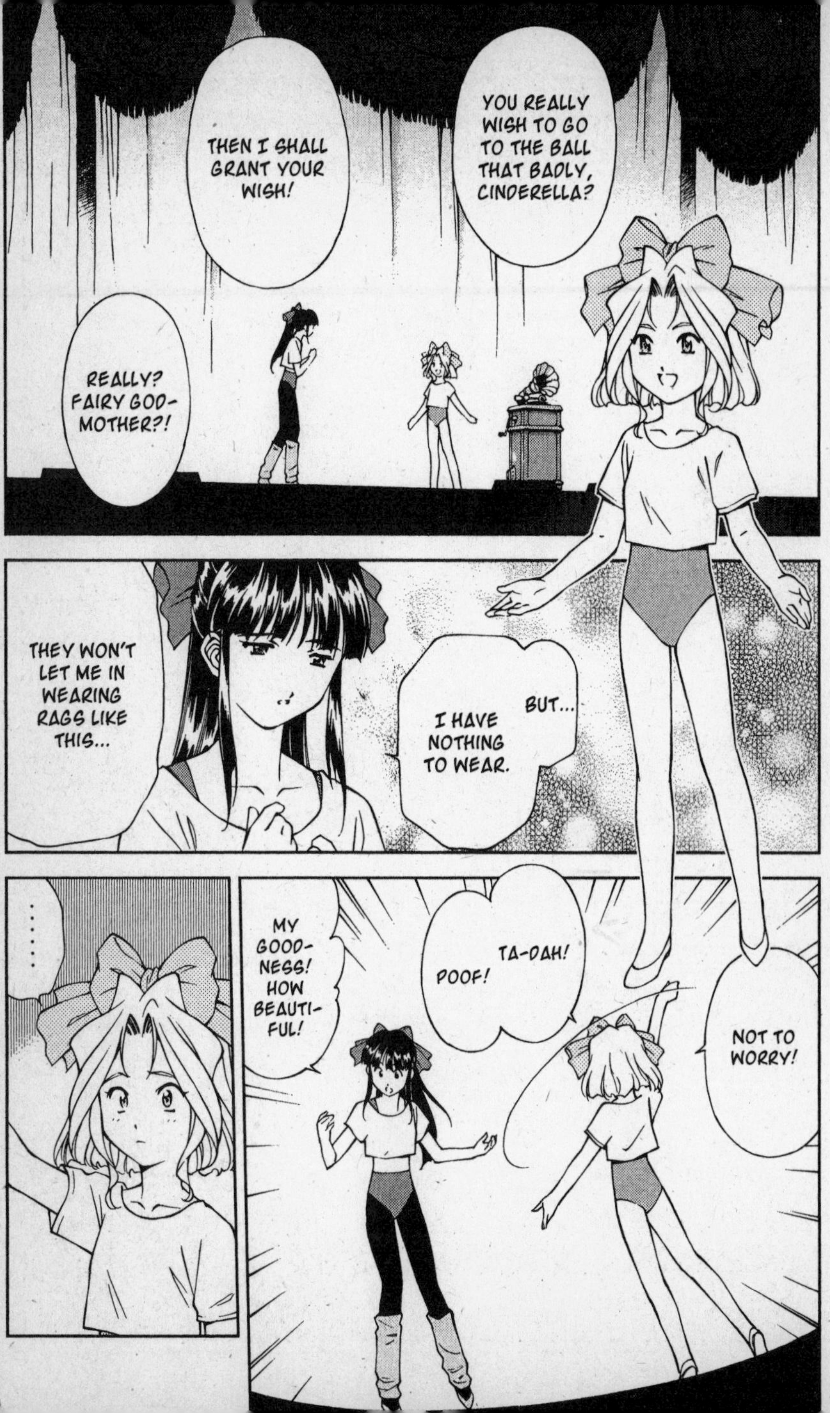
YOU REALLY WISH TO GO TO THE BALL THAT BADLY, CINDERELLA?
THEN I SHALL GRANT YOUR WISH!
REALLY? FAIRY GOD-MOTHER?!
BUT...
I HAVE NOTHING TO WEAR.
THEY WON'T LET ME IN WEARING RAGS LIKE THIS...
NOT TO WORRY!
TA-DAH!
POOF!
MY GOOD-NESS! HOW BEAUTI-FUL!
......

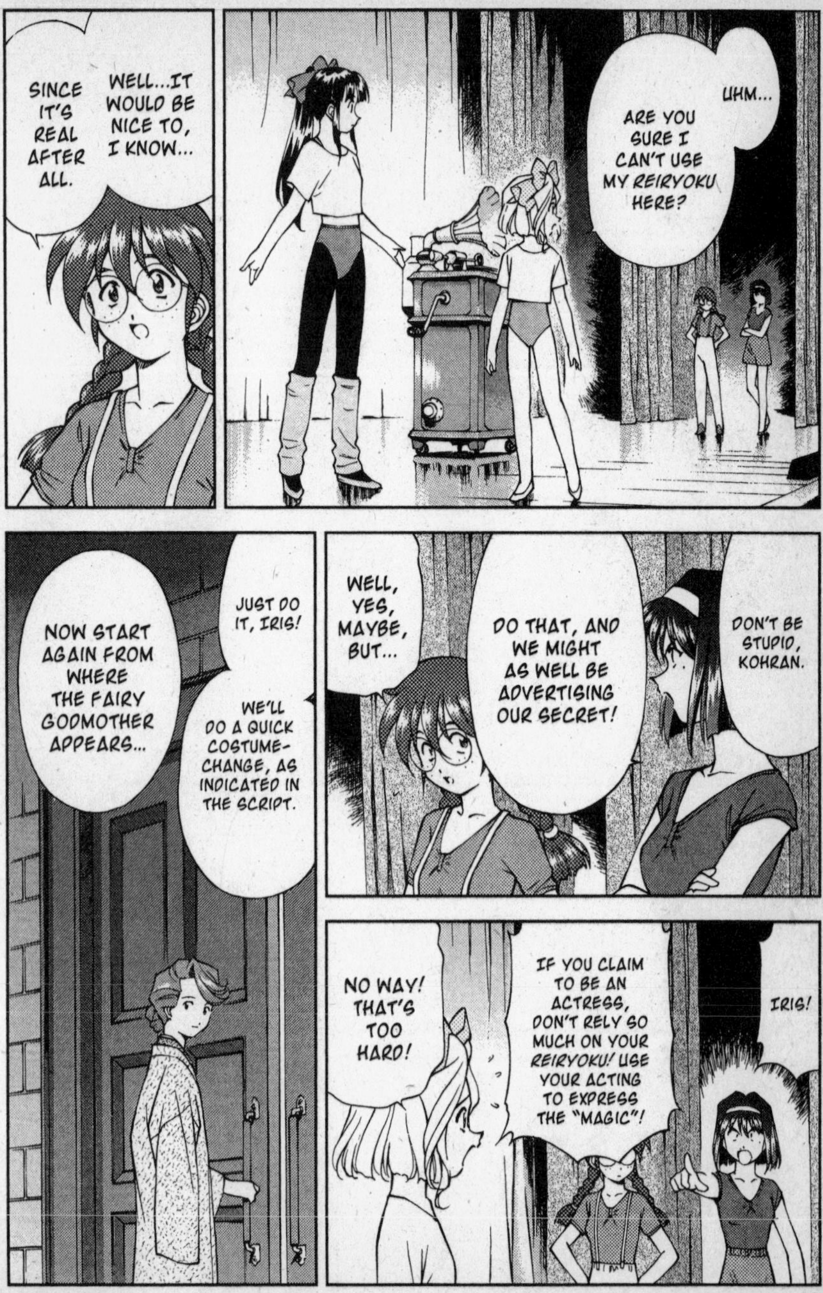
UHM...
ARE YOU SURE I CAN'T USE MY *REIRYOKU* HERE?
WELL...IT WOULD BE NICE TO, I KNOW...
SINCE IT'S REAL AFTER ALL.
DON'T BE STUPID, KOHRAN.
DO THAT, AND WE MIGHT AS WELL BE ADVERTISING OUR SECRET!
WELL, YES, MAYBE, BUT...
IRIS!
IF YOU CLAIM TO BE AN ACTRESS, DON'T RELY SO MUCH ON YOUR *REIRYOKU*! USE YOUR ACTING TO EXPRESS THE "MAGIC"!
NO WAY! THAT'S TOO HARD!
JUST DO IT, IRIS!
NOW START AGAIN FROM WHERE THE FAIRY GODMOTHER APPEARS...
WE'LL DO A QUICK COSTUME-CHANGE, AS INDICATED IN THE SCRIPT.

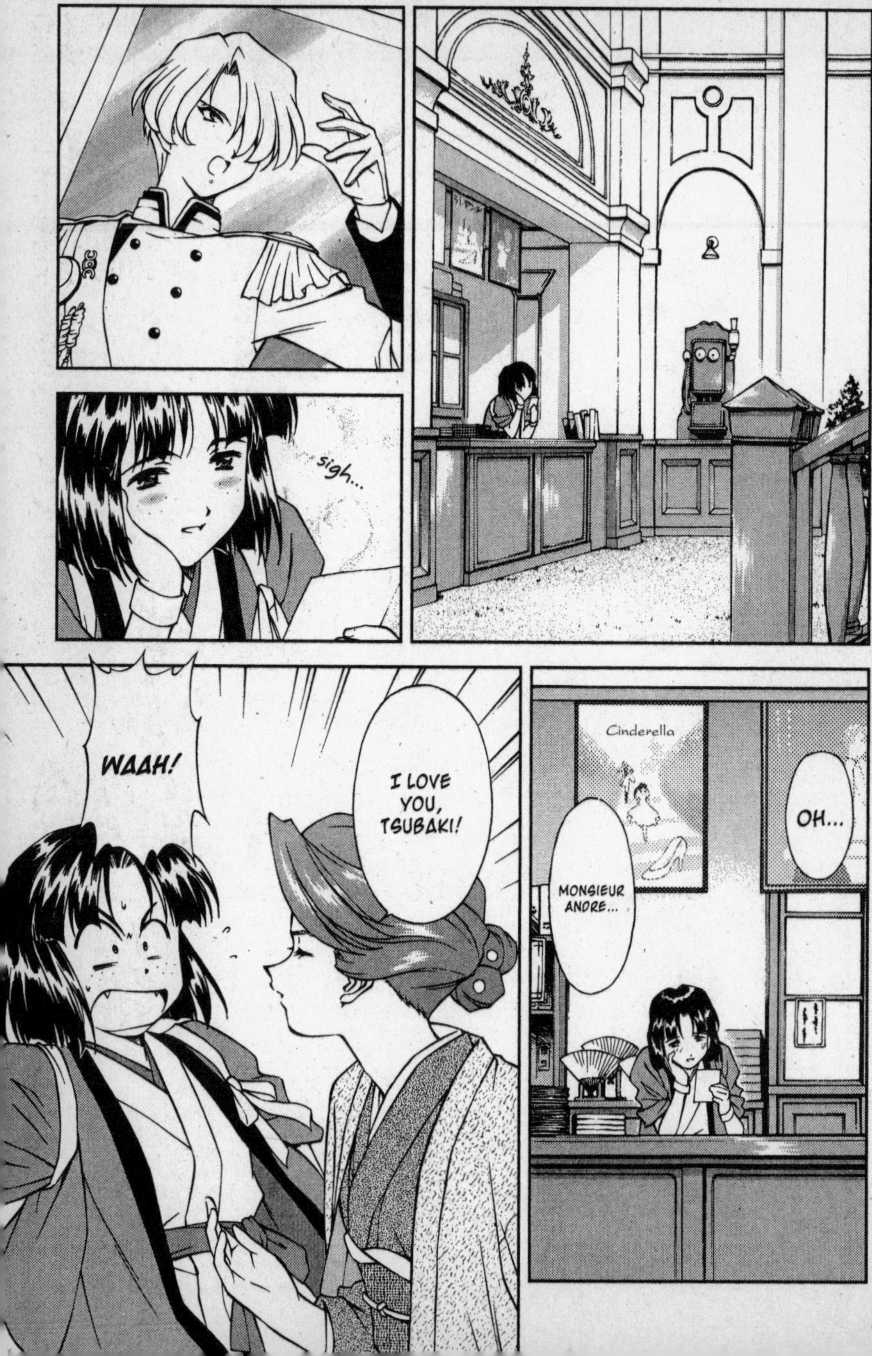
sigh...
Cinderella
OH...
MONSIEUR ANDRE...
I LOVE YOU, TSUBAKI!
WAAH!

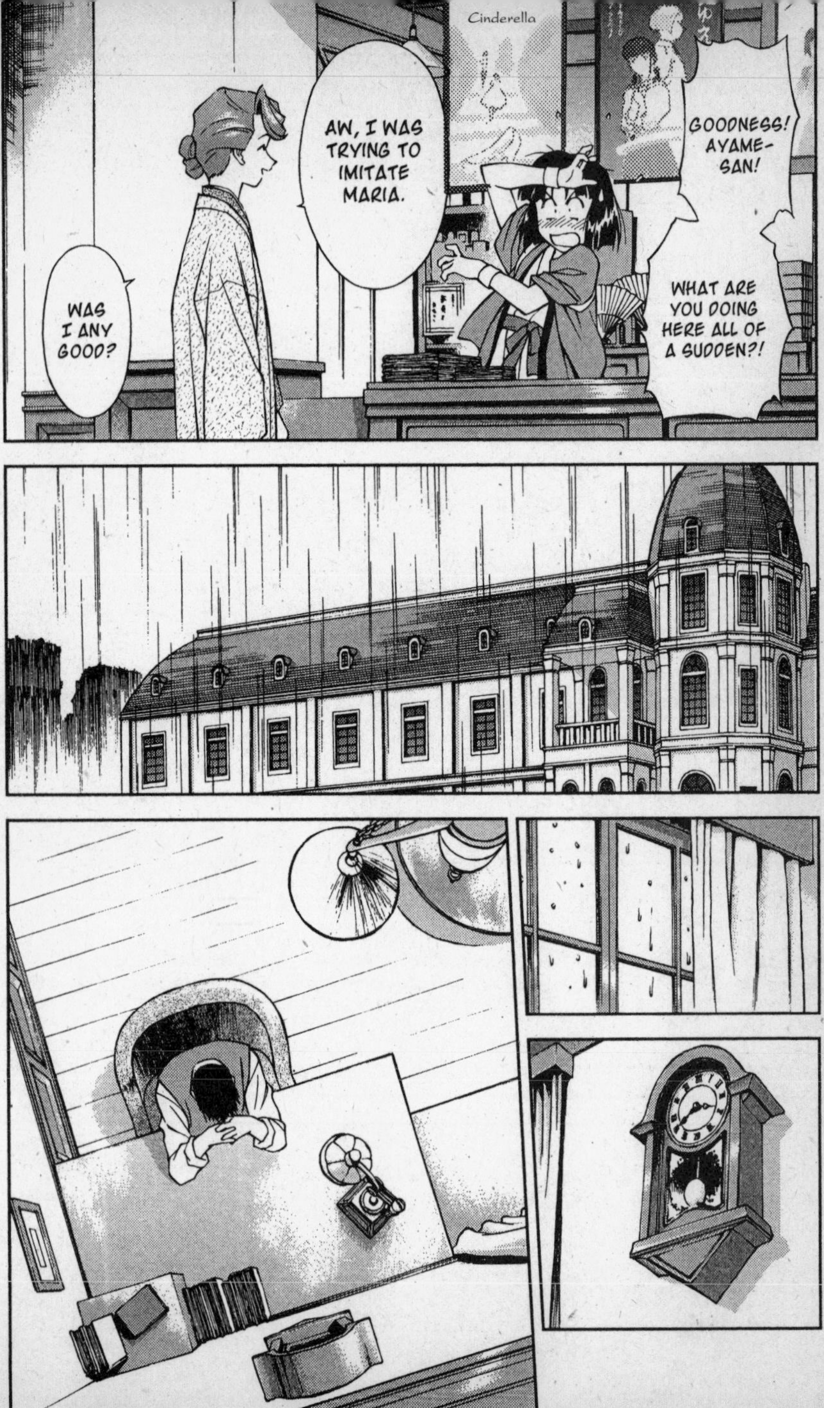
GOODNESS! AYAME-SAN!
WHAT ARE YOU DOING HERE ALL OF A SUDDEN?!
AW, I WAS TRYING TO IMITATE MARIA.
WAS I ANY GOOD?

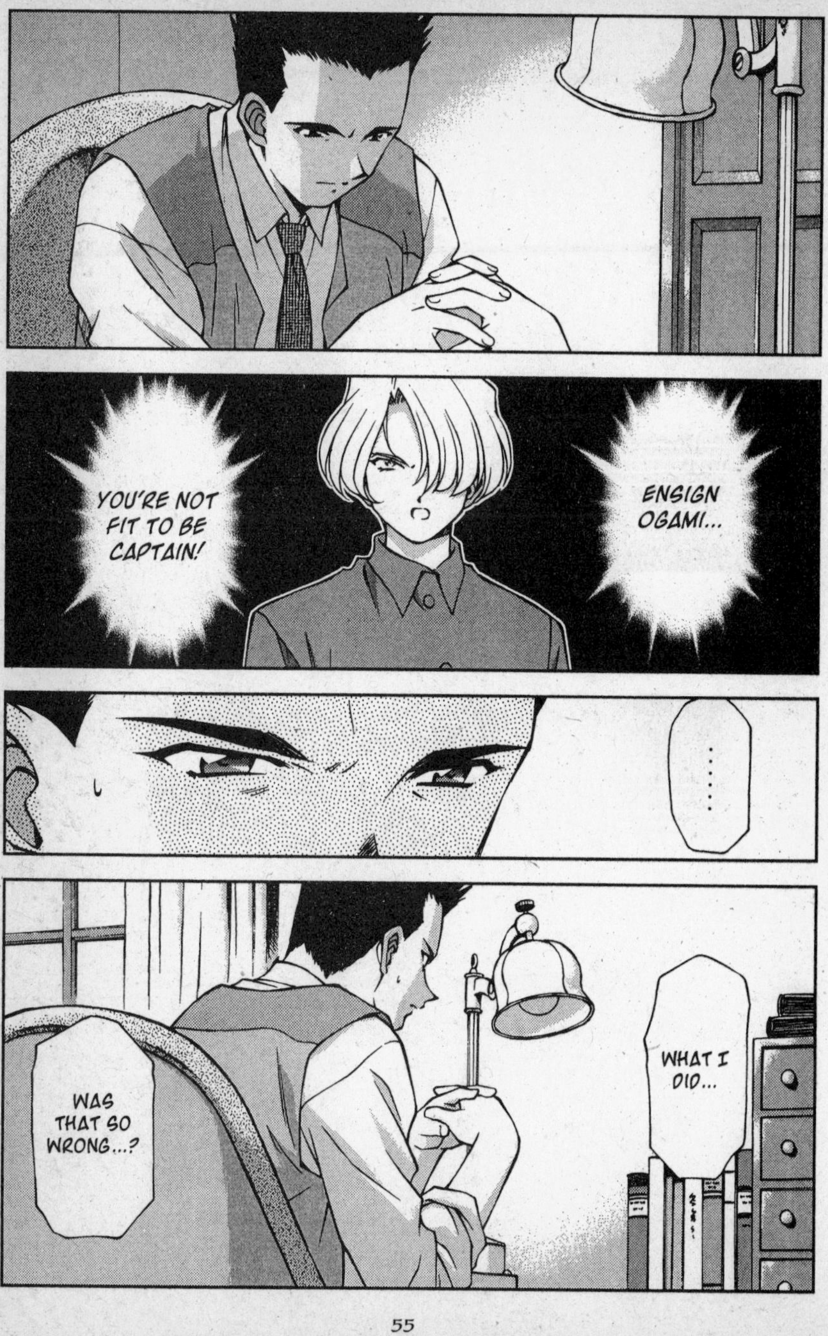
ENSIGN OGAMI...
YOU'RE NOT FIT TO BE CAPTAIN!
......
WHAT I DID...
WAS THAT SO WRONG...?

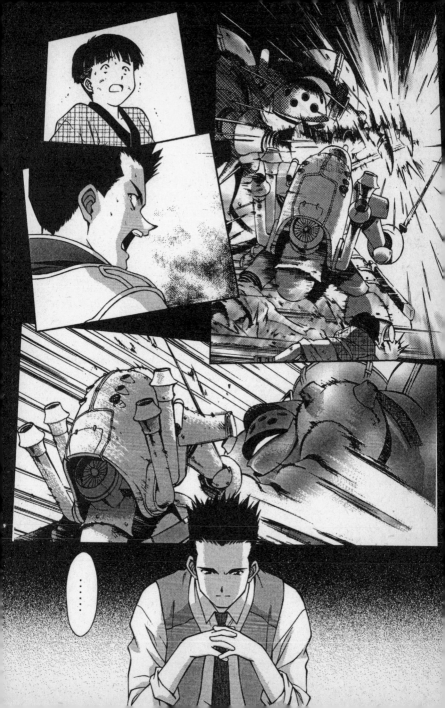

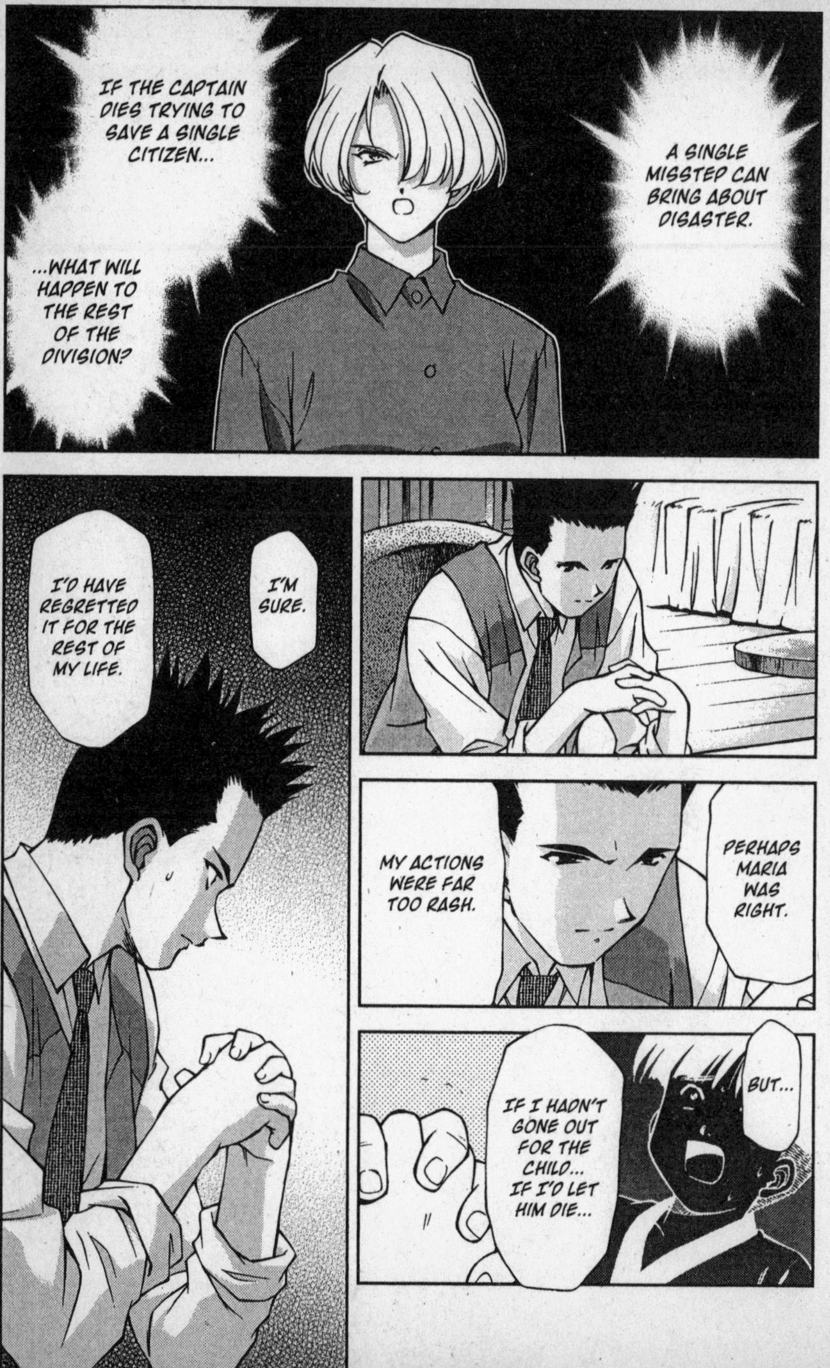
A SINGLE MISSTEP CAN BRING ABOUT DISASTER.
IF THE CAPTAIN DIES TRYING TO SAVE A SINGLE CITIZEN...
...WHAT WILL HAPPEN TO THE REST OF THE DIVISION?
PERHAPS MARIA WAS RIGHT.
MY ACTIONS WERE FAR TOO RASH.
BUT...
IF I HADN'T GONE OUT FOR THE CHILD... IF I'D LET HIM DIE...
I'M SURE.
I'D HAVE REGRETTED IT FOR THE REST OF MY LIFE.

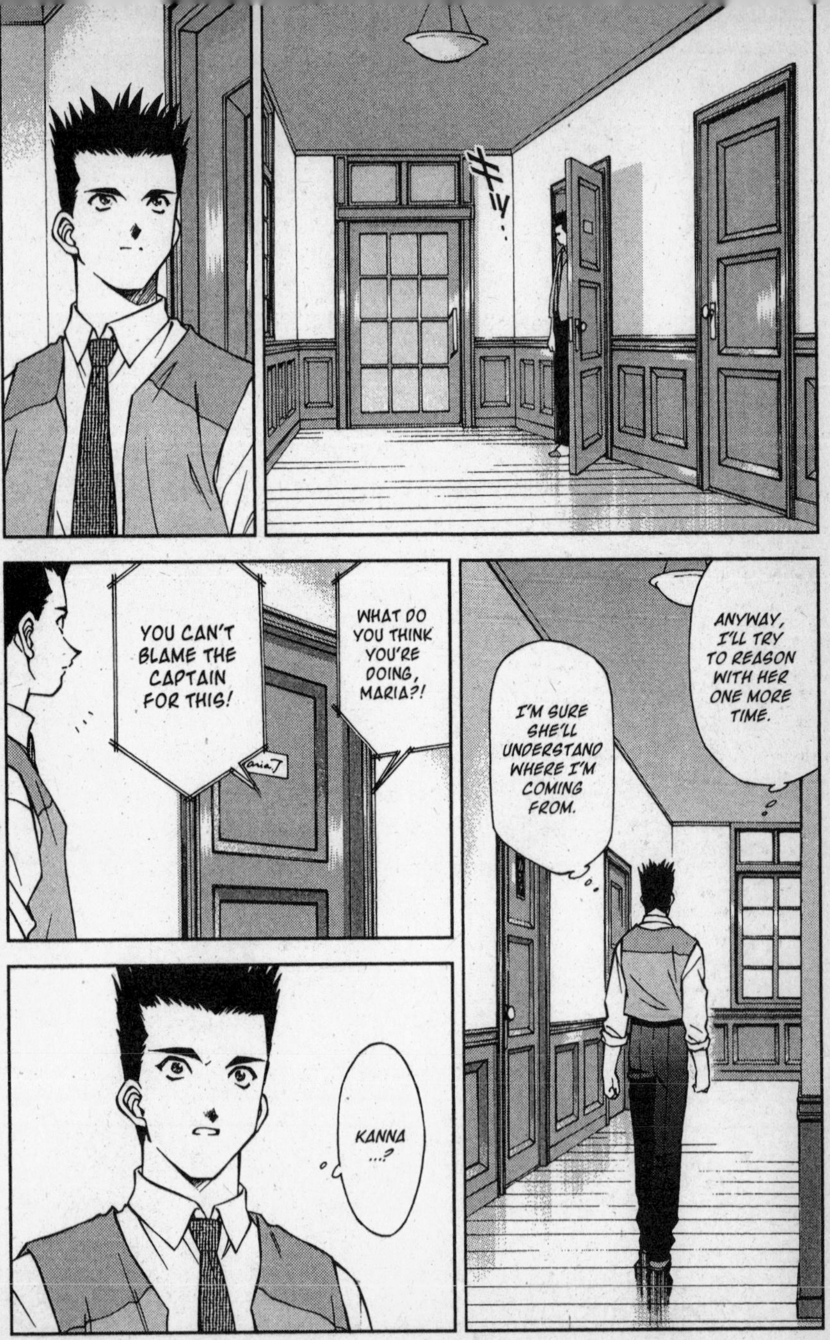
ANYWAY, I'LL TRY TO REASON WITH HER ONE MORE TIME.
I'M SURE SHE'LL UNDERSTAND WHERE I'M COMING FROM.
WHAT DO YOU THINK YOU'RE DOING, MARIA?!
YOU CAN'T BLAME THE CAPTAIN FOR THIS!
...
KANNA...?

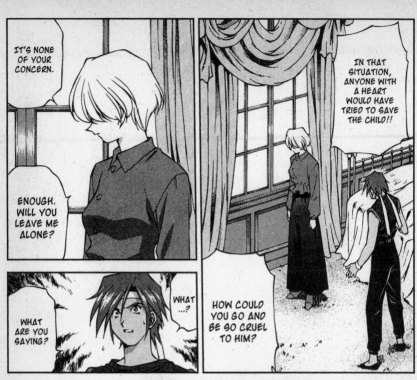

IN THAT SITUATION, ANYONE WITH A HEART WOULD HAVE TRIED TO SAVE THE CHILD!!
HOW COULD YOU GO AND BE SO CRUEL TO HIM?
IT'S NONE OF YOUR CONCERN.
ENOUGH. WILL YOU LEAVE ME ALONE?
WHAT ...?
WHAT ARE YOU SAYING?
WE'VE BEEN FRIENDS FOREVER, YET YOU DARE SPEAK TO ME THAT WAY?
AREN'T WE COMRADES IN ARMS?

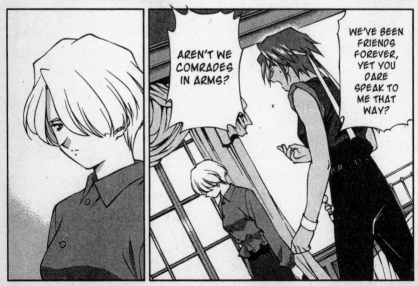

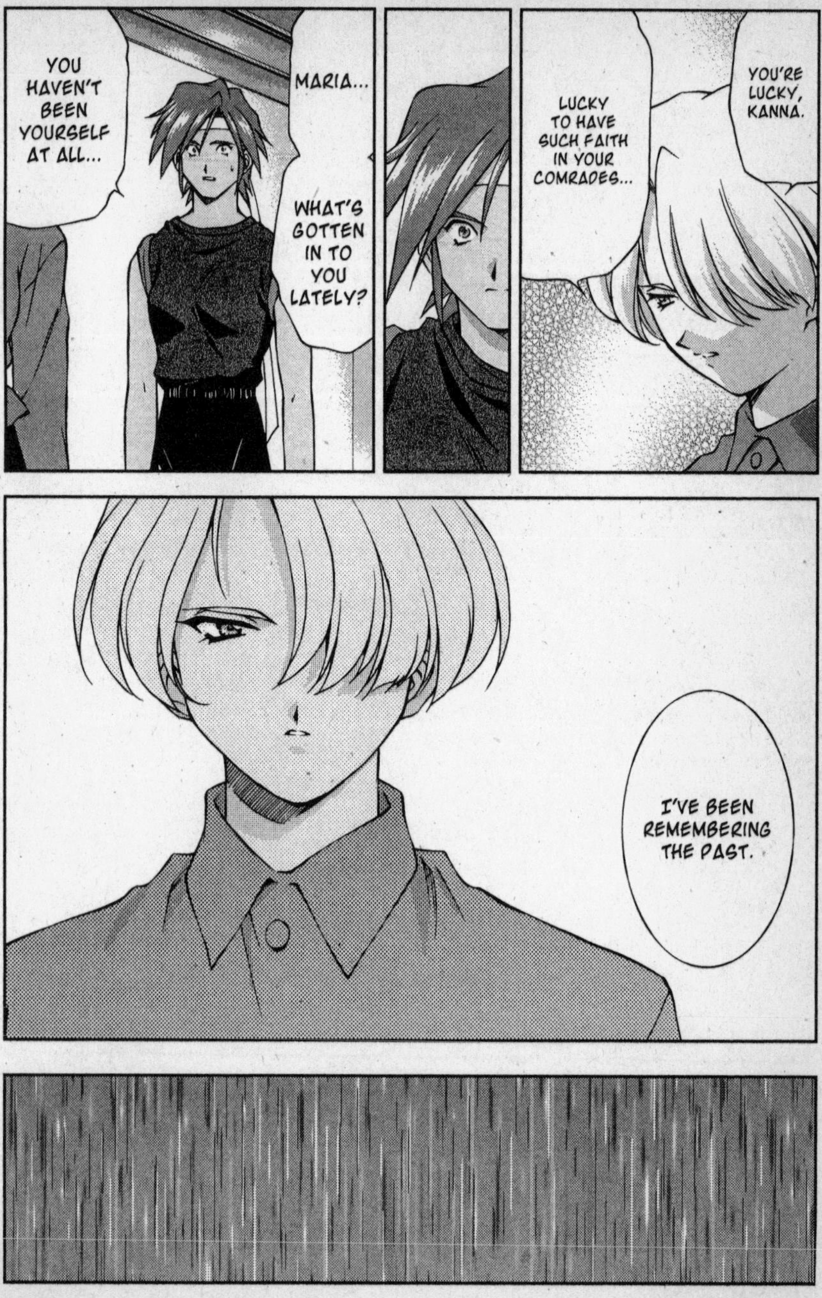
YOU'RE LUCKY, KANNA.
LUCKY TO HAVE SUCH FAITH IN YOUR COMRADES...
MARIA...
WHAT'S GOTTEN IN TO YOU LATELY?
YOU HAVEN'T BEEN YOURSELF AT ALL...
I'VE BEEN REMEMBERING THE PAST.

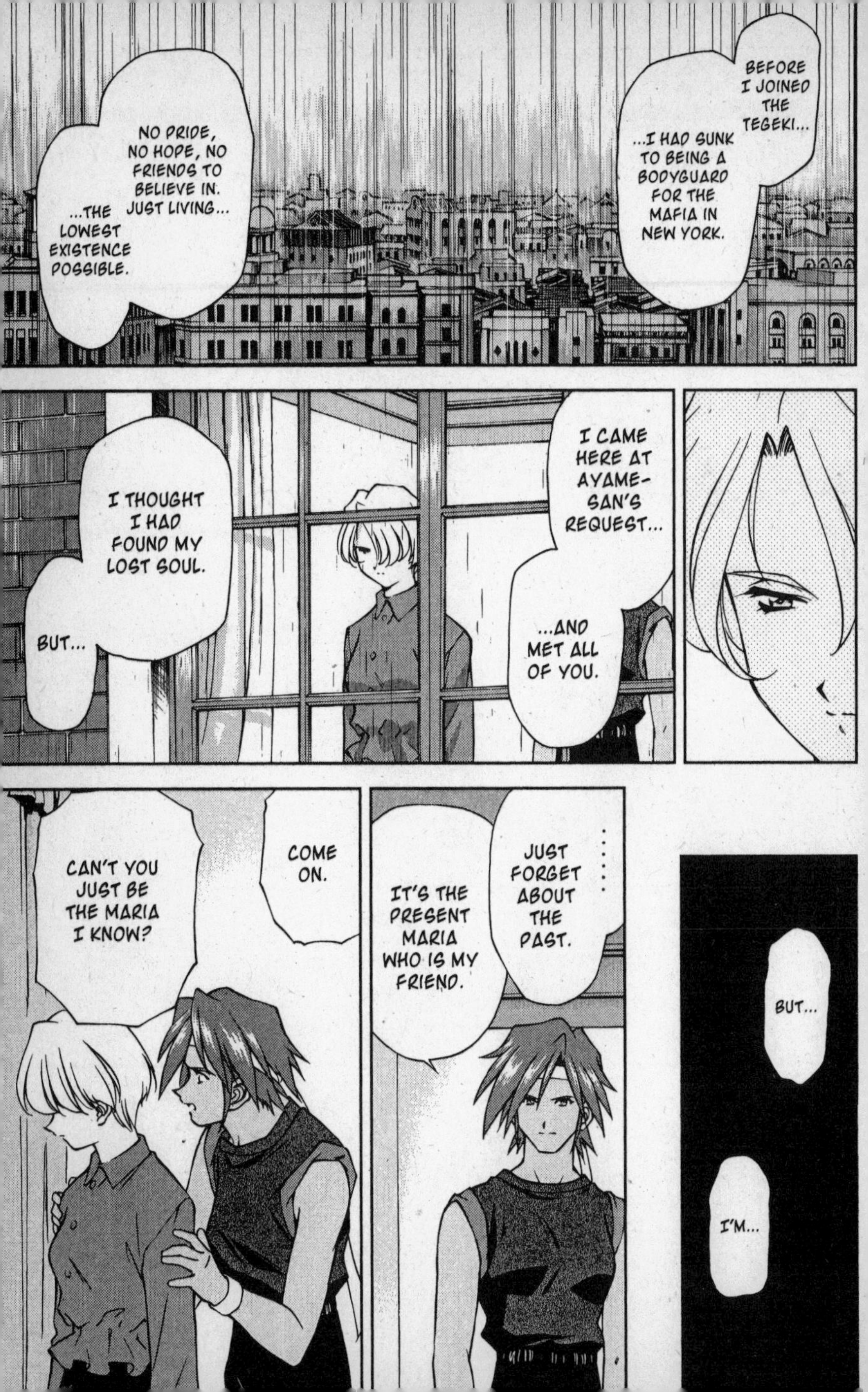
BEFORE I JOINED THE TEGEKI...
...I HAD SUNK TO BEING A BODYGUARD FOR THE MAFIA IN NEW YORK.
NO PRIDE, NO HOPE, NO FRIENDS TO BELIEVE IN. JUST LIVING...
...THE LOWEST EXISTENCE POSSIBLE.
I CAME HERE AT AYAME-SAN'S REQUEST...
...AND MET ALL OF YOU.
I THOUGHT I HAD FOUND MY LOST SOUL.
BUT...
BUT...
I'M...
......
JUST FORGET ABOUT THE PAST.
IT'S THE PRESENT MARIA WHO IS MY FRIEND.
COME ON.
CAN'T YOU JUST BE THE MARIA I KNOW?

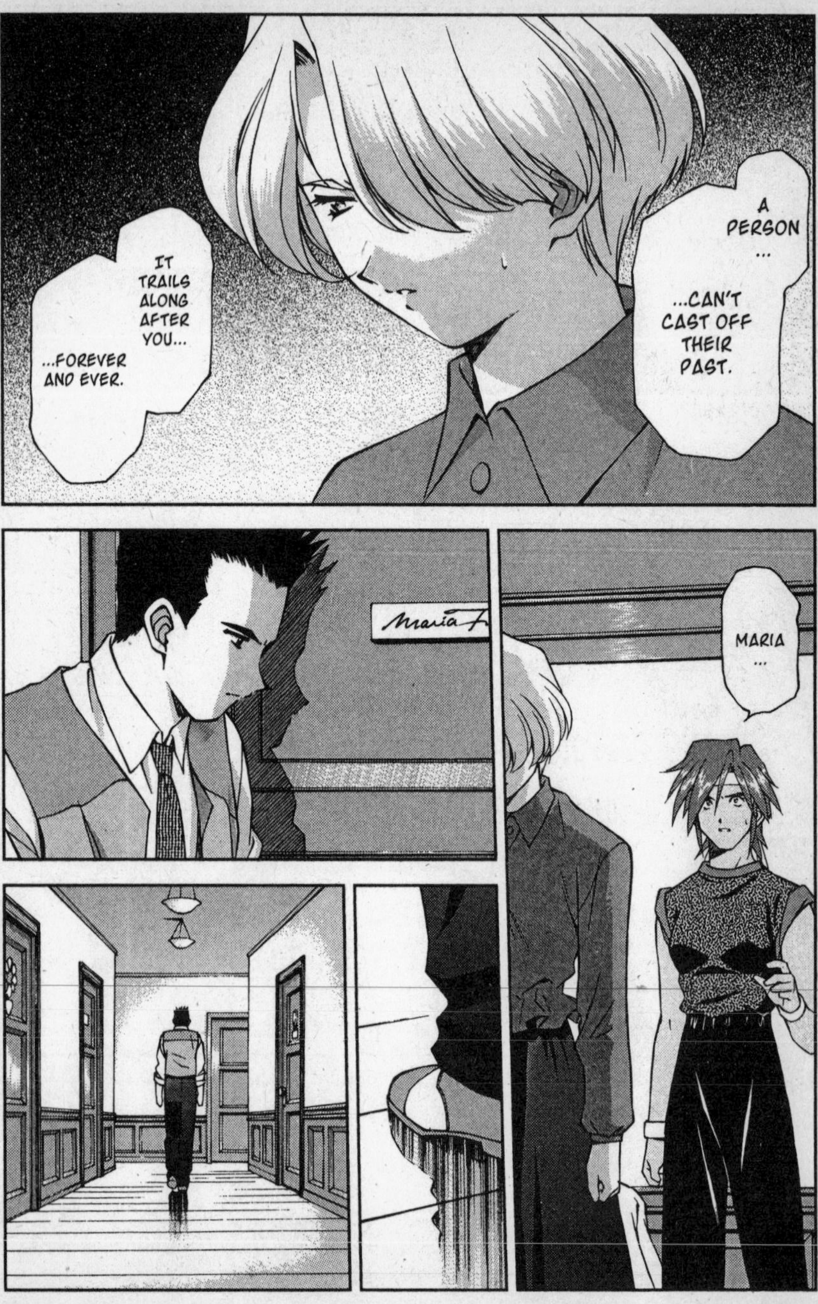
A PERSON ...
...CAN'T CAST OFF THEIR PAST.
IT TRAILS ALONG AFTER YOU...
...FOREVER AND EVER.
MARIA ...

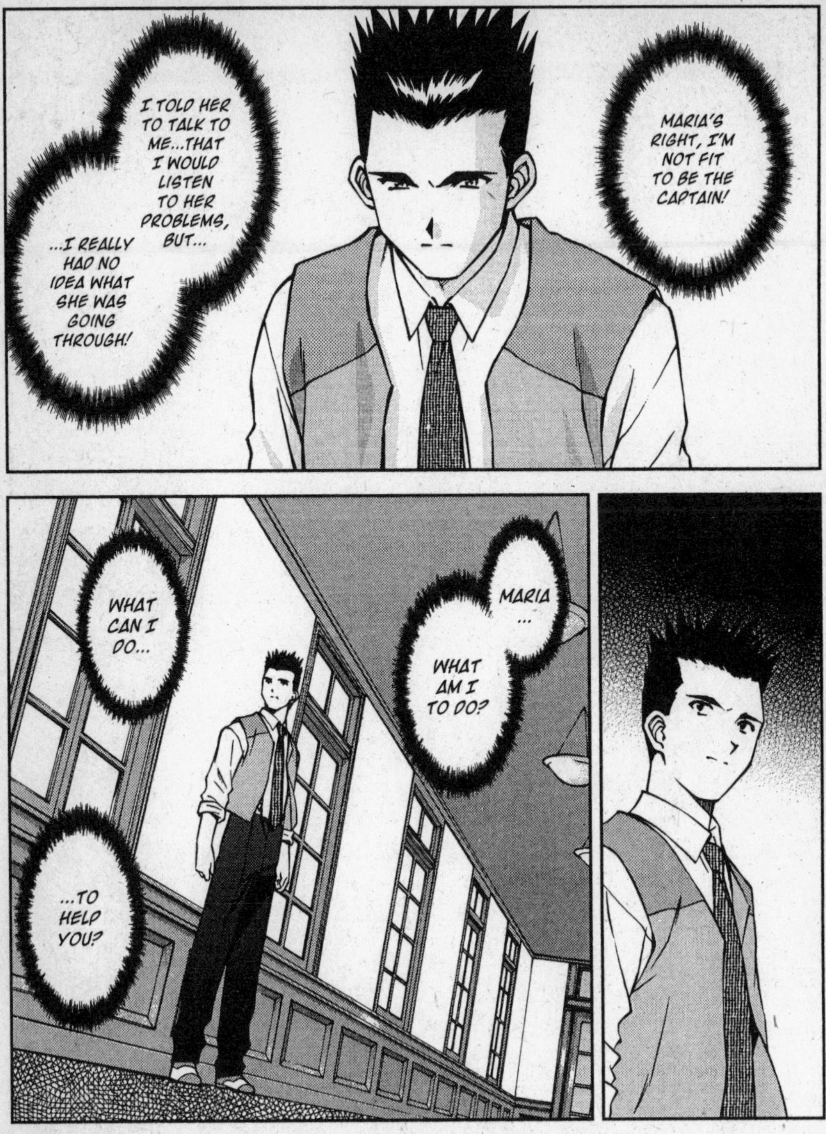
MARIA'S RIGHT, I'M NOT FIT TO BE THE CAPTAIN!
I TOLD HER TO TALK TO ME...THAT I WOULD LISTEN TO HER PROBLEMS, BUT...
...I REALLY HAD NO IDEA WHAT SHE WAS GOING THROUGH!
MARIA ...
WHAT AM I TO DO?
WHAT CAN I DO...
...TO HELP YOU?

[redacted]

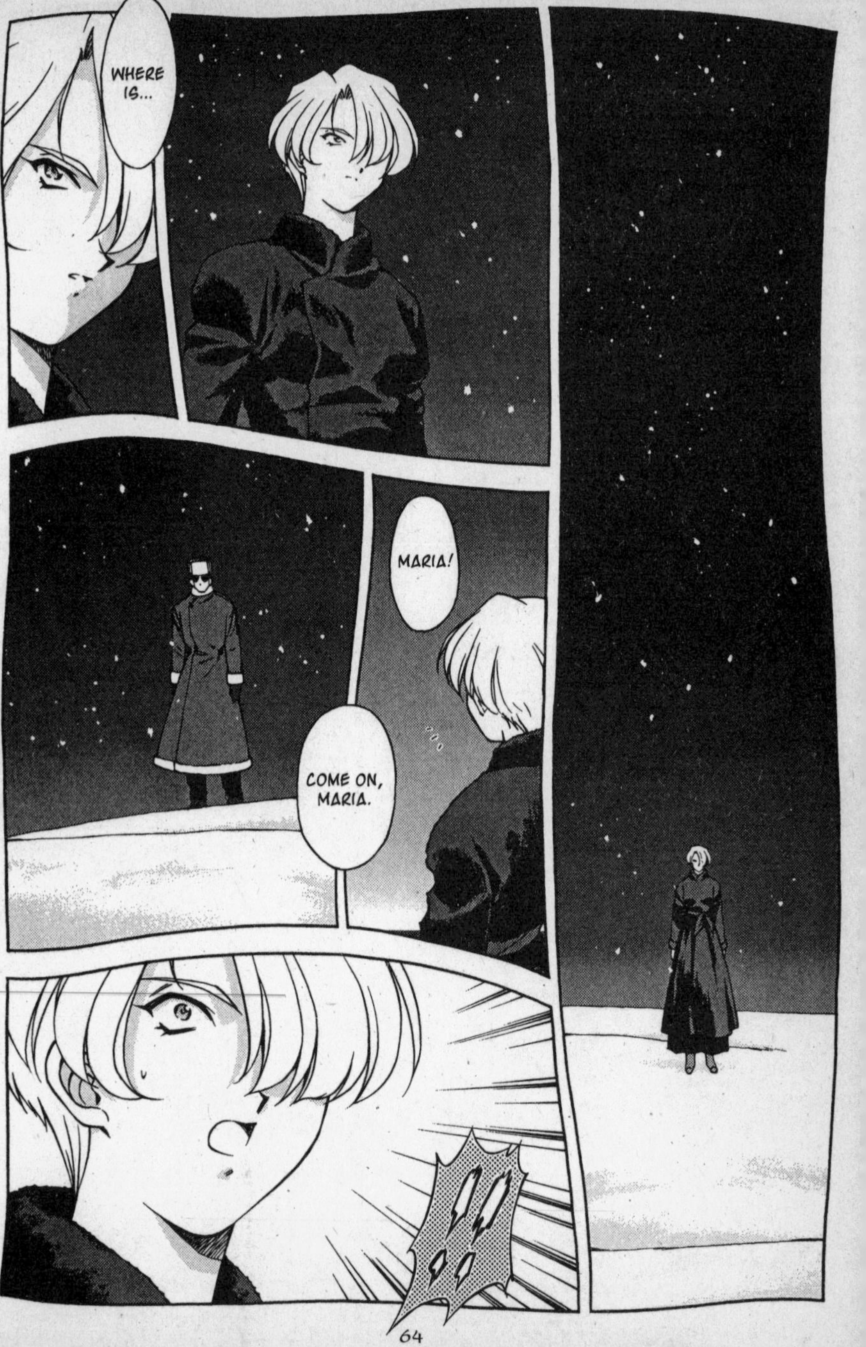
WHERE IS...
MARIA!
COME ON, MARIA.

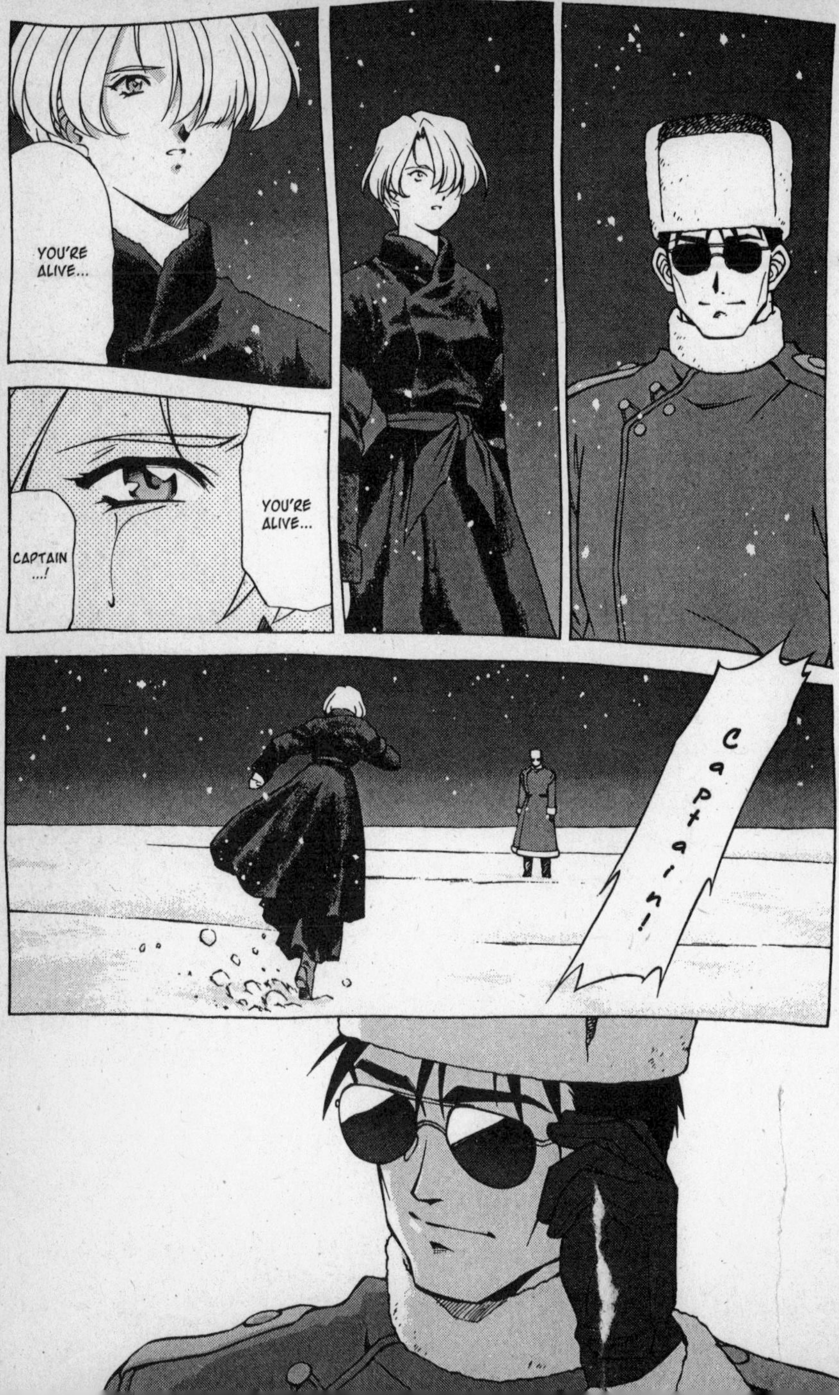
YOU'RE ALIVE...
YOU'RE ALIVE...
CAPTAIN ...!
Captain!

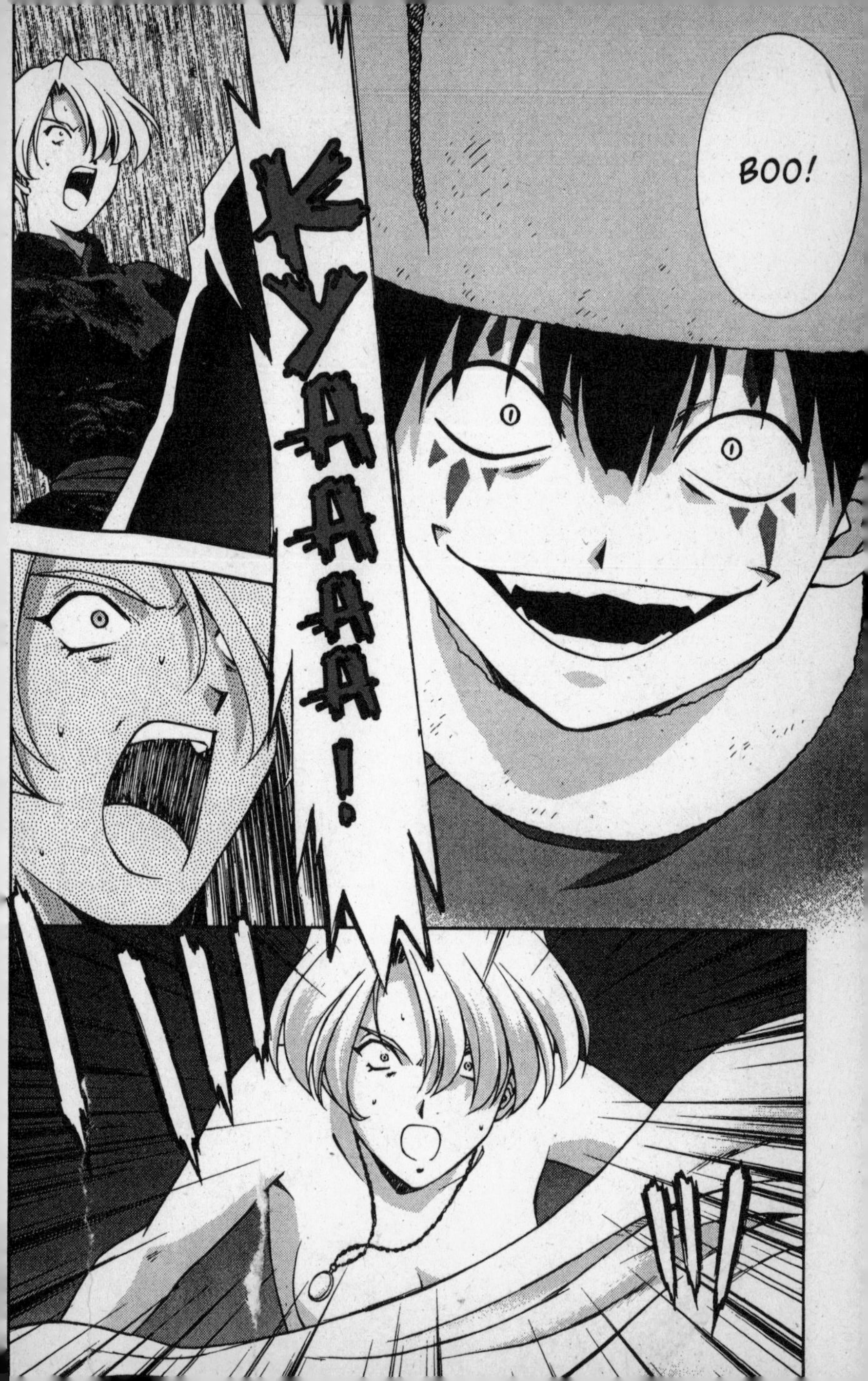
BOO!
KYAAAAA!

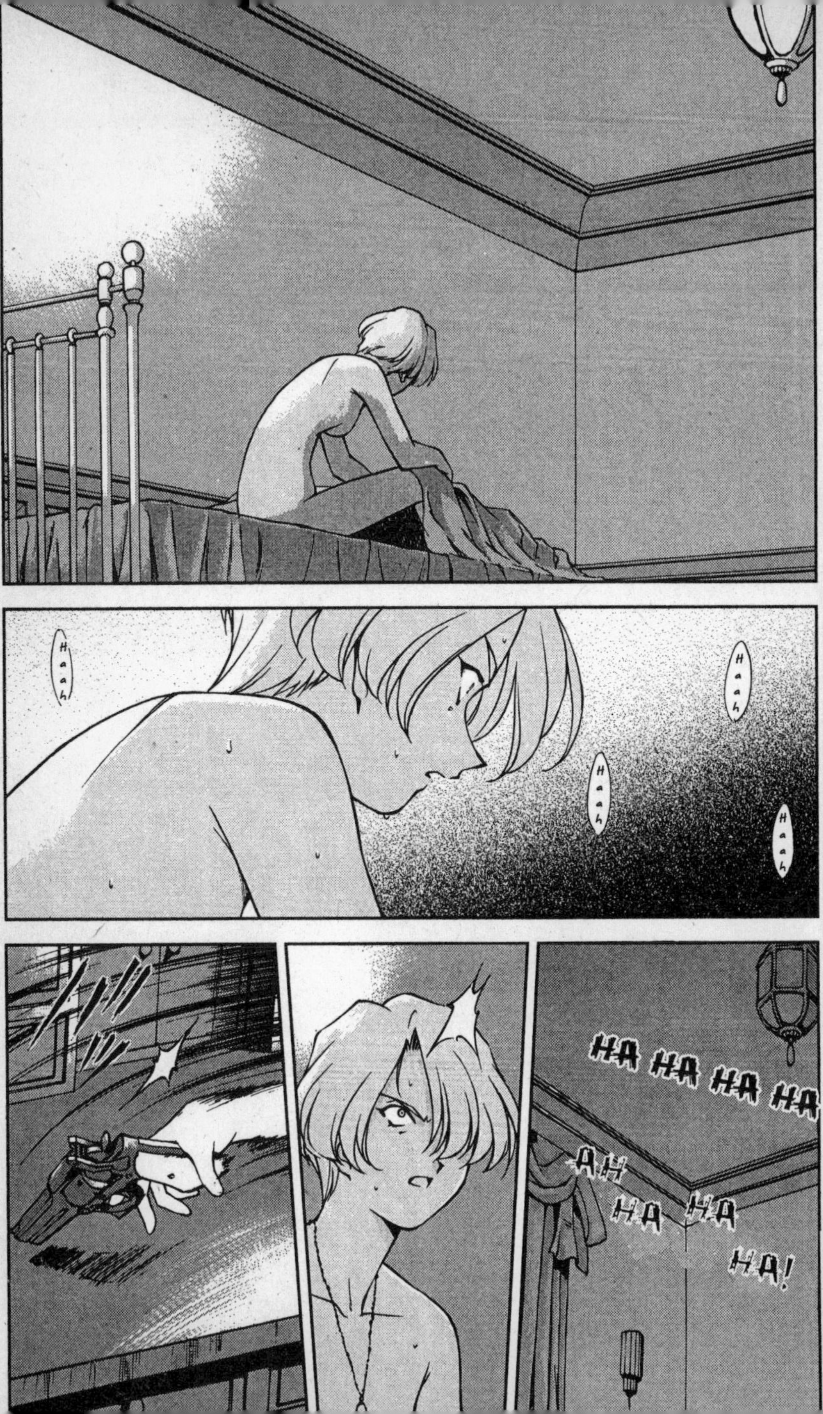
Haah
Haah
Haah
Haah
HA HA HA HA
AH HA HA HA!

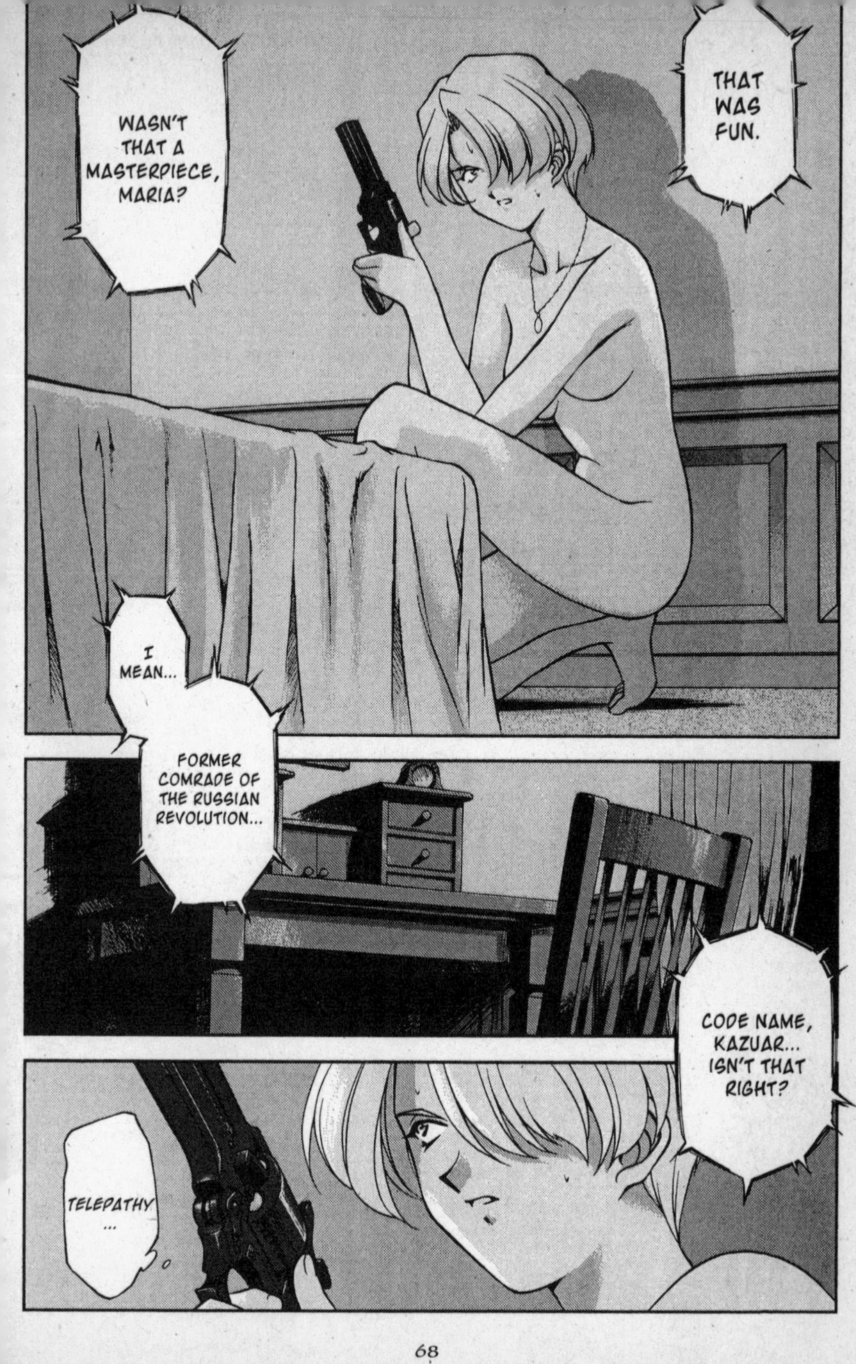
THAT WAS FUN.
WASN'T THAT A MASTERPIECE, MARIA?
I MEAN...
FORMER COMRADE OF THE RUSSIAN REVOLUTION...
CODE NAME, KAZUAR... ISN'T THAT RIGHT?
TELEPATHY...

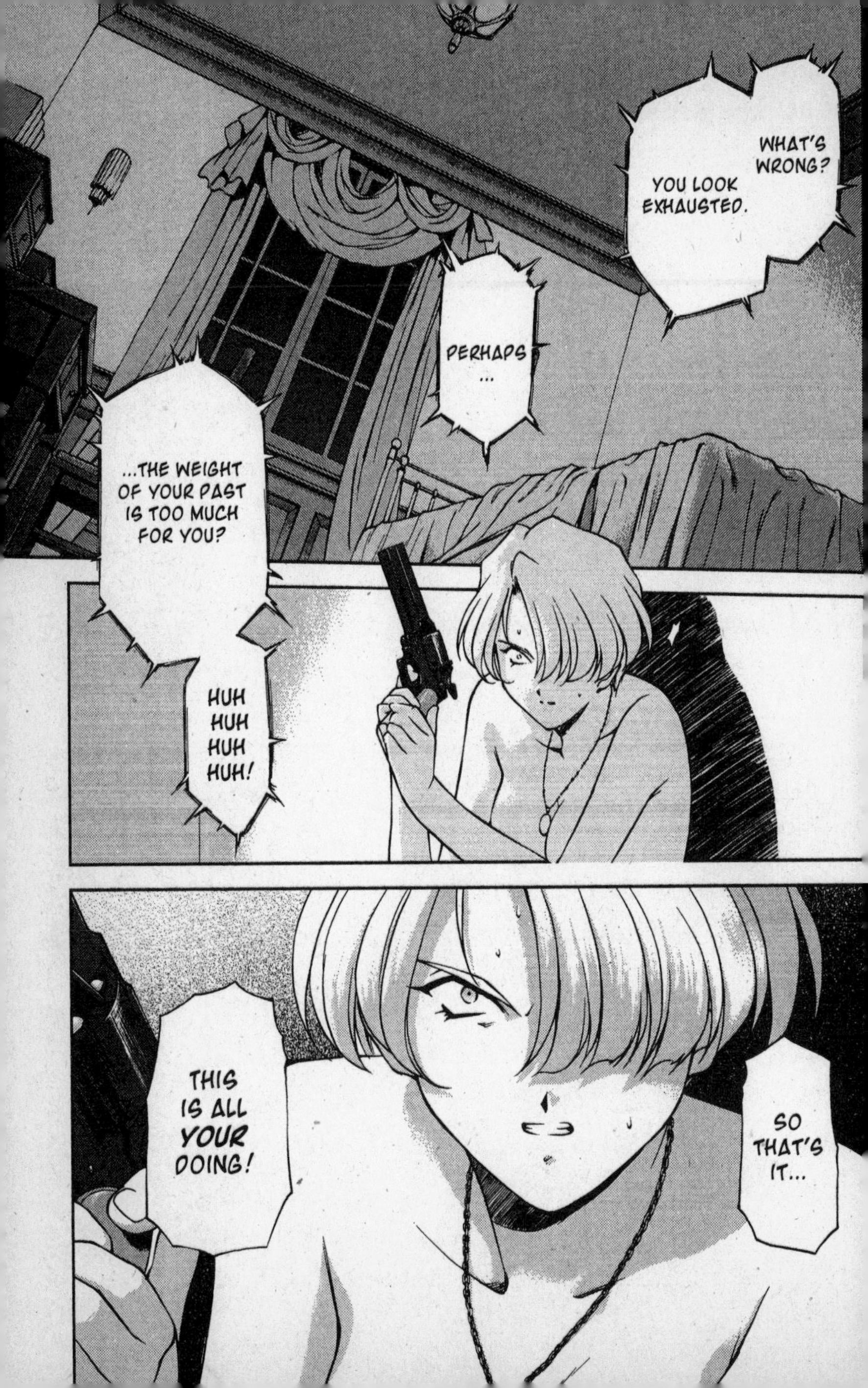
WHAT'S WRONG?
YOU LOOK EXHAUSTED.
PERHAPS ...
...THE WEIGHT OF YOUR PAST IS TOO MUCH FOR YOU?
HUH HUH HUH HUH!
SO THAT'S IT...
THIS IS ALL *YOUR* DOING!

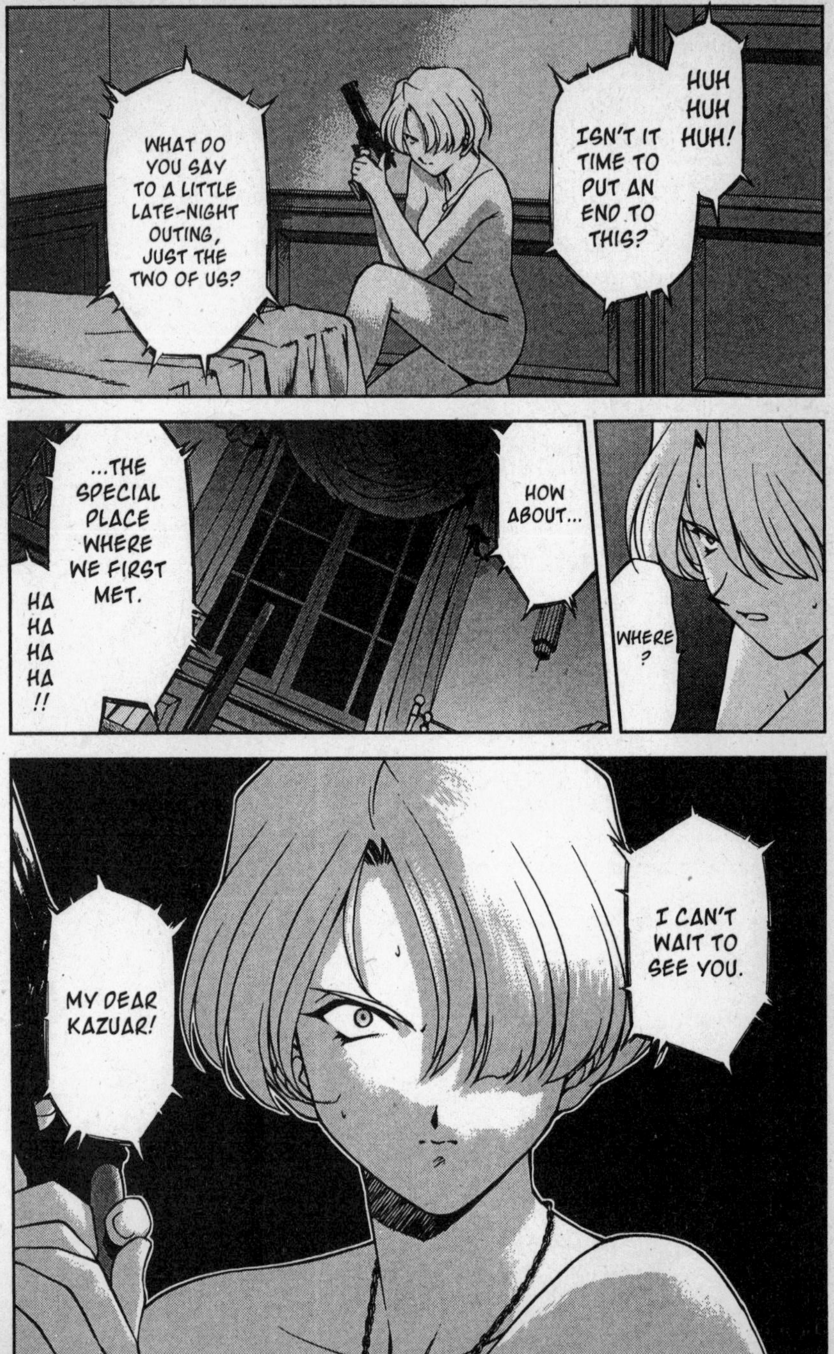
HUH HUH HUH!
ISN'T IT TIME TO PUT AN END TO THIS?
WHAT DO YOU SAY TO A LITTLE LATE-NIGHT OUTING, JUST THE TWO OF US?
WHERE?
HOW ABOUT...
...THE SPECIAL PLACE WHERE WE FIRST MET.
HA HA HA HA!!
I CAN'T WAIT TO SEE YOU.
MY DEAR KAZUAR!

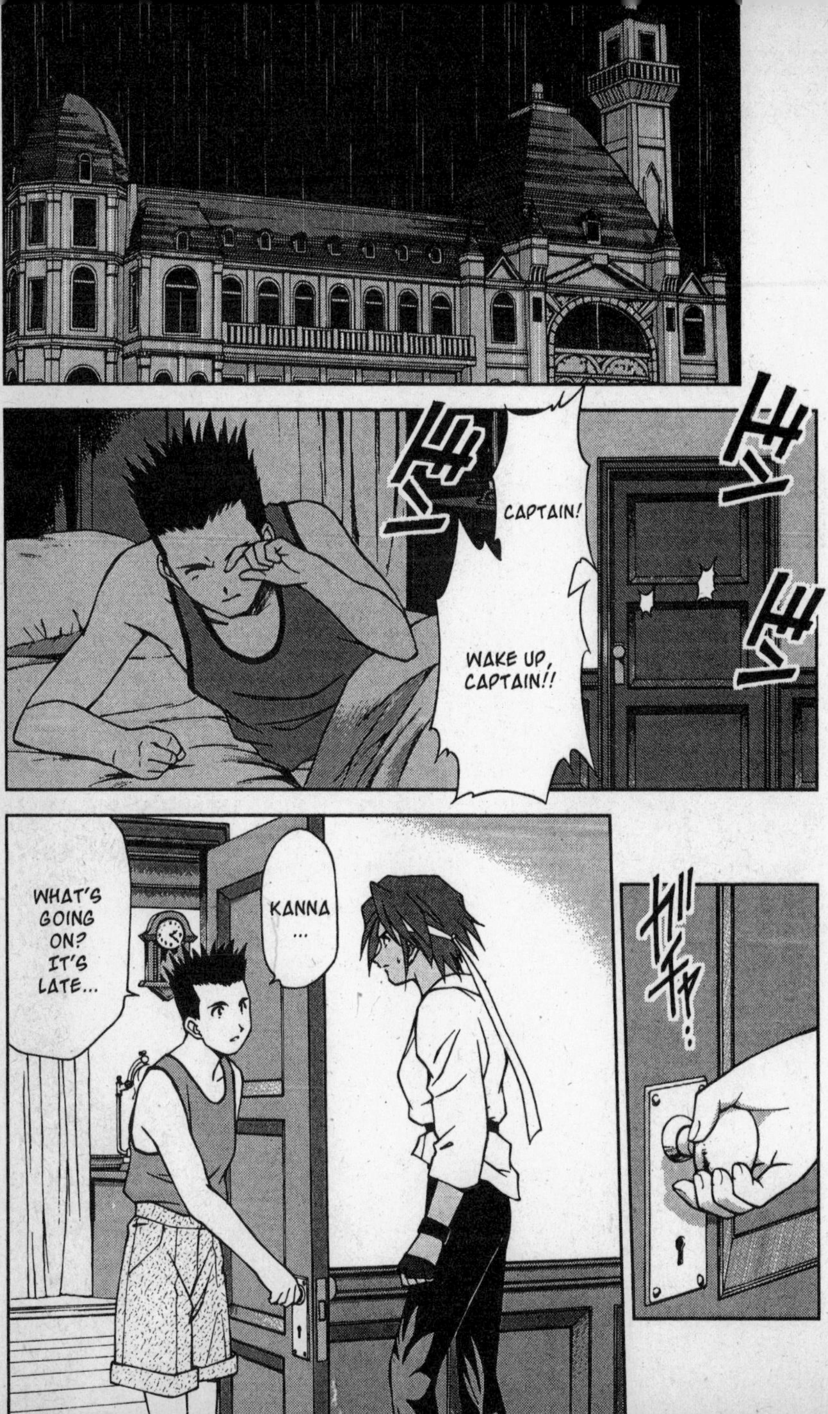
CAPTAIN!
WAKE UP, CAPTAIN!!
KANNA ...
WHAT'S GOING ON? IT'S LATE...

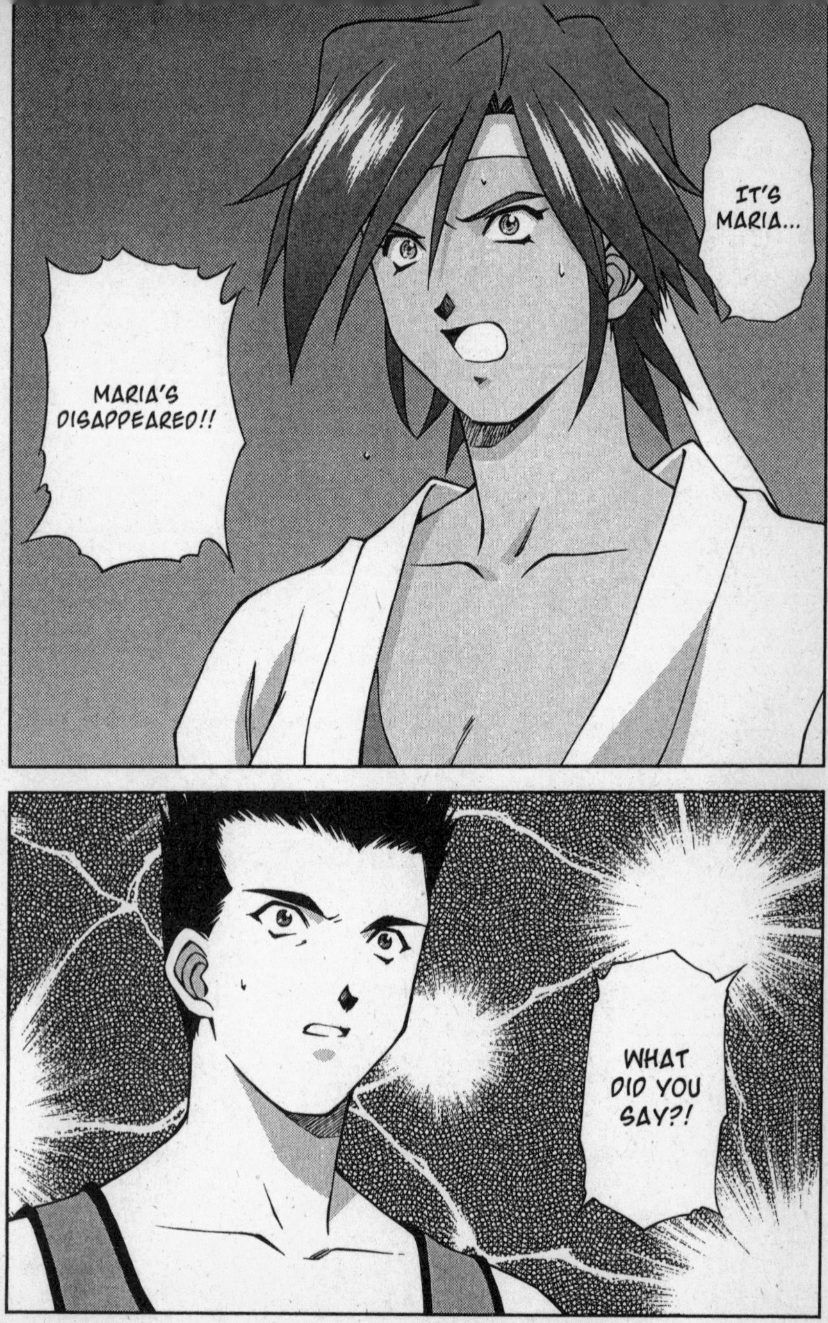
IT'S MARIA...
MARIA'S DISAPPEARED!!
WHAT DID YOU SAY?!

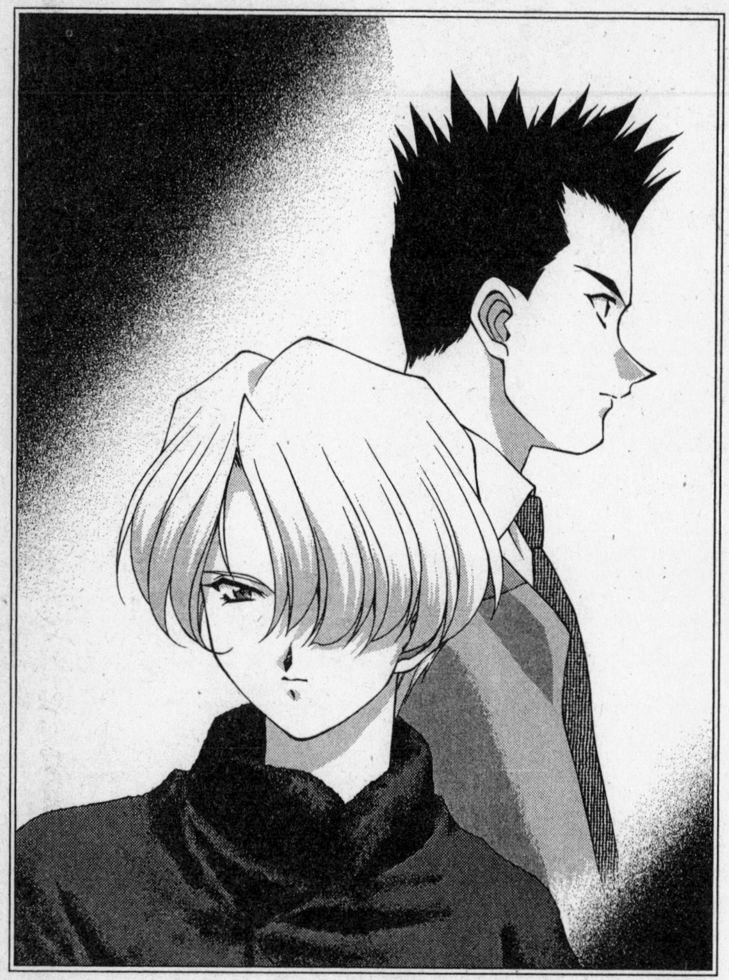

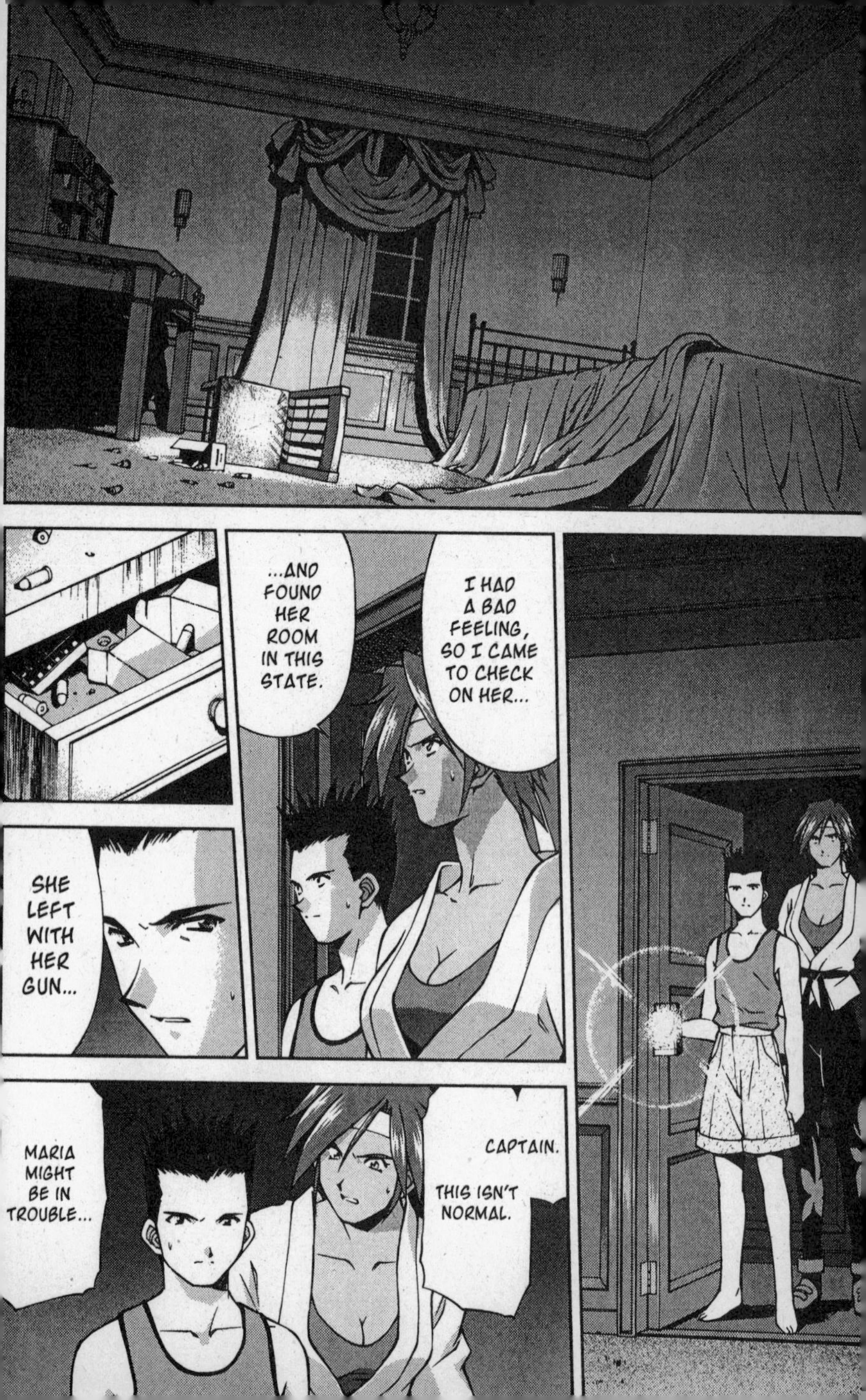
I HAD A BAD FEELING, SO I CAME TO CHECK ON HER...
...AND FOUND HER ROOM IN THIS STATE.
SHE LEFT WITH HER GUN...
CAPTAIN.
THIS ISN'T NORMAL.
MARIA MIGHT BE IN TROUBLE...

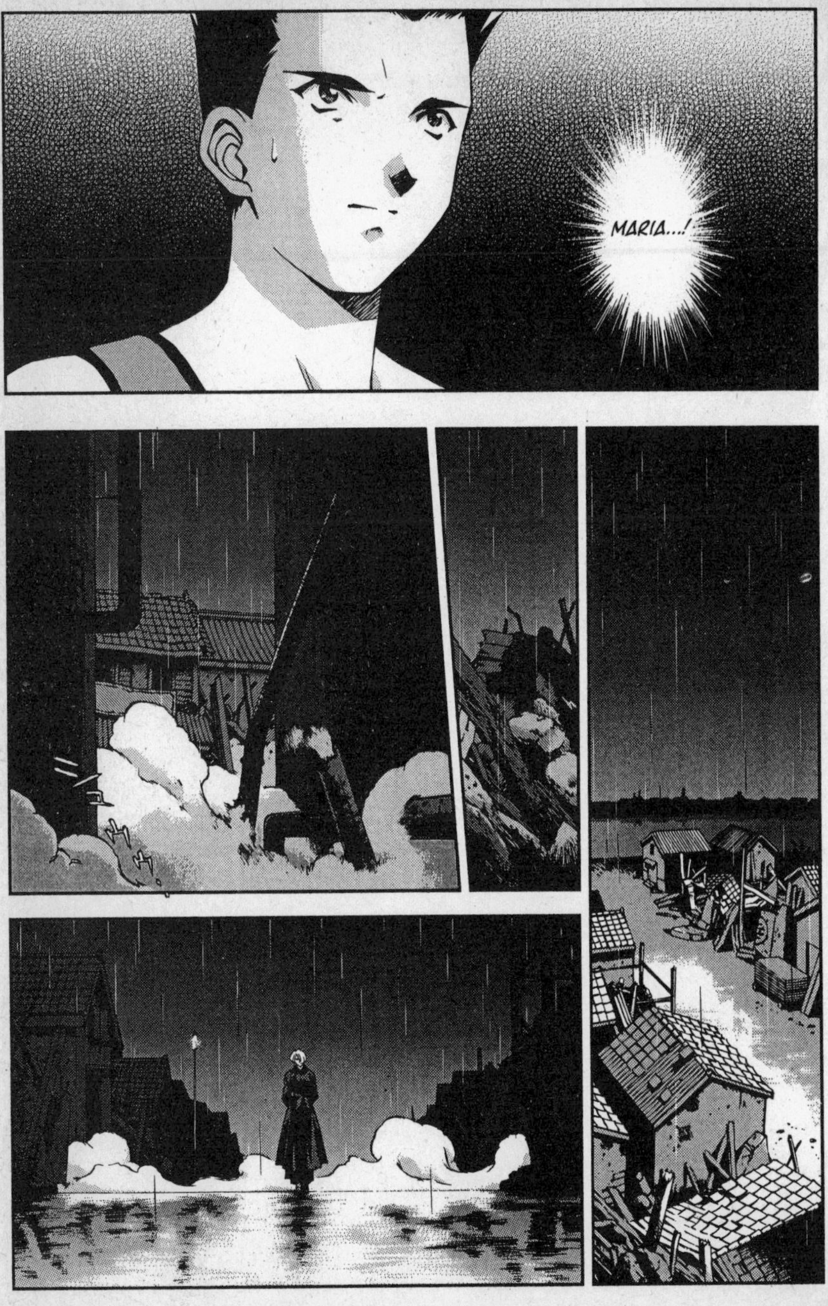
MARIA...!

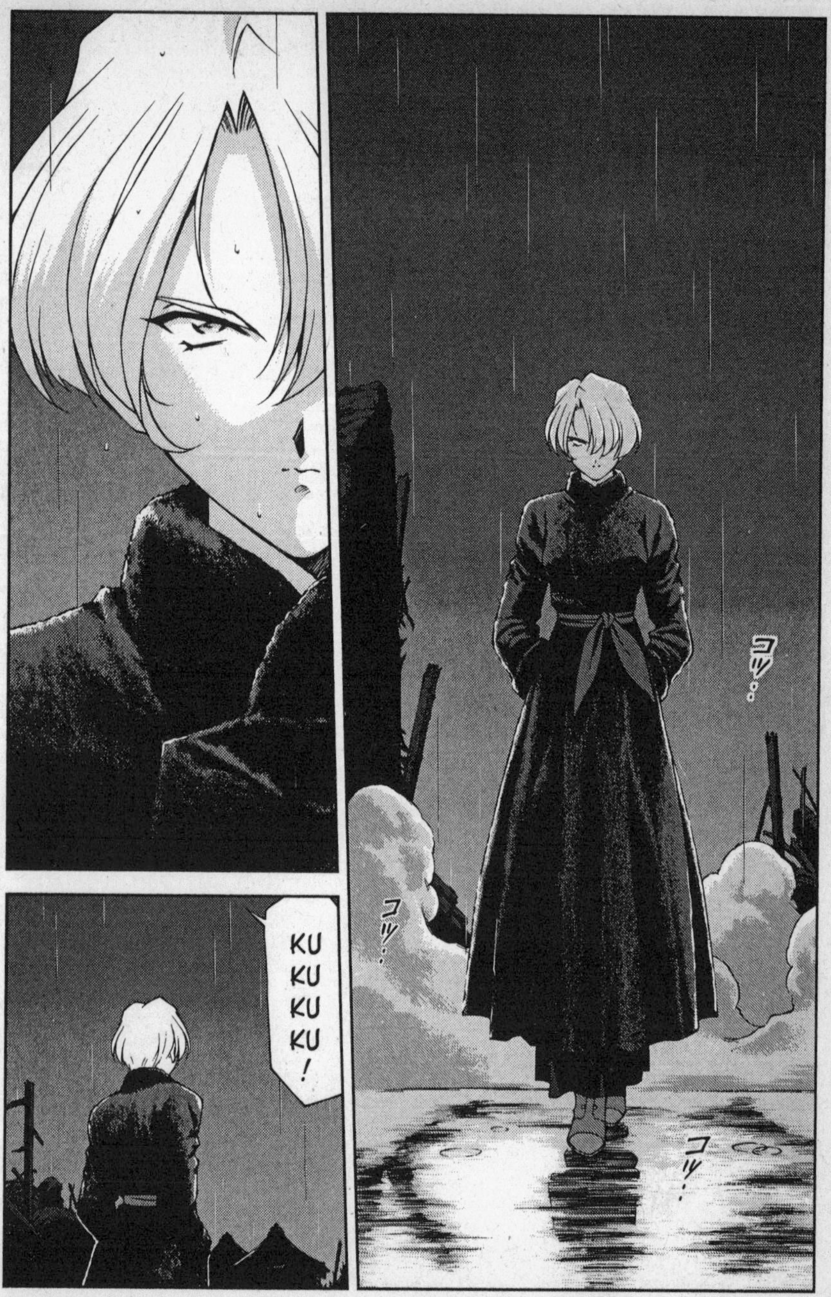
コツ。。
コツ・・
コツ!・
KU KU KU KU!

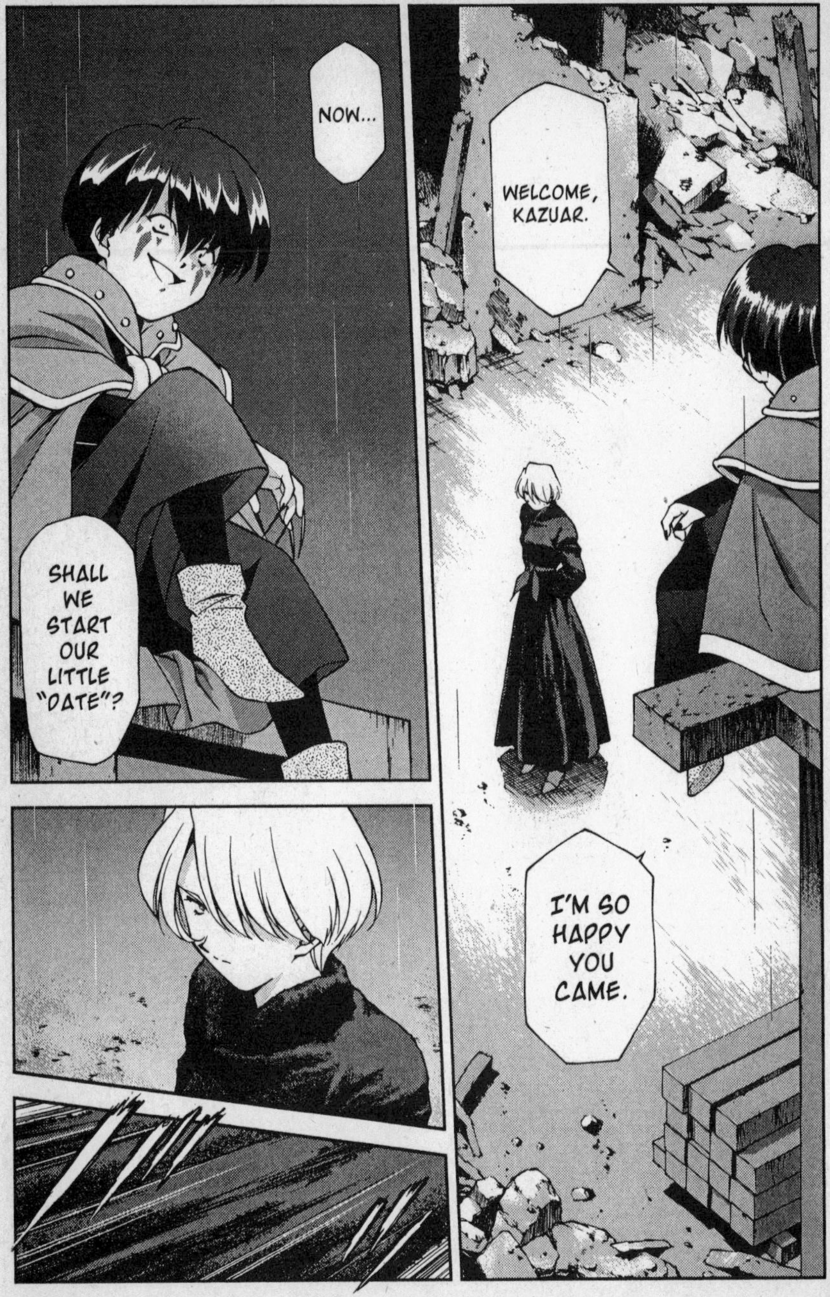
WELCOME, KAZUAR.
I'M SO HAPPY YOU CAME.
NOW...
SHALL WE START OUR LITTLE "DATE"?

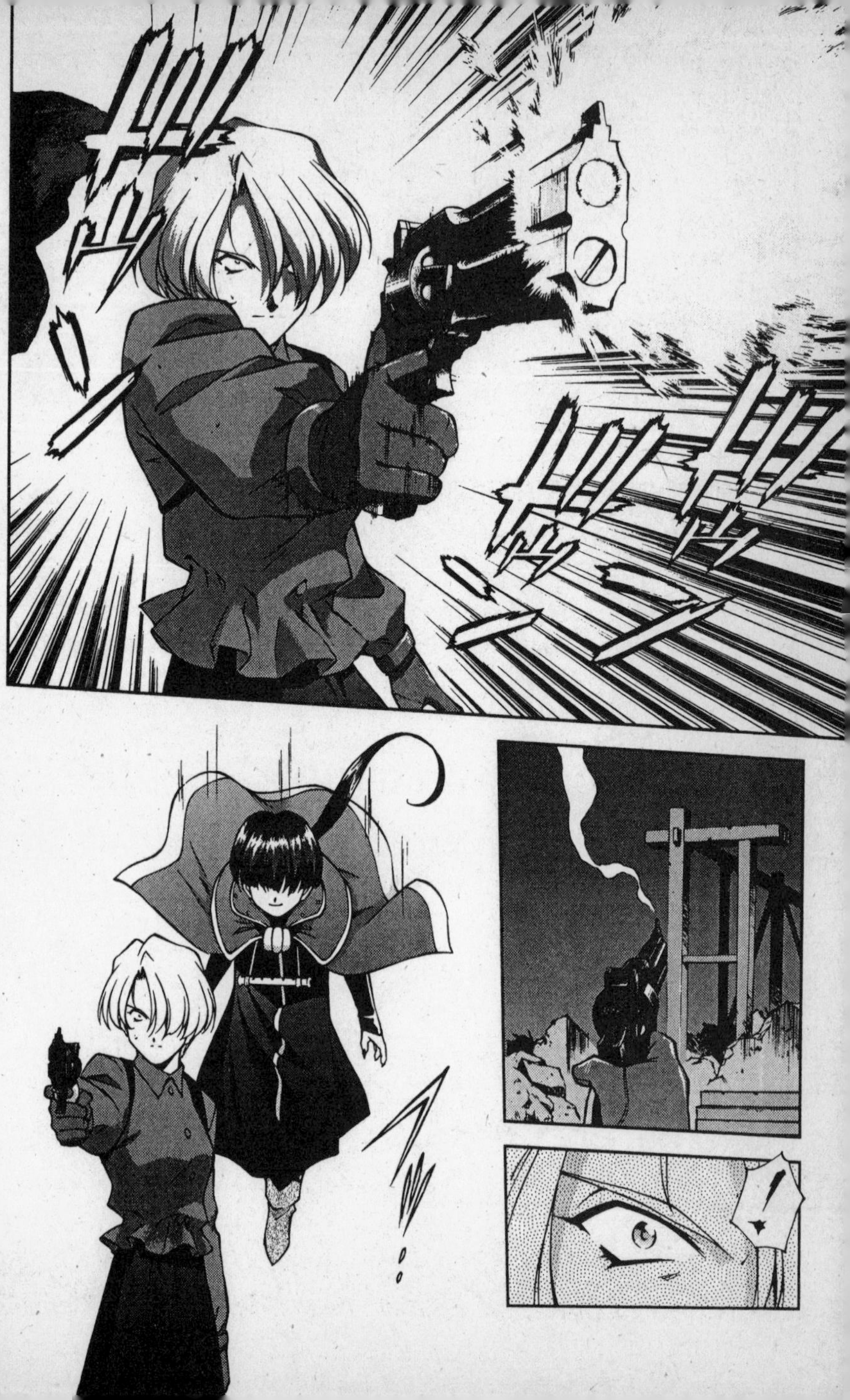
!

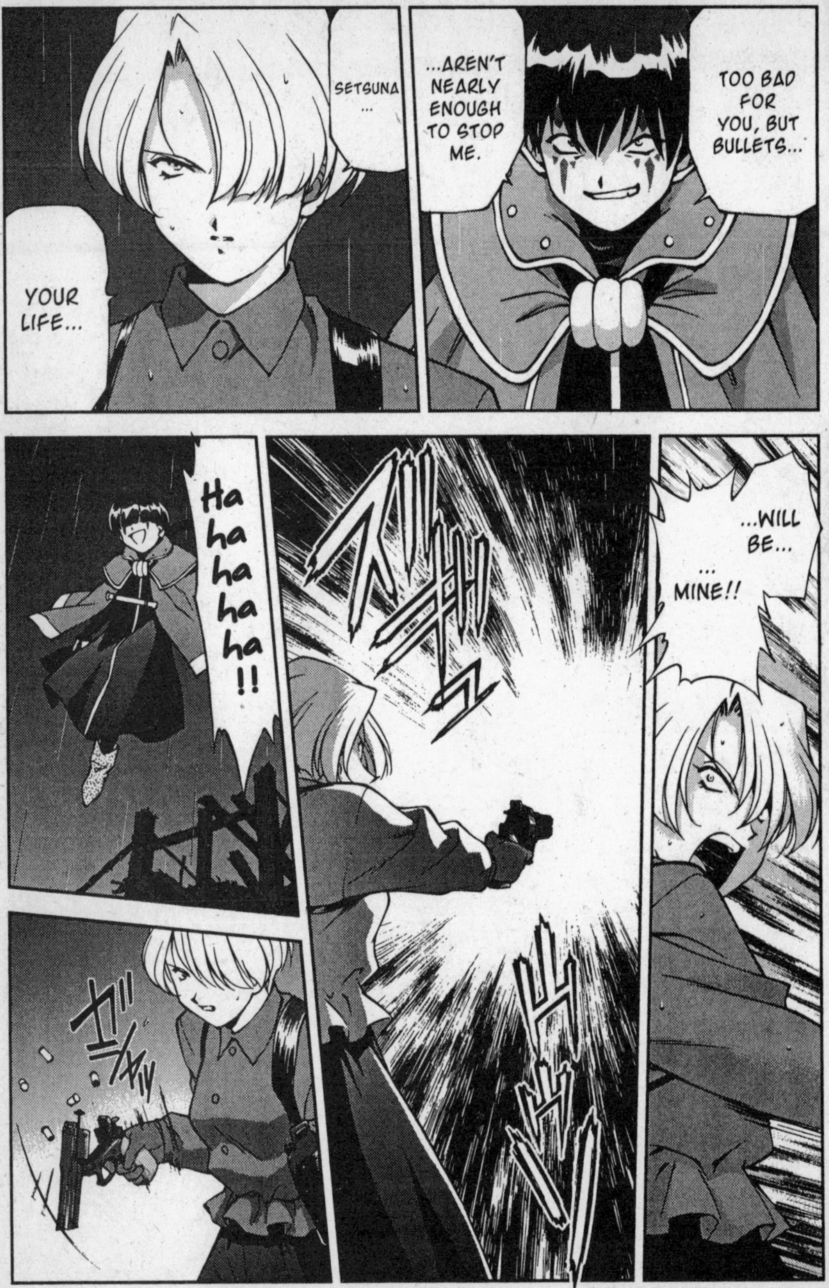
TOO BAD FOR YOU, BUT BULLETS...
...AREN'T NEARLY ENOUGH TO STOP ME.
SETSUNA ...
YOUR LIFE...
...WILL BE...
... MINE!!
Ha ha ha ha ha !!

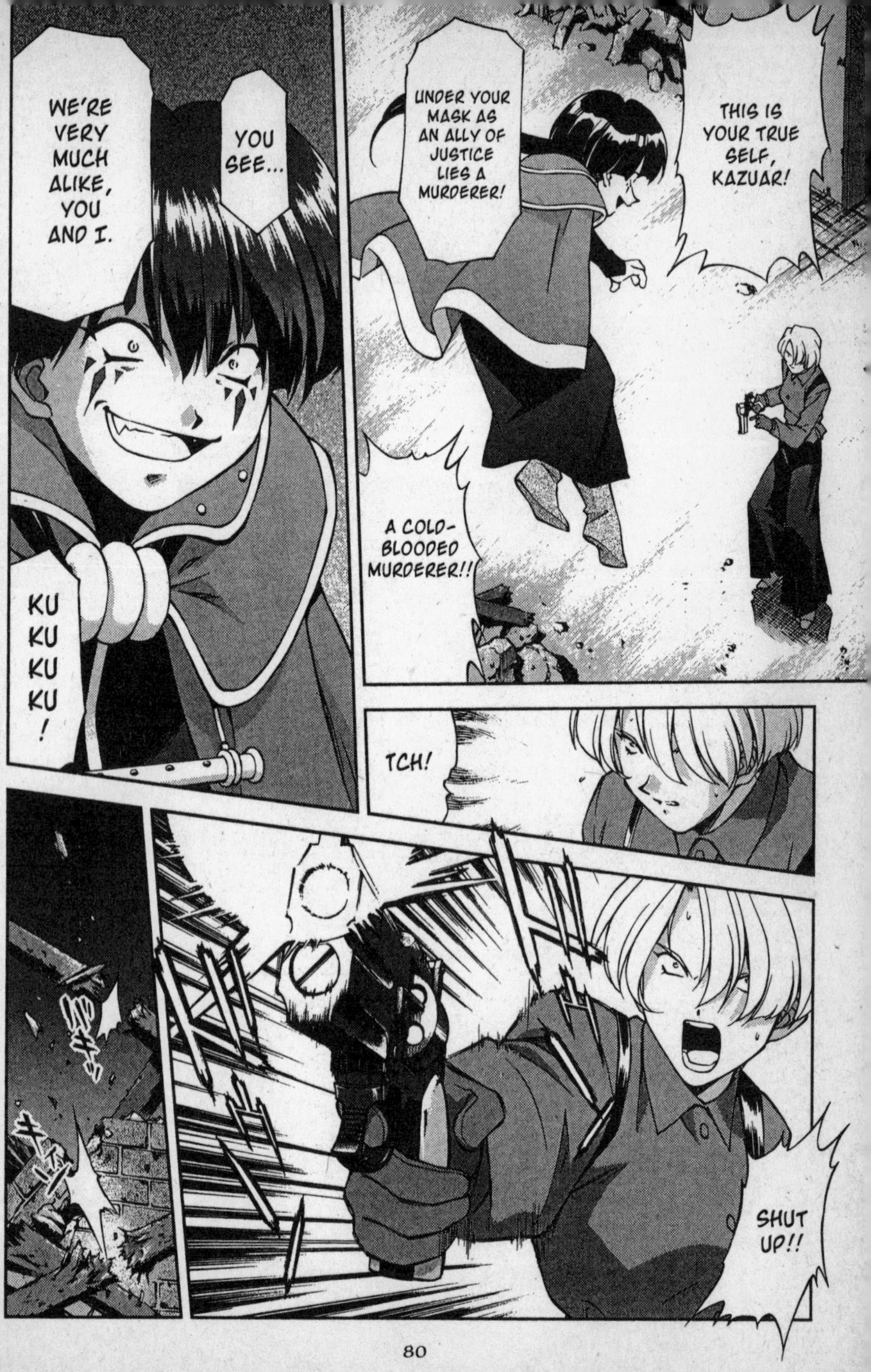
THIS IS YOUR TRUE SELF, KAZUAR!
UNDER YOUR MASK AS AN ALLY OF JUSTICE LIES A MURDERER!
A COLD-BLOODED MURDERER!!
TCH!
YOU SEE...
WE'RE VERY MUCH ALIKE, YOU AND I.
KU KU KU KU!
SHUT UP!!

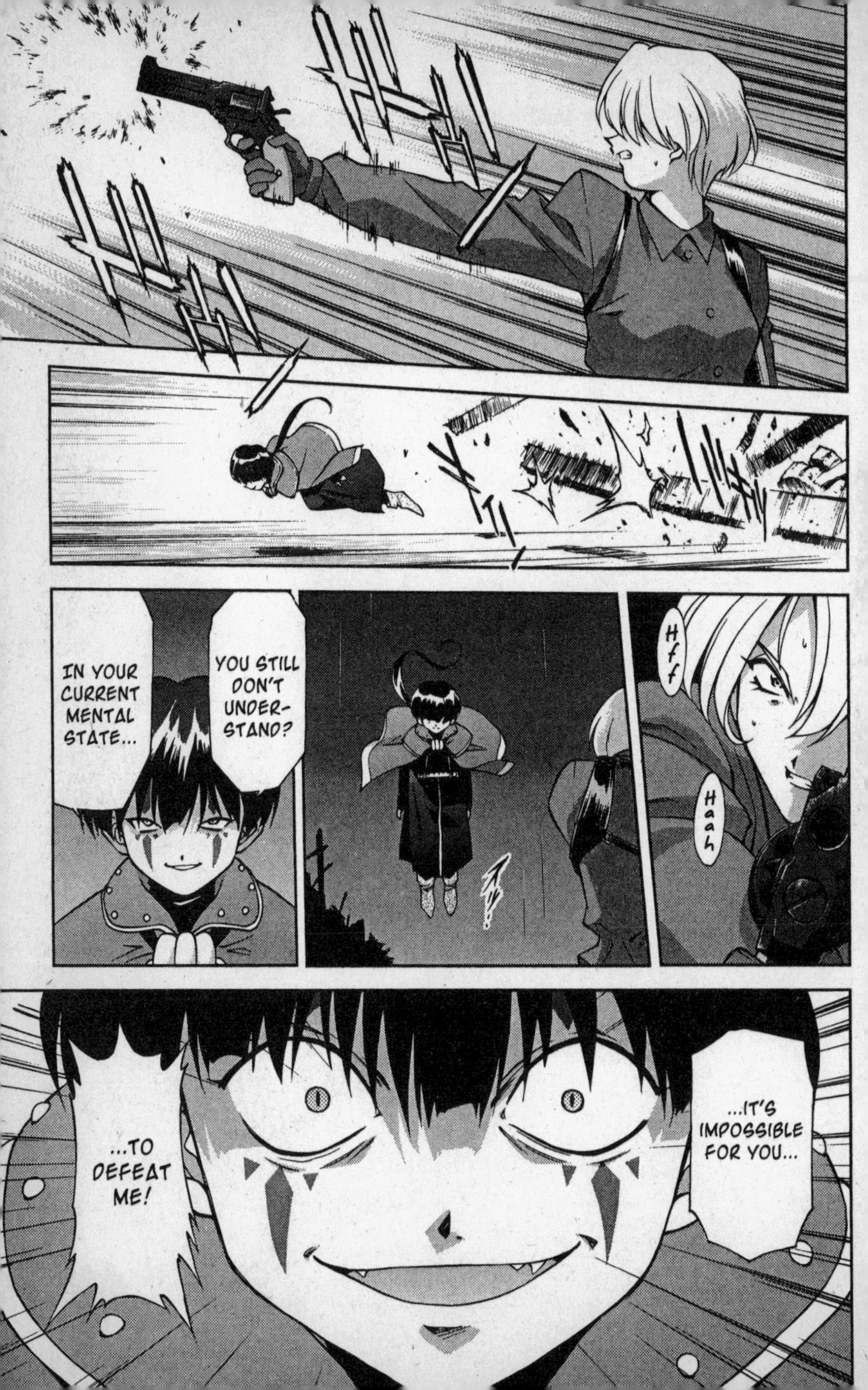
Hff
Haah
YOU STILL DON'T UNDER-STAND?
IN YOUR CURRENT MENTAL STATE...
...IT'S IMPOSSIBLE FOR YOU...
...TO DEFEAT ME!

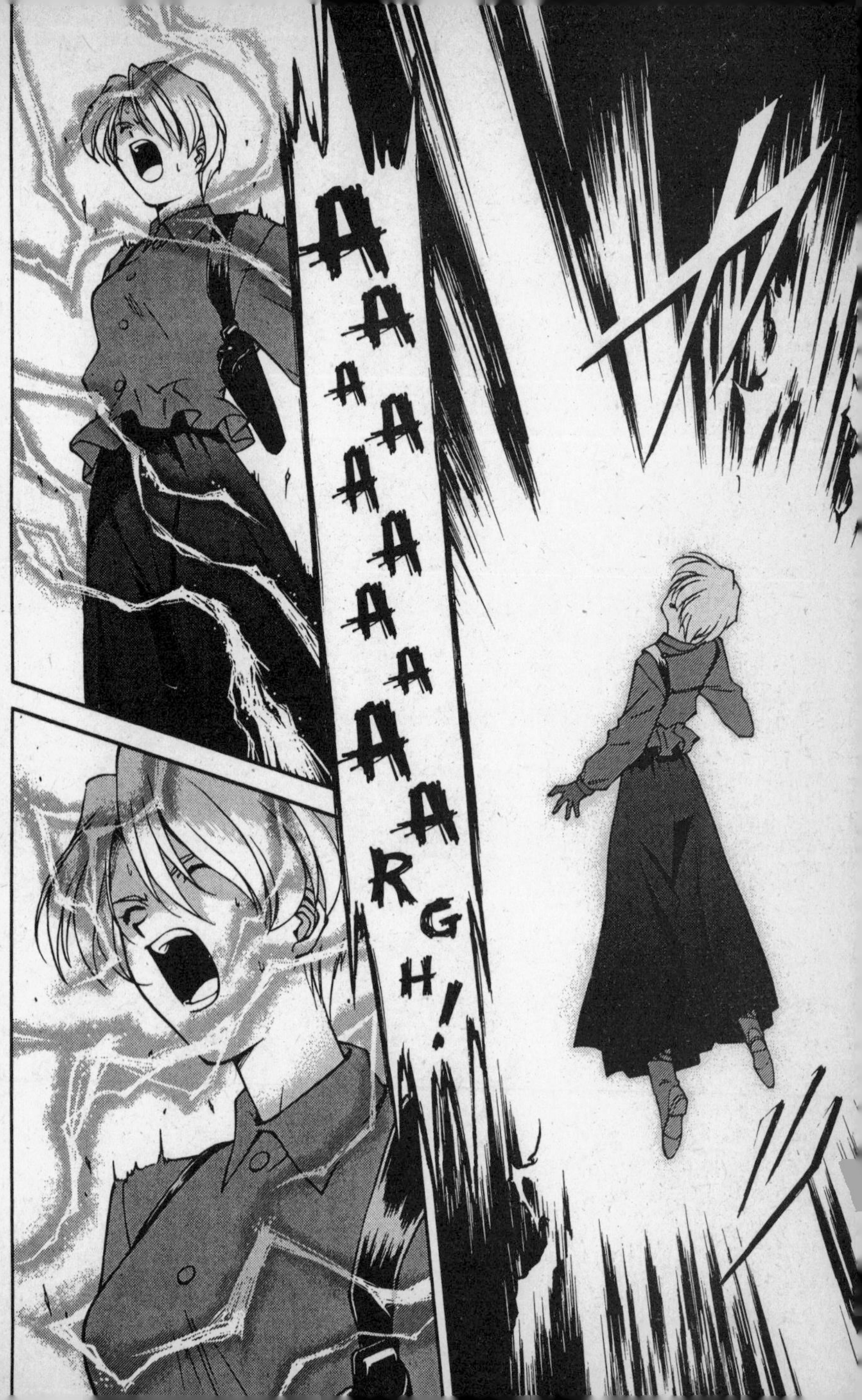
AAAAAAAAAAAARGH!

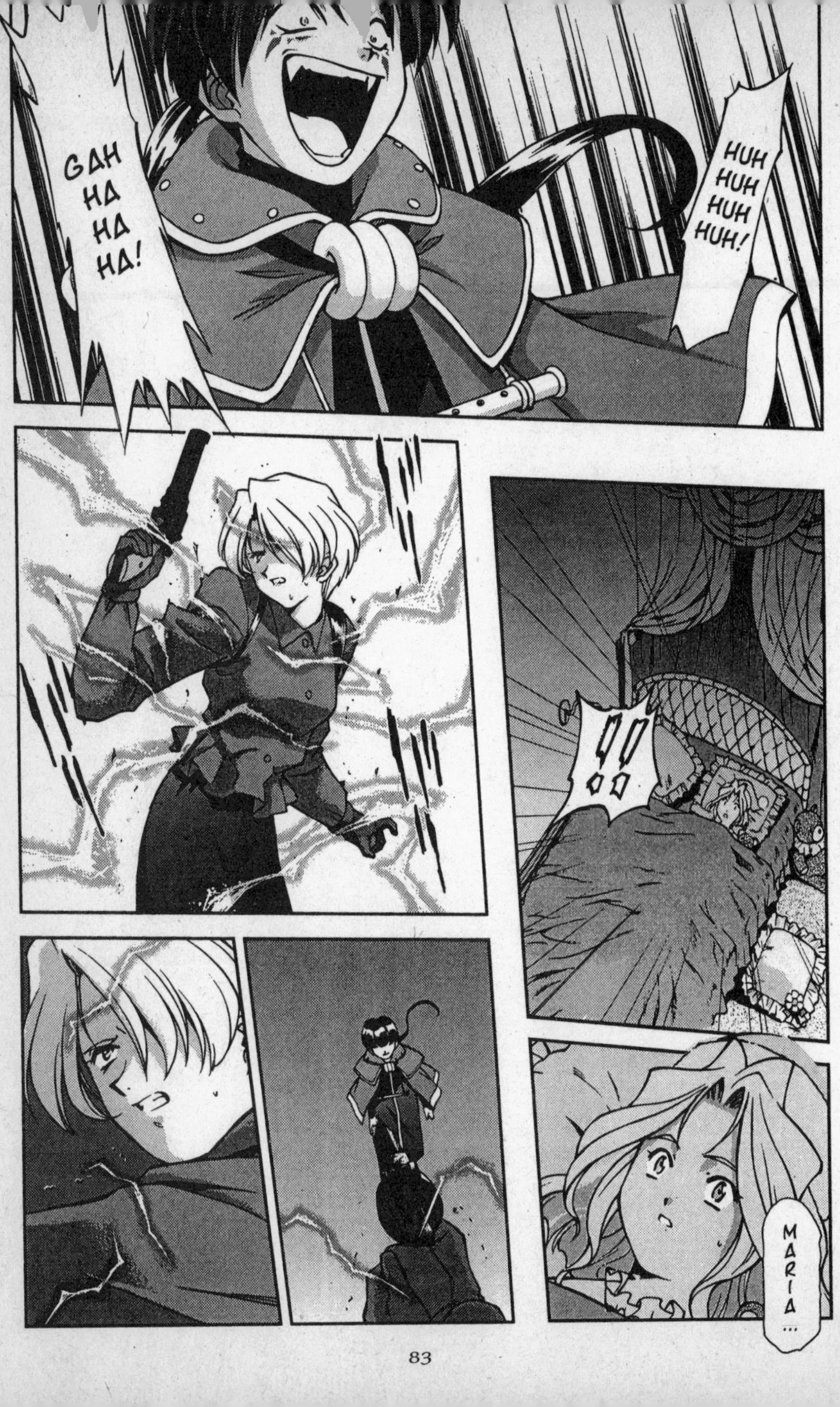
HUH HUH HUH HUH!
GAH HA HA HA!
!!
MARIA...

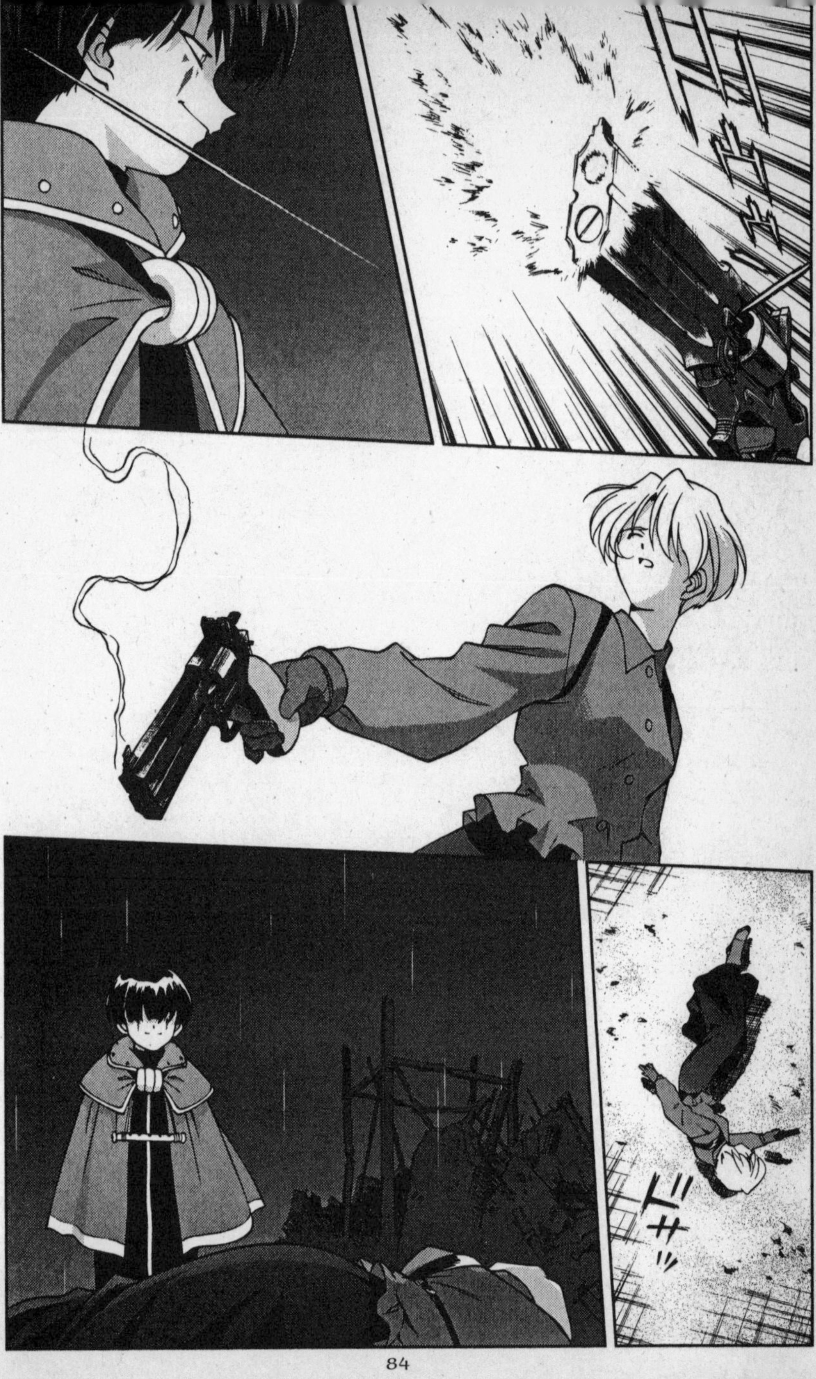
ドサッ

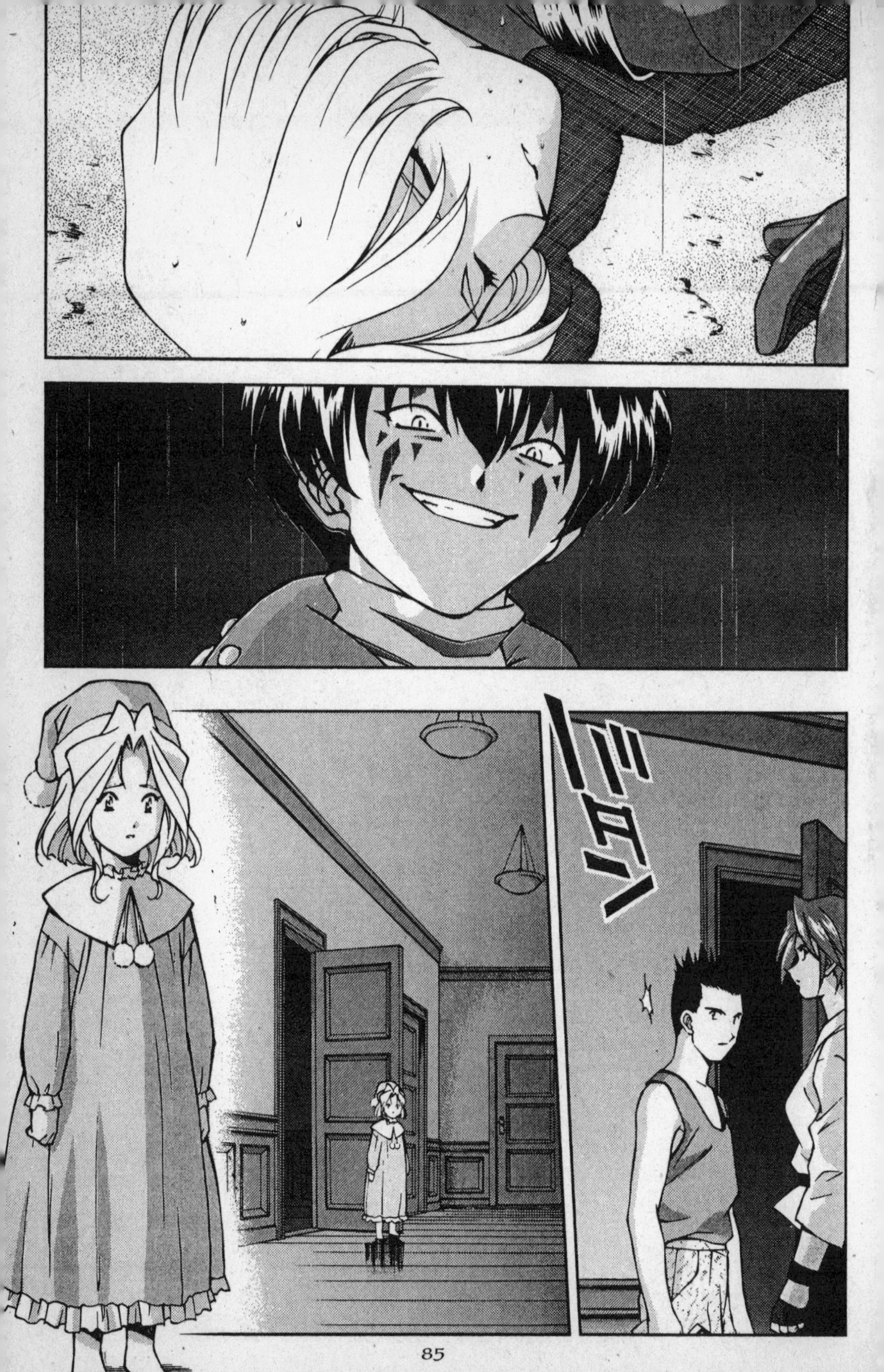
バタン

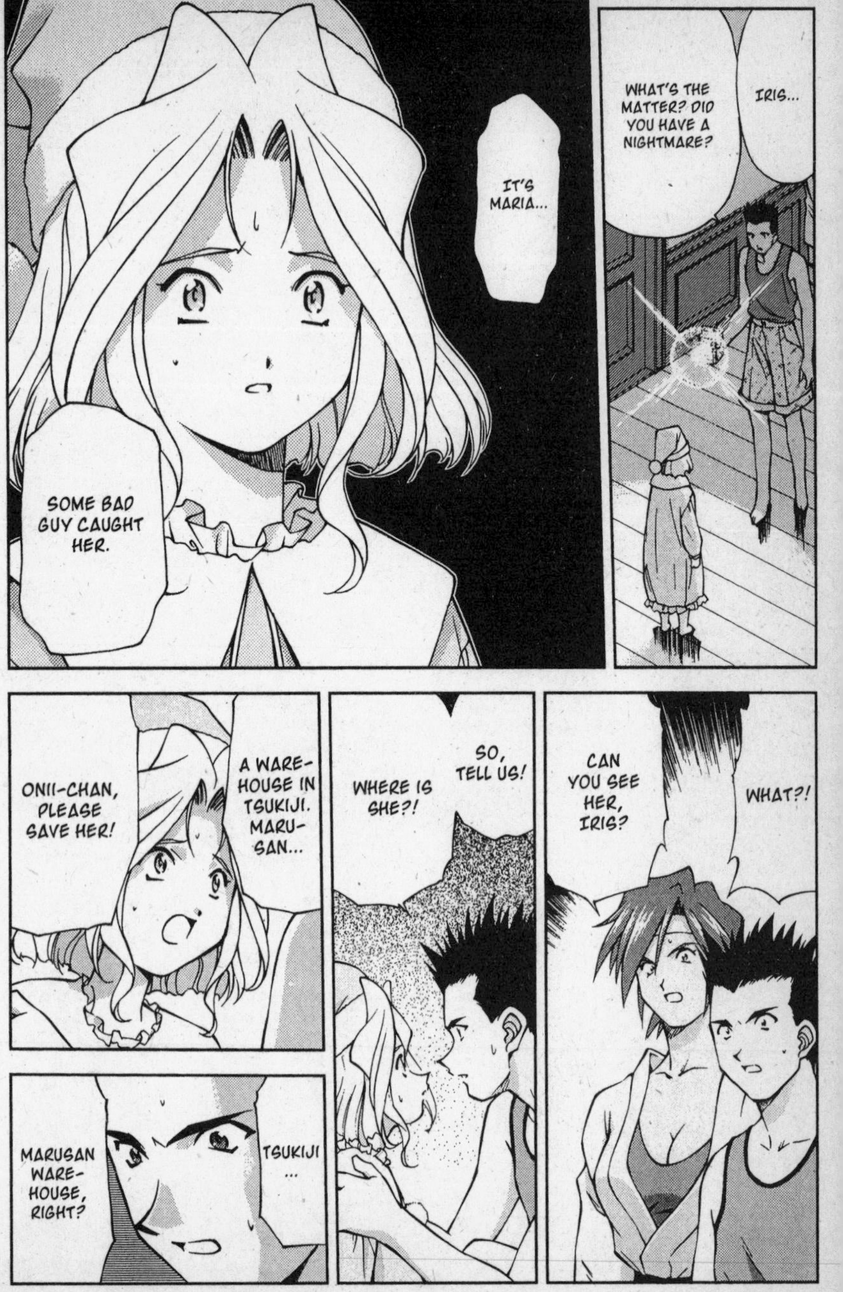
IRIS...
WHAT'S THE MATTER? DID YOU HAVE A NIGHTMARE?
IT'S MARIA...
SOME BAD GUY CAUGHT HER.
WHAT?!
CAN YOU SEE HER, IRIS?
SO, TELL US!
WHERE IS SHE?!
A WARE-HOUSE IN TSUKIJI. MARU-SAN...
ONII-CHAN, PLEASE SAVE HER!
TSUKIJI...
MARUSAN WARE-HOUSE, RIGHT?

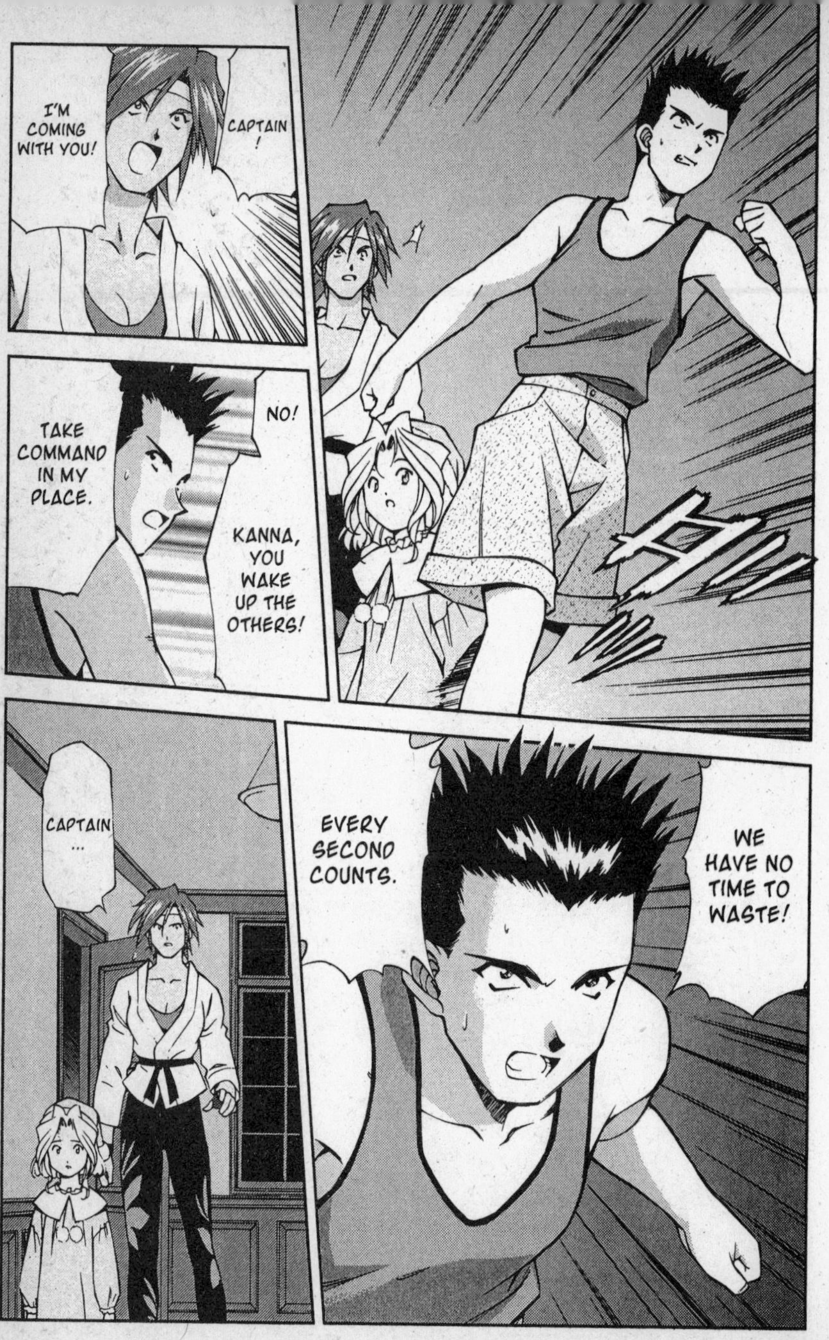
CAPTAIN !
I'M COMING WITH YOU!
NO!
TAKE COMMAND IN MY PLACE.
KANNA, YOU WAKE UP THE OTHERS!
WE HAVE NO TIME TO WASTE!
EVERY SECOND COUNTS.
CAPTAIN ...

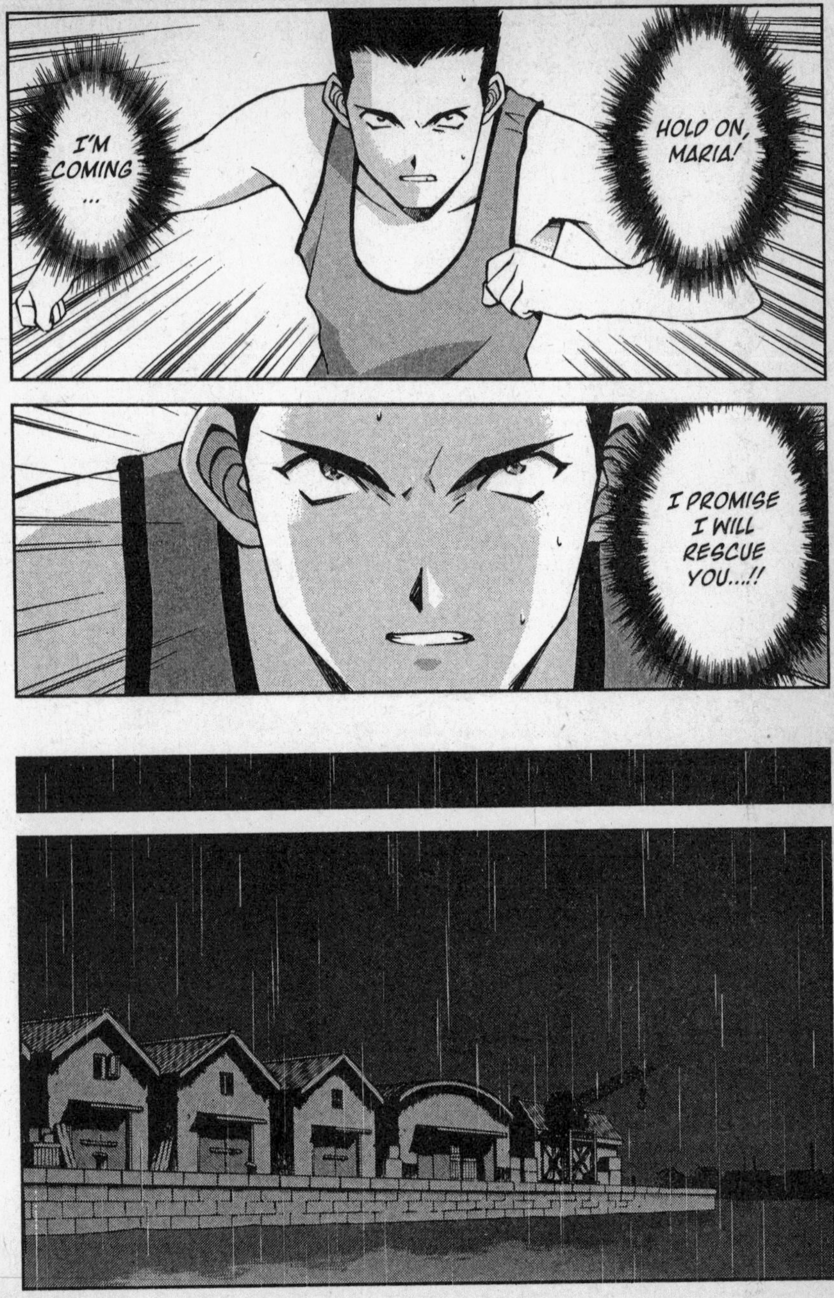
HOLD ON, MARIA!
I'M COMING ...
I PROMISE I WILL RESCUE YOU...!!

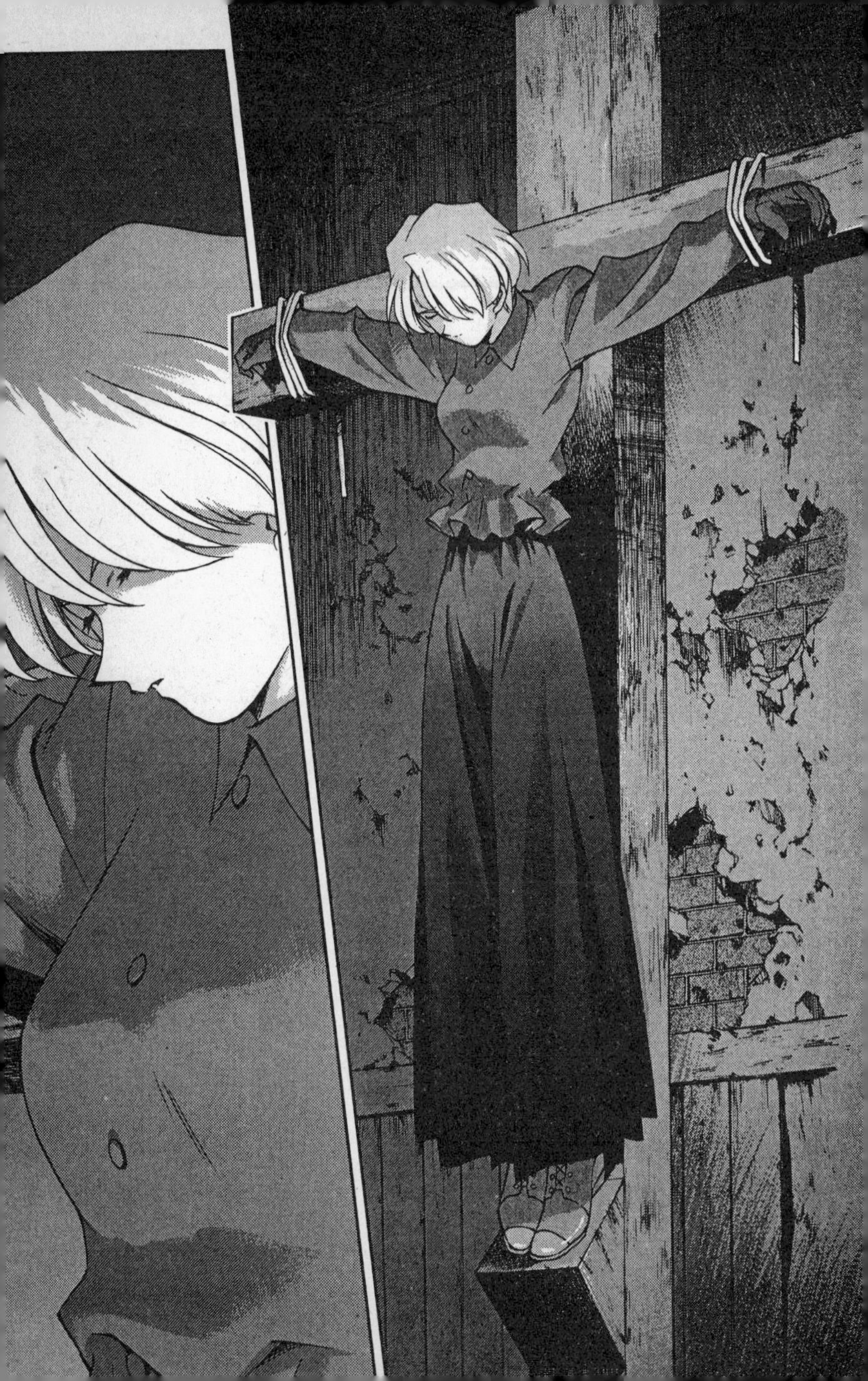

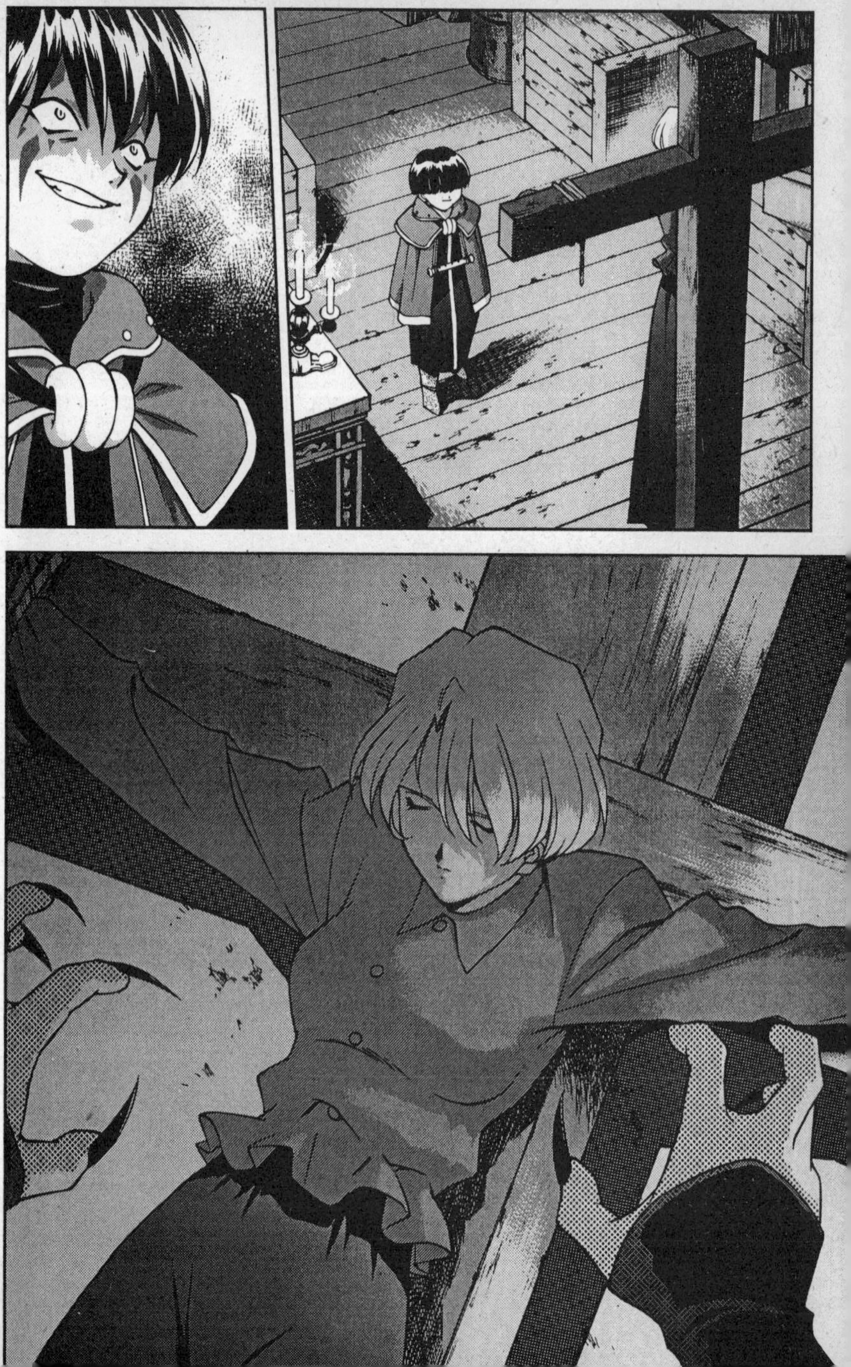

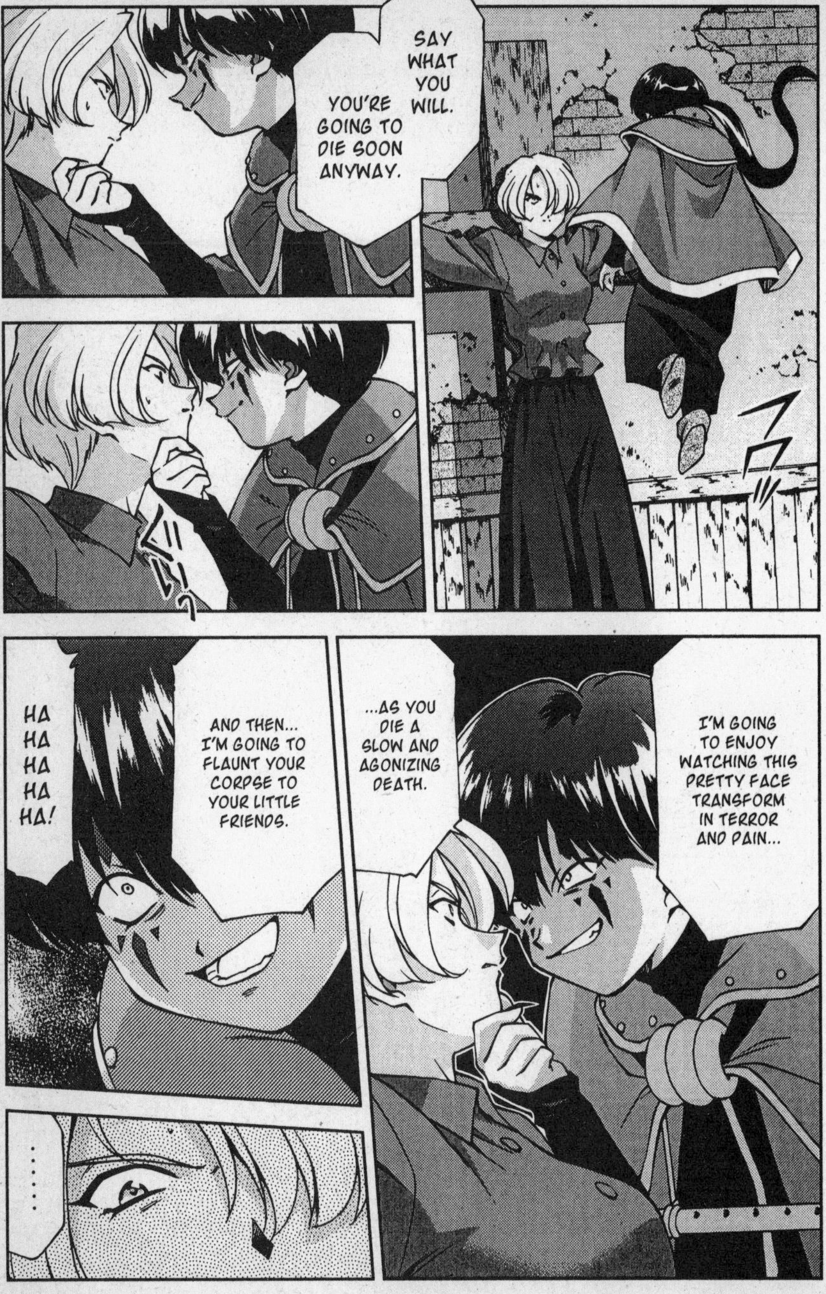
SAY WHAT YOU WILL.
YOU'RE GOING TO DIE SOON ANYWAY.
I'M GOING TO ENJOY WATCHING THIS PRETTY FACE TRANSFORM IN TERROR AND PAIN...
...AS YOU DIE A SLOW AND AGONIZING DEATH.
AND THEN... I'M GOING TO FLAUNT YOUR CORPSE TO YOUR LITTLE FRIENDS.
HA HA HA HA HA!
......

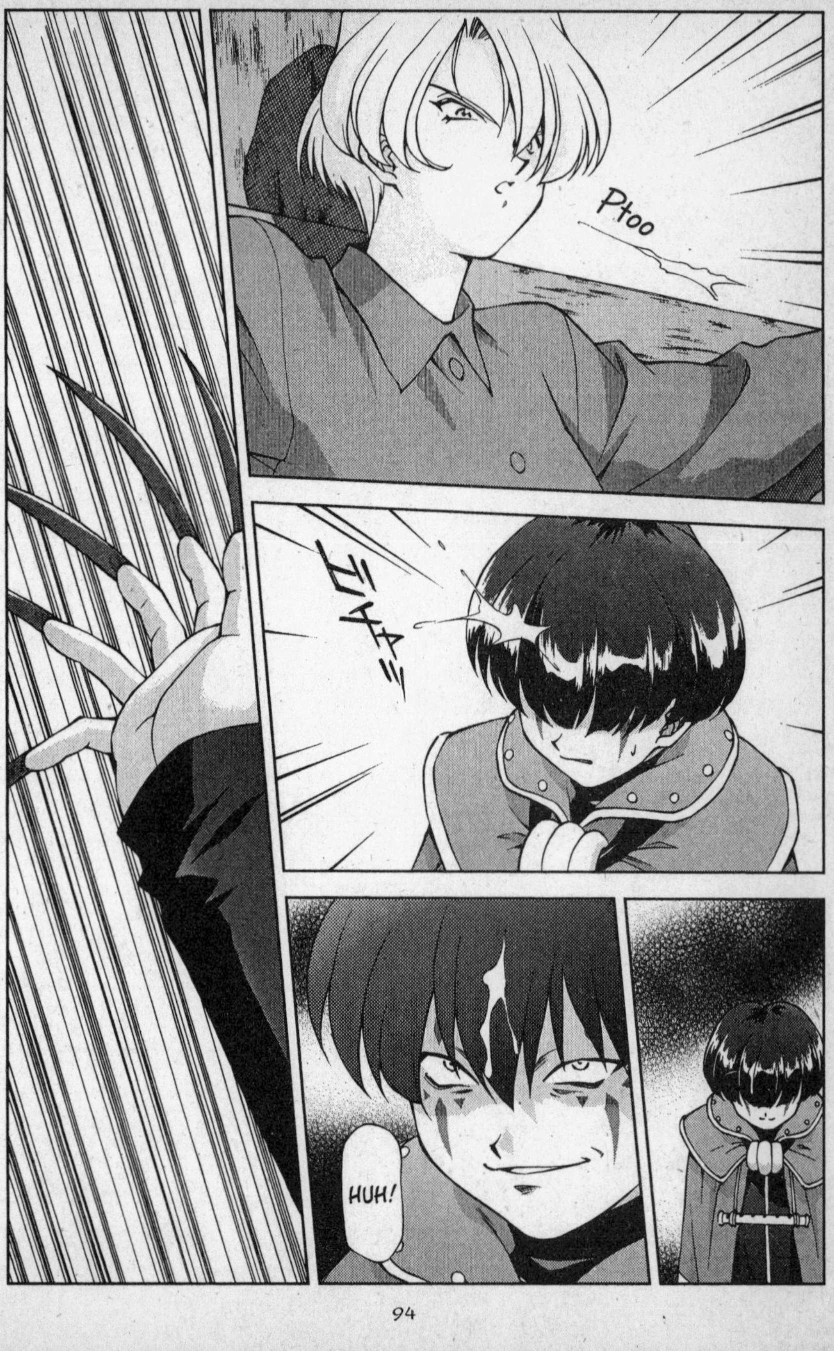
Ptoo
HUH!

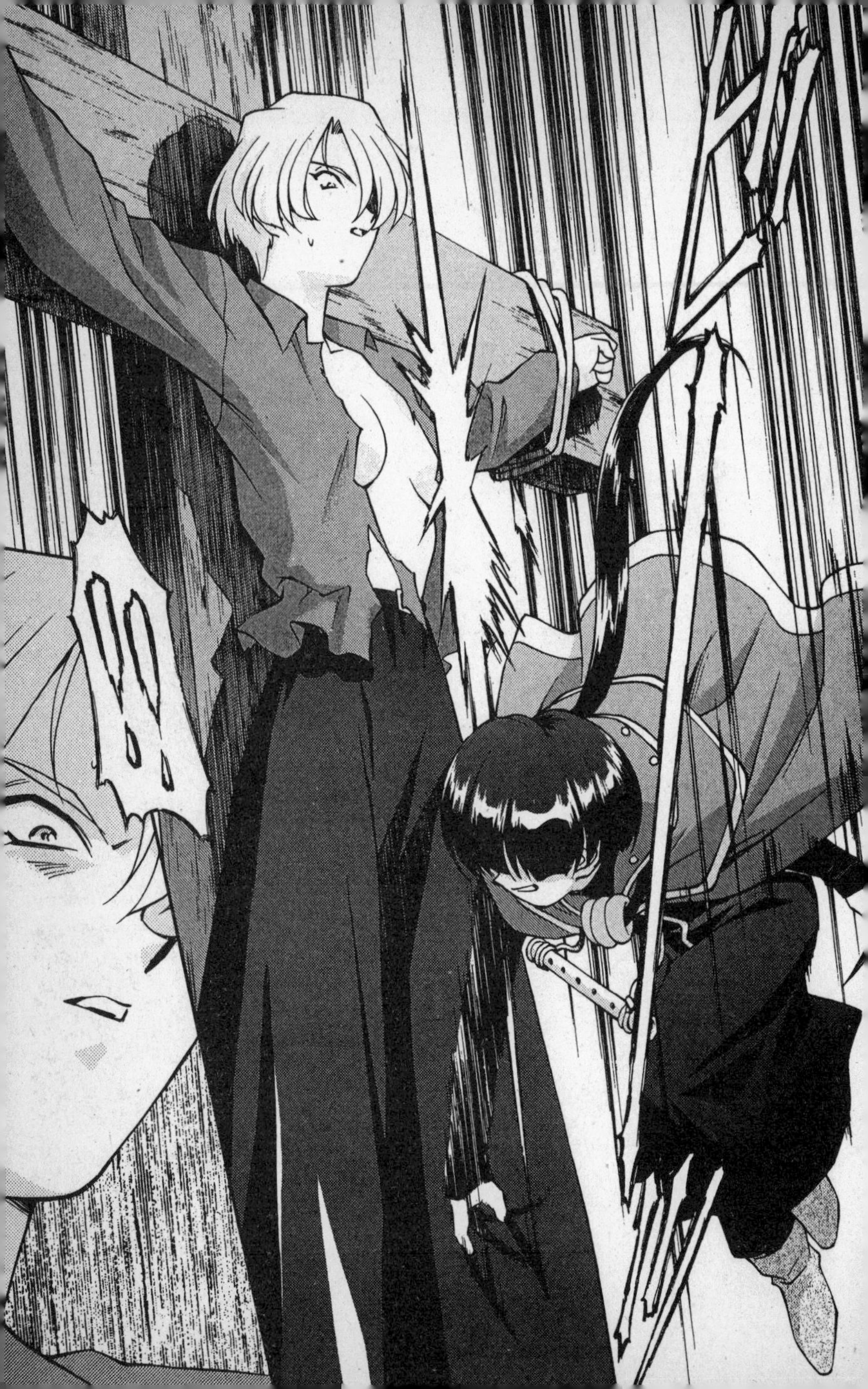
!!

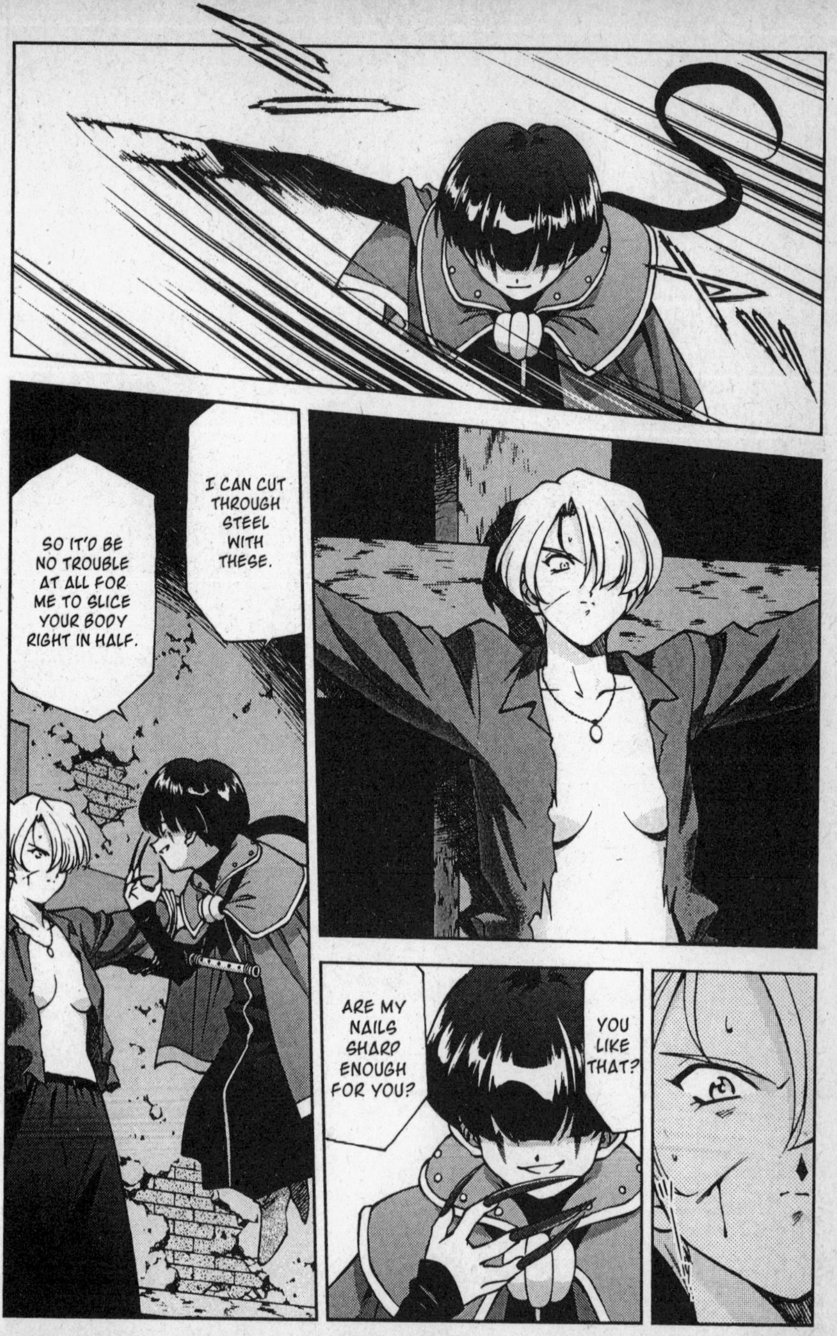
YOU LIKE THAT?
ARE MY NAILS SHARP ENOUGH FOR YOU?
I CAN CUT THROUGH STEEL WITH THESE.
SO IT'D BE NO TROUBLE AT ALL FOR ME TO SLICE YOUR BODY RIGHT IN HALF.

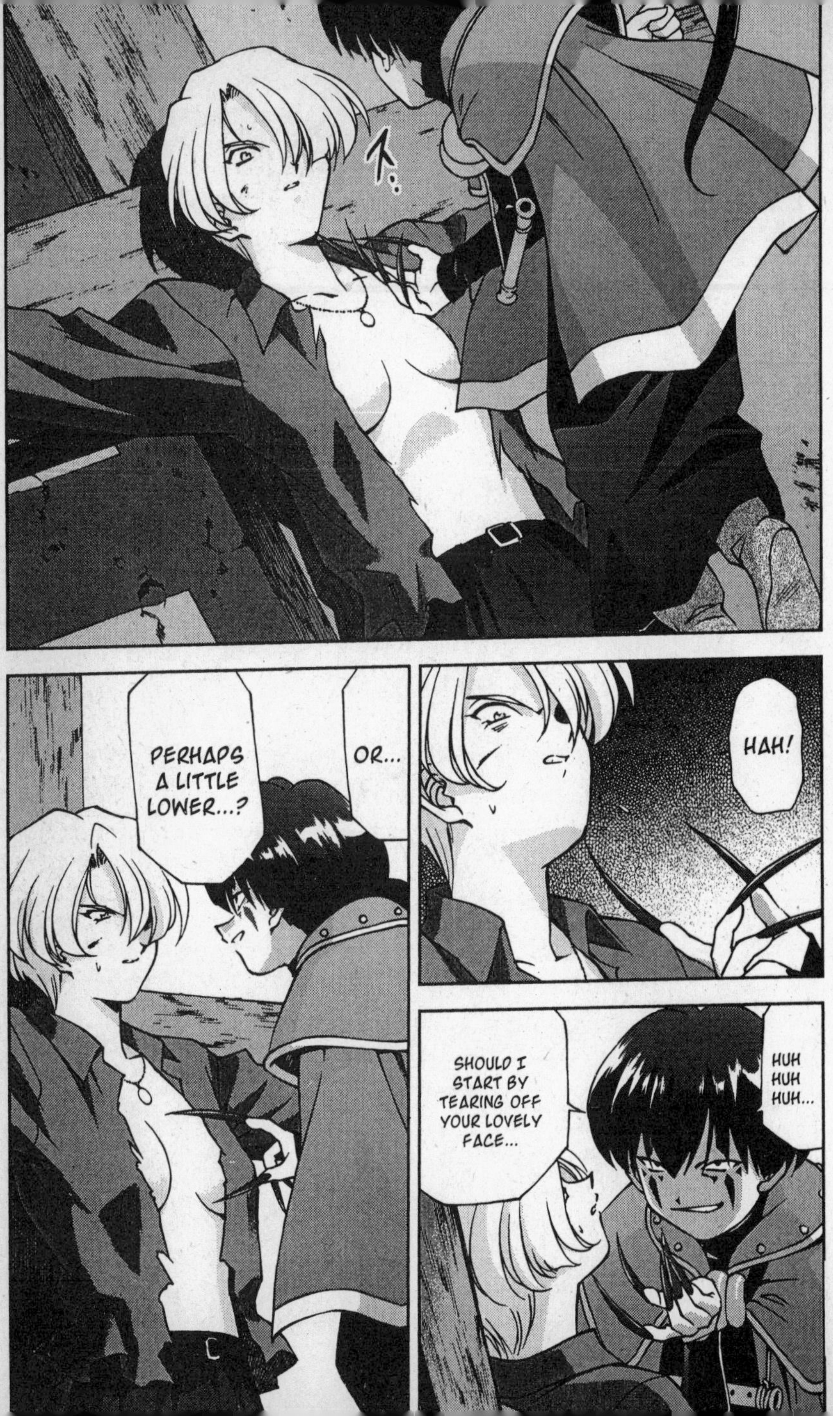
HAH!
HUH HUH HUH...
SHOULD I START BY TEARING OFF YOUR LOVELY FACE...
OR...
PERHAPS A LITTLE LOWER...?

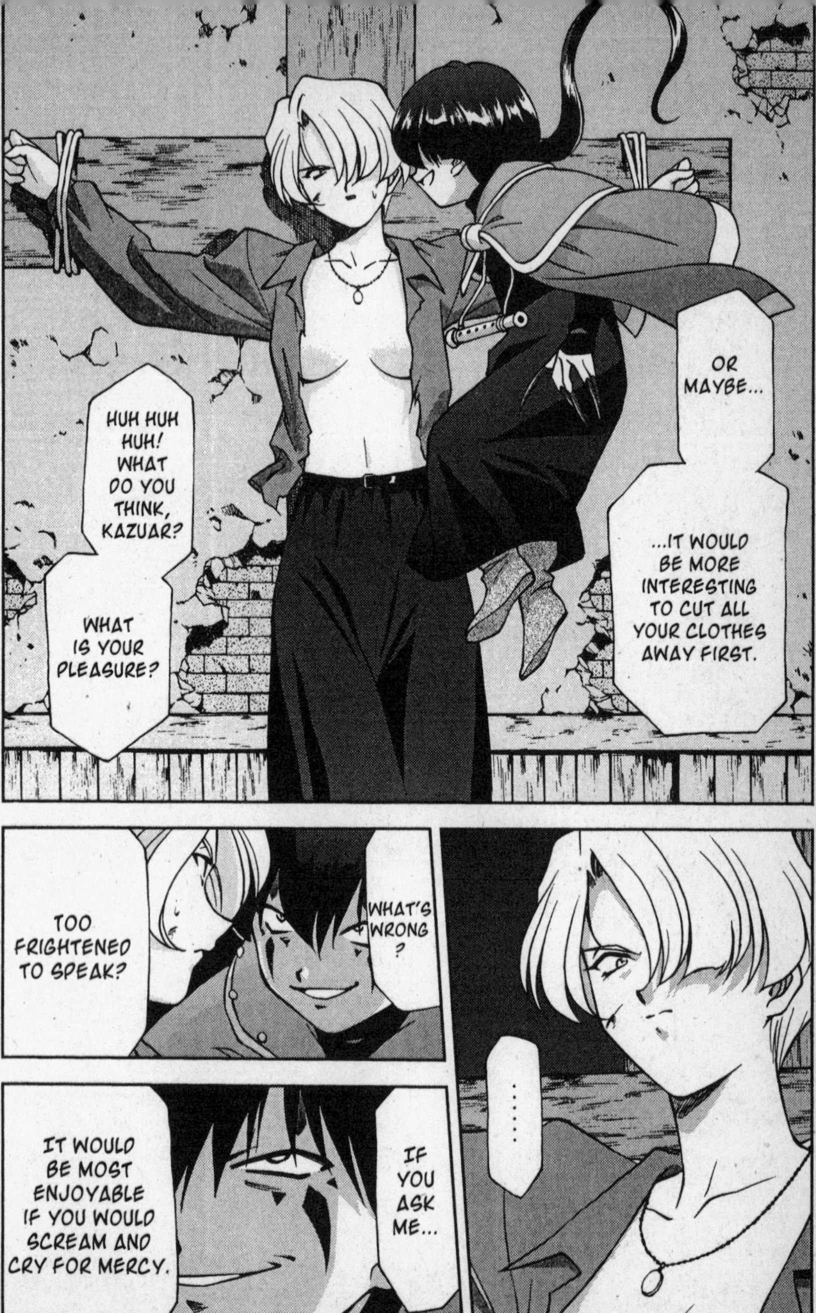
OR MAYBE...
...IT WOULD BE MORE INTERESTING TO CUT ALL YOUR CLOTHES AWAY FIRST.
HUH HUH HUH! WHAT DO YOU THINK, KAZUAR?
WHAT IS YOUR PLEASURE?
......
WHAT'S WRONG?
TOO FRIGHTENED TO SPEAK?
IF YOU ASK ME...
IT WOULD BE MOST ENJOYABLE IF YOU WOULD SCREAM AND CRY FOR MERCY.

98

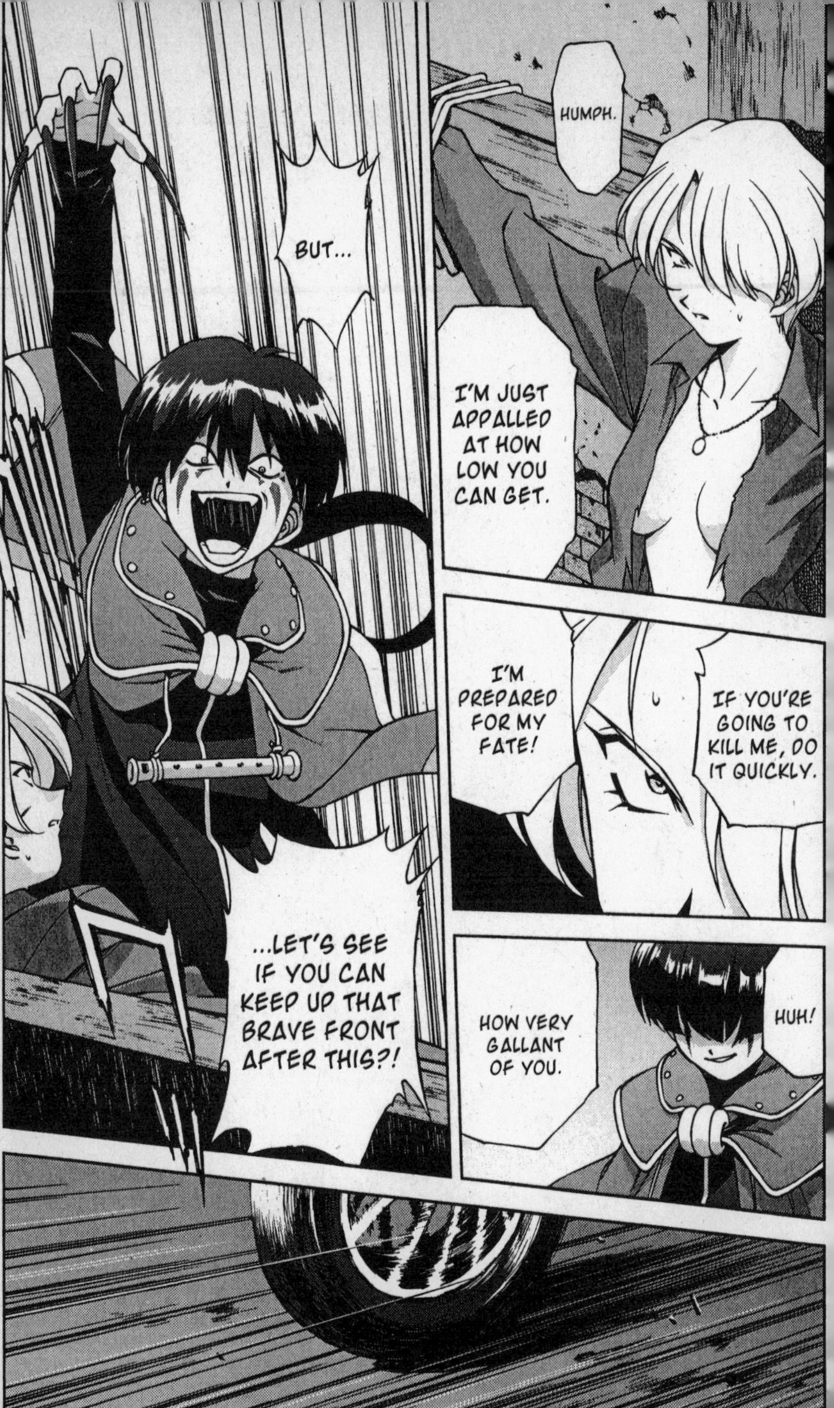
HUMPH.
I'M JUST APPALLED AT HOW LOW YOU CAN GET.
IF YOU'RE GOING TO KILL ME, DO IT QUICKLY.
I'M PREPARED FOR MY FATE!
HUH!
HOW VERY GALLANT OF YOU.
BUT...
...LET'S SEE IF YOU CAN KEEP UP THAT BRAVE FRONT AFTER THIS?!

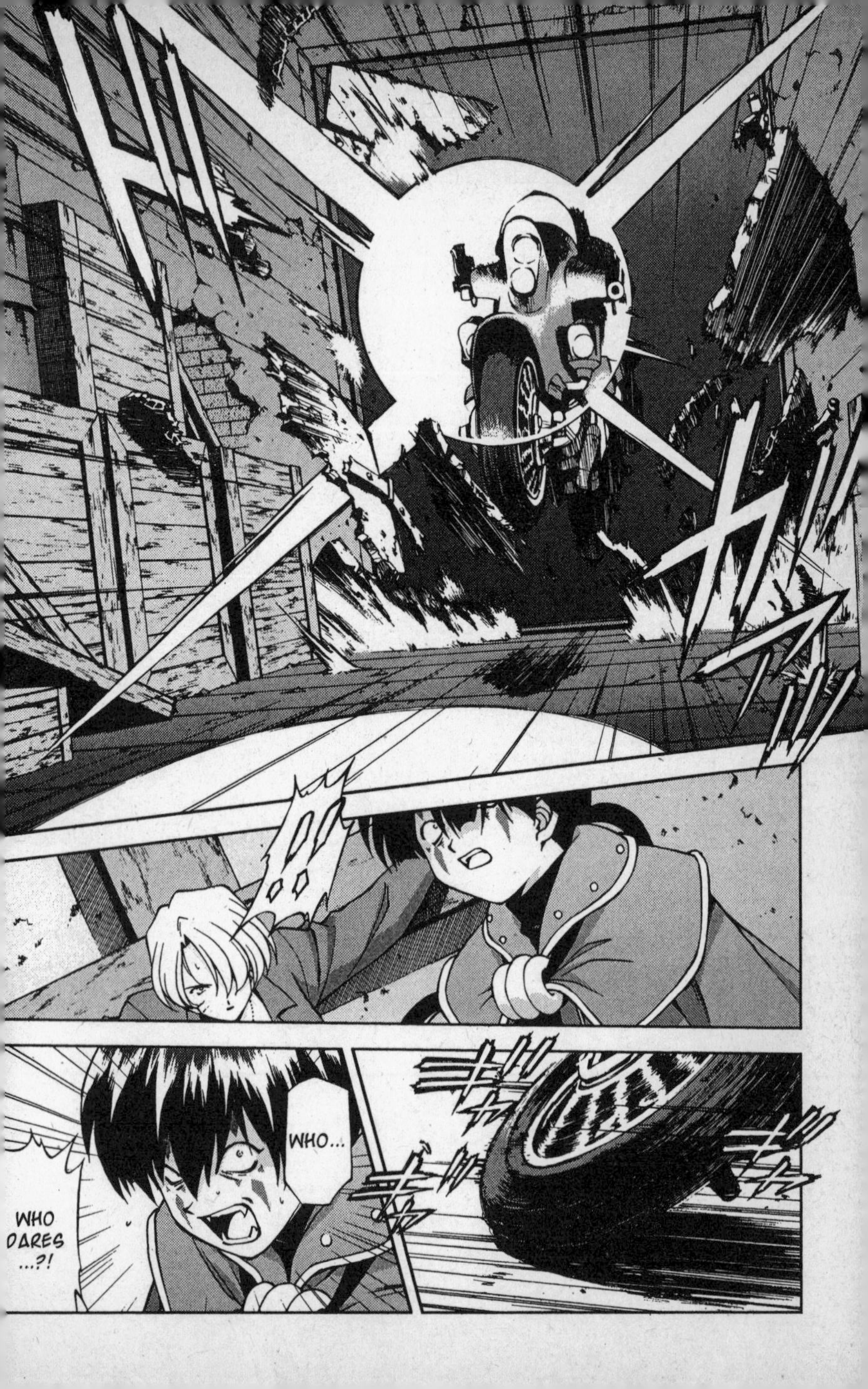
WHO...
WHO DARES ...?!

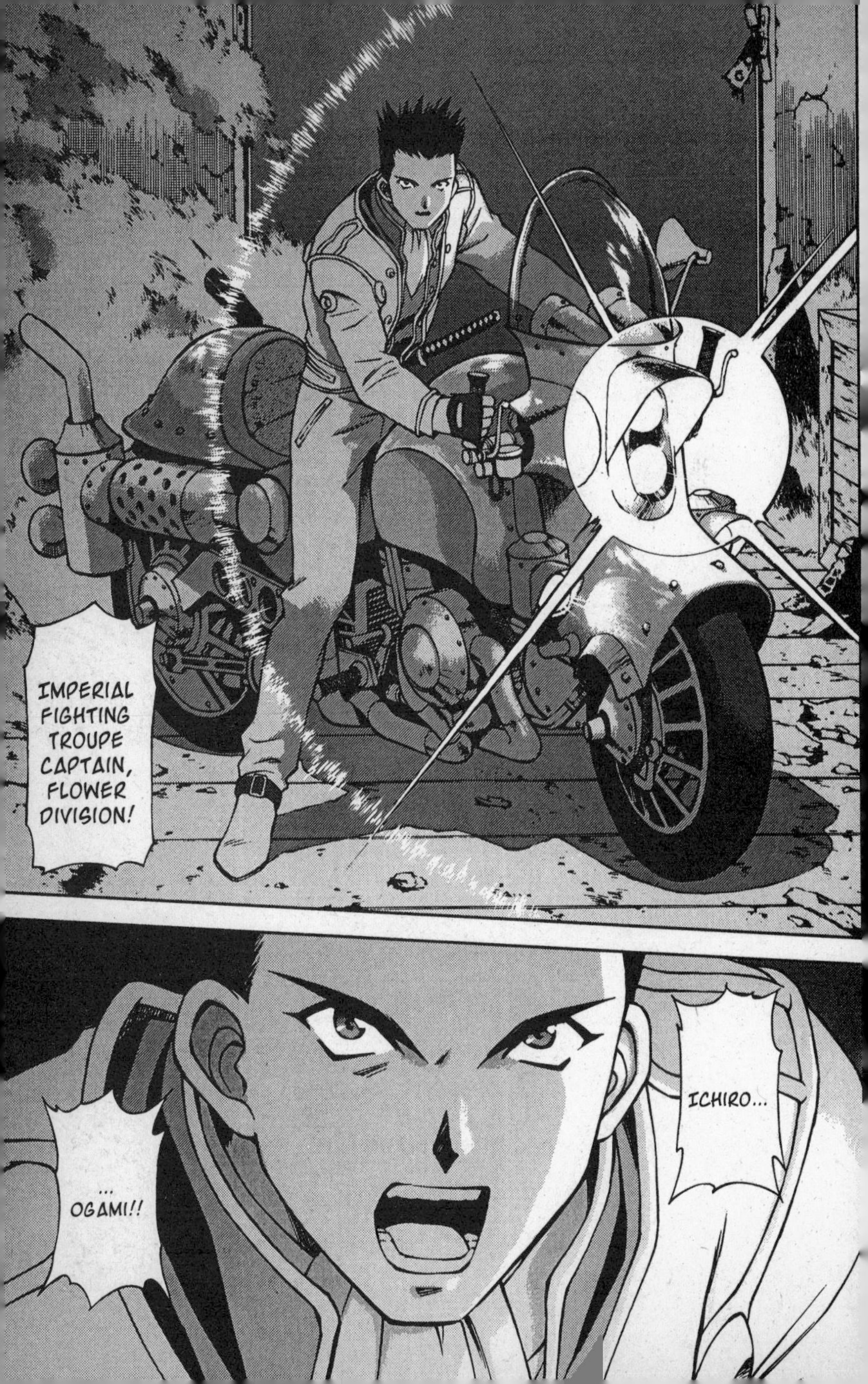
IMPERIAL FIGHTING TROUPE CAPTAIN, FLOWER DIVISION!
ICHIRO...
...OGAMI!!

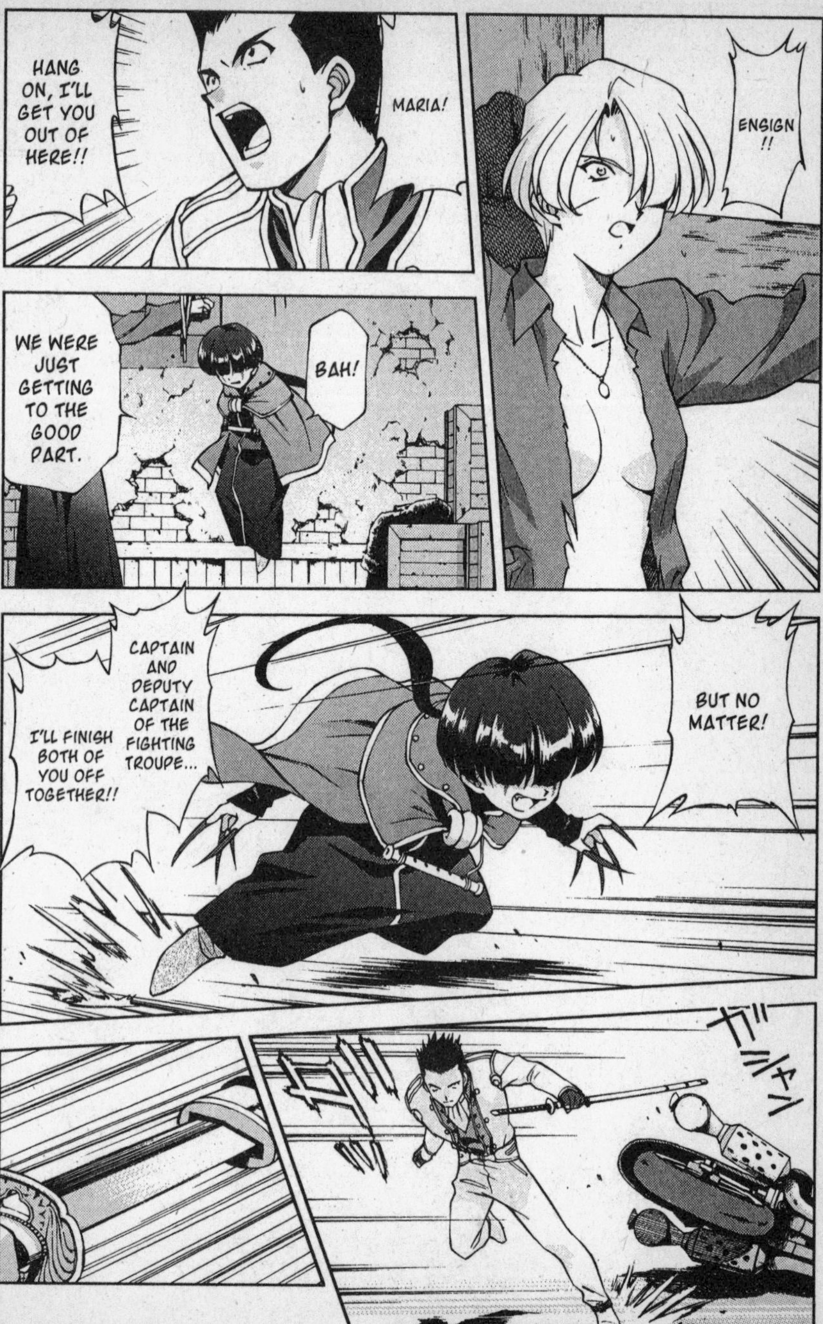
ENSIGN!!
MARIA!
HANG ON, I'LL GET YOU OUT OF HERE!!
BAH!
WE WERE JUST GETTING TO THE GOOD PART.
BUT NO MATTER!
CAPTAIN AND DEPUTY CAPTAIN OF THE FIGHTING TROUPE...
I'LL FINISH BOTH OF YOU OFF TOGETHER!!
ガシャン

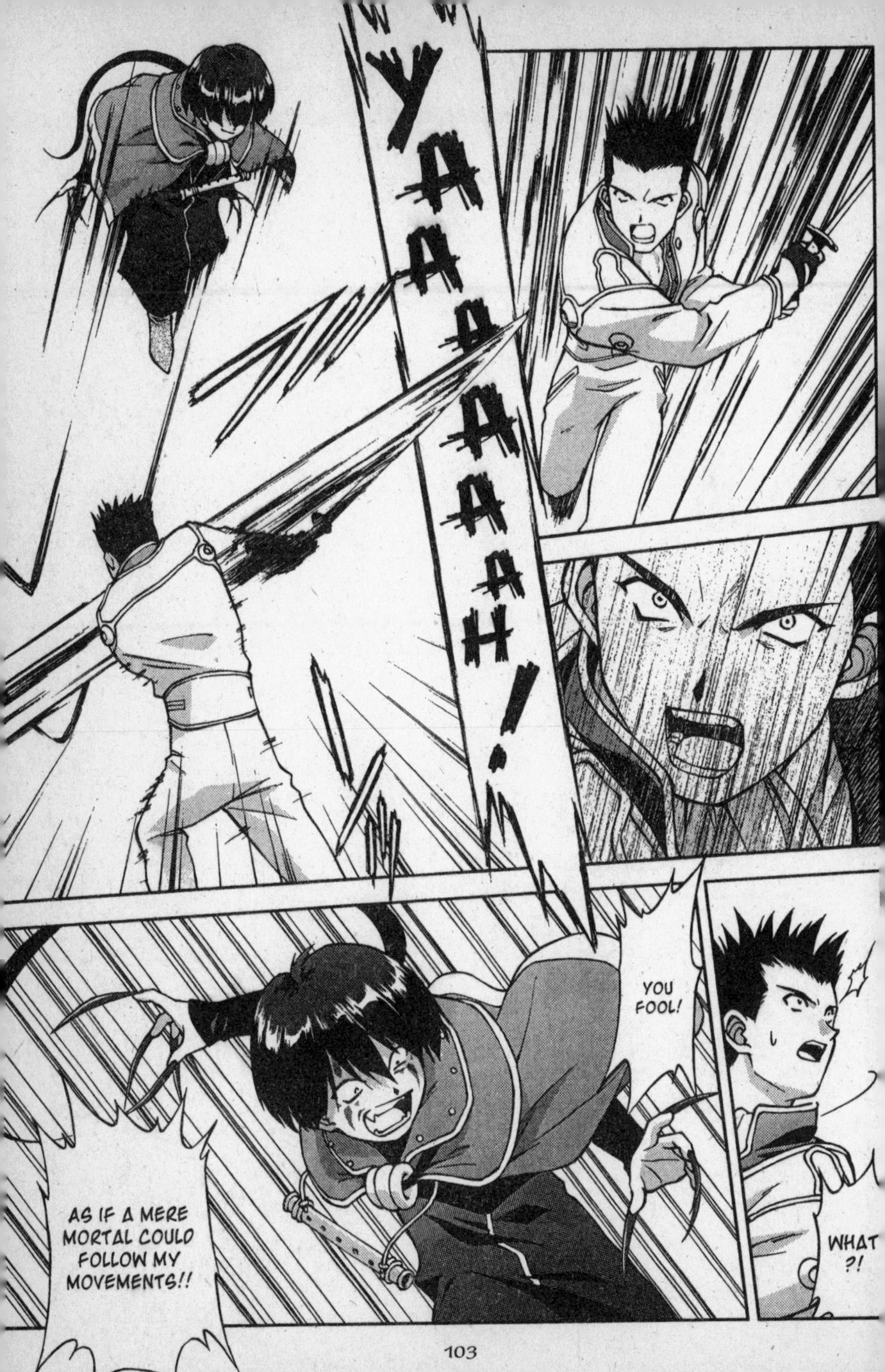

YAAAAAAAH!!
WHAT?!
YOU FOOL!
AS IF A MERE MORTAL COULD FOLLOW MY MOVEMENTS!!

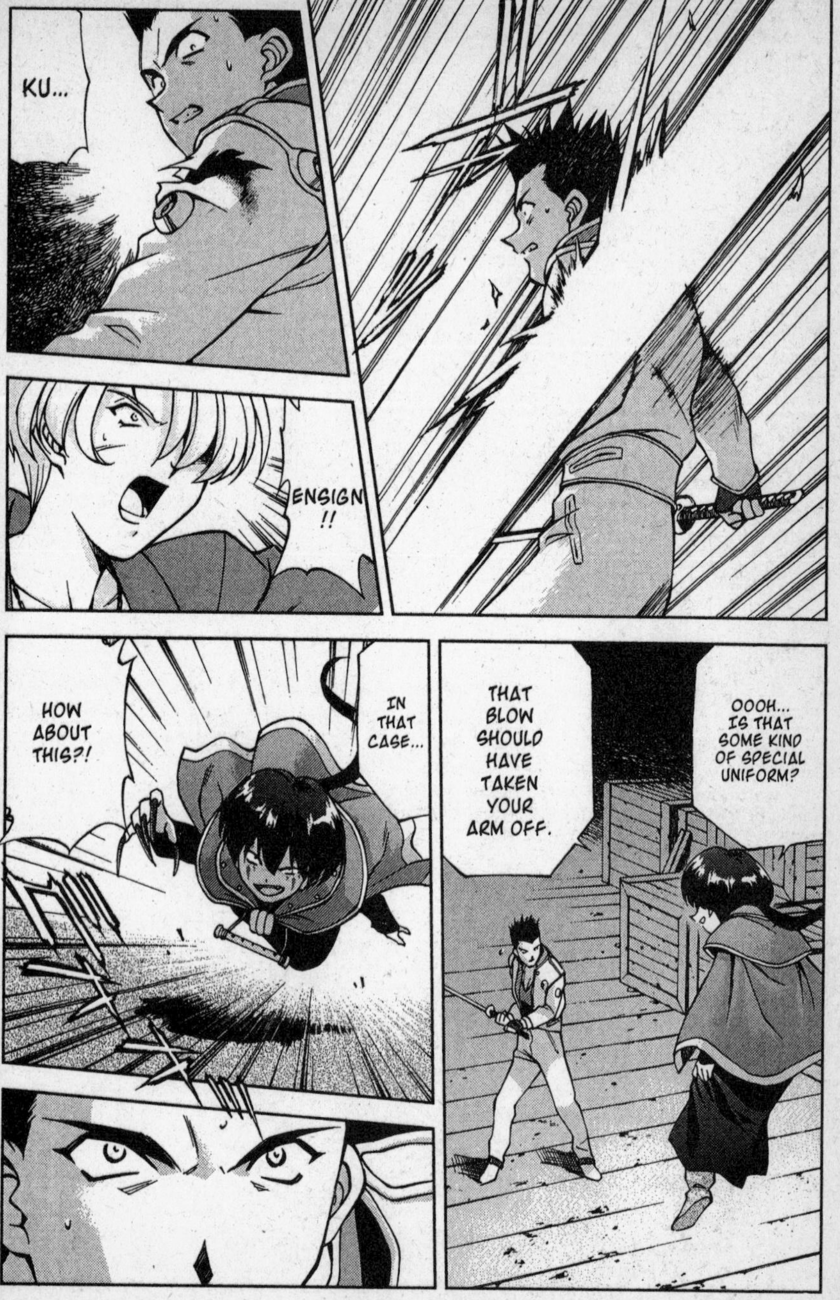
KU...
ENSIGN !!
OOOH... IS THAT SOME KIND OF SPECIAL UNIFORM?
THAT BLOW SHOULD HAVE TAKEN YOUR ARM OFF.
IN THAT CASE...
HOW ABOUT THIS?!

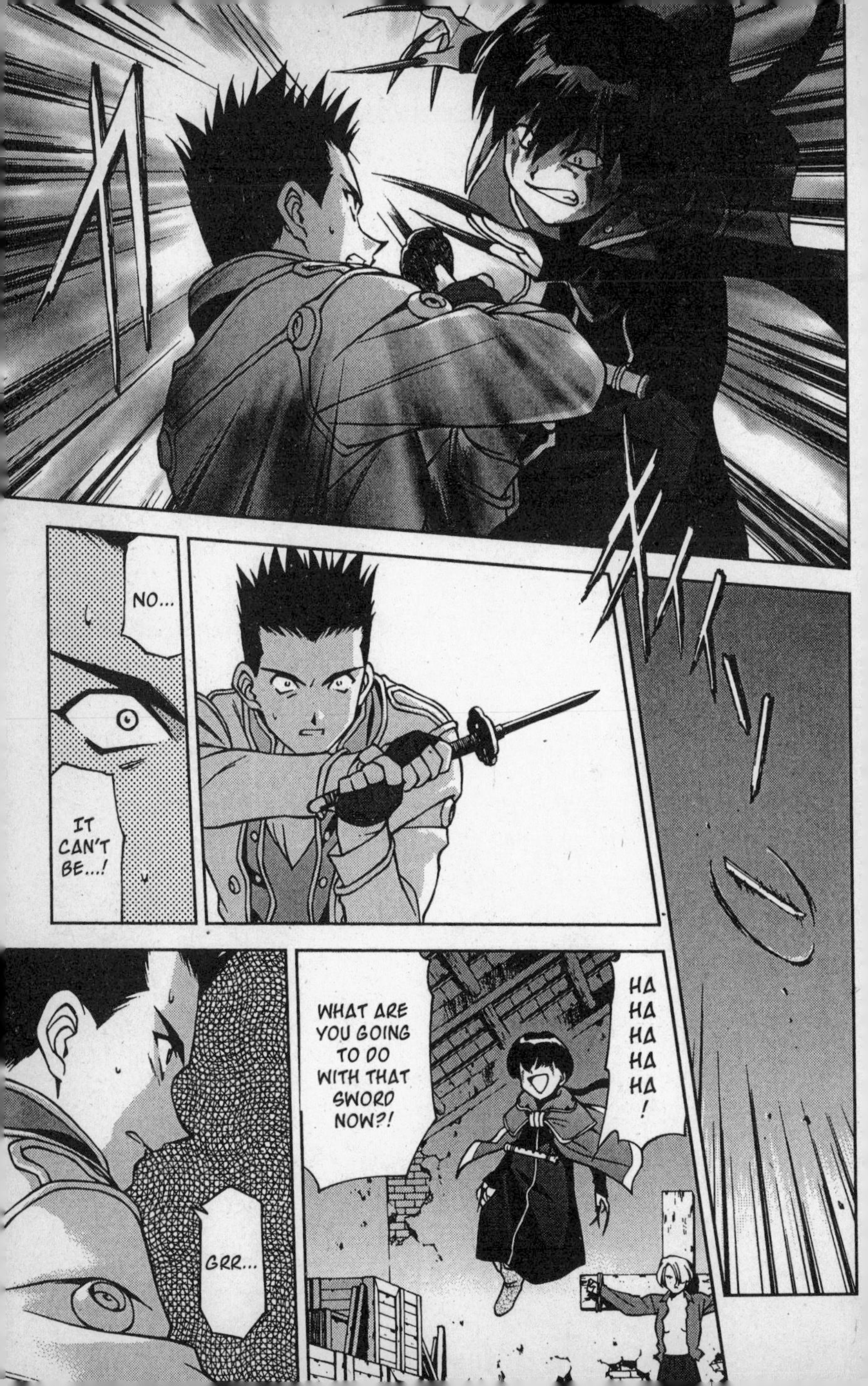
NO...
IT CAN'T BE...!
HA HA HA HA HA!
WHAT ARE YOU GOING TO DO WITH THAT SWORD NOW?!
GRR...

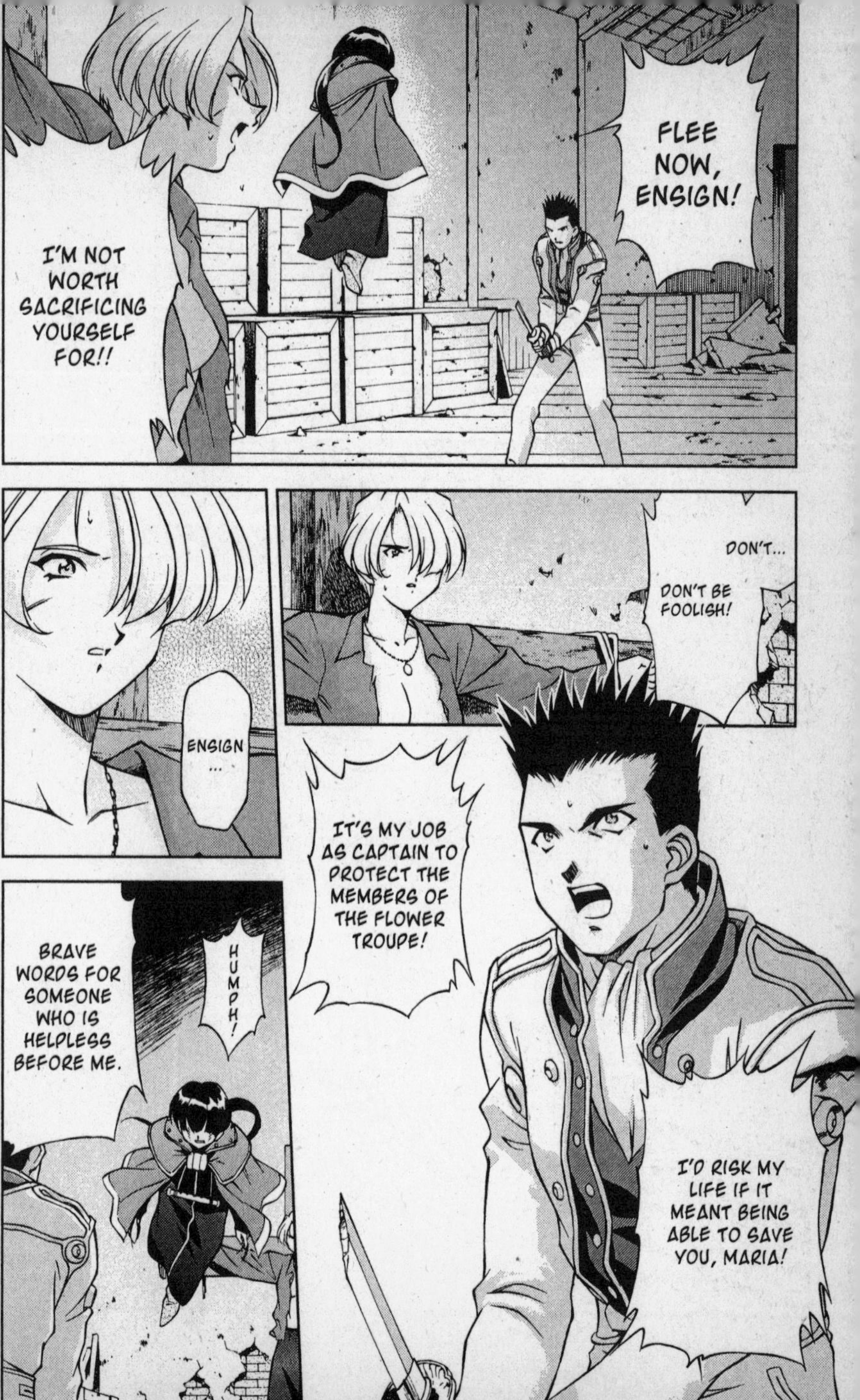
FLEE NOW, ENSIGN!
I'M NOT WORTH SACRIFICING YOURSELF FOR!!
DON'T...
DON'T BE FOOLISH!
ENSIGN...
IT'S MY JOB AS CAPTAIN TO PROTECT THE MEMBERS OF THE FLOWER TROUPE!
I'D RISK MY LIFE IF IT MEANT BEING ABLE TO SAVE YOU, MARIA!
HUMPH!
BRAVE WORDS FOR SOMEONE WHO IS HELPLESS BEFORE ME.

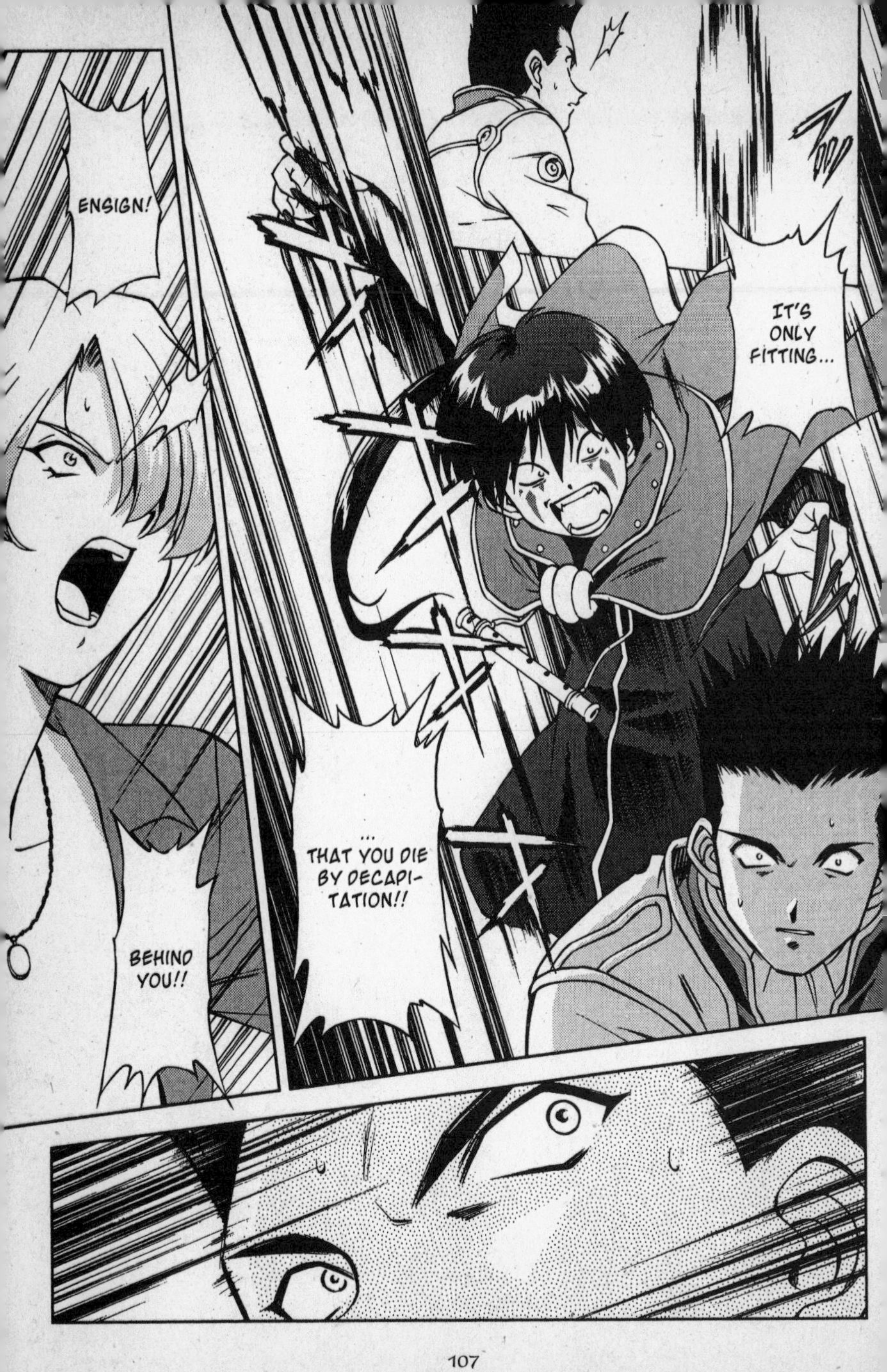
IT'S ONLY FITTING...
... THAT YOU DIE BY DECAPI-TATION!!
ENSIGN!
BEHIND YOU!!

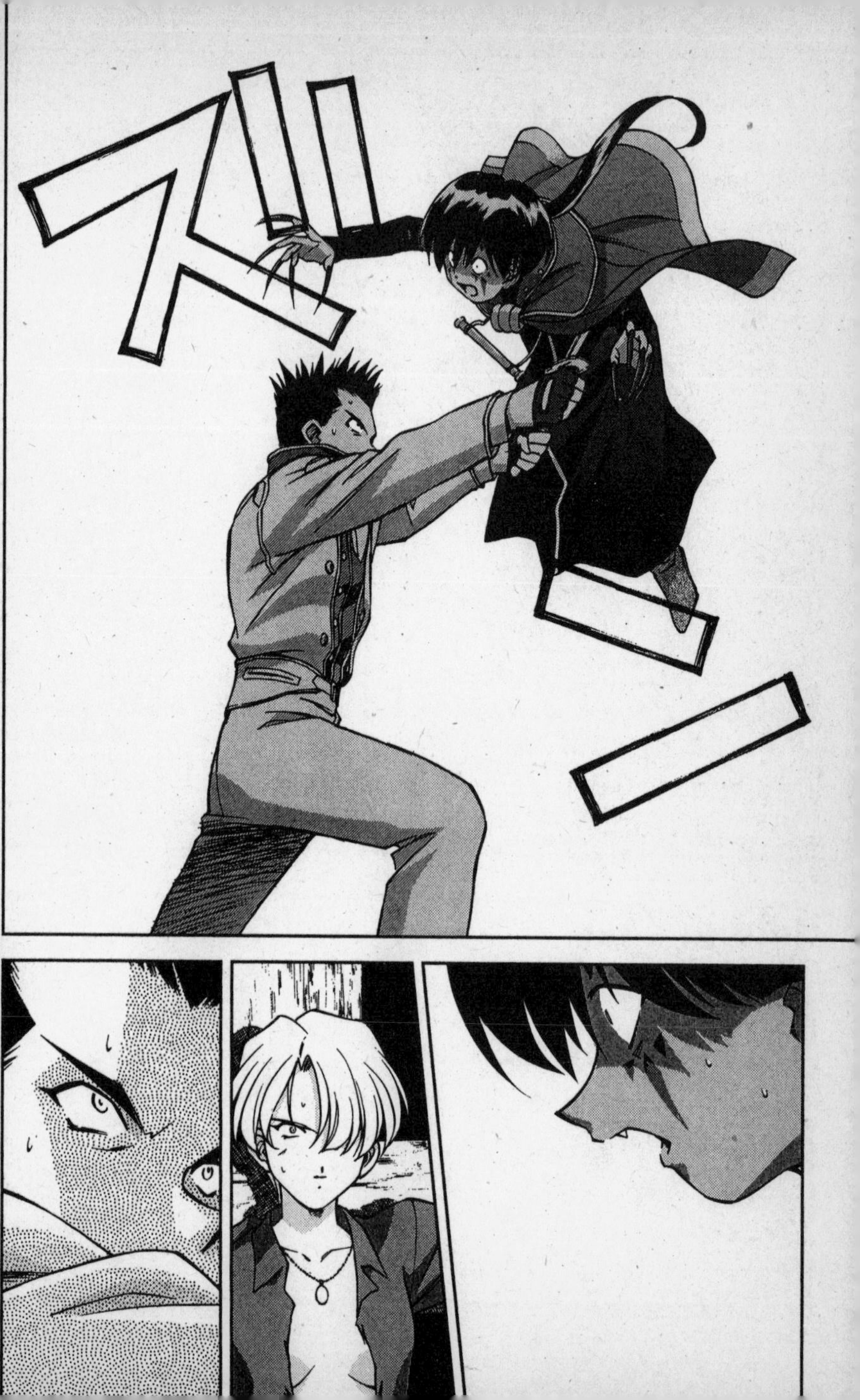

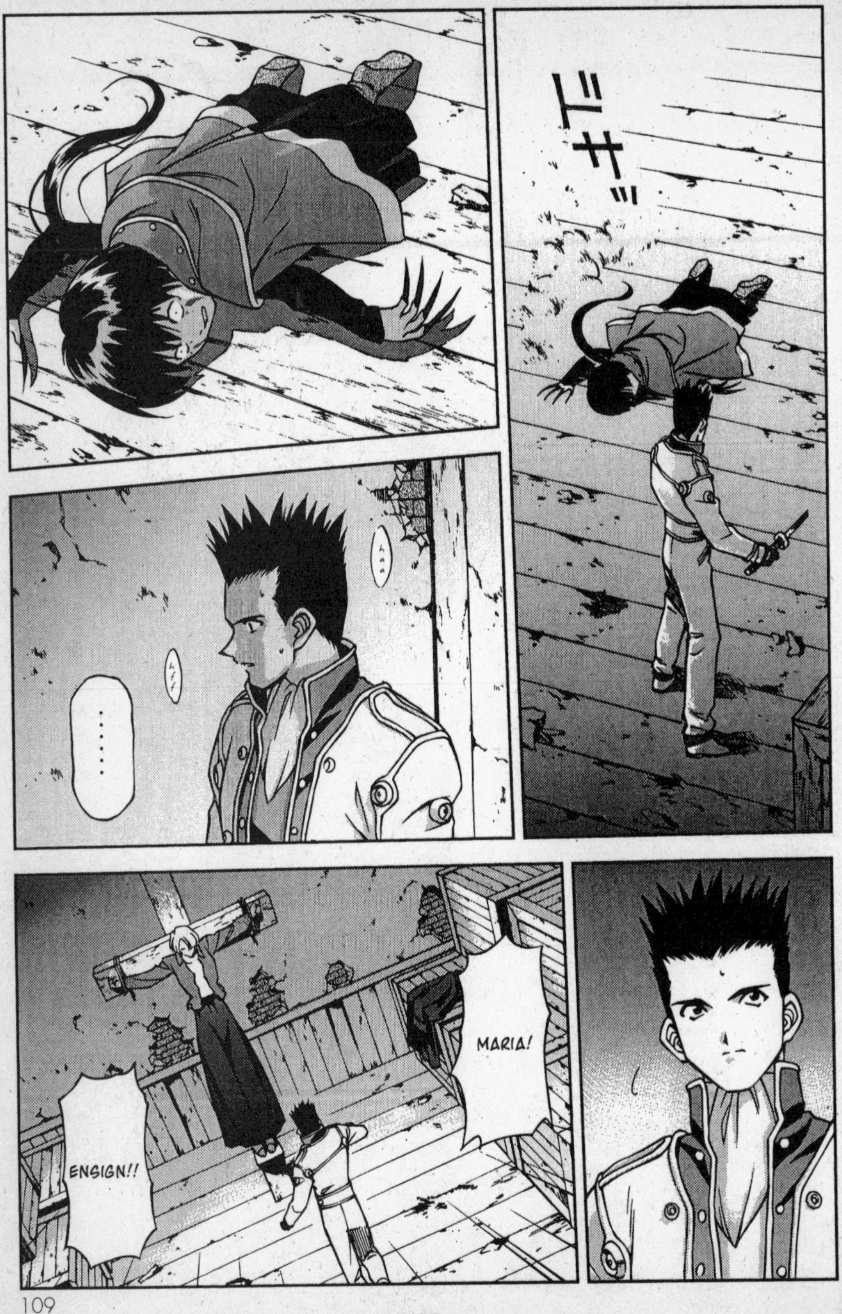
ドサッ
......
MARIA!
ENSIGN!!

109

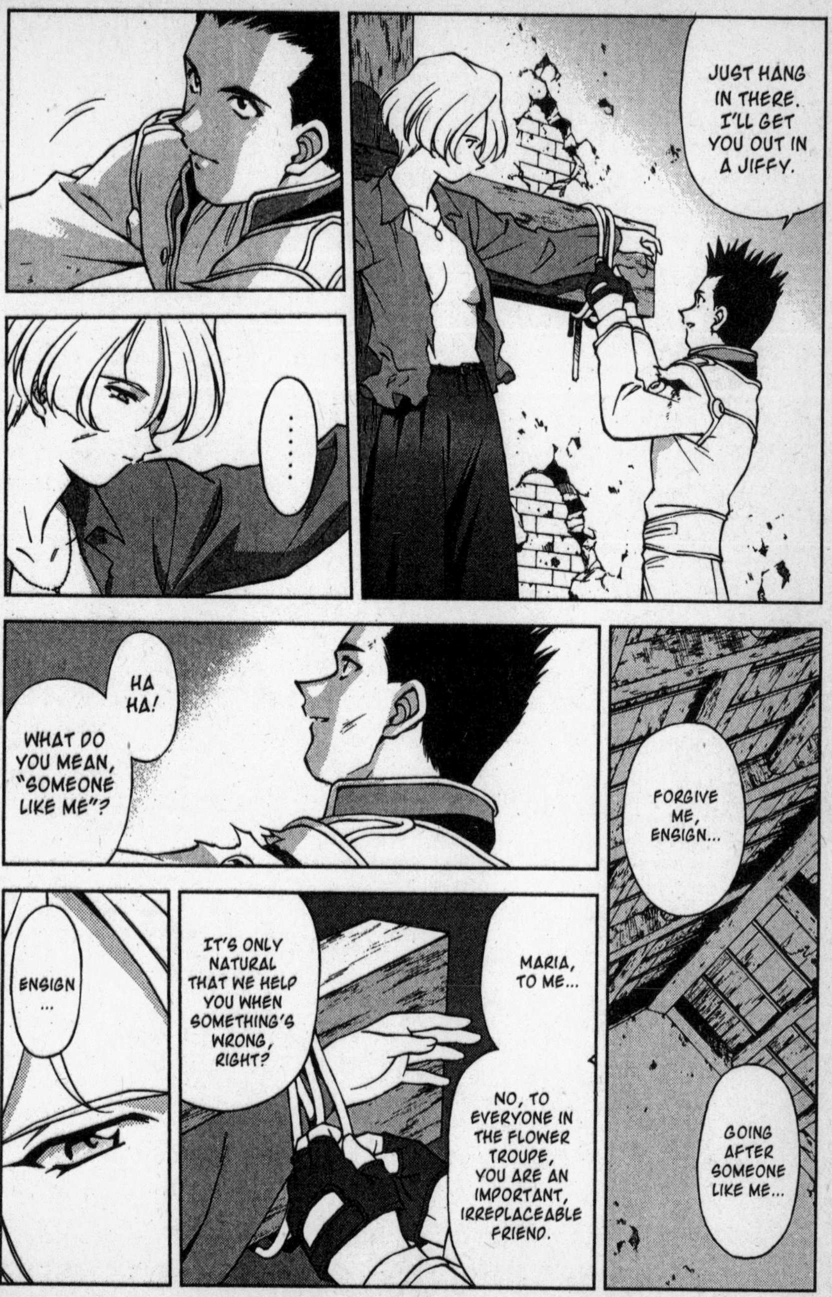
JUST HANG IN THERE. I'LL GET YOU OUT IN A JIFFY.
......
FORGIVE ME, ENSIGN...
GOING AFTER SOMEONE LIKE ME...
HA HA!
WHAT DO YOU MEAN, "SOMEONE LIKE ME"?
MARIA, TO ME...
NO, TO EVERYONE IN THE FLOWER TROUPE, YOU ARE AN IMPORTANT, IRREPLACEABLE FRIEND.
IT'S ONLY NATURAL THAT WE HELP YOU WHEN SOMETHING'S WRONG, RIGHT?
ENSIGN ...

110

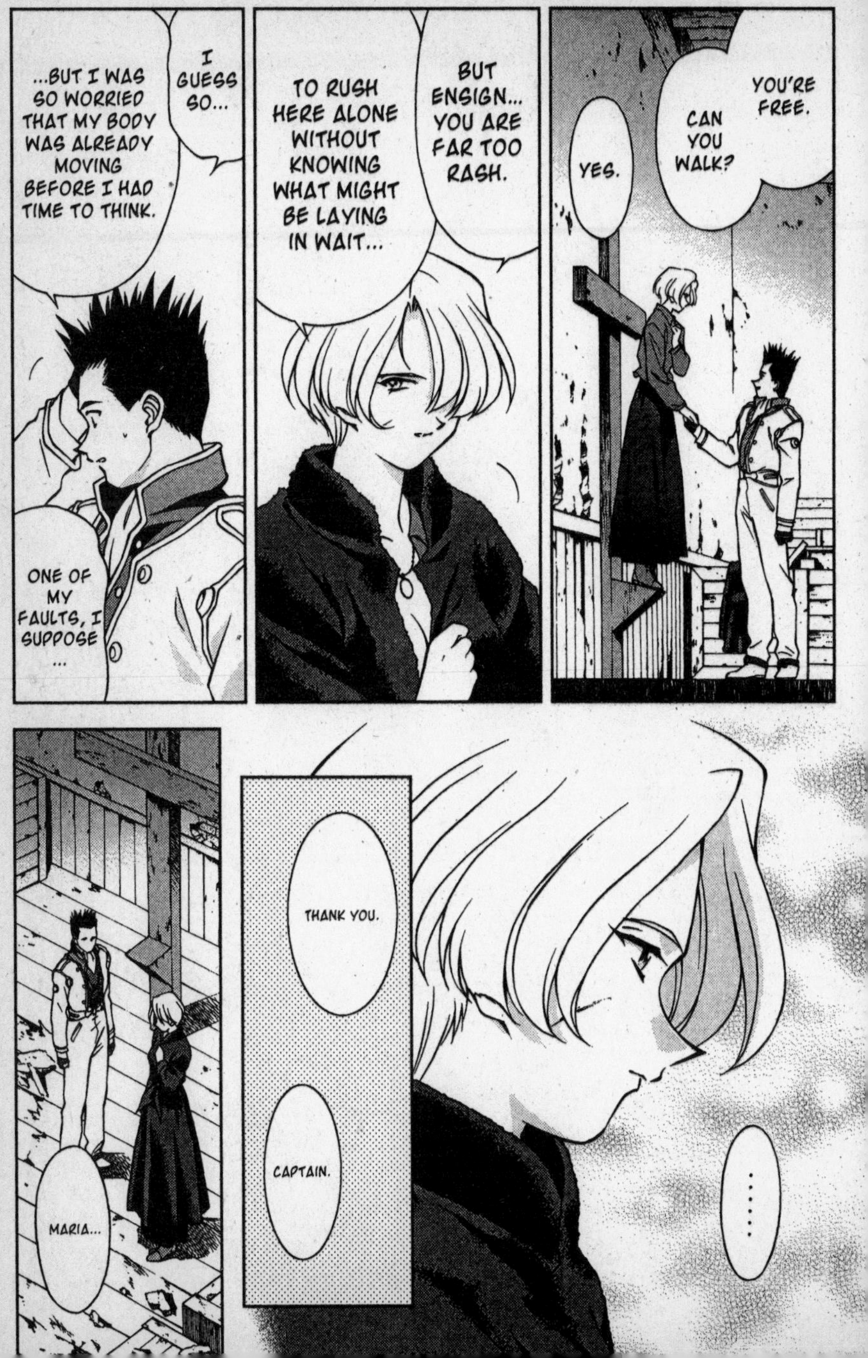
YOU'RE FREE.
CAN YOU WALK?
YES.
BUT ENSIGN... YOU ARE FAR TOO RASH.
TO RUSH HERE ALONE WITHOUT KNOWING WHAT MIGHT BE LAYING IN WAIT...
I GUESS SO...
...BUT I WAS SO WORRIED THAT MY BODY WAS ALREADY MOVING BEFORE I HAD TIME TO THINK.
ONE OF MY FAULTS, I SUPPOSE ...
......
THANK YOU.
CAPTAIN.
MARIA...

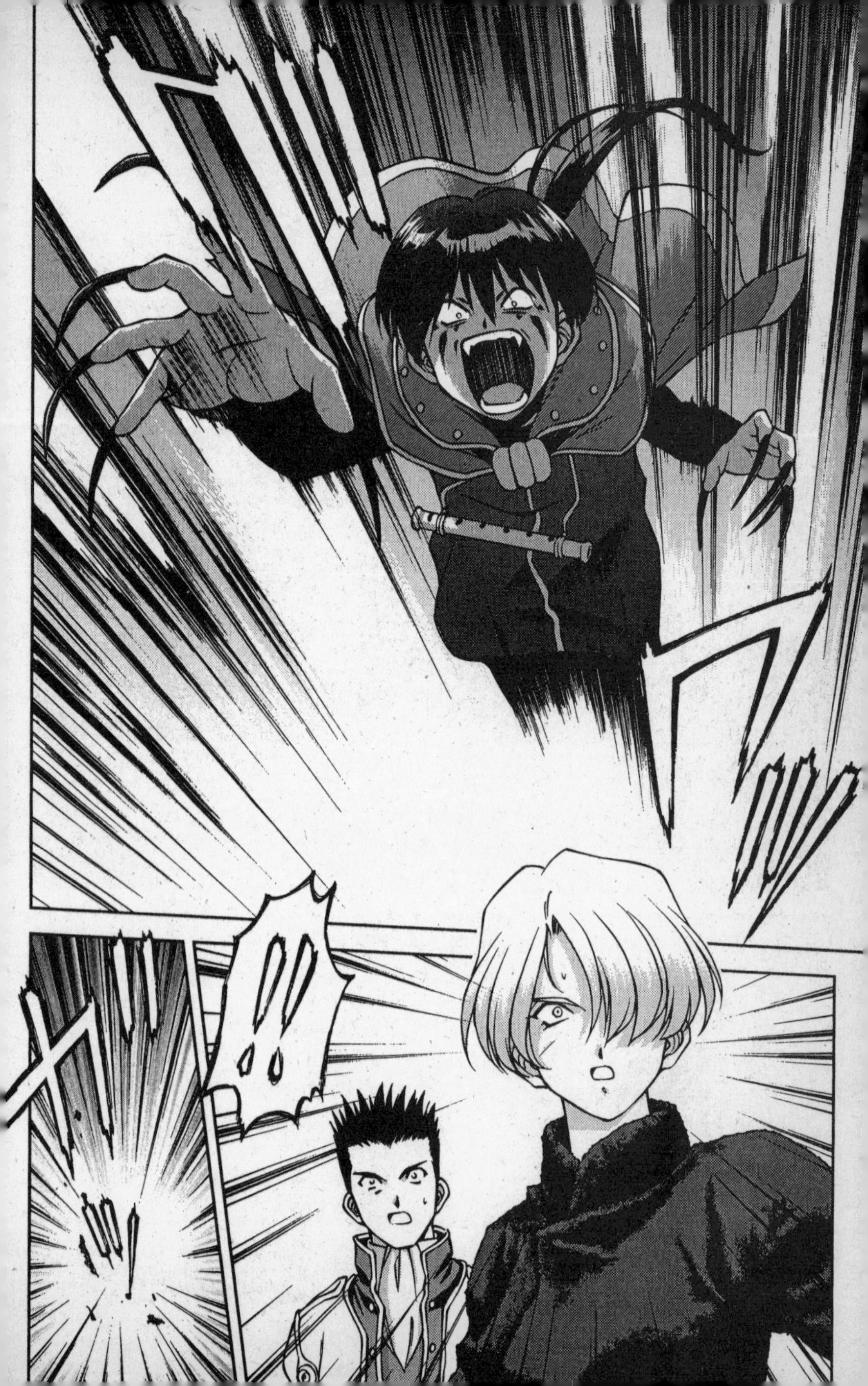
!!

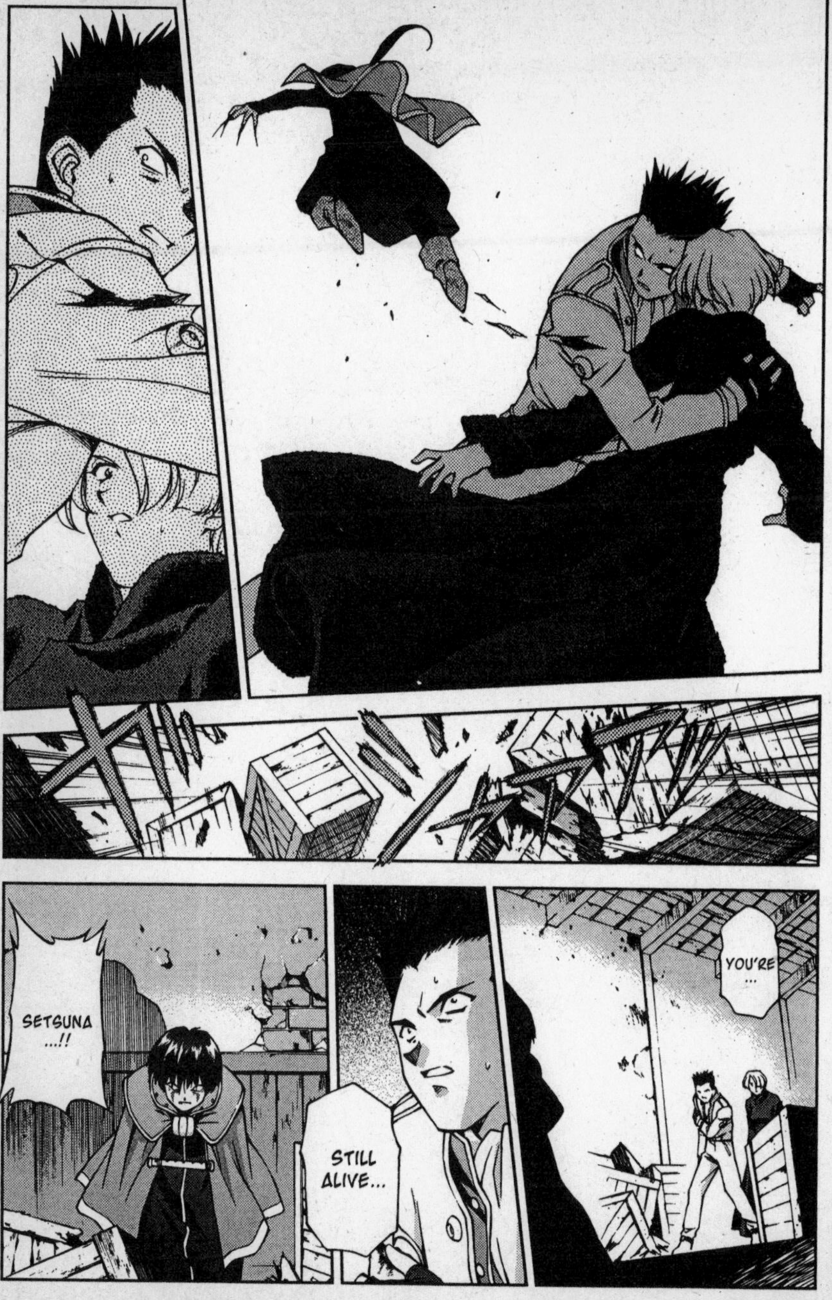
YOU'RE ...
STILL ALIVE...
SETSUNA ...!!

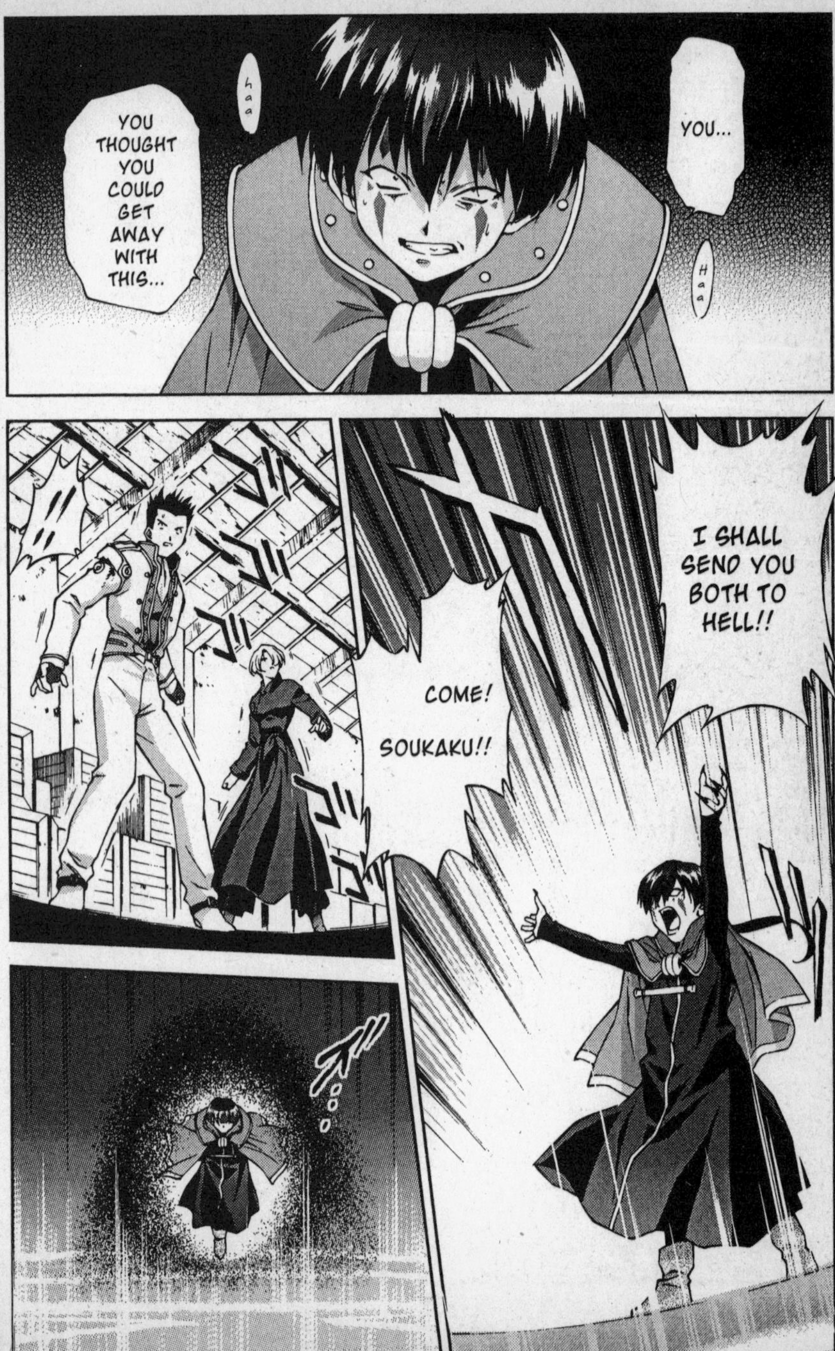
YOU...
Haa
haa
YOU THOUGHT YOU COULD GET AWAY WITH THIS...
I SHALL SEND YOU BOTH TO HELL!!
COME!
SOUKAKU!!

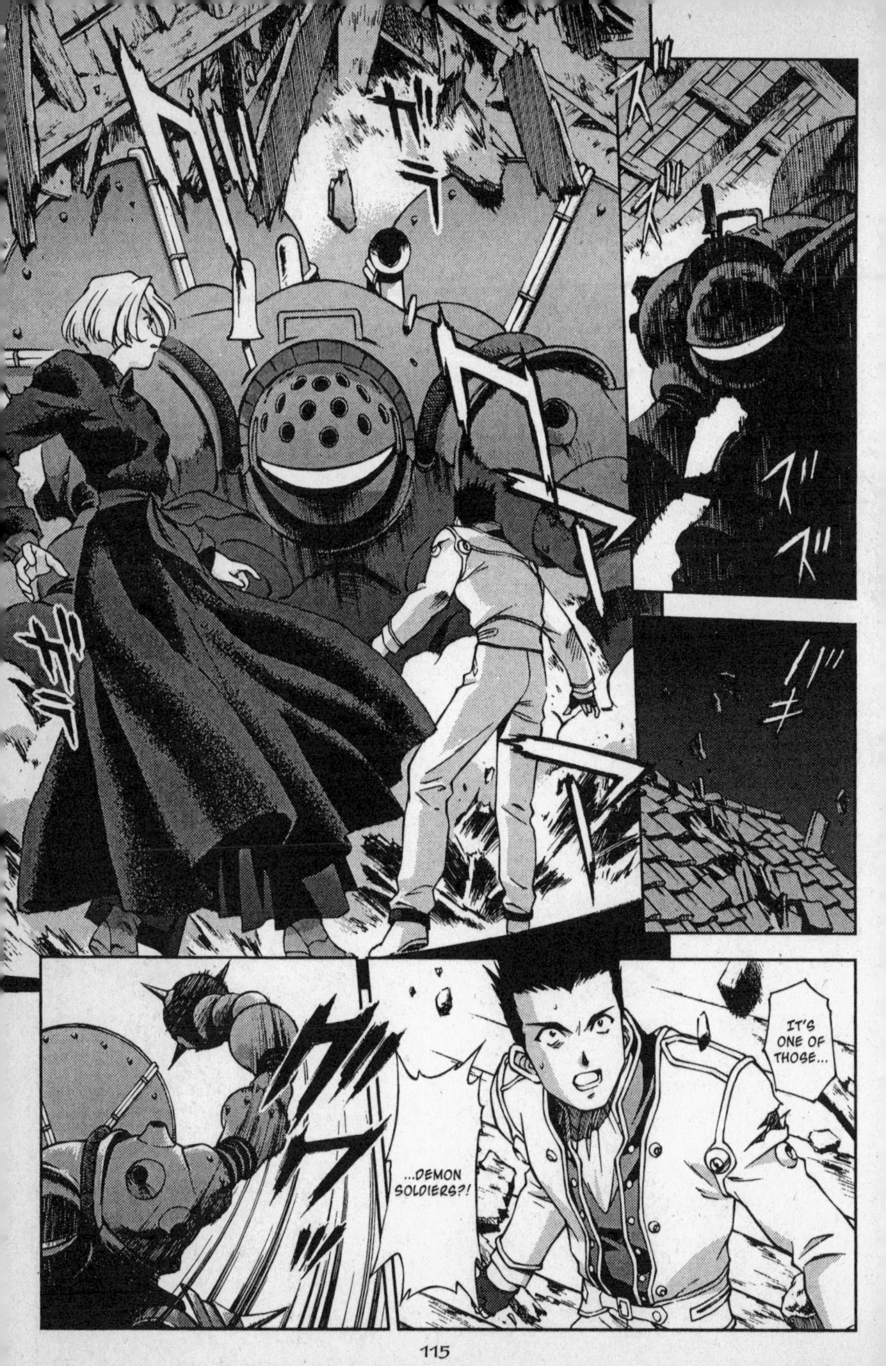
IT'S ONE OF THOSE...
...DEMON SOLDIERS?!

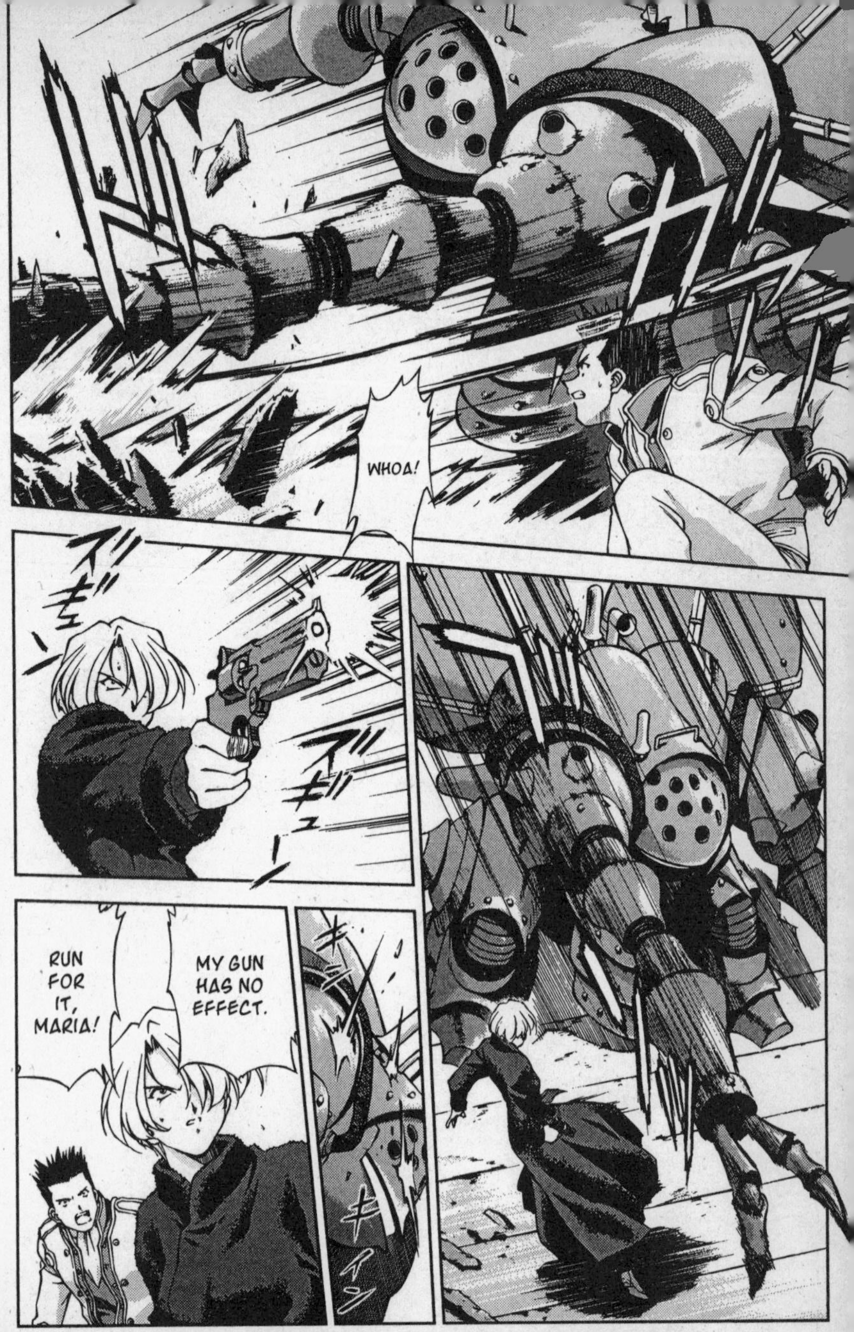
WHOA!
MY GUN HAS NO EFFECT.
RUN FOR IT, MARIA!

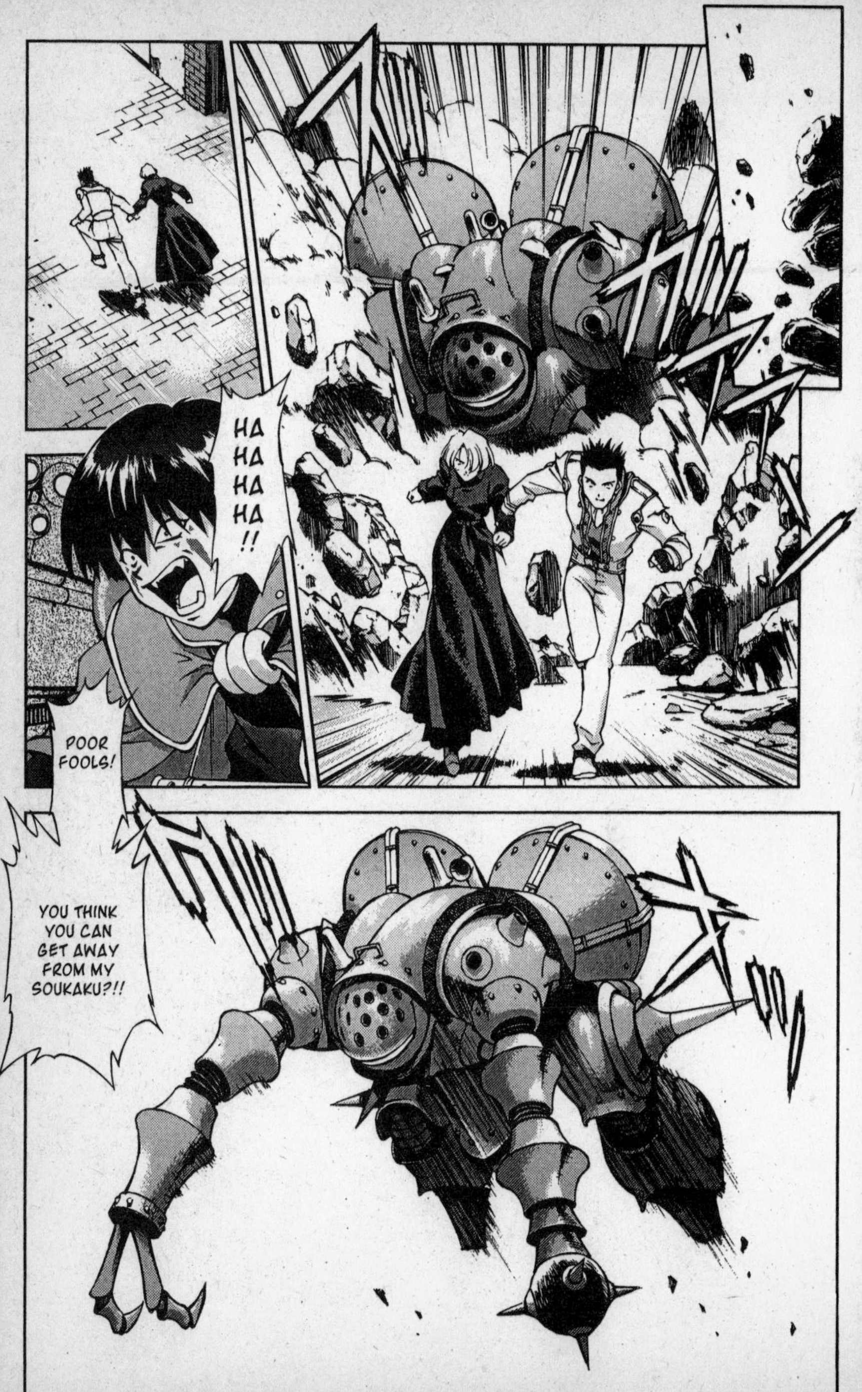
HA HA HA HA!!
POOR FOOLS!
YOU THINK YOU CAN GET AWAY FROM MY SOUKAKU?!!

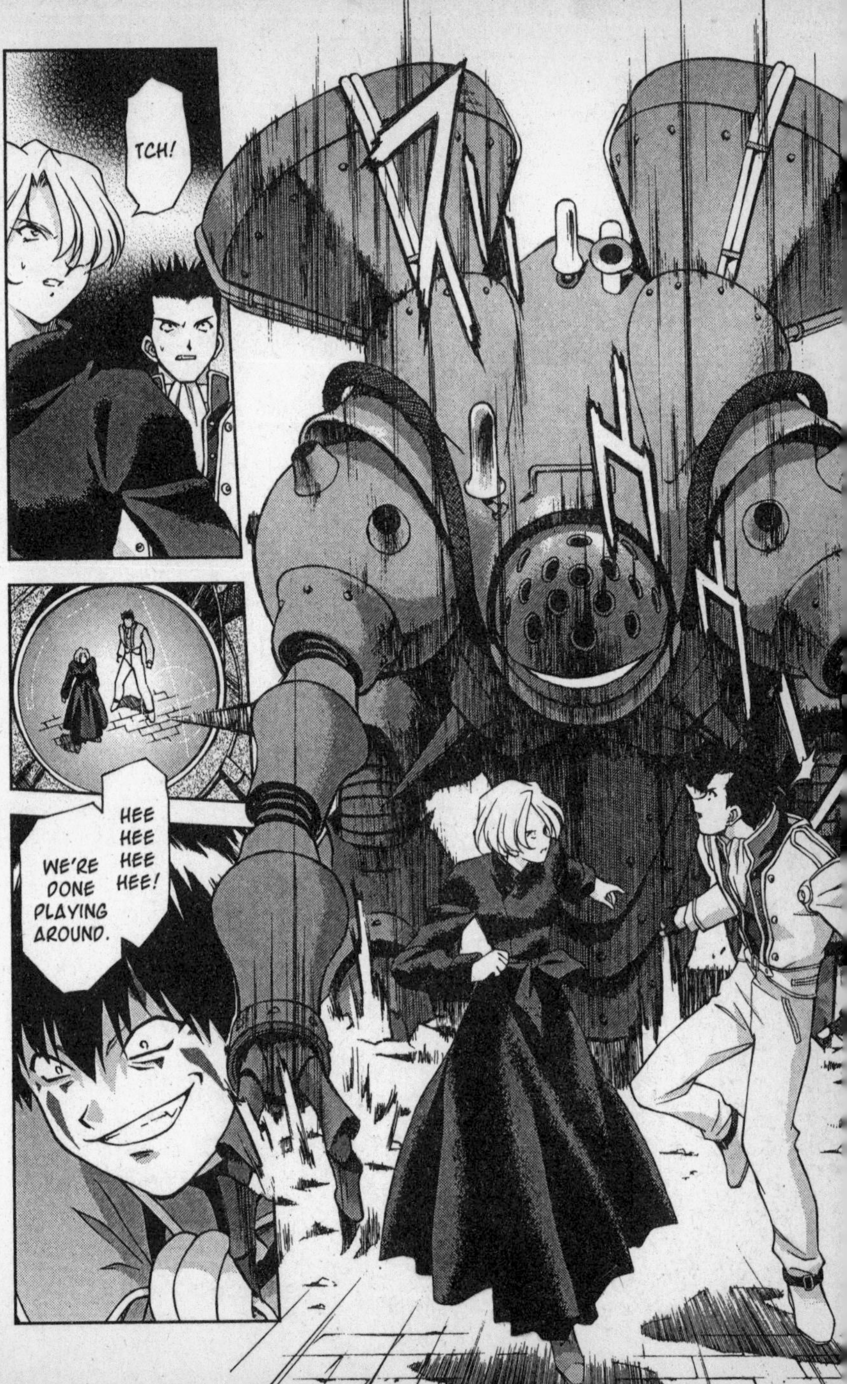
TCH!
HEE HEE HEE HEE!
WE'RE DONE PLAYING AROUND.

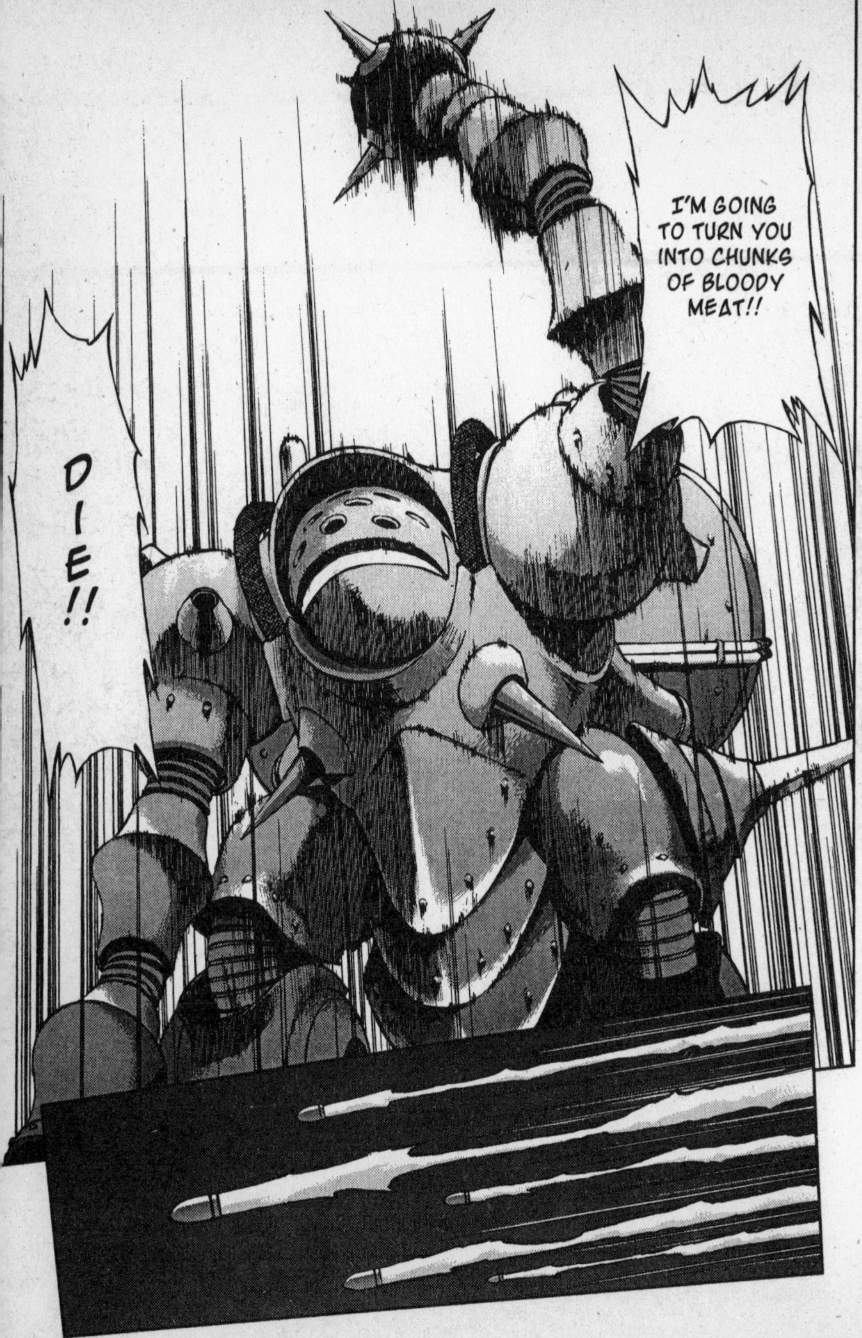
I'M GOING TO TURN YOU INTO CHUNKS OF BLOODY MEAT!!
DIE!!

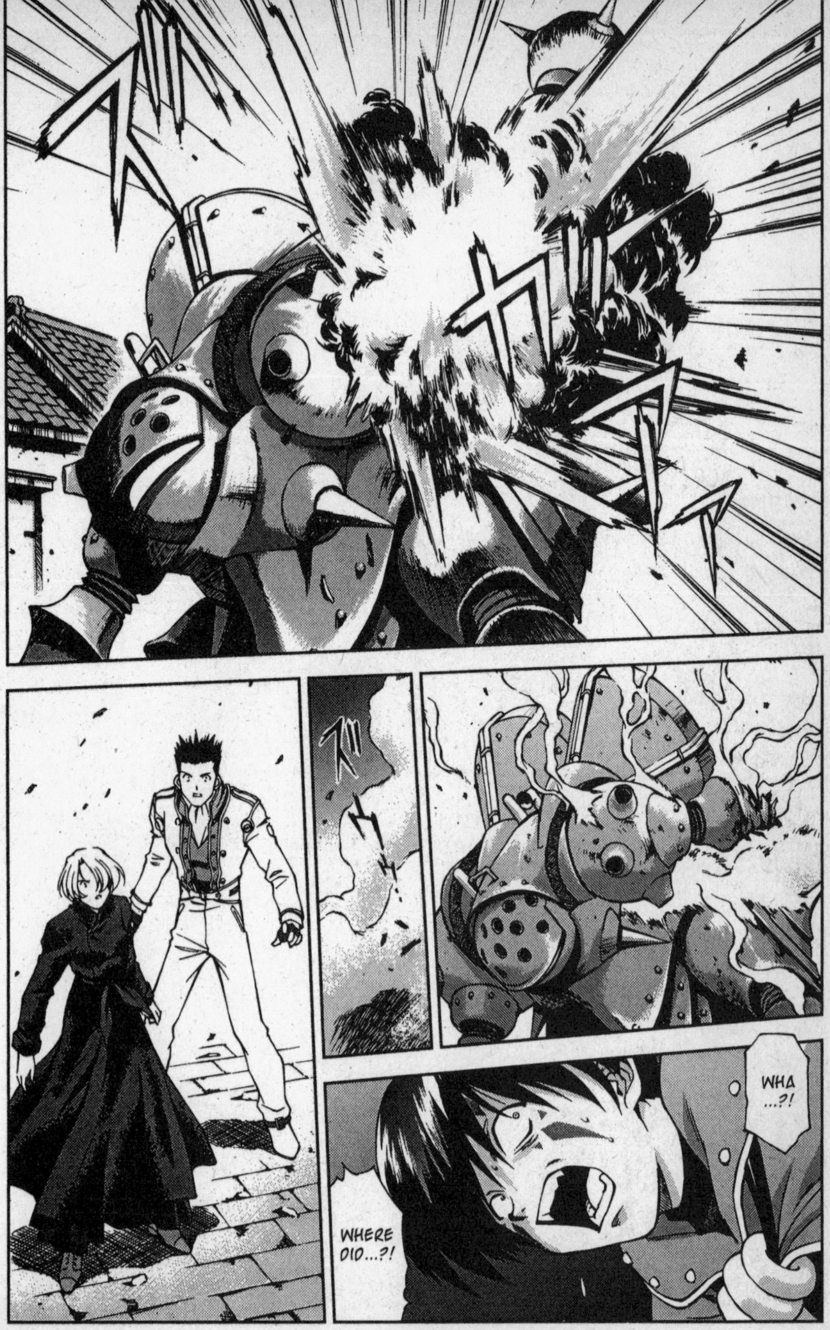
WHA ...?!
WHERE DID...?!

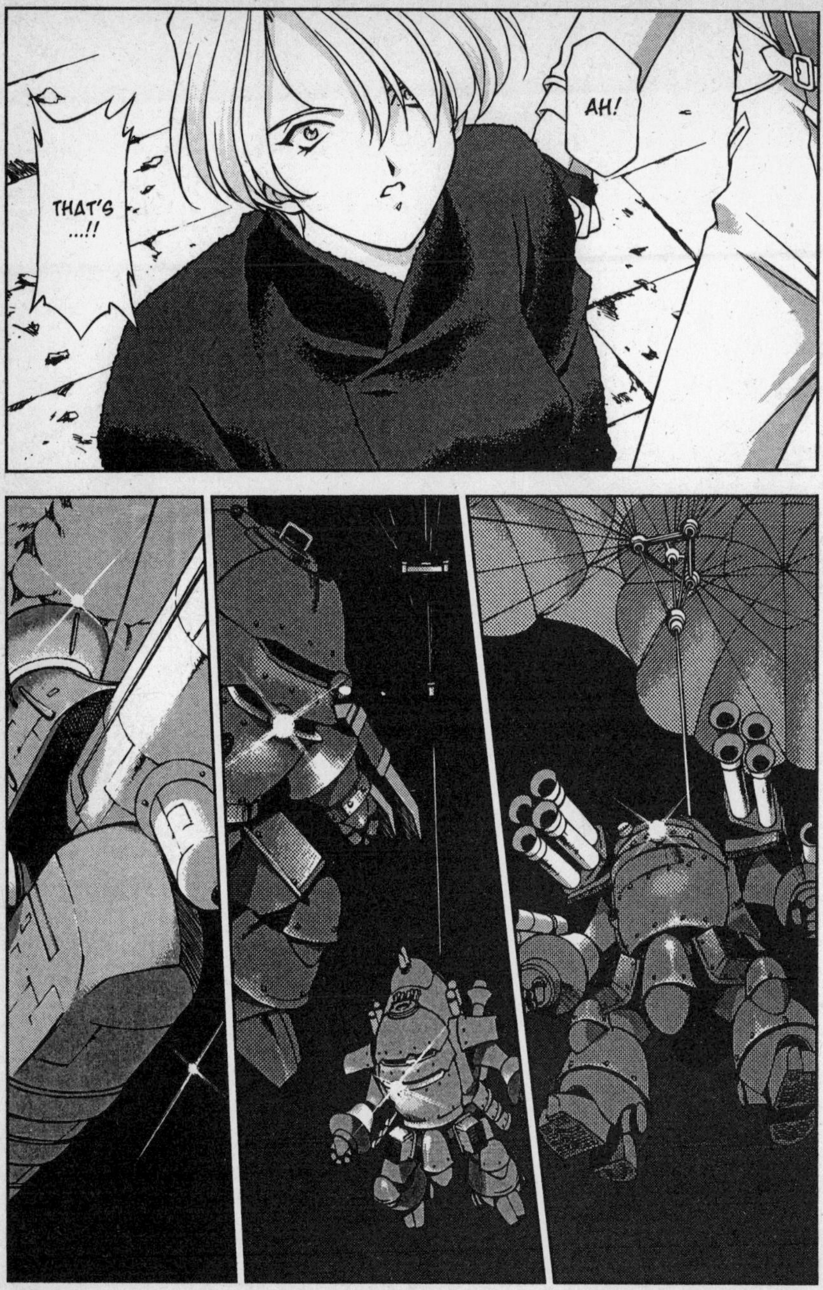
AH!
THAT'S ...!!

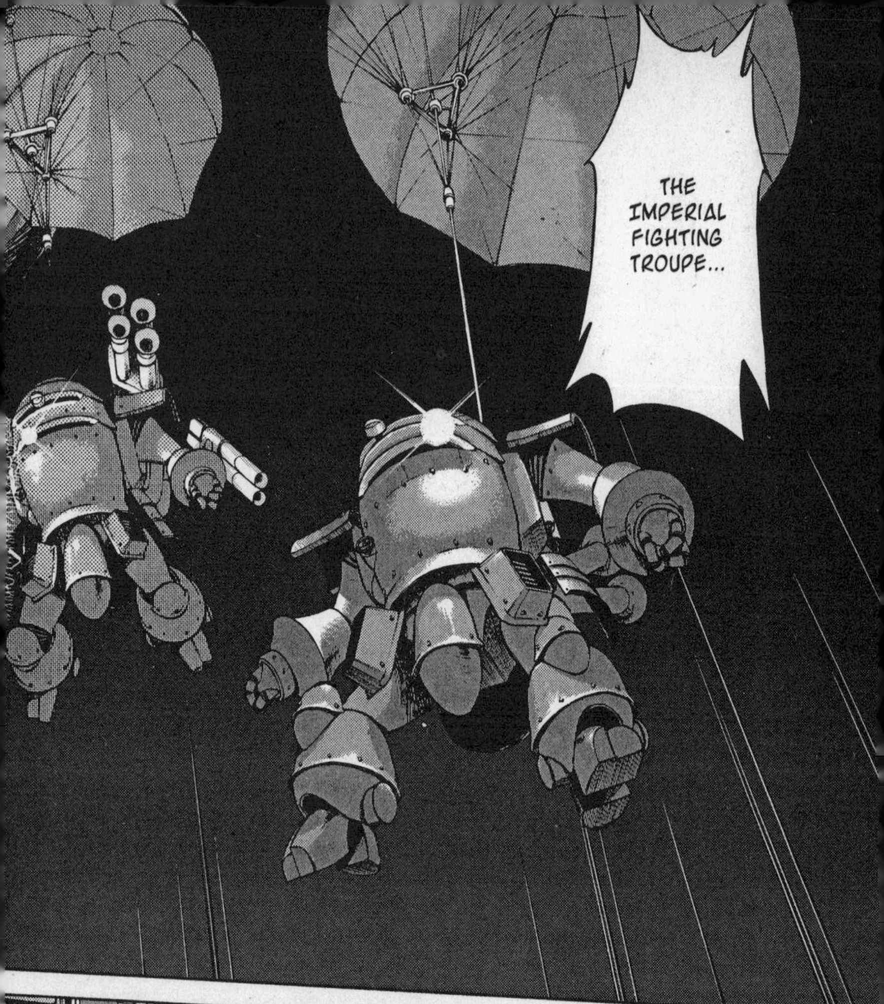
THE IMPERIAL FIGHTING TROUPE...

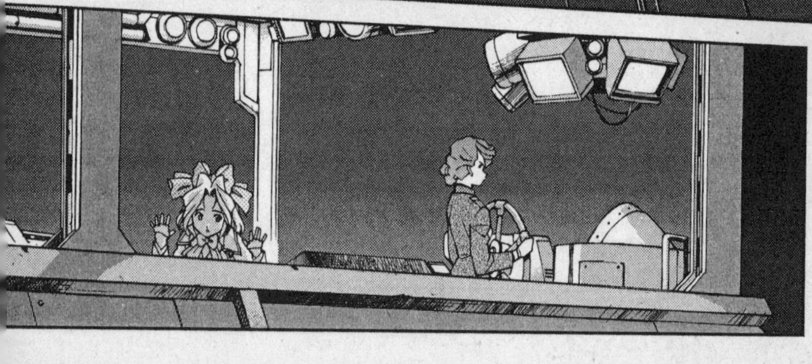

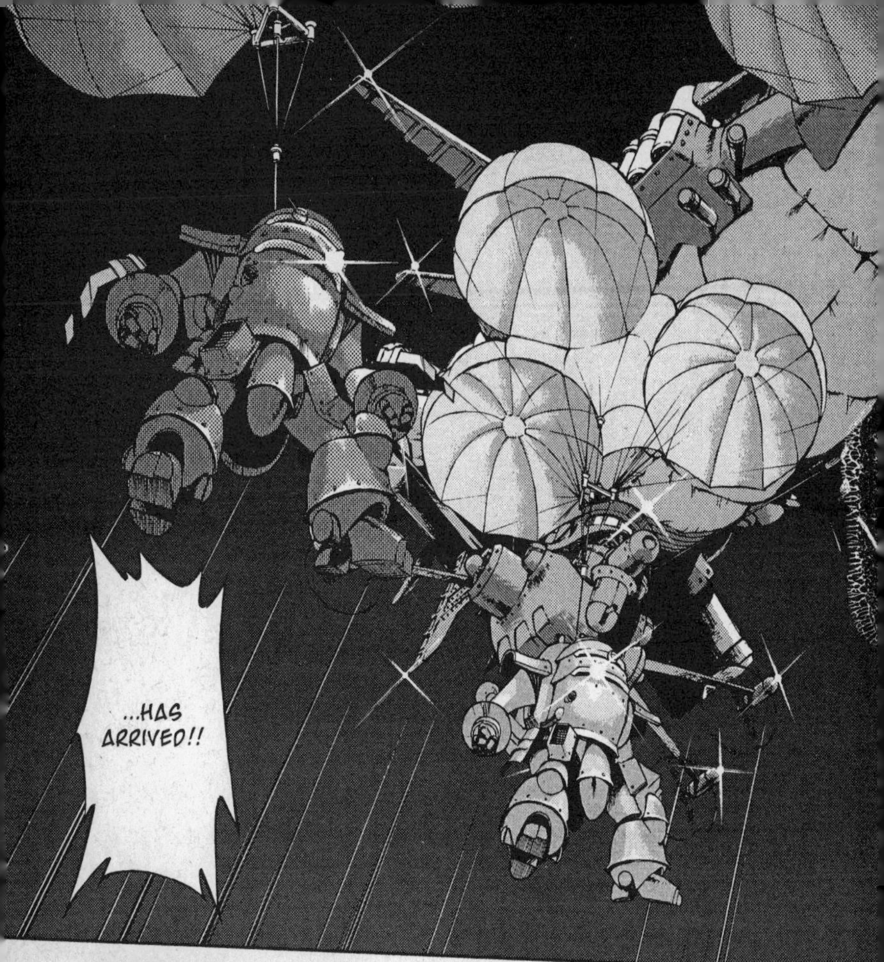
...HAS ARRIVED!!

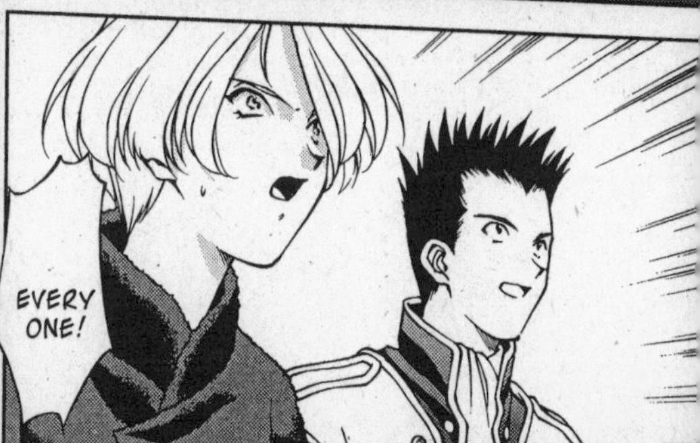
EVERY ONE!

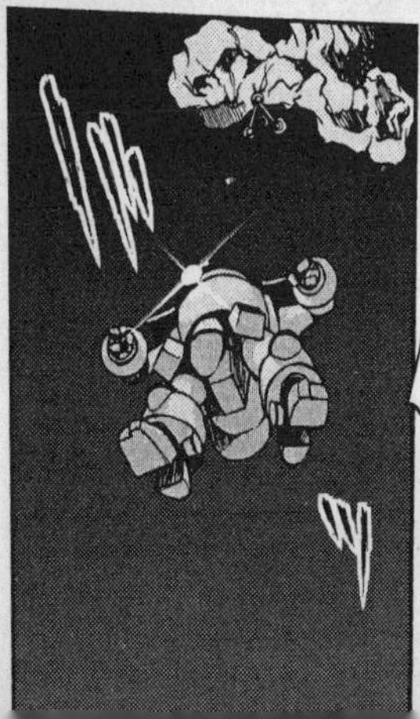

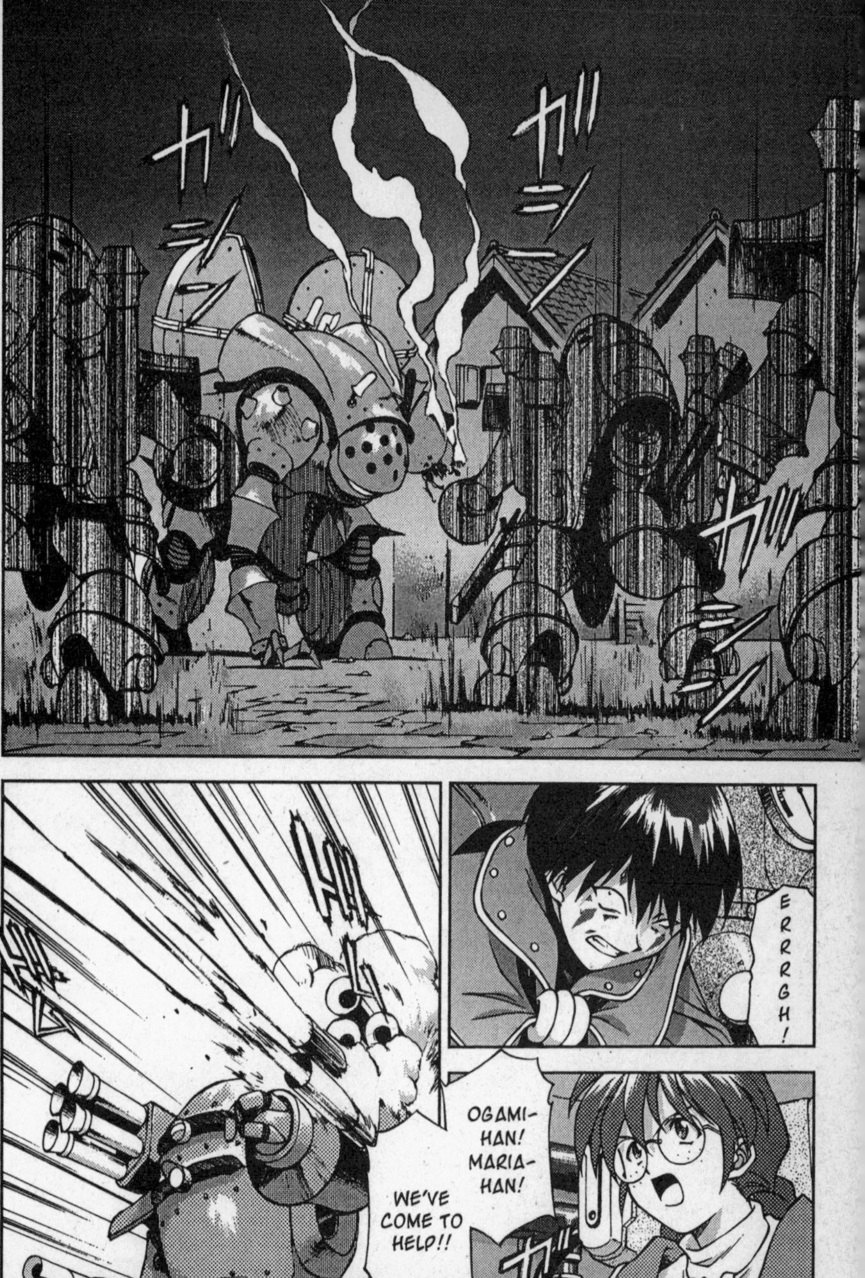
ERRRGH!
OGAMI-HAN! MARIA-HAN!
WE'VE COME TO HELP!!

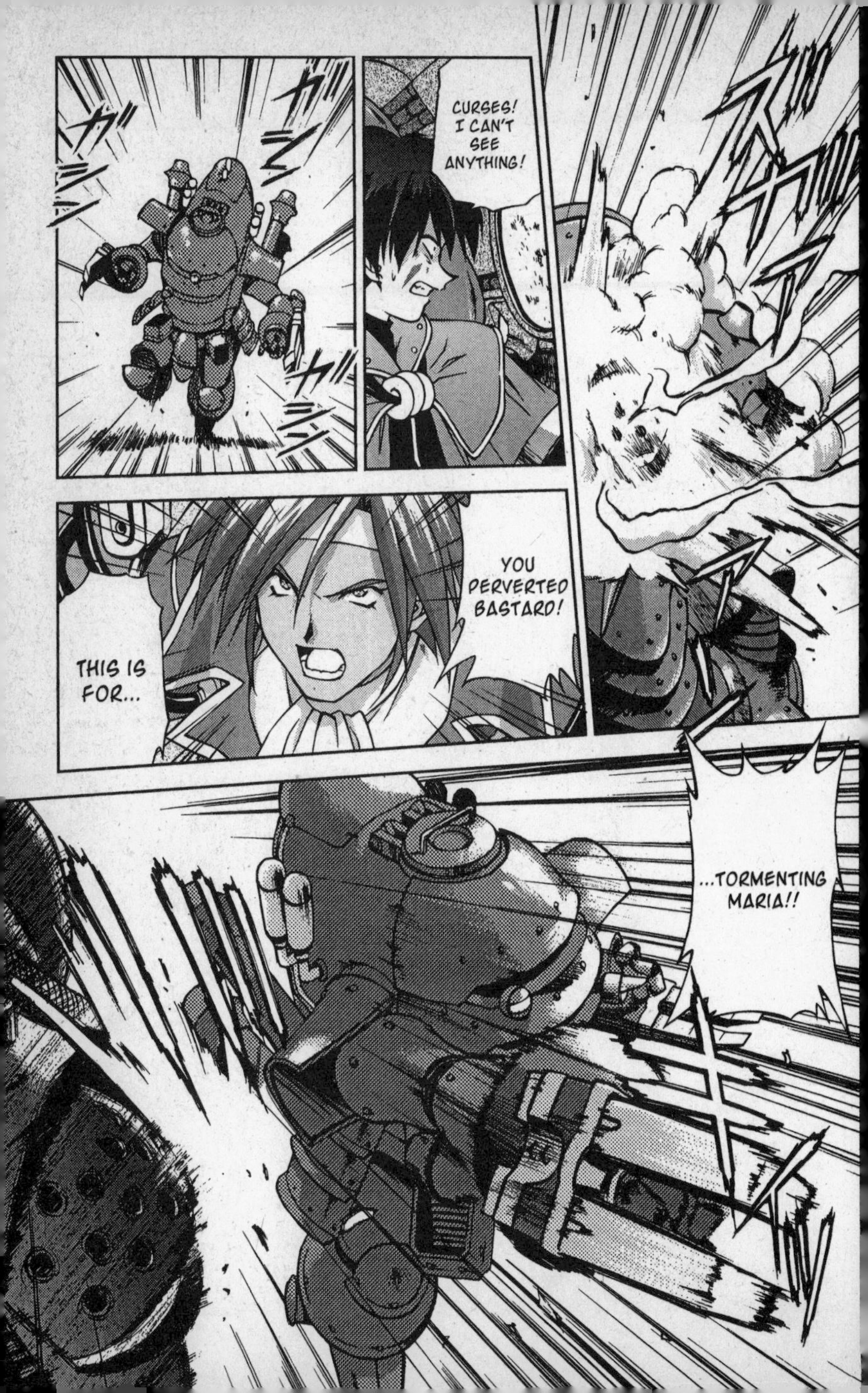
CURSES! I CAN'T SEE ANYTHING!
YOU PERVERTED BASTARD!
THIS IS FOR...
...TORMENTING MARIA!!

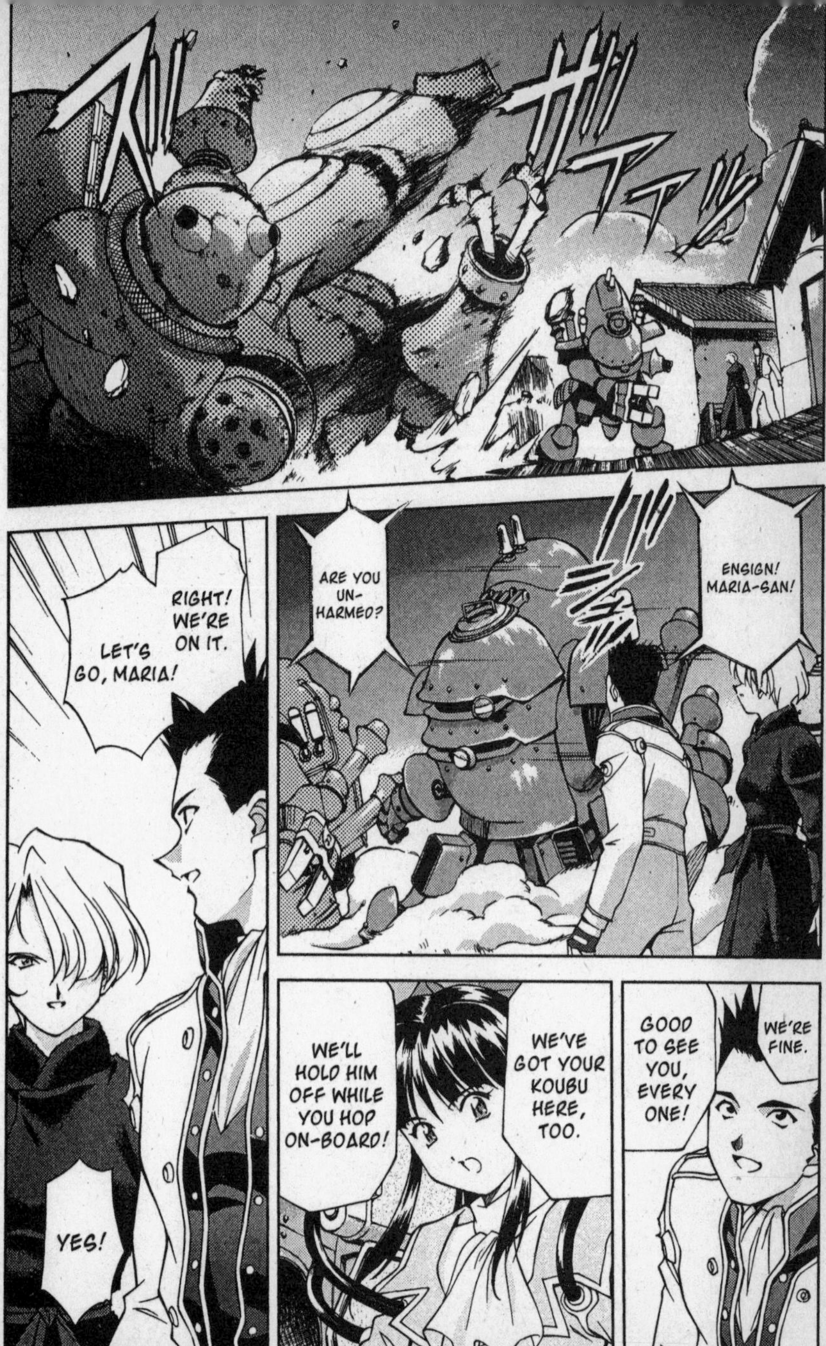
ENSIGN! MARIA-SAN!
ARE YOU UN-HARMED?
WE'RE FINE.
GOOD TO SEE YOU, EVERY ONE!
WE'VE GOT YOUR KOUBU HERE, TOO.
WE'LL HOLD HIM OFF WHILE YOU HOP ON-BOARD!
RIGHT! WE'RE ON IT.
LET'S GO, MARIA!
YES!

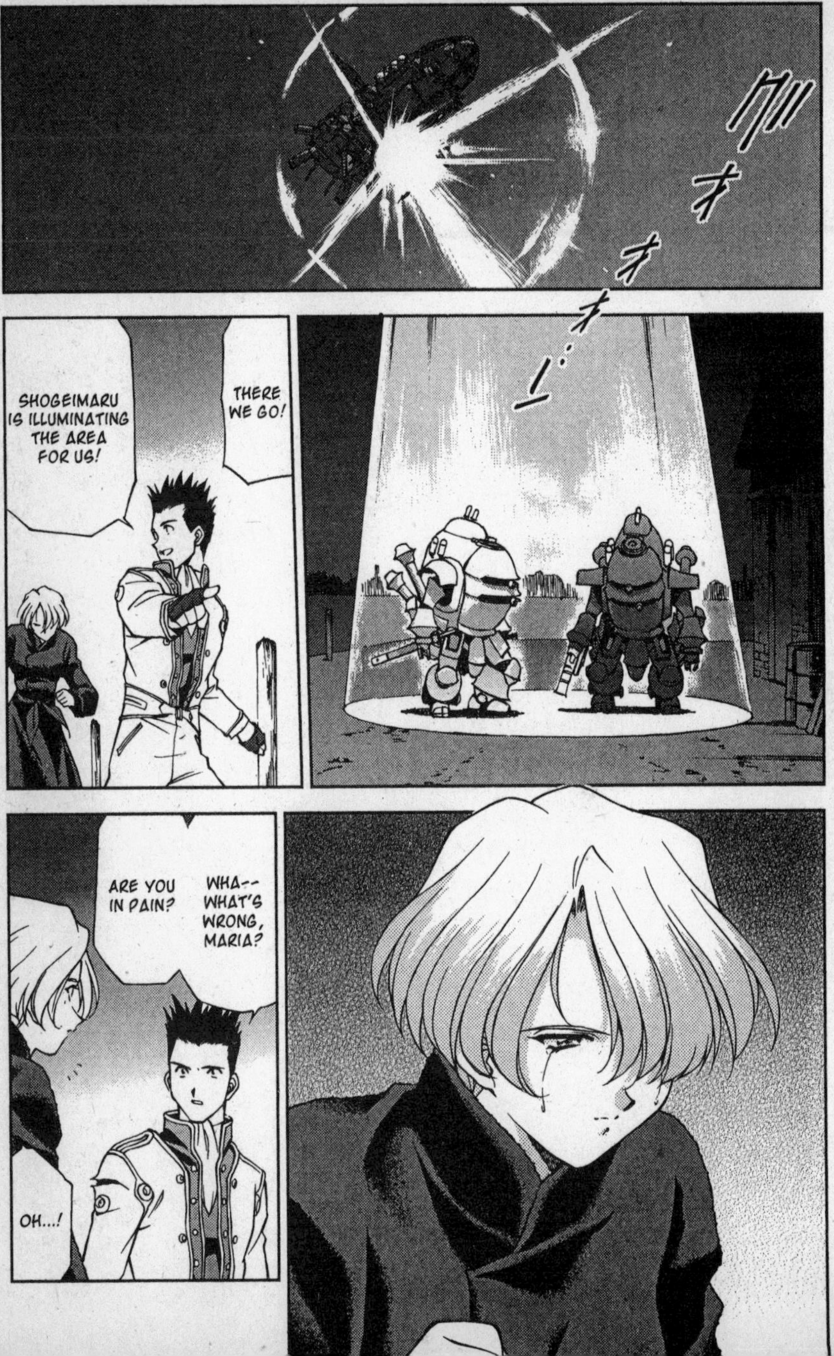
グオオオォ…ン
THERE WE GO!
SHOGEIMARU IS ILLUMINATING THE AREA FOR US!
WHA-- WHAT'S WRONG, MARIA?
ARE YOU IN PAIN?
OH...!

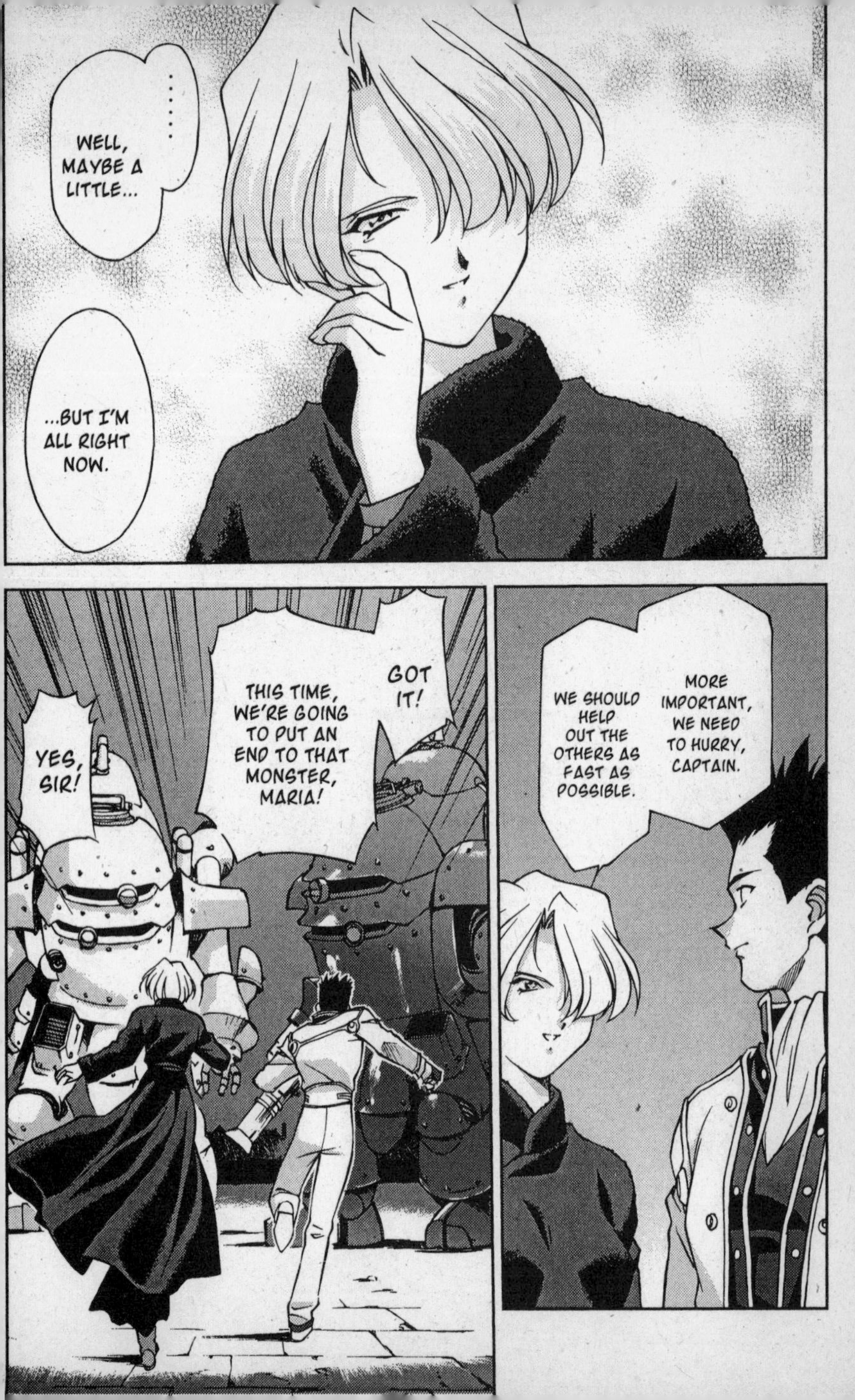
......
WELL, MAYBE A LITTLE...
...BUT I'M ALL RIGHT NOW.
MORE IMPORTANT, WE NEED TO HURRY, CAPTAIN.
WE SHOULD HELP OUT THE OTHERS AS FAST AS POSSIBLE.
GOT IT!
THIS TIME, WE'RE GOING TO PUT AN END TO THAT MONSTER, MARIA!
YES, SIR!

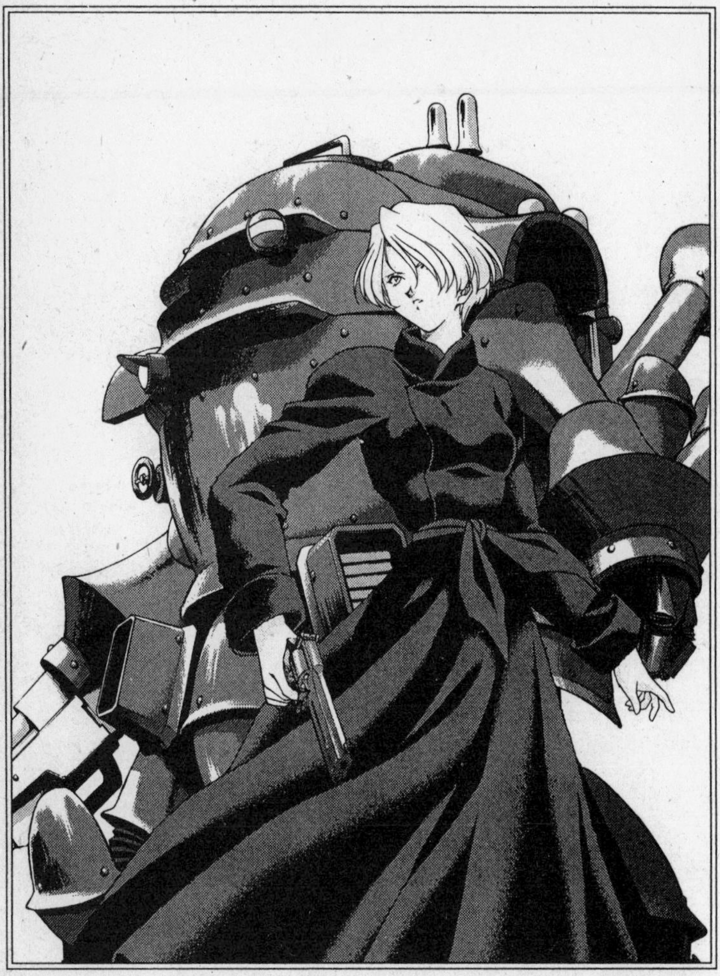

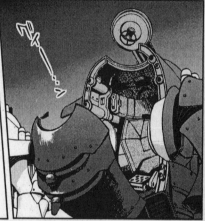

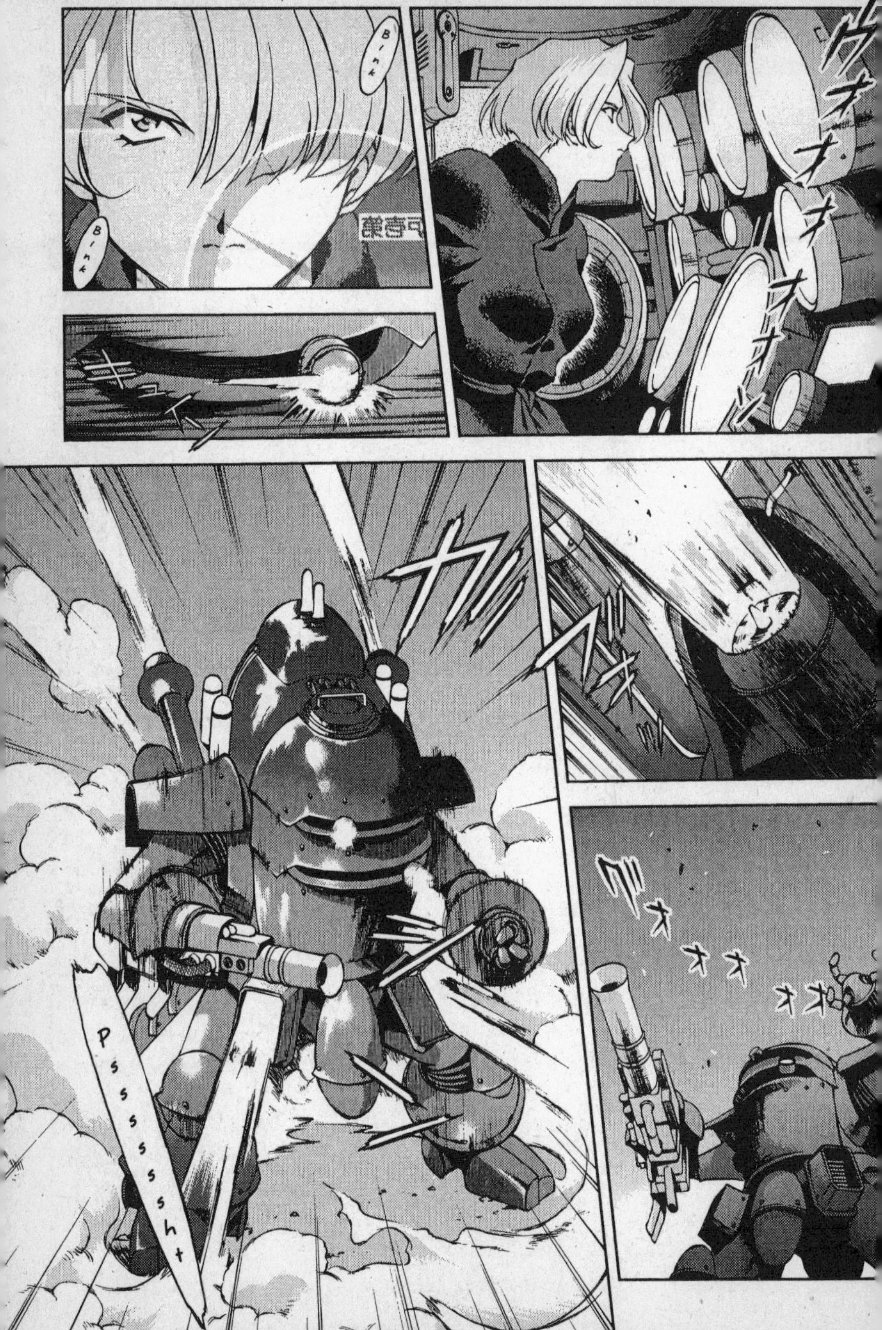
Blink
Blink
Psssssht

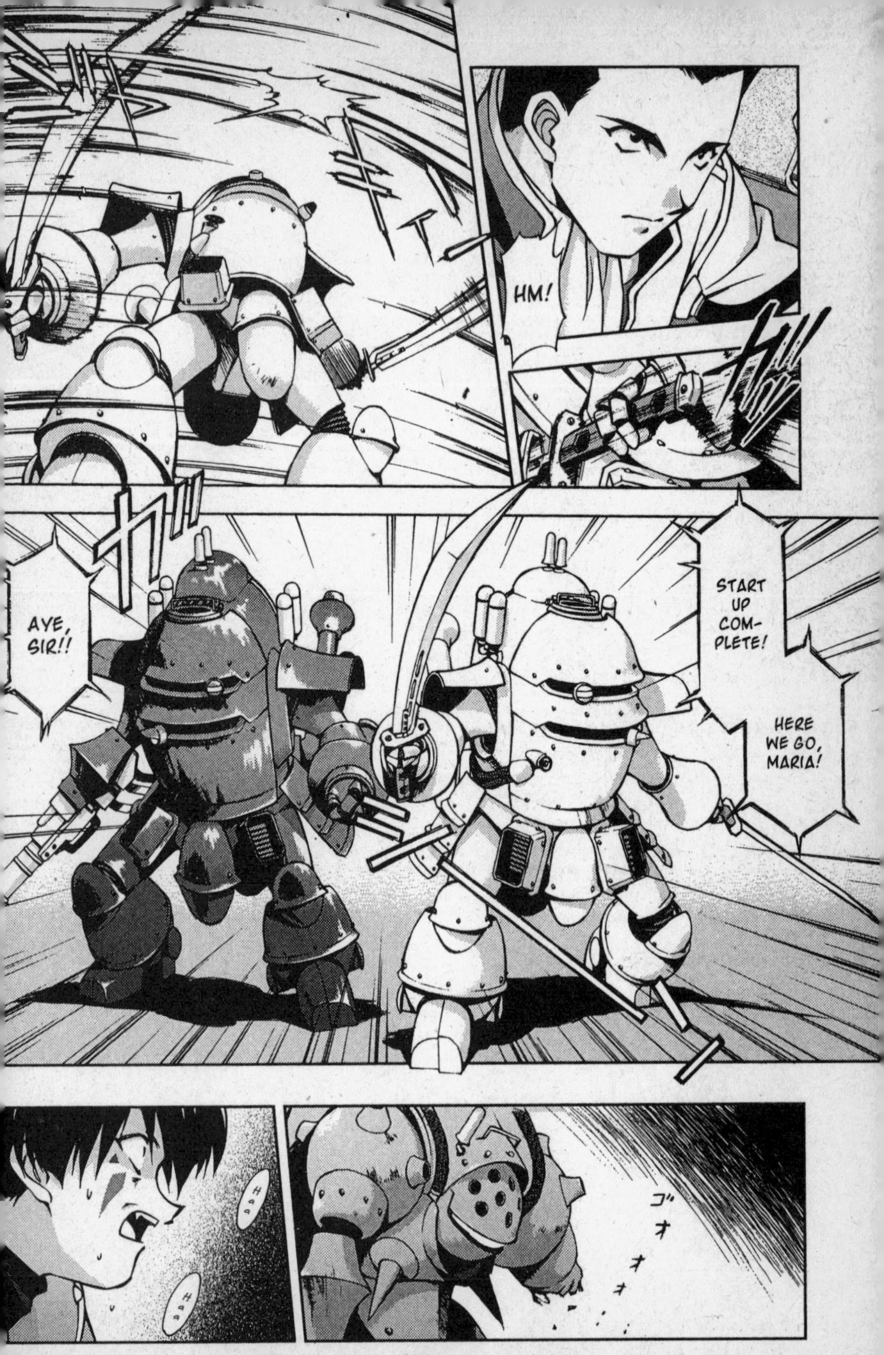
HM!
START UP COMPLETE!
HERE WE GO, MARIA!
AYE, SIR!!
ゴオォォ

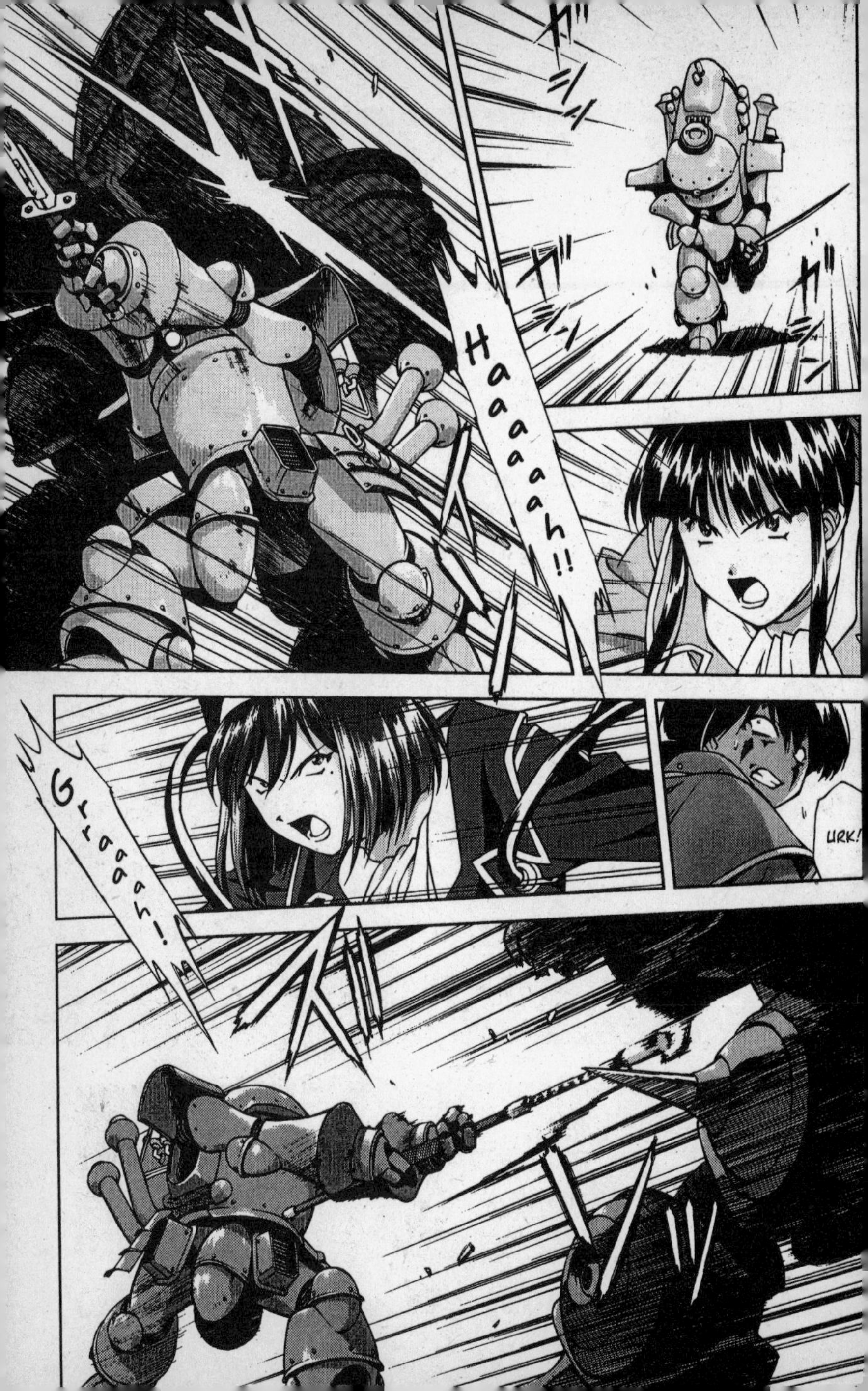
Haaaaaah!!
URK!
Grraaaah!

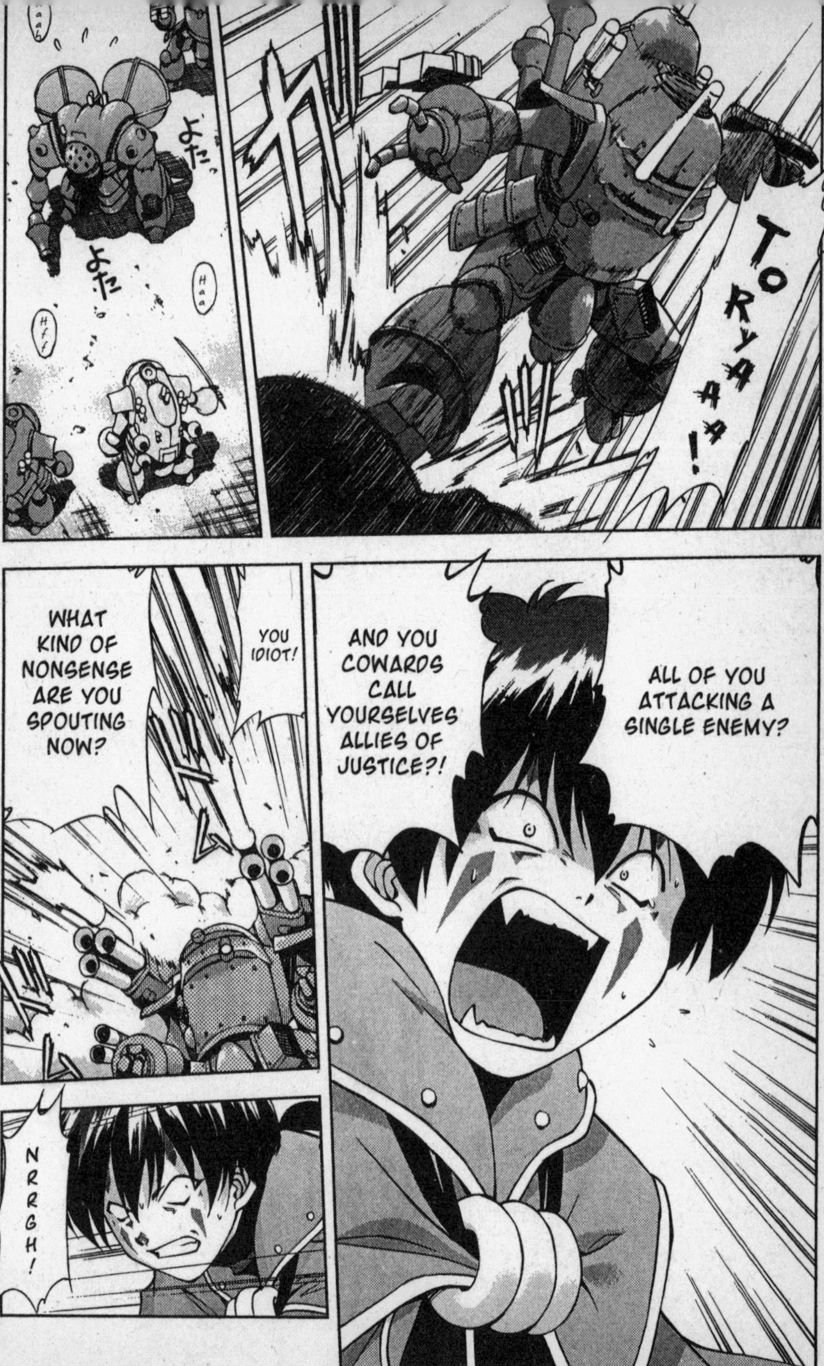
TORYAAA!
aah
よたっ
よた
Haa
Hff
ALL OF YOU ATTACKING A SINGLE ENEMY?
AND YOU COWARDS CALL YOURSELVES ALLIES OF JUSTICE?!
YOU IDIOT!
WHAT KIND OF NONSENSE ARE YOU SPOUTING NOW?
NRRGH!

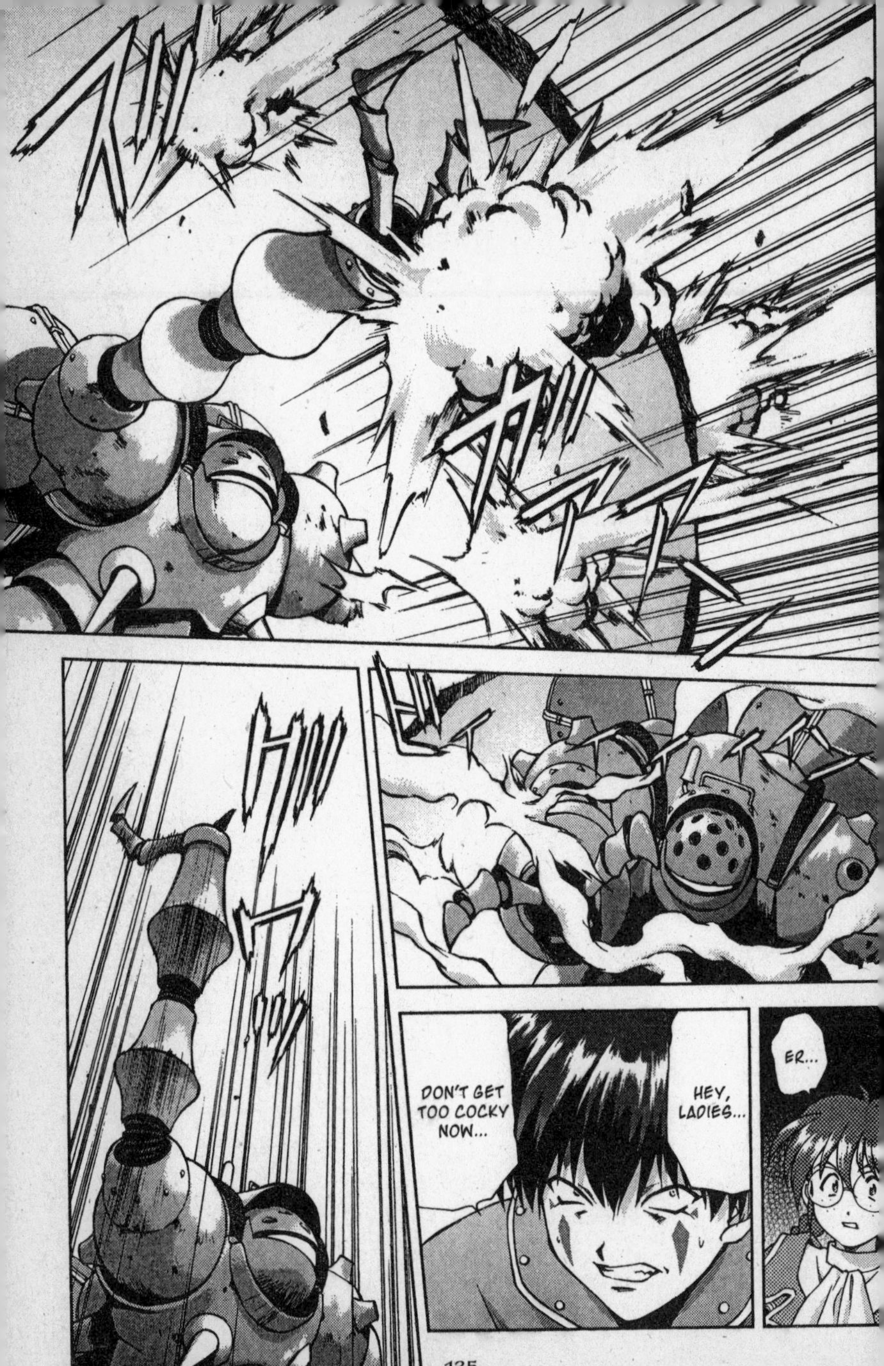
ER...
HEY, LADIES...
DON'T GET TOO COCKY NOW...

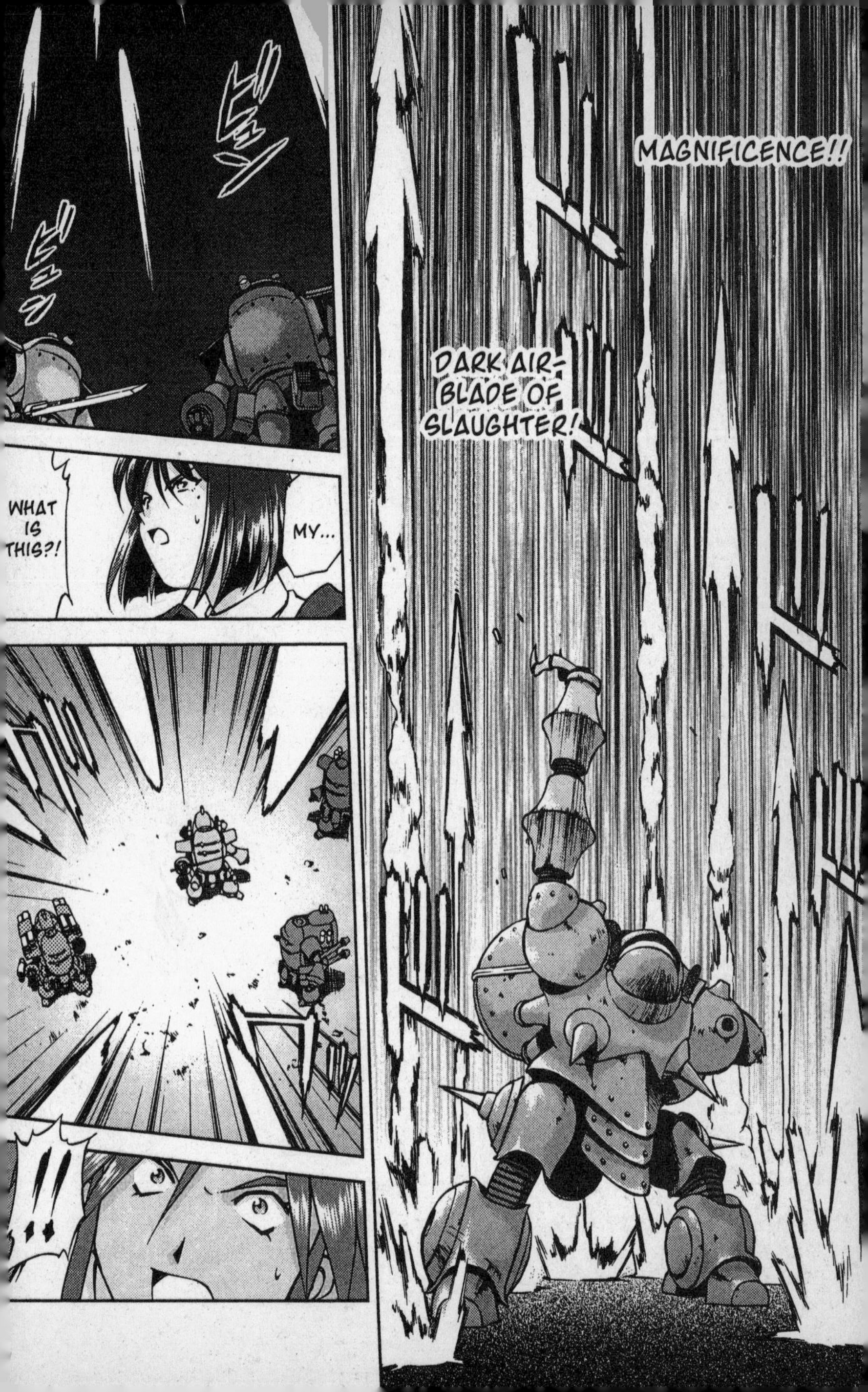
MAGNIFICENCE!!
DARK AIR-BLADE OF SLAUGHTER!
MY...
WHAT IS THIS?!
!!

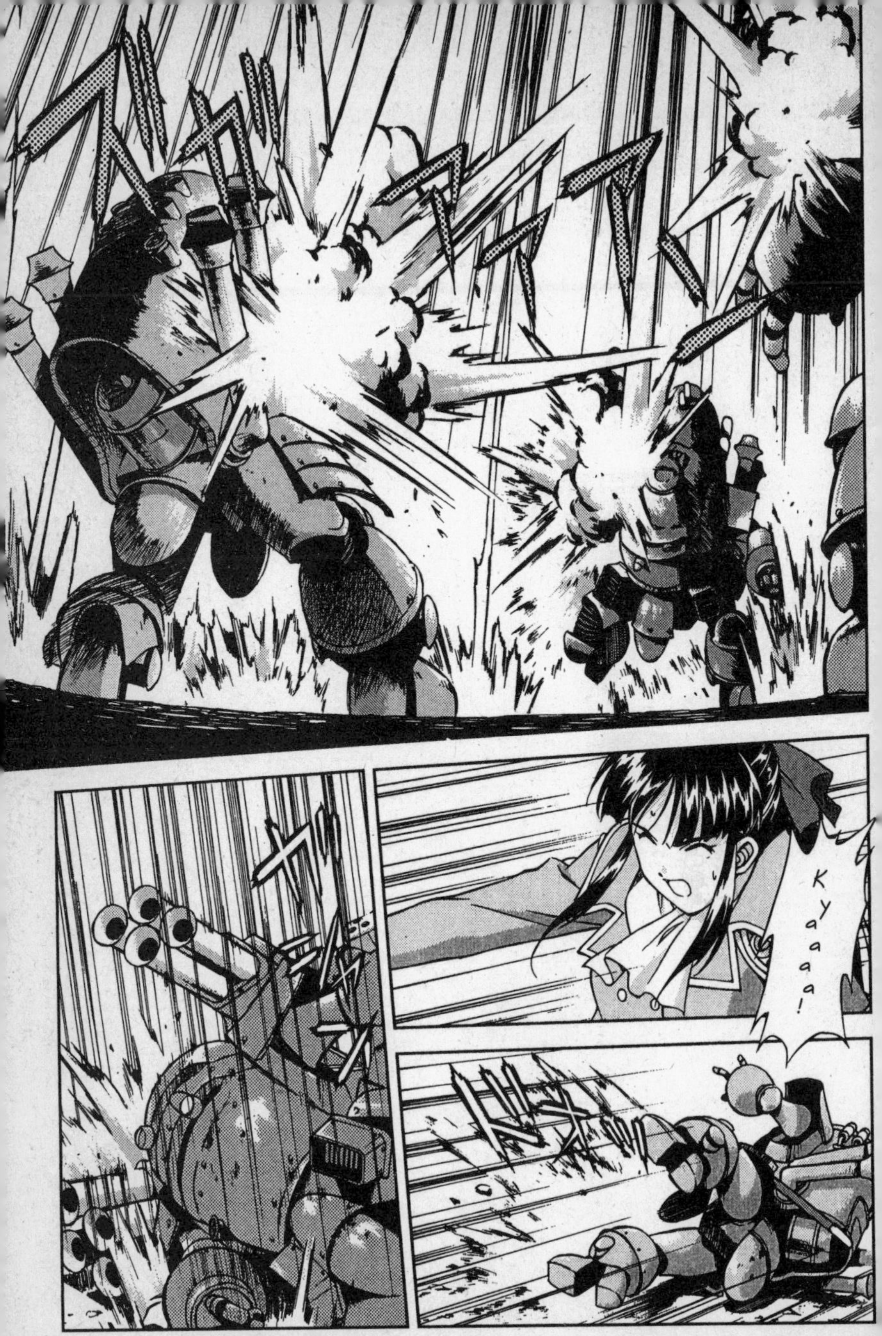
Kyaaaaa!

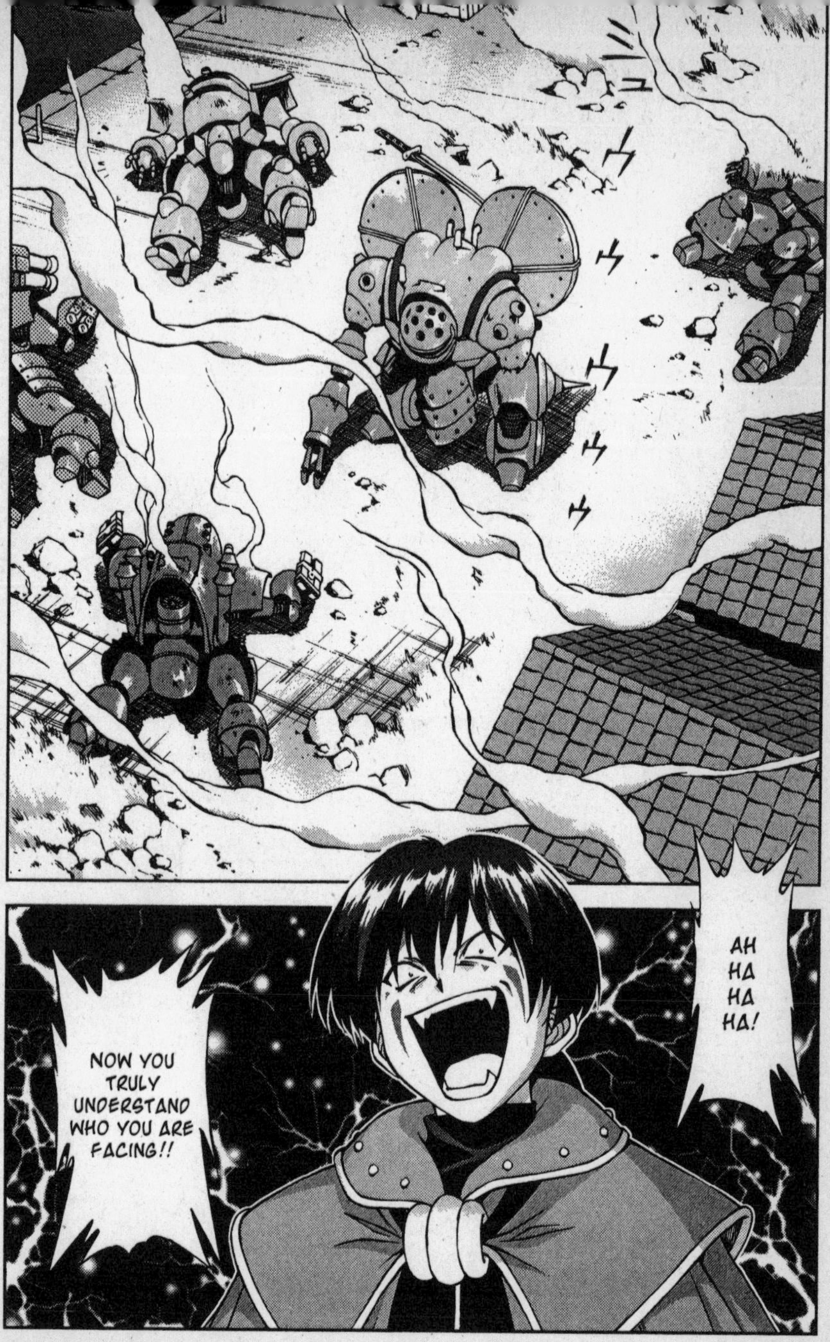
AH HA HA HA!
NOW YOU TRULY UNDERSTAND WHO YOU ARE FACING!!

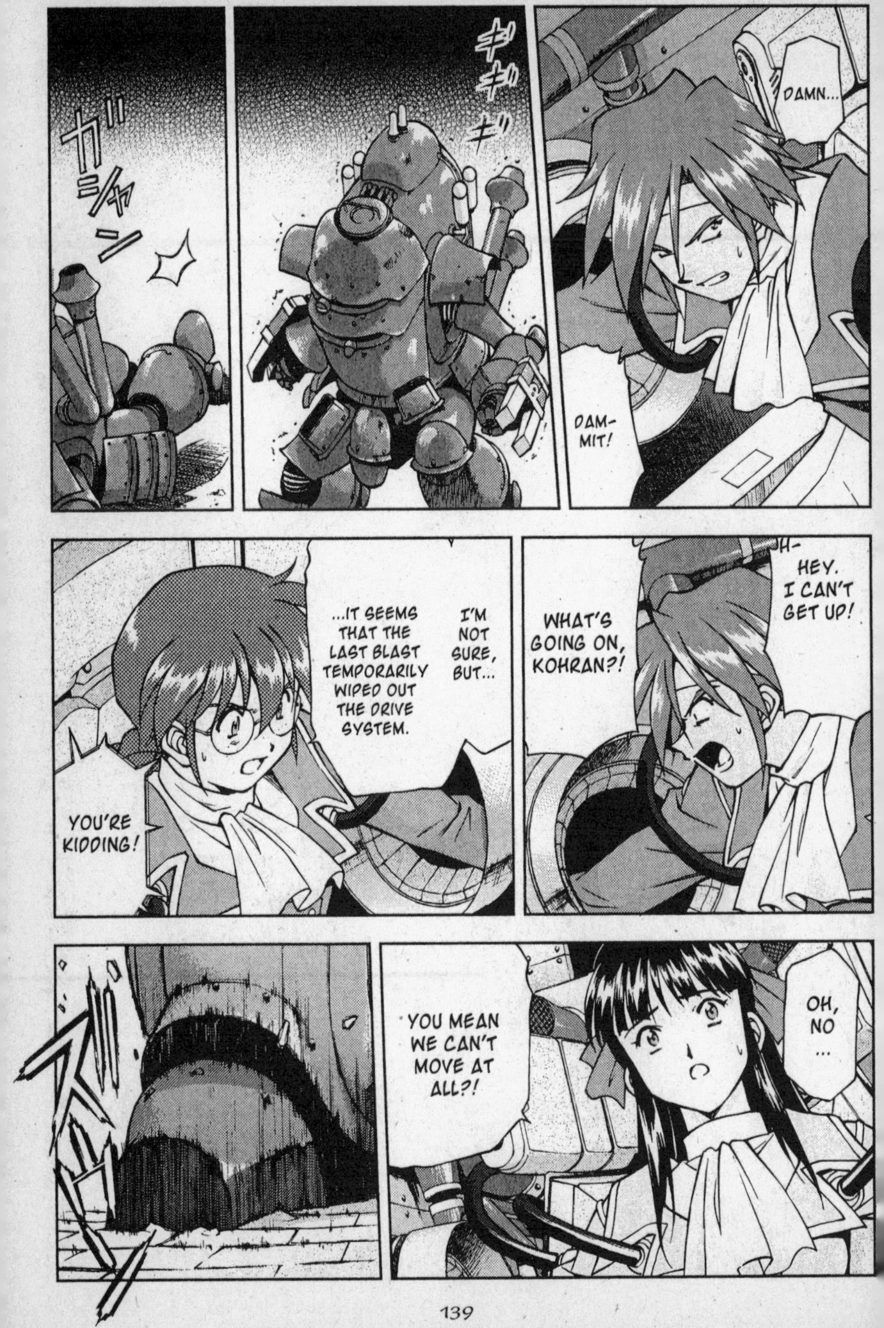
DAMN...
DAM-MIT!
ギギギ
ガシャン
H-HEY. I CAN'T GET UP!
WHAT'S GOING ON, KOHRAN?!
I'M NOT SURE, BUT...
...IT SEEMS THAT THE LAST BLAST TEMPORARILY WIPED OUT THE DRIVE SYSTEM.
YOU'RE KIDDING!
OH, NO ...
YOU MEAN WE CAN'T MOVE AT ALL?!

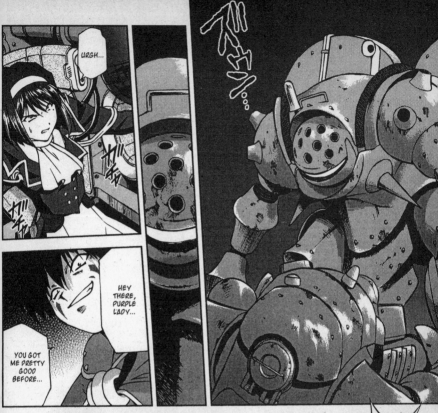

URGH...

HEY, THERE, PURPLE LADY...

YOU GOT ME PRETTY GOOD BEFORE...

...SO HERE'S SOME PAYBACK!

AARGH!

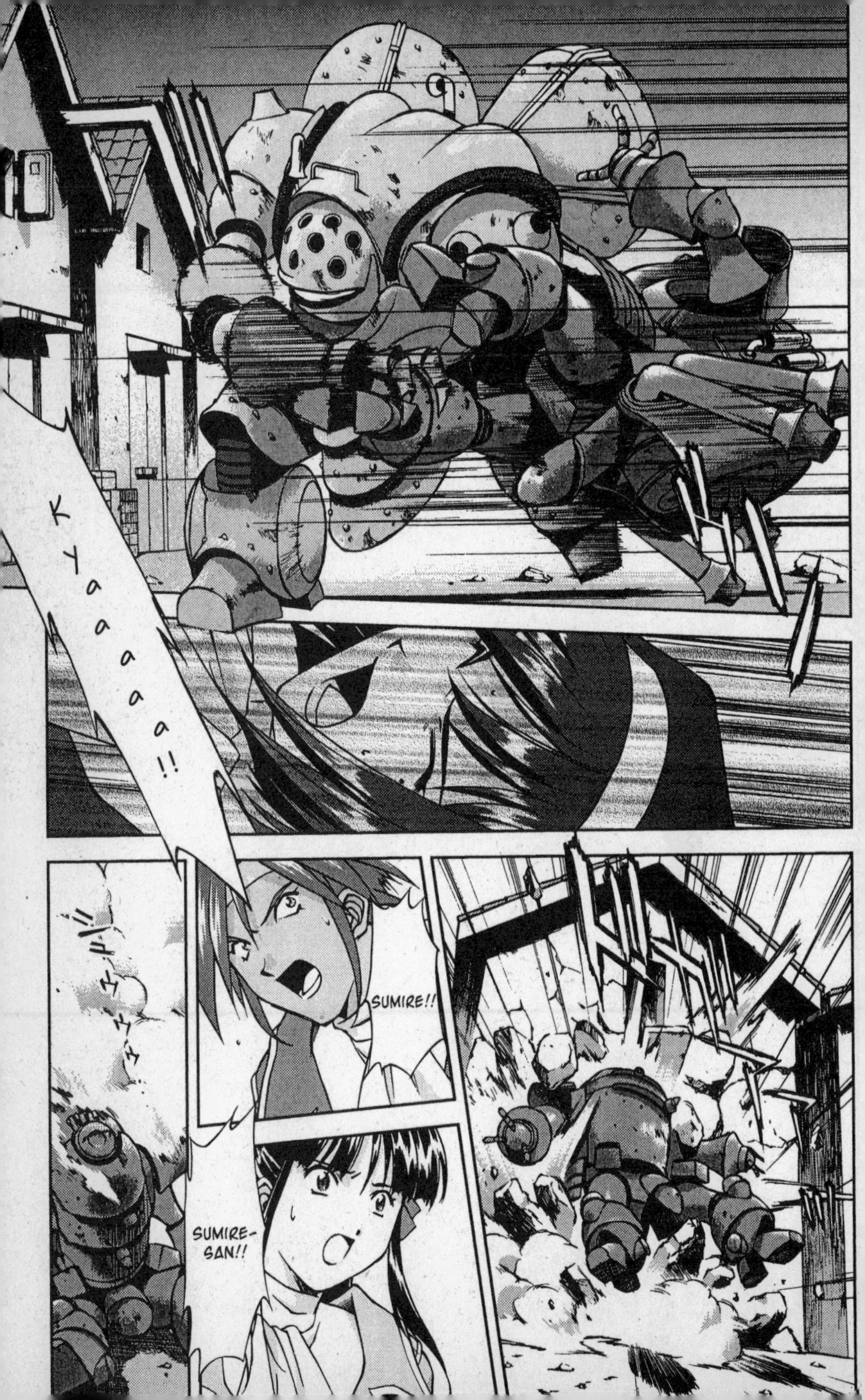
KYaaaaa!!
SUMIRE!!
SUMIRE-SAN!!

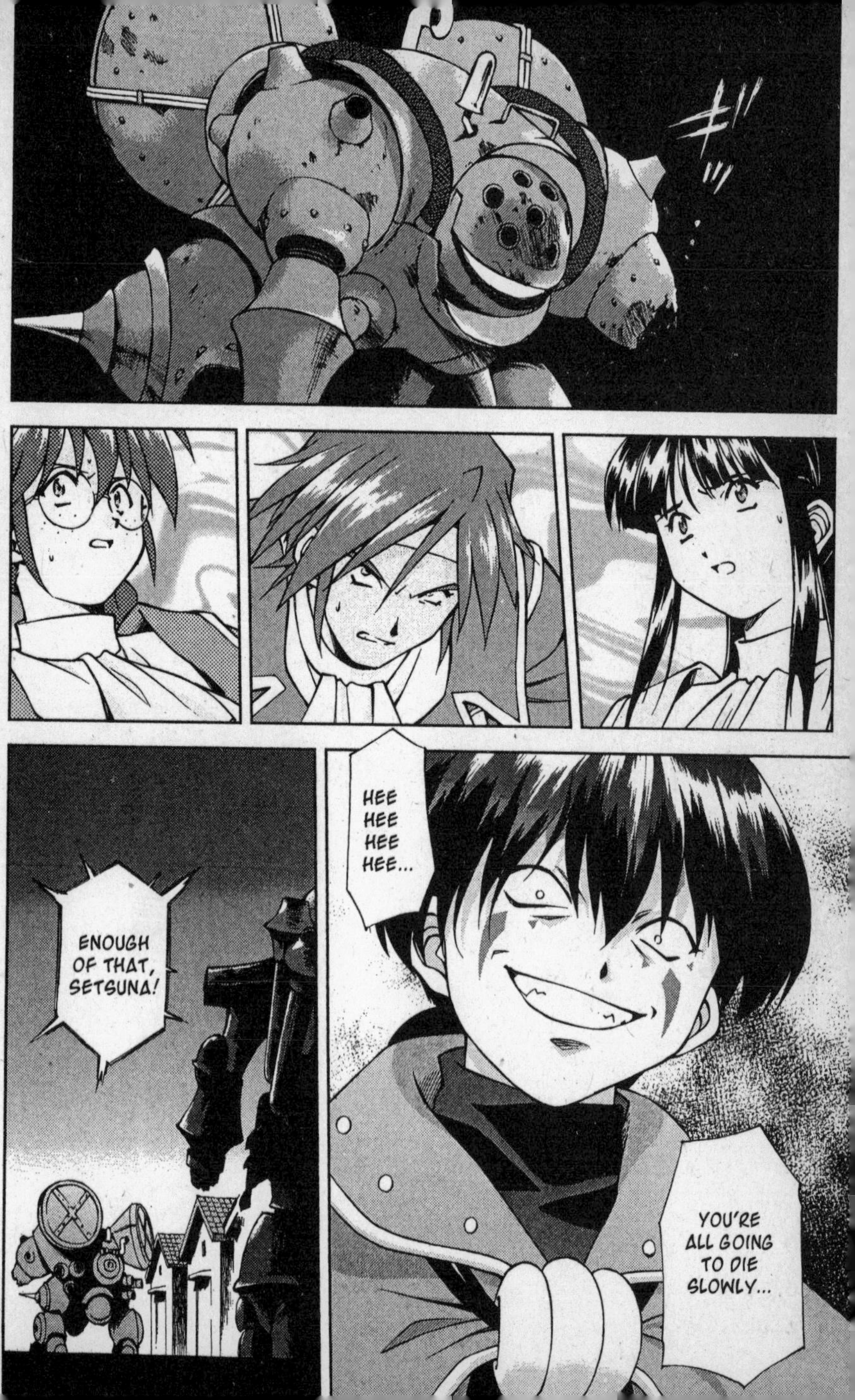
HEE HEE HEE HEE...
YOU'RE ALL GOING TO DIE SLOWLY...
ENOUGH OF THAT, SETSUNA!

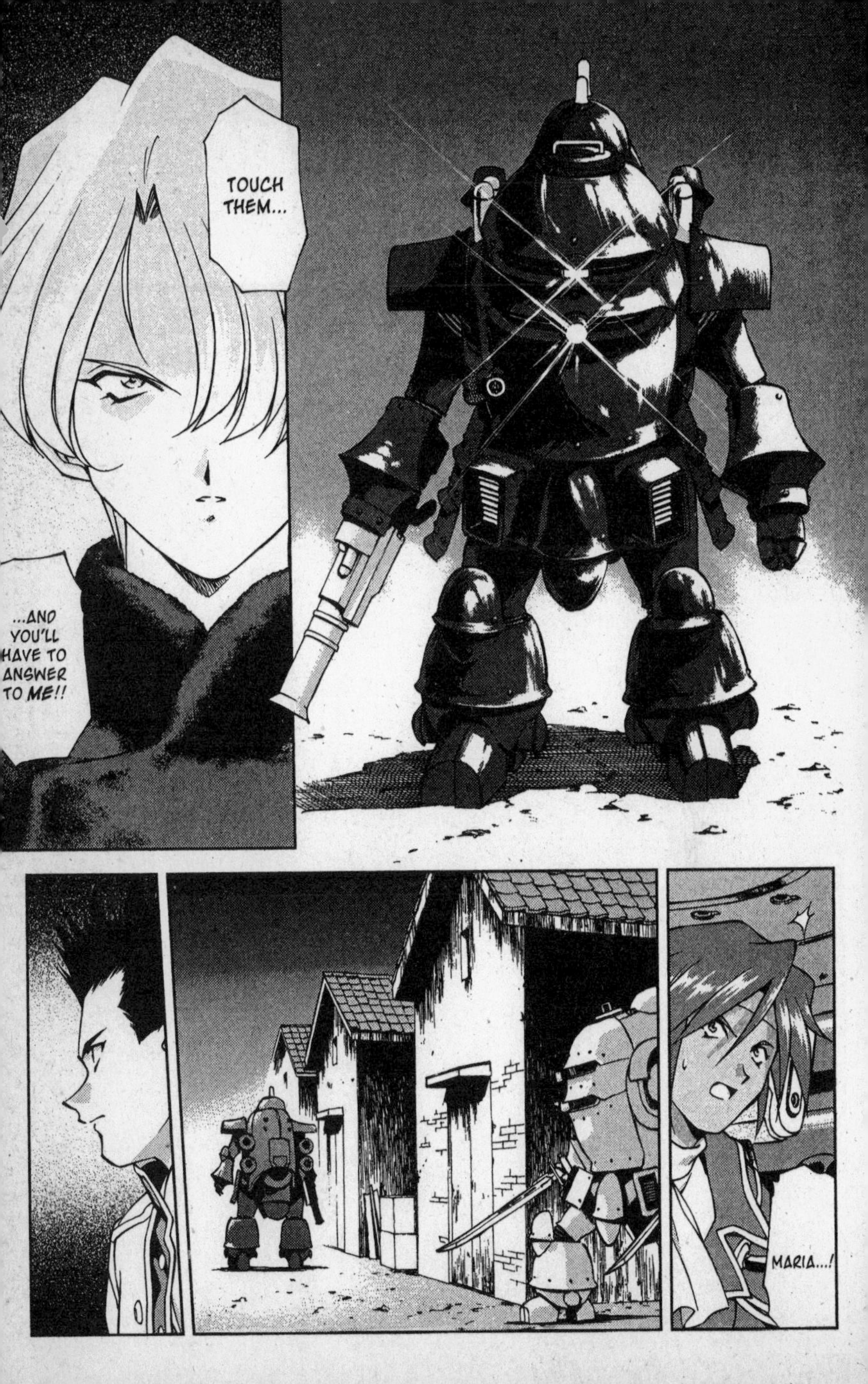
TOUCH THEM...
...AND YOU'LL HAVE TO ANSWER TO *ME*!!
MARIA...!

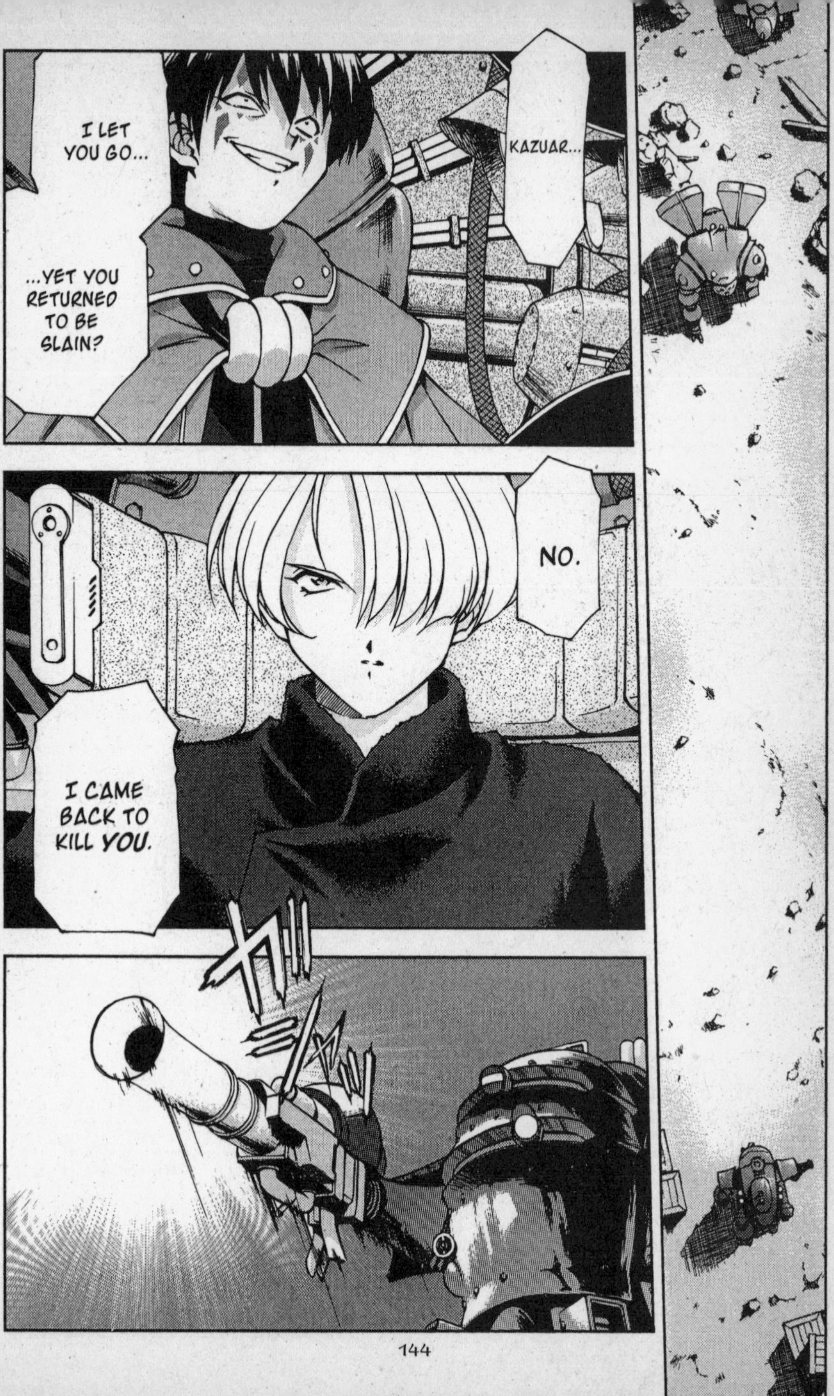
KAZUAR...
I LET YOU GO...
...YET YOU RETURNED TO BE SLAIN?
NO.
I CAME BACK TO KILL *YOU*.

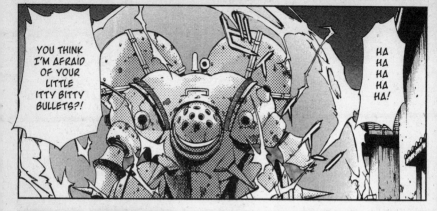

YOU THINK I'M AFRAID OF YOUR LITTLE ITTY BITTY BULLETS?!

HA HA HA HA!

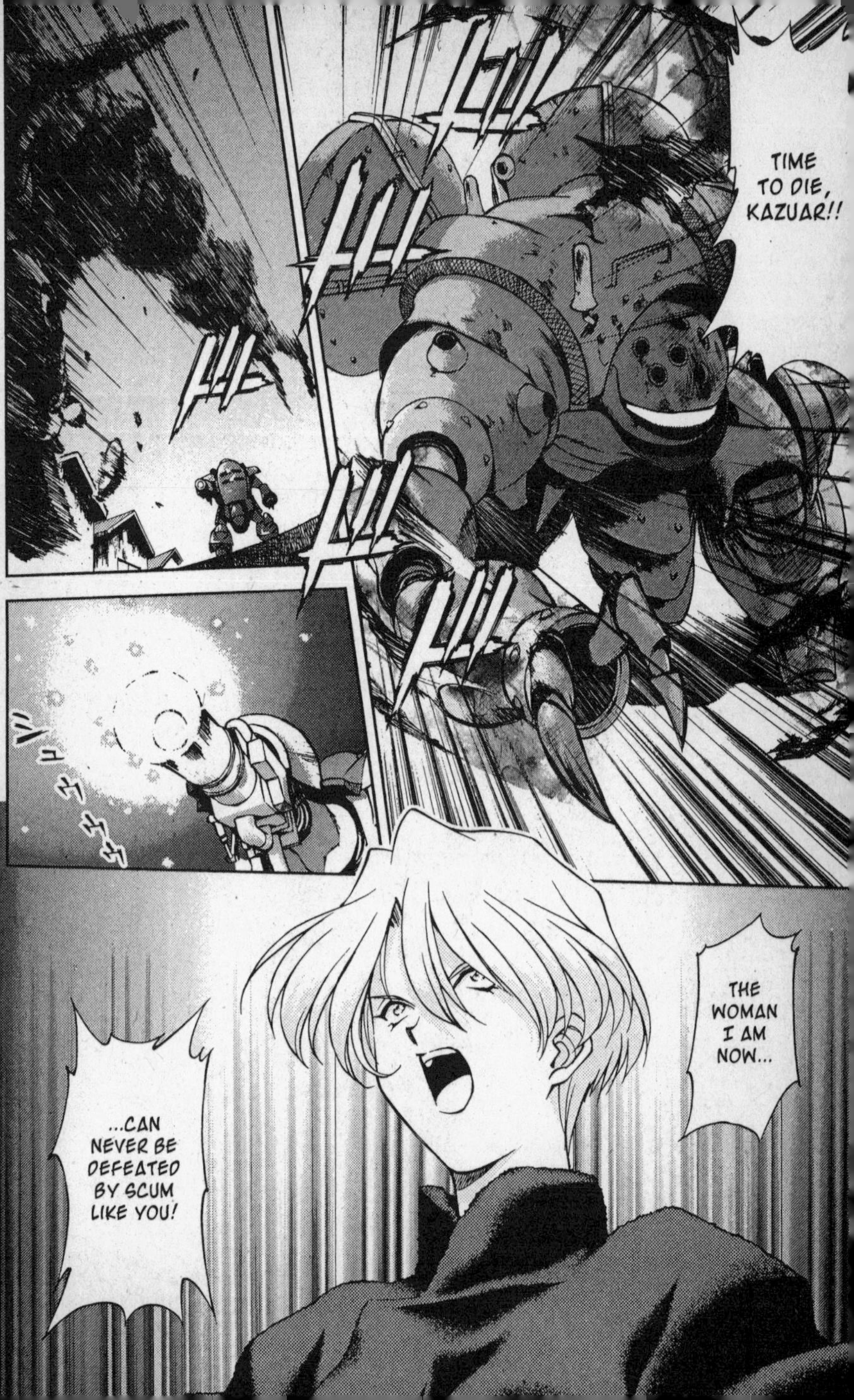
TIME TO DIE, KAZUAR!!
THE WOMAN I AM NOW...
...CAN NEVER BE DEFEATED BY SCUM LIKE YOU!

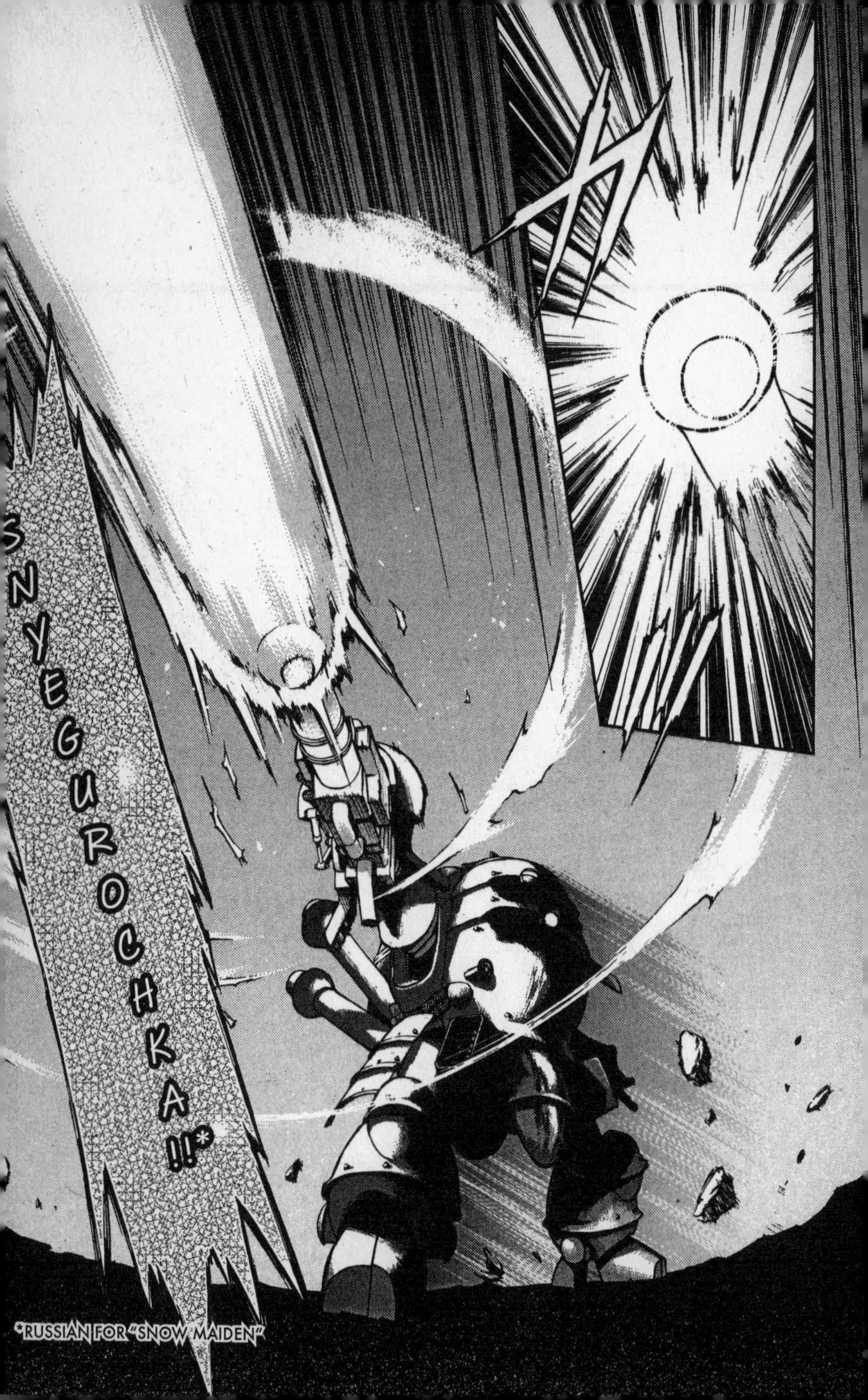
SNYEGUROCHKA!!*
*RUSSIAN FOR "SNOW MAIDEN"

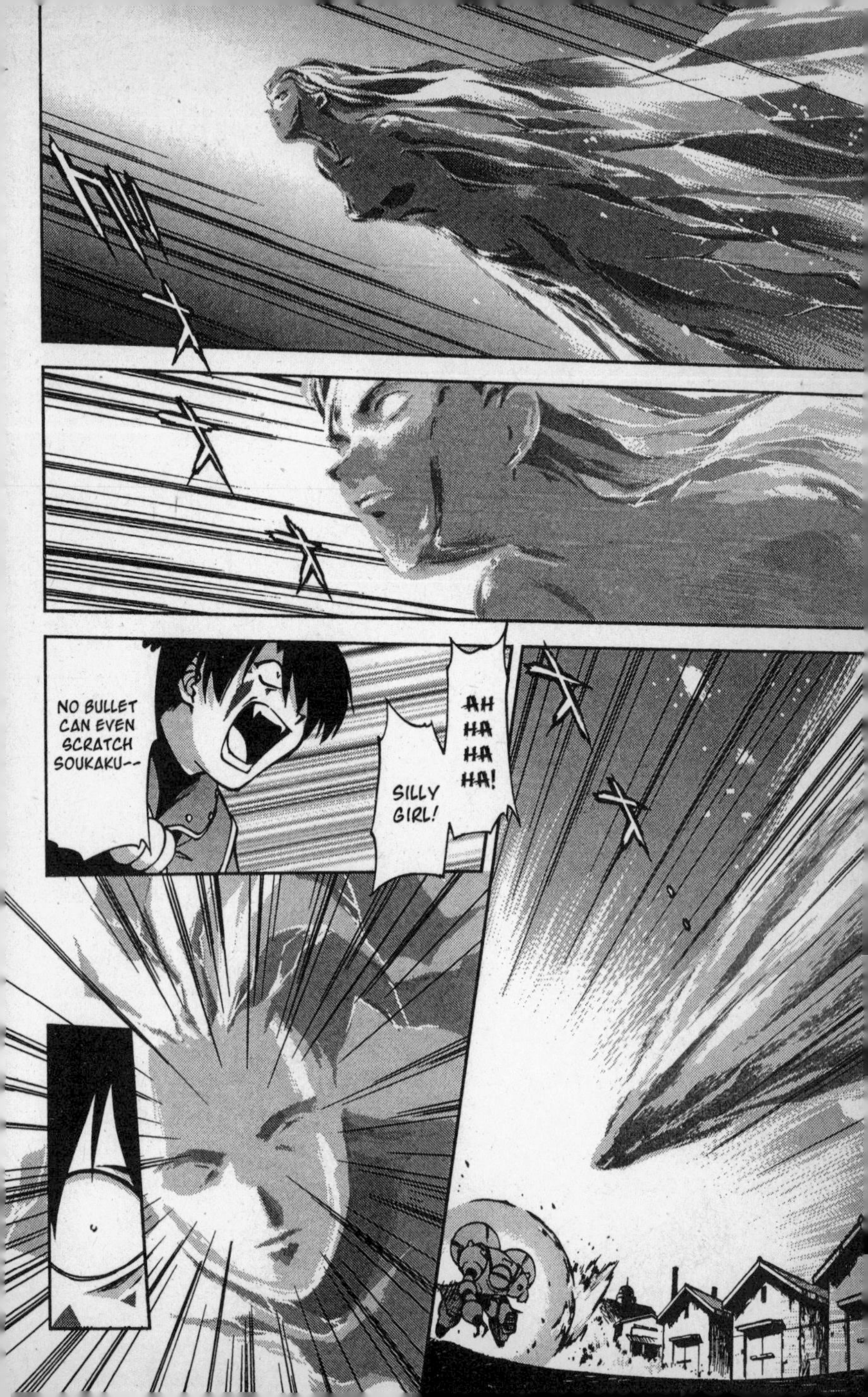
AH HA HA HA!
SILLY GIRL!
NO BULLET CAN EVEN SCRATCH SOUKAKU--

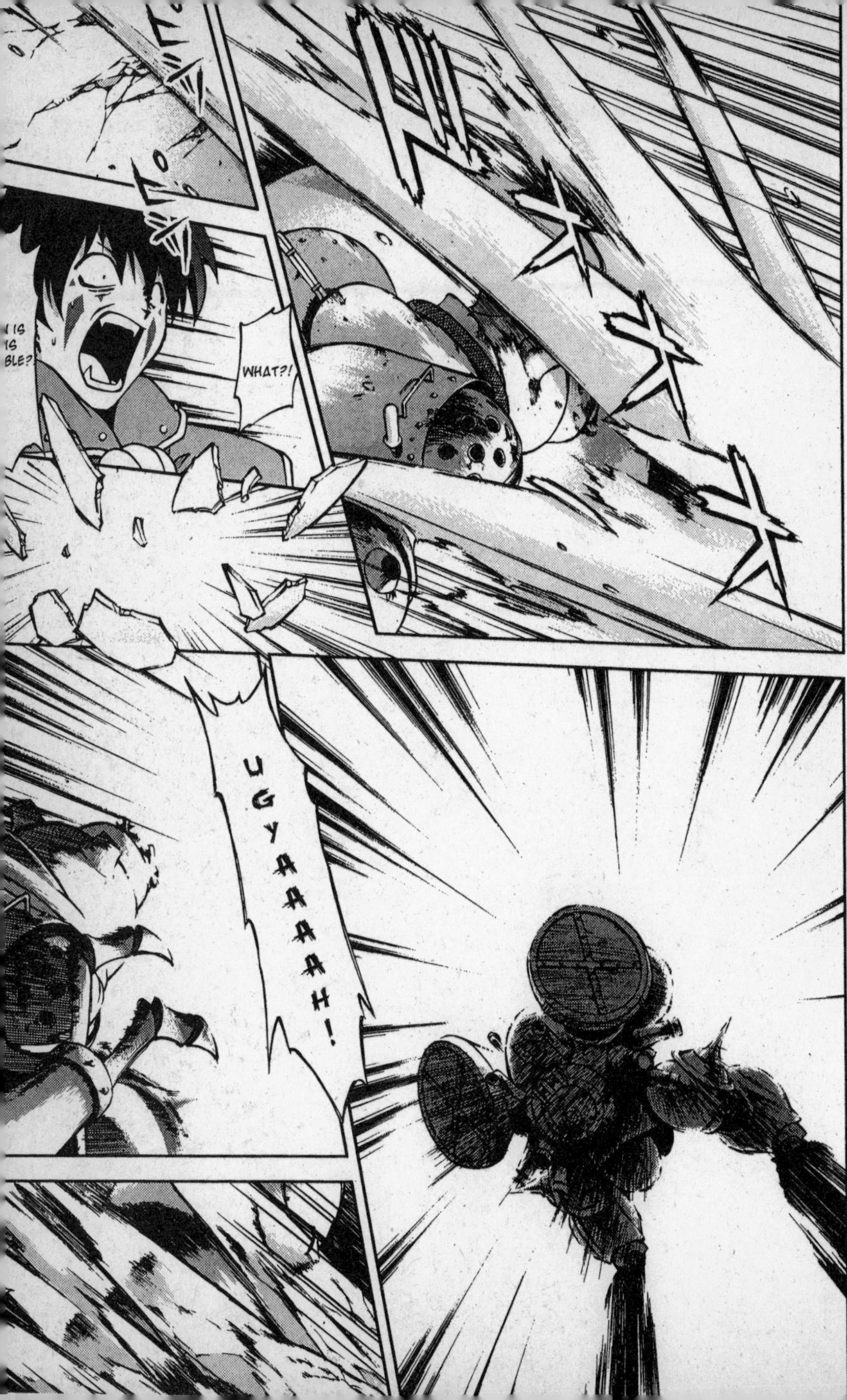
WHAT?!
UGYAAAAAH!

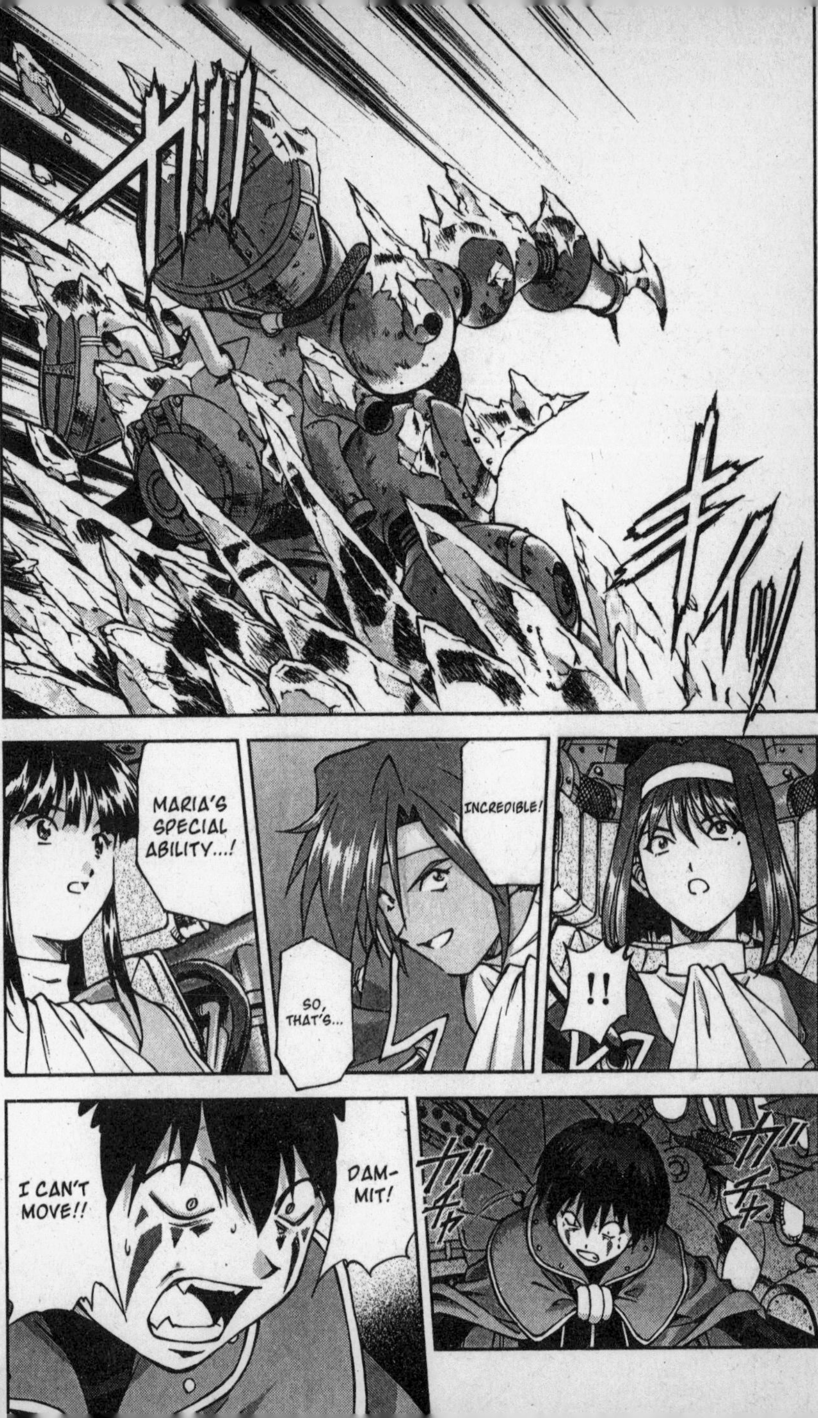
!!
INCREDIBLE!
SO, THAT'S...
MARIA'S SPECIAL ABILITY...!
DAM-MIT!
I CAN'T MOVE!!

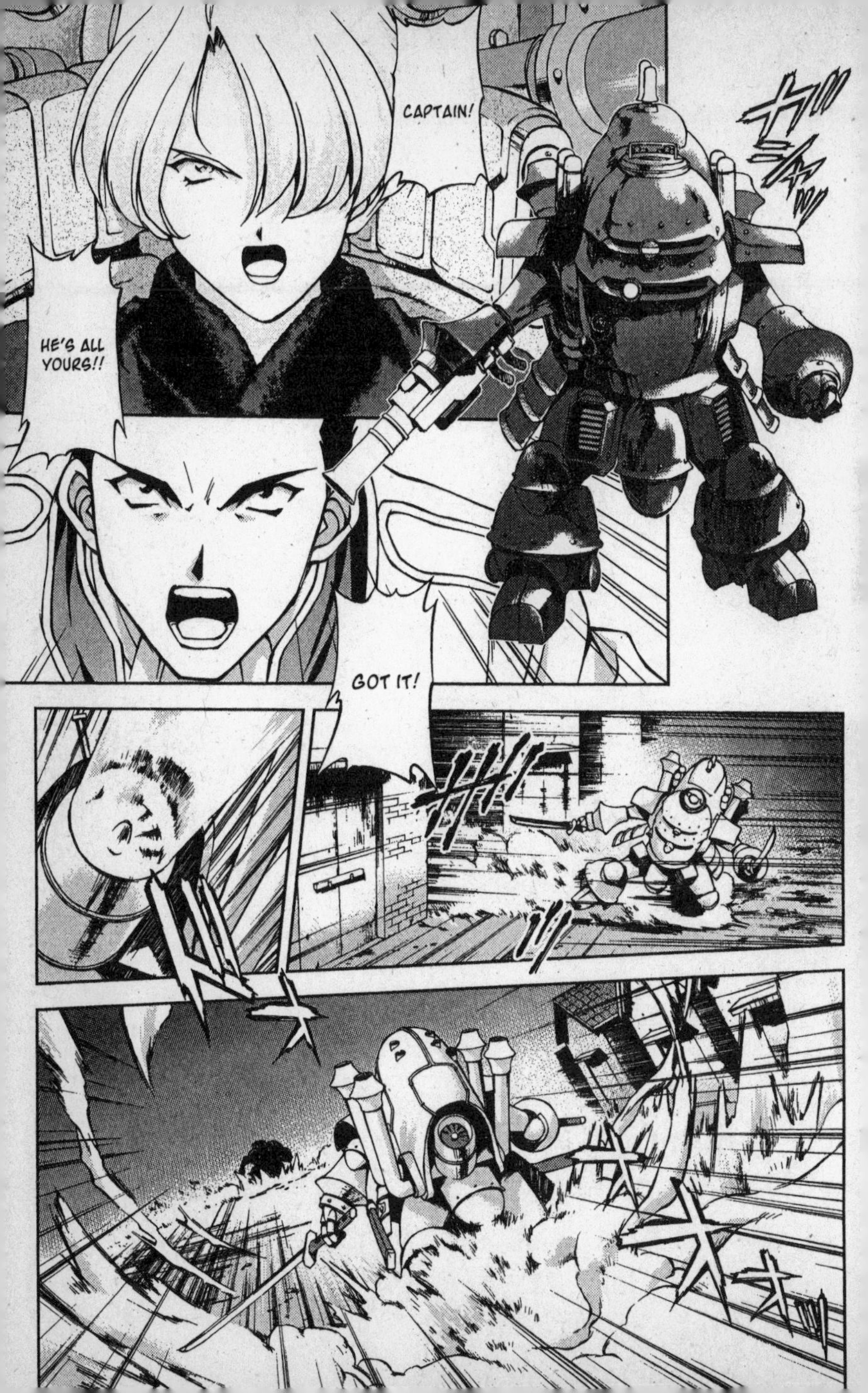
CAPTAIN!
HE'S ALL YOURS!!
GOT IT!

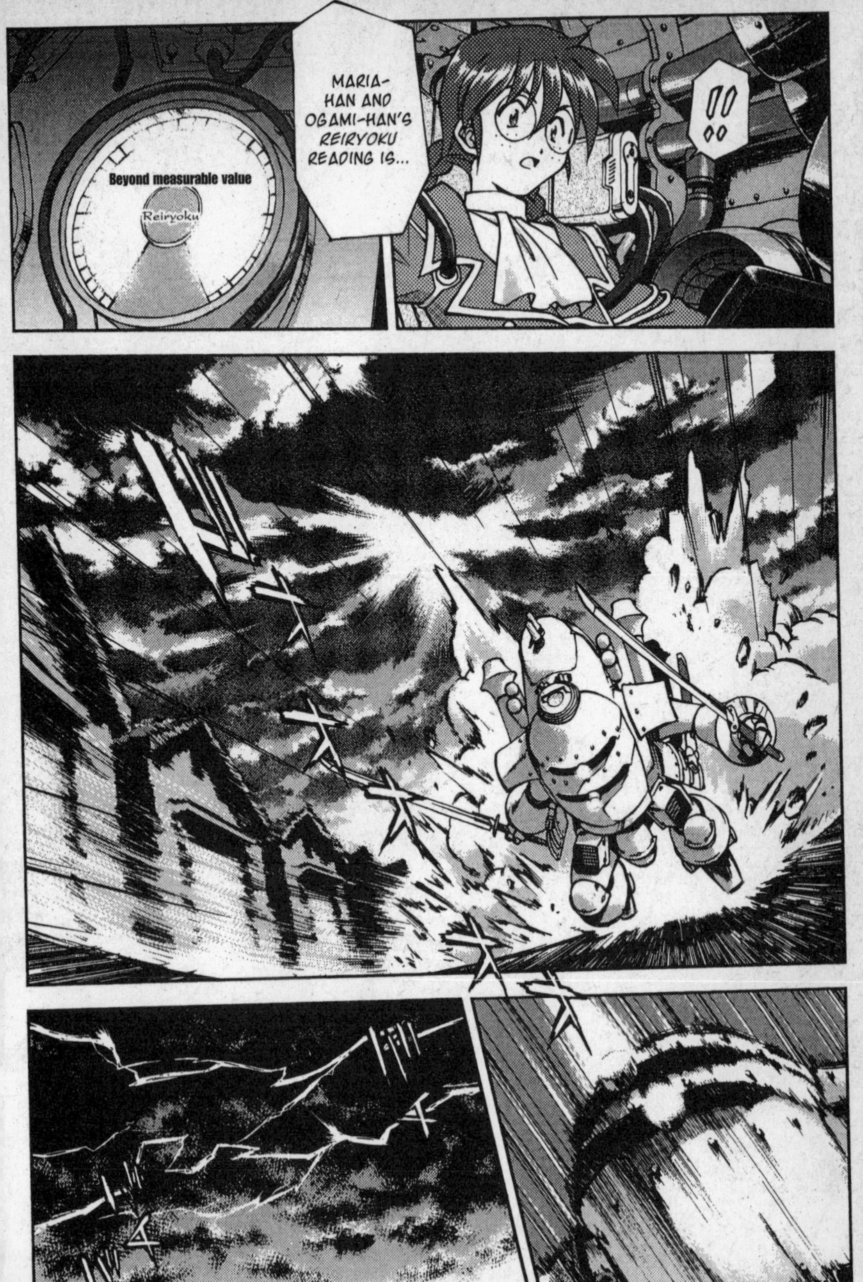
!!
MARIA-HAN AND OGAMI-HAN'S REIRYOKU READING IS...
Beyond measurable value
Reiryoku

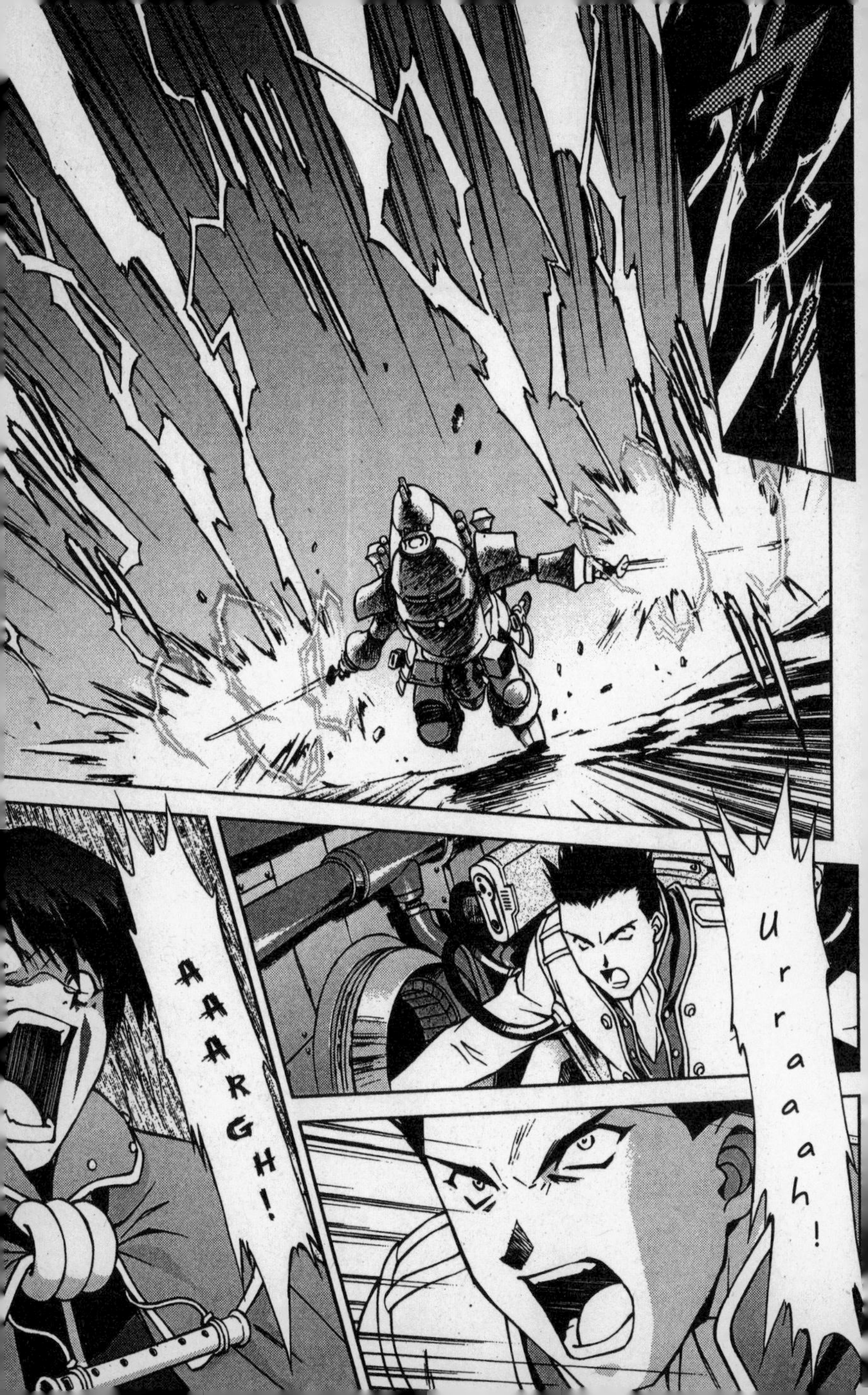
Urraaah!
AAARGH!

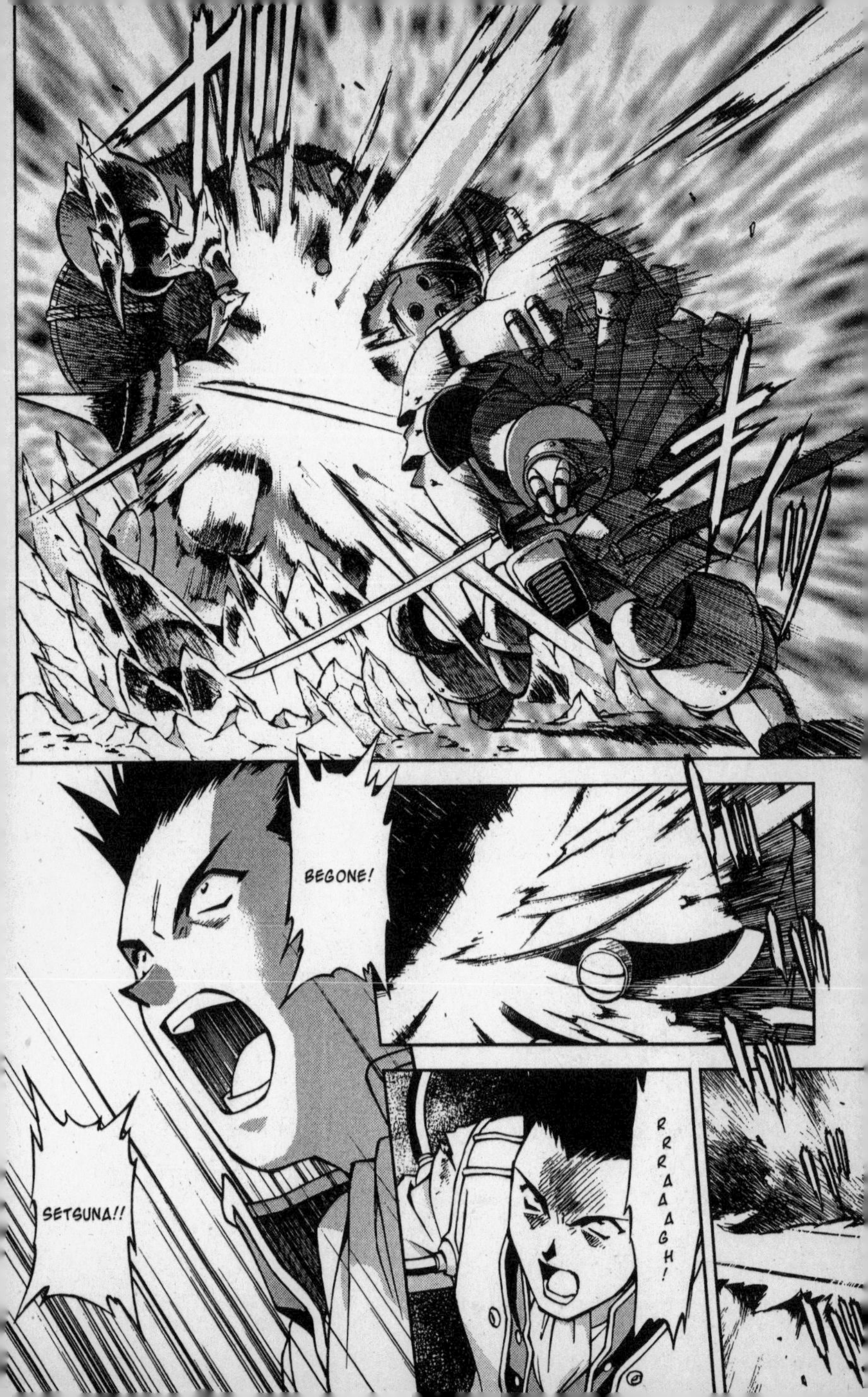
BEGONE!
RRRAAAGH!
SETSUNA!!

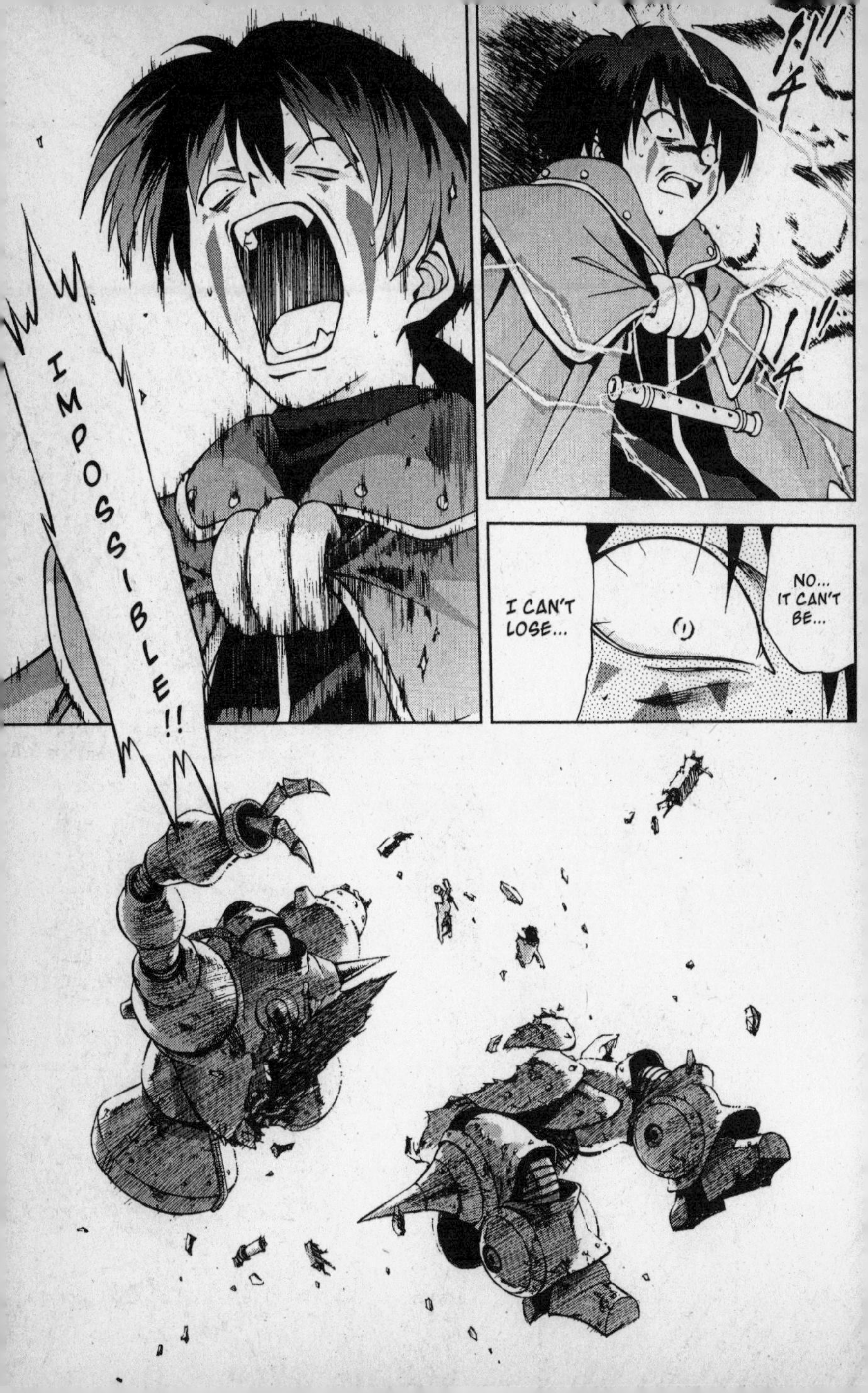
NO... IT CAN'T BE...
I CAN'T LOSE...
IMPOSSIBLE!!

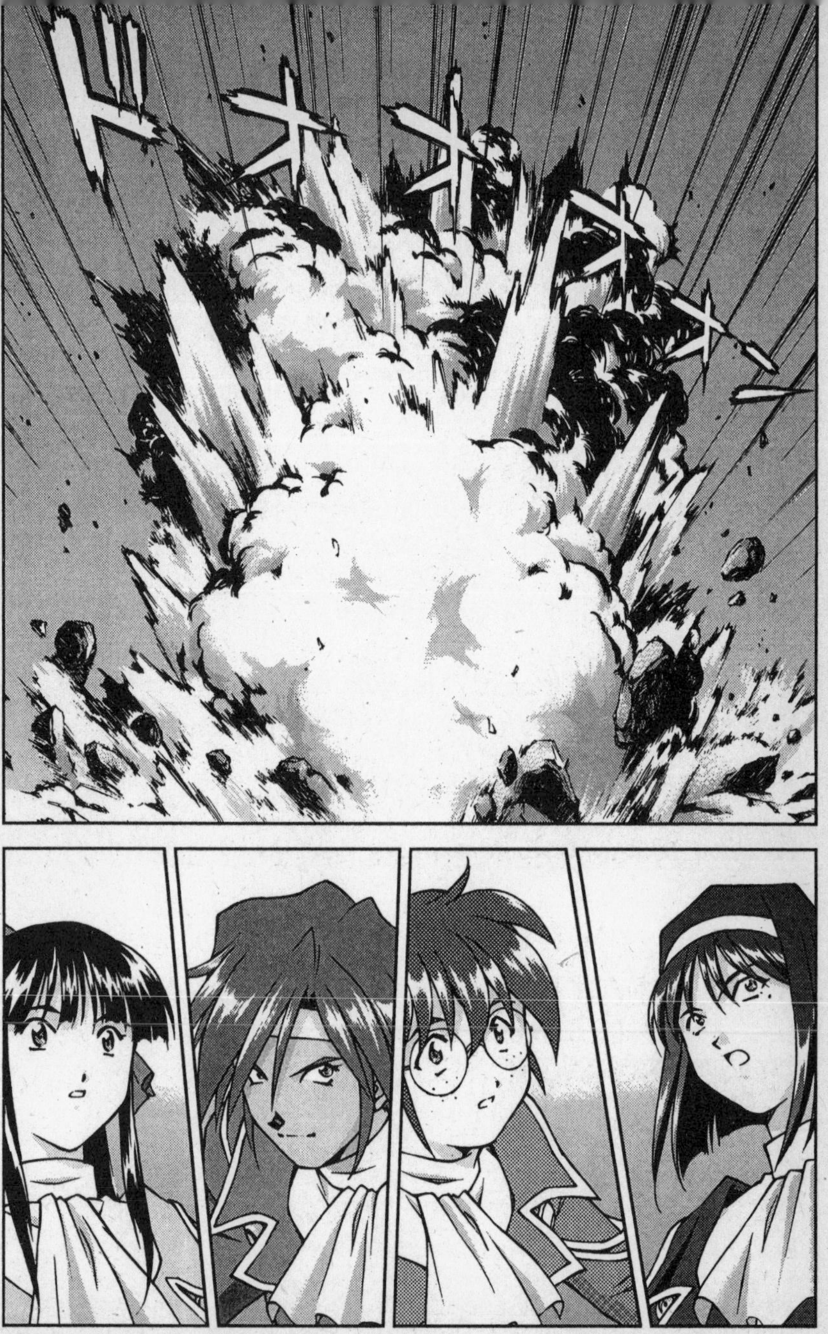

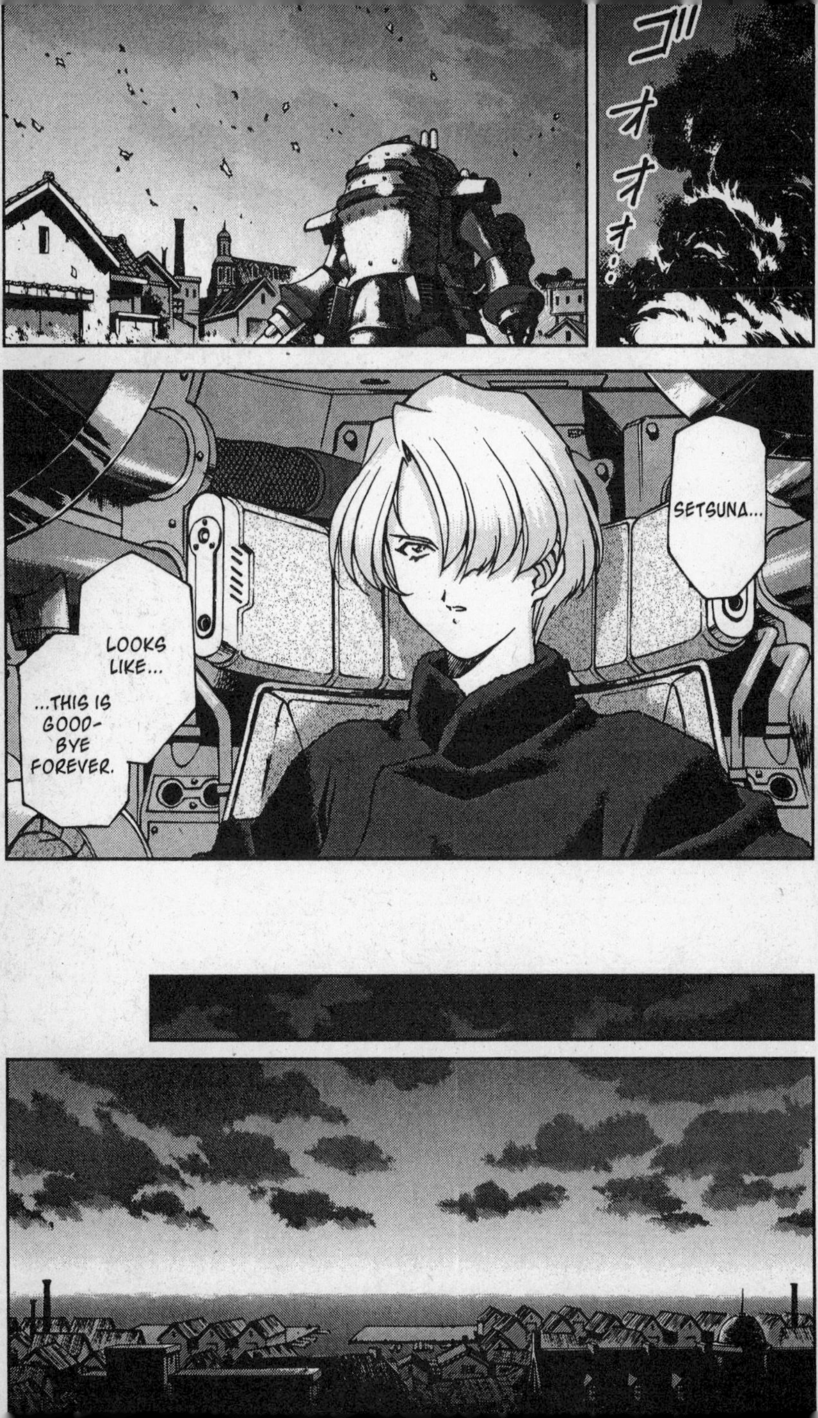
ゴオオオ…
SETSUNA...
LOOKS LIKE...
...THIS IS GOOD-BYE FOREVER.

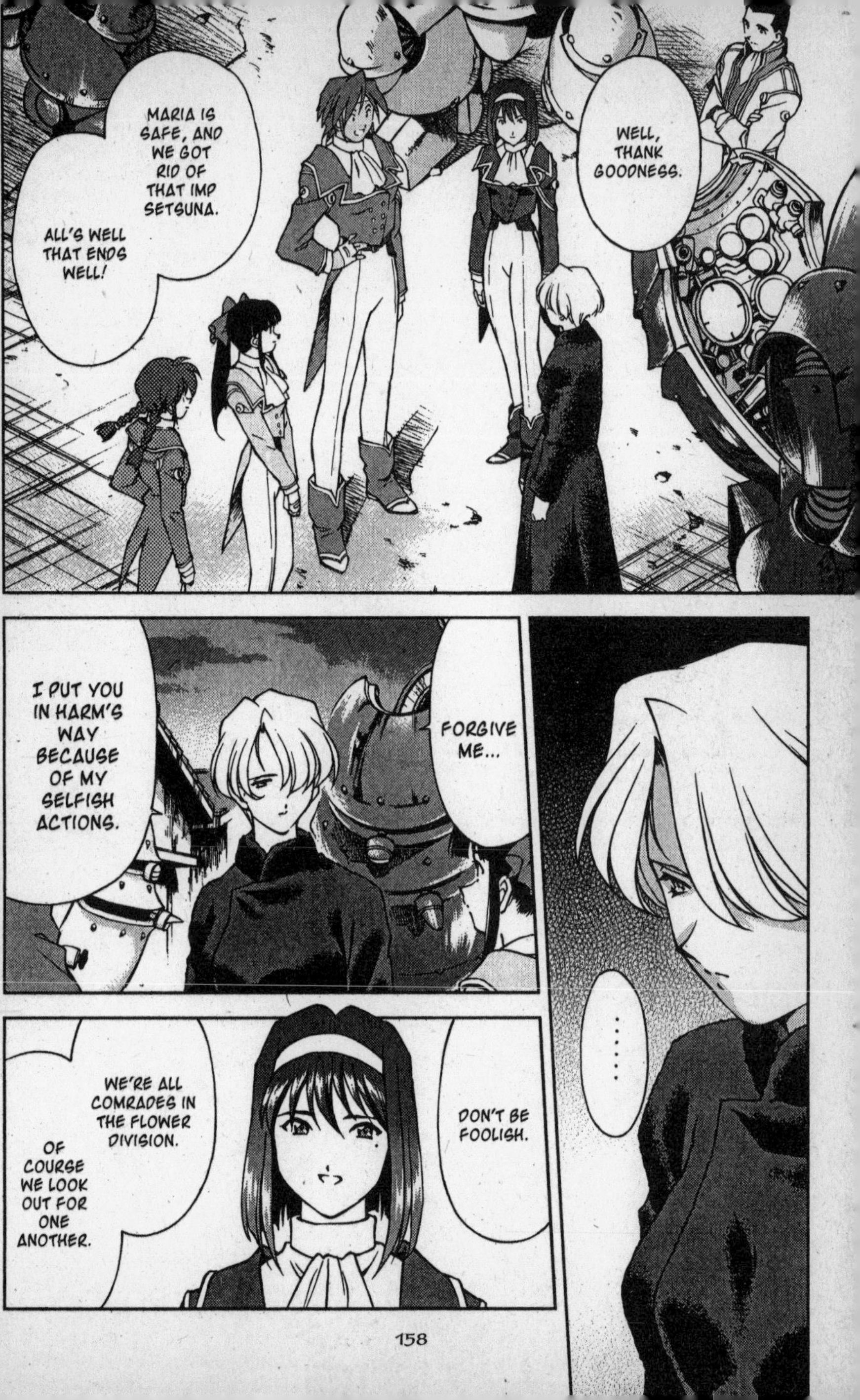
WELL, THANK GOODNESS.
MARIA IS SAFE, AND WE GOT RID OF THAT IMP SETSUNA.
ALL'S WELL THAT ENDS WELL!
......
FORGIVE ME...
I PUT YOU IN HARM'S WAY BECAUSE OF MY SELFISH ACTIONS.
DON'T BE FOOLISH.
WE'RE ALL COMRADES IN THE FLOWER DIVISION.
OF COURSE WE LOOK OUT FOR ONE ANOTHER.

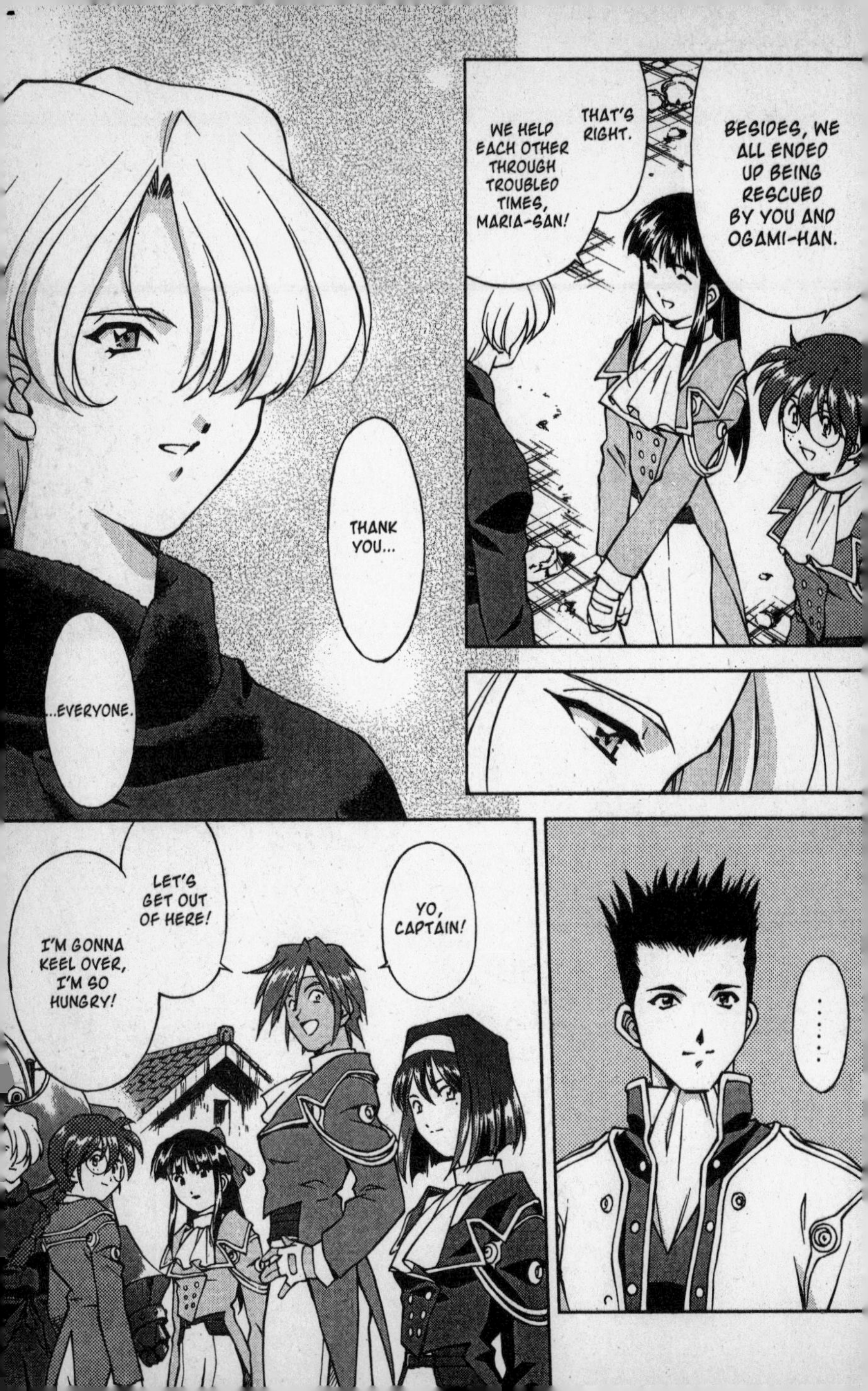
BESIDES, WE ALL ENDED UP BEING RESCUED BY YOU AND OGAMI-HAN.
THAT'S RIGHT.
WE HELP EACH OTHER THROUGH TROUBLED TIMES, MARIA-SAN!
THANK YOU...
...EVERYONE.
......
YO, CAPTAIN!
LET'S GET OUT OF HERE!
I'M GONNA KEEL OVER, I'M SO HUNGRY!

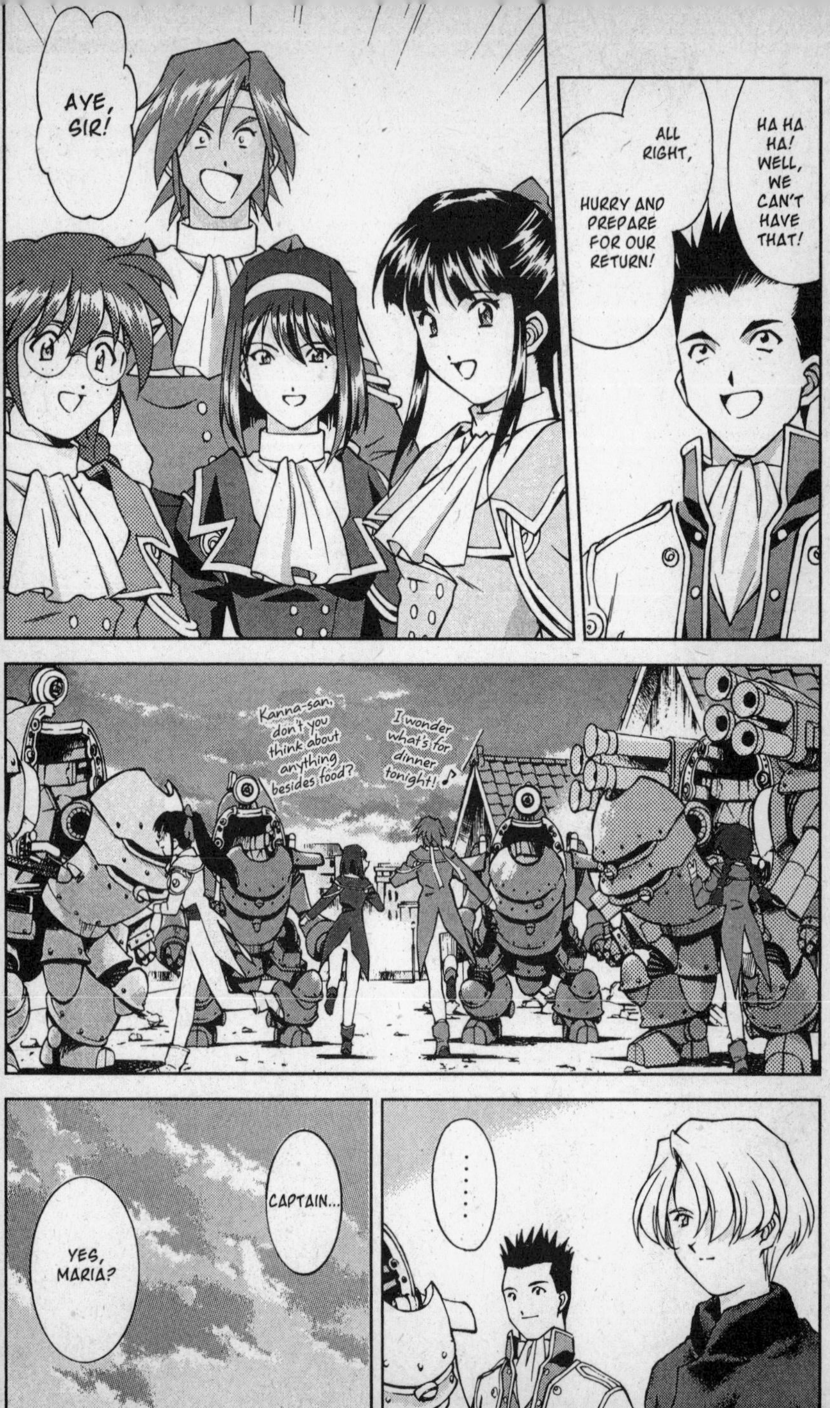
HA HA HA! WELL, WE CAN'T HAVE THAT!
ALL RIGHT, HURRY AND PREPARE FOR OUR RETURN!
AYE, SIR!
I wonder what's for dinner tonight! ♪
Kanna-san, don't you think about anything besides food?
......
CAPTAIN...
YES, MARIA?

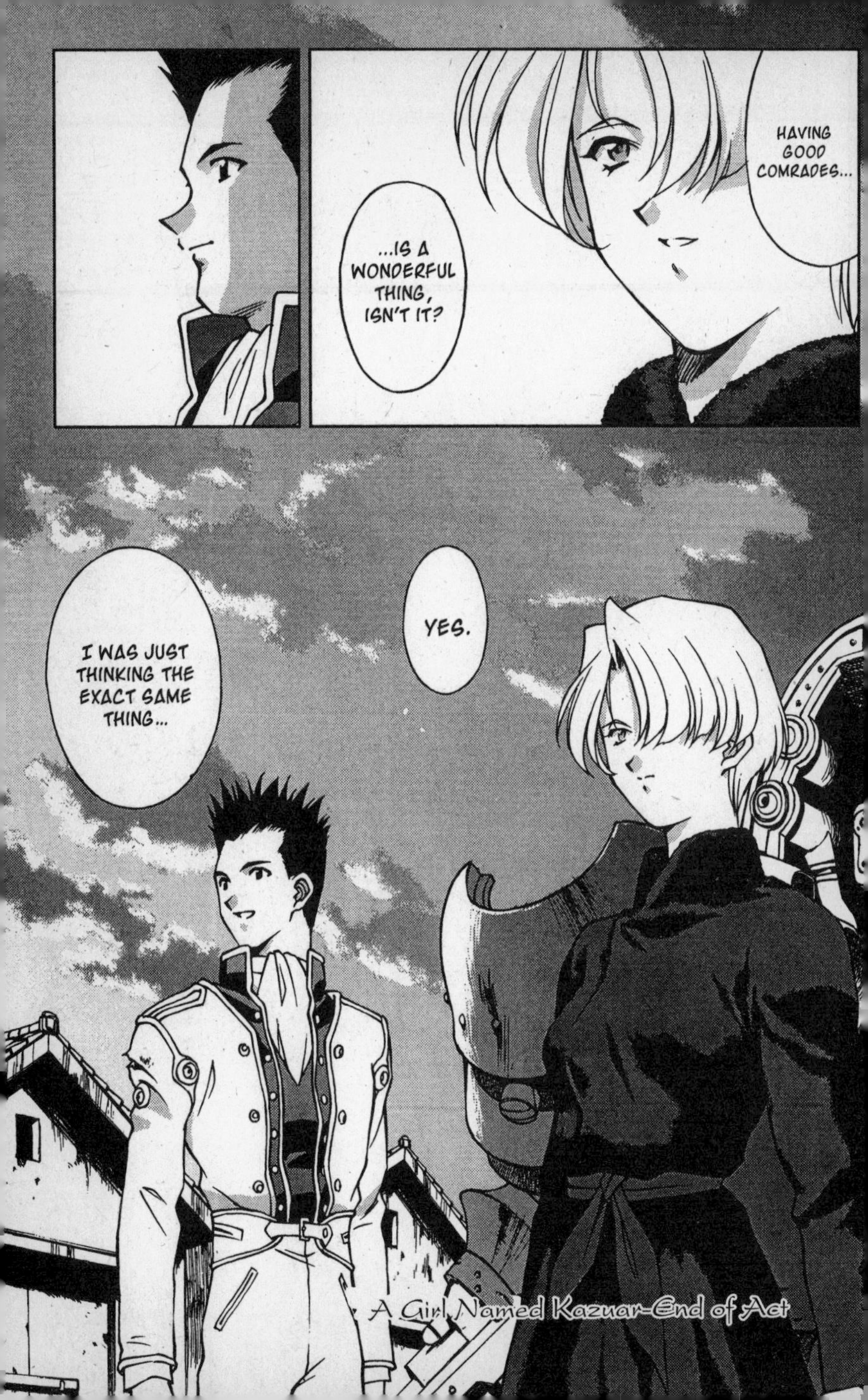
HAVING GOOD COMRADES...
...IS A WONDERFUL THING, ISN'T IT?
YES.
I WAS JUST THINKING THE EXACT SAME THING...
A Girl Named Kazuar-End of Act

Imperial Fighting Troupe

アイリス＆紅蘭

Iris and Kohran

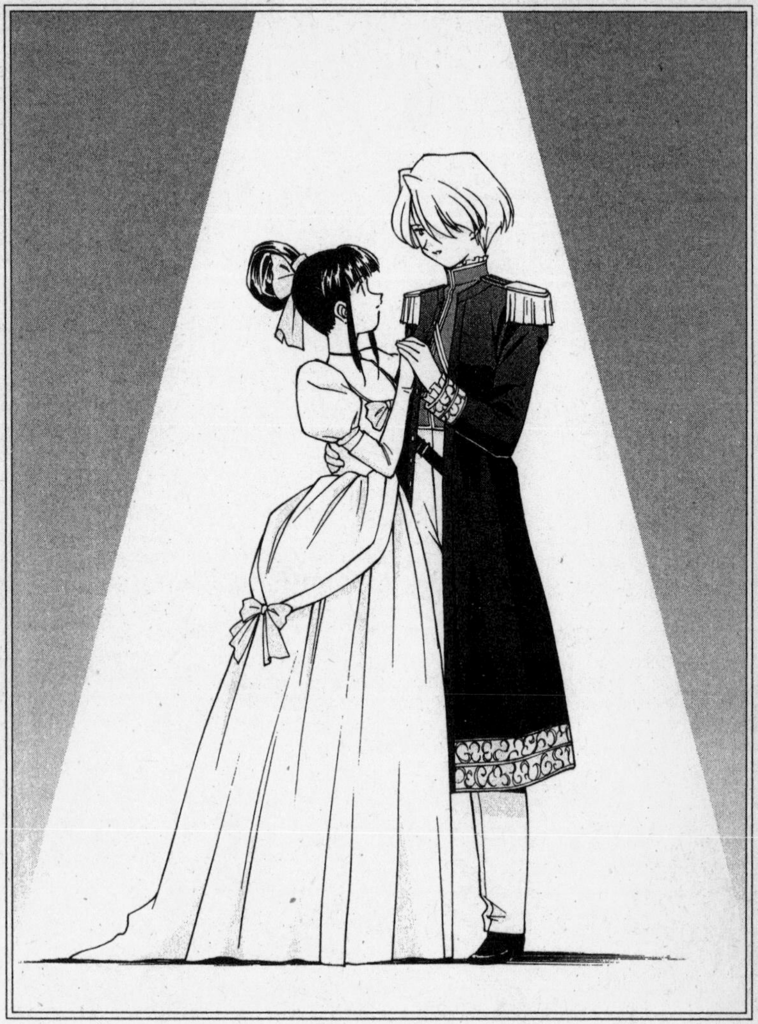

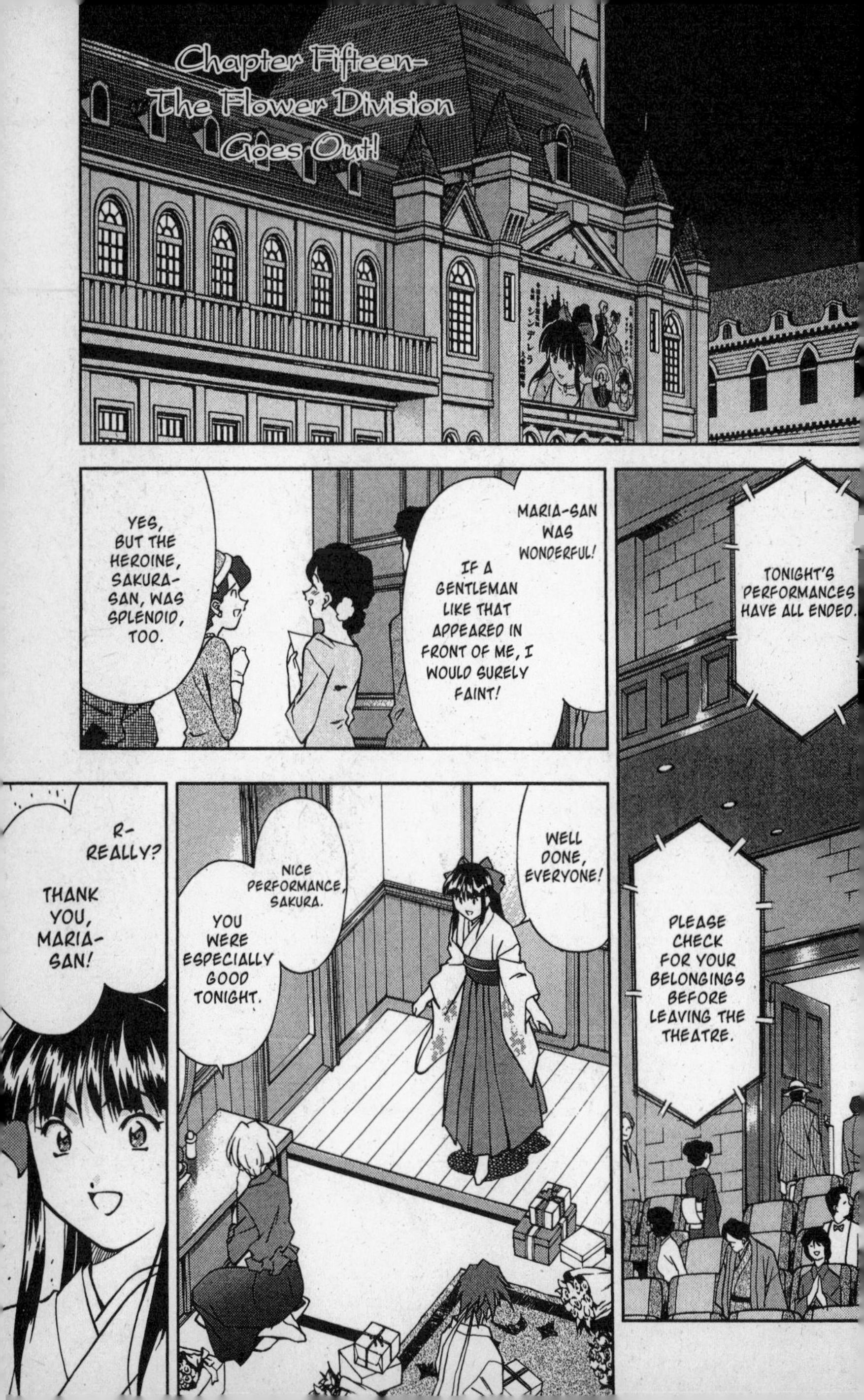
Chapter Fifteen-
The Flower Division
Goes Out!
TONIGHT'S PERFORMANCES HAVE ALL ENDED.
MARIA-SAN WAS WONDERFUL!
IF A GENTLEMAN LIKE THAT APPEARED IN FRONT OF ME, I WOULD SURELY FAINT!
YES, BUT THE HEROINE, SAKURA-SAN, WAS SPLENDID, TOO.
PLEASE CHECK FOR YOUR BELONGINGS BEFORE LEAVING THE THEATRE.
WELL DONE, EVERYONE!
NICE PERFORMANCE, SAKURA.
YOU WERE ESPECIALLY GOOD TONIGHT.
R-REALLY?
THANK YOU, MARIA-SAN!

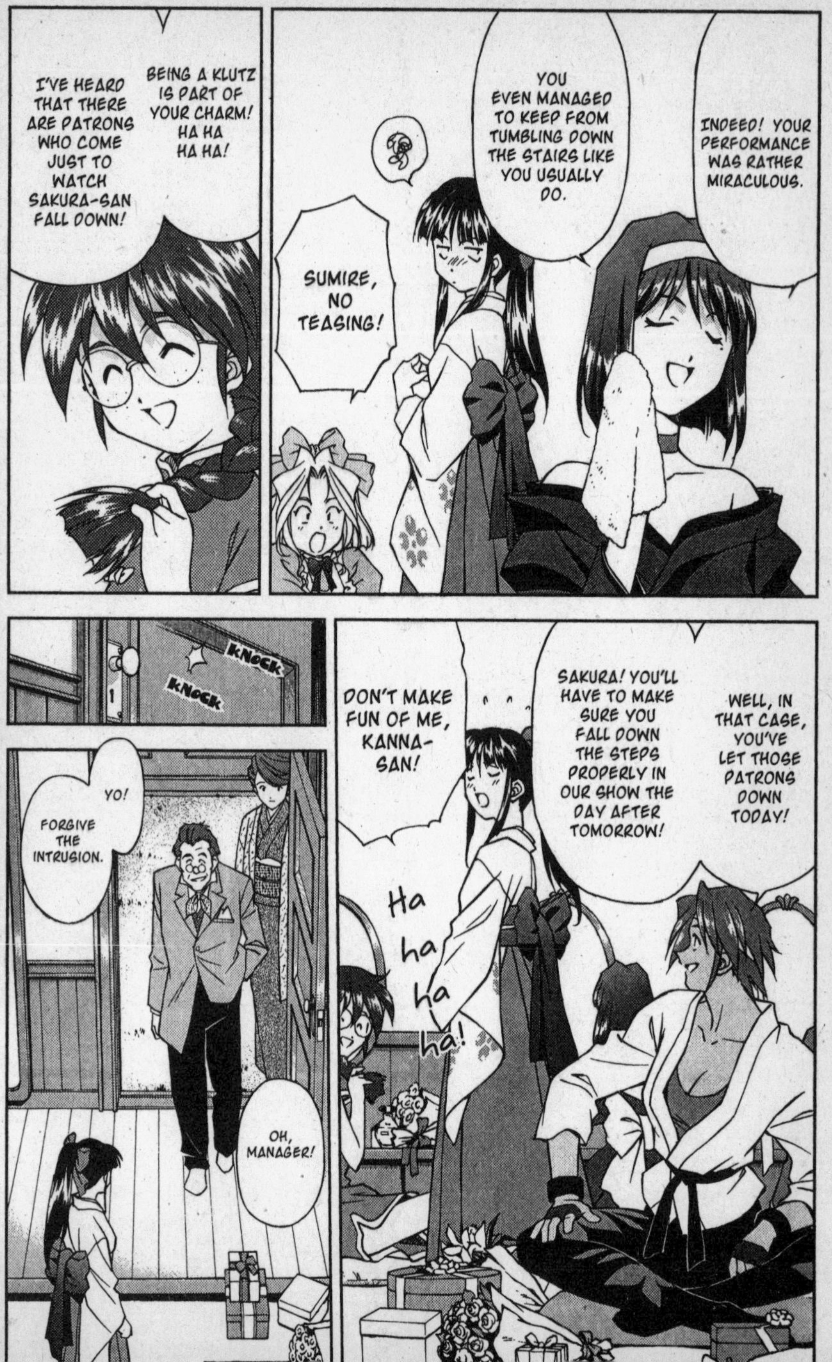
INDEED! YOUR PERFORMANCE WAS RATHER MIRACULOUS.
YOU EVEN MANAGED TO KEEP FROM TUMBLING DOWN THE STAIRS LIKE YOU USUALLY DO.
SUMIRE, NO TEASING!
BEING A KLUTZ IS PART OF YOUR CHARM! HA HA HA HA!
I'VE HEARD THAT THERE ARE PATRONS WHO COME JUST TO WATCH SAKURA-SAN FALL DOWN!
WELL, IN THAT CASE, YOU'VE LET THOSE PATRONS DOWN TODAY!
SAKURA! YOU'LL HAVE TO MAKE SURE YOU FALL DOWN THE STEPS PROPERLY IN OUR SHOW THE DAY AFTER TOMORROW!
DON'T MAKE FUN OF ME, KANNA-SAN!
Ha ha ha ha!
KNOCK
KNOCK
YO!
FORGIVE THE INTRUSION.
OH, MANAGER!

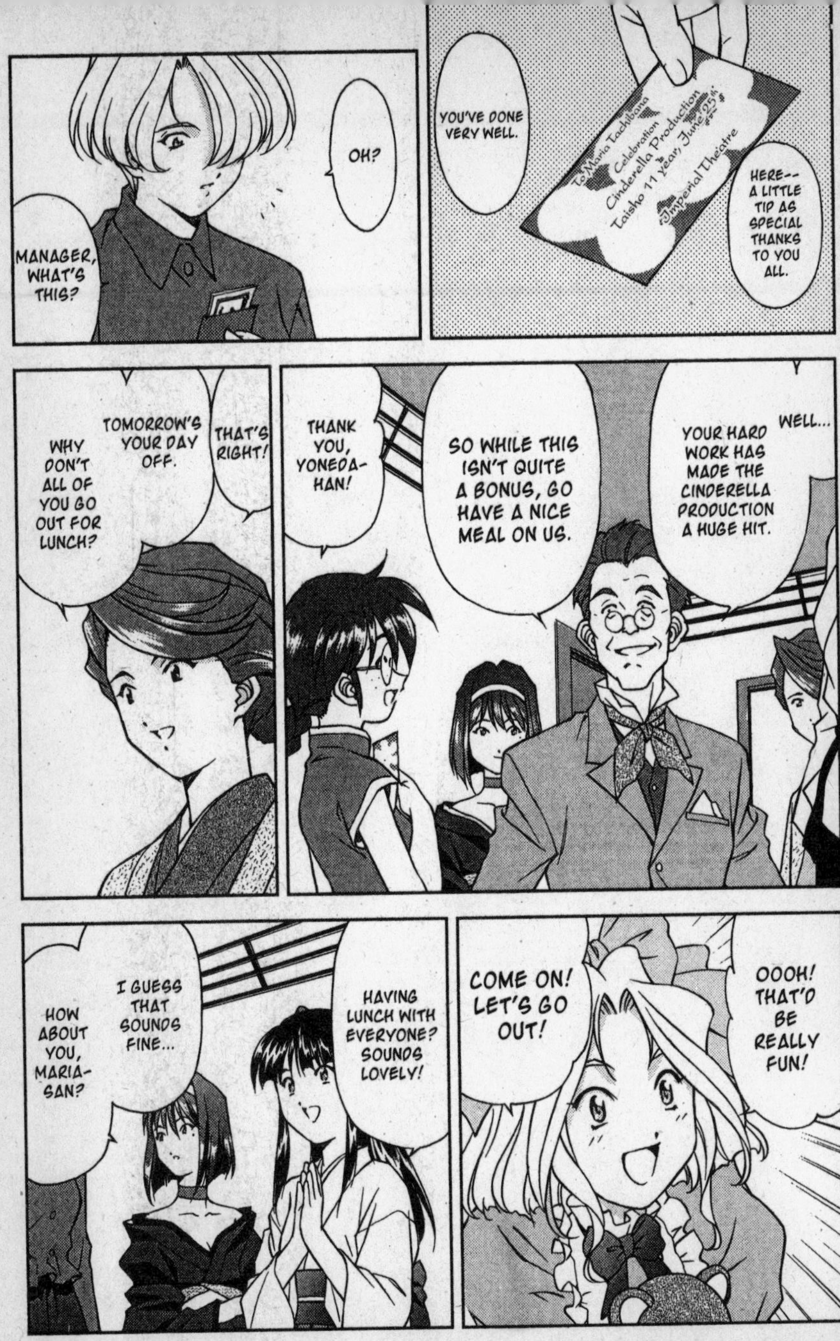
YOU'VE DONE VERY WELL.
To Maria Tachibana
Celebration
Cinderella Production
Taisho 11 year, June 25th
Imperial Theatre
HERE-- A LITTLE TIP AS SPECIAL THANKS TO YOU ALL.
OH?
MANAGER, WHAT'S THIS?
WELL...
YOUR HARD WORK HAS MADE THE CINDERELLA PRODUCTION A HUGE HIT.
SO WHILE THIS ISN'T QUITE A BONUS, GO HAVE A NICE MEAL ON US.
THANK YOU, YONEDA-HAN!
THAT'S RIGHT!
TOMORROW'S YOUR DAY OFF.
WHY DON'T ALL OF YOU GO OUT FOR LUNCH?
OOOH! THAT'D BE REALLY FUN!
COME ON! LET'S GO OUT!
HAVING LUNCH WITH EVERYONE? SOUNDS LOVELY!
I GUESS THAT SOUNDS FINE...
HOW ABOUT YOU, MARIA-SAN?

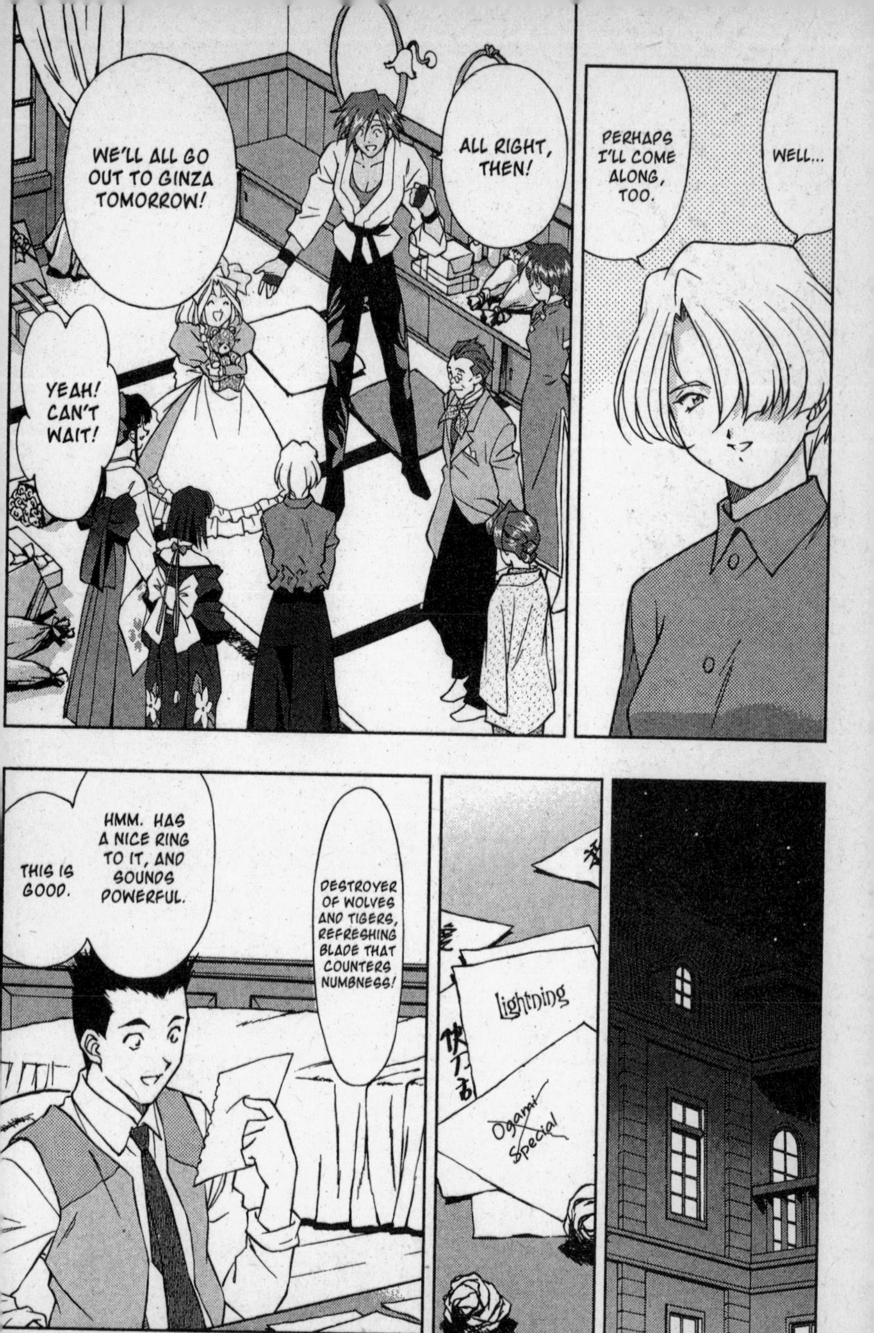
WELL...
PERHAPS I'LL COME ALONG, TOO.
ALL RIGHT, THEN!
WE'LL ALL GO OUT TO GINZA TOMORROW!
YEAH! CAN'T WAIT!
Lightning
Ogami Special
DESTROYER OF WOLVES AND TIGERS, REFRESHING BLADE THAT COUNTERS NUMBNESS!
HMM. HAS A NICE RING TO IT, AND SOUNDS POWERFUL.
THIS IS GOOD.

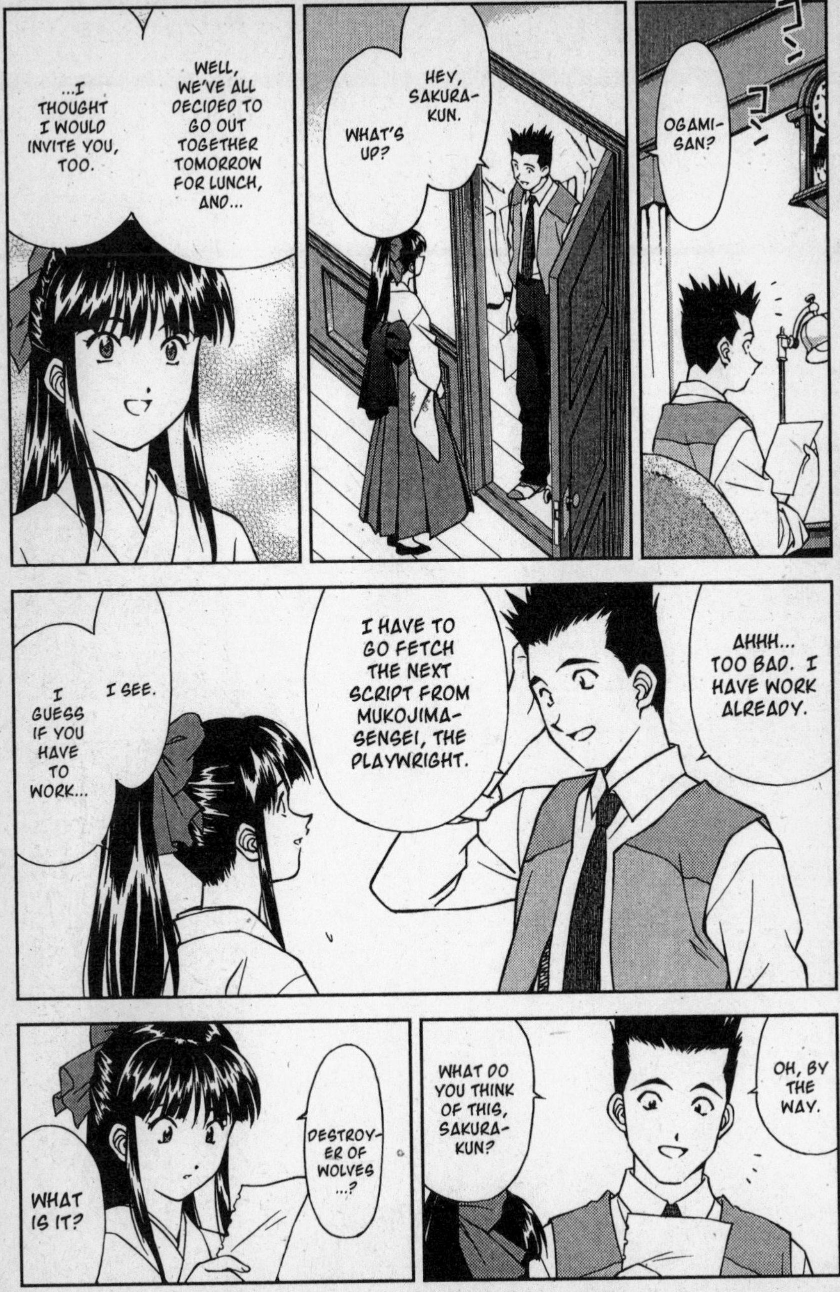
OGAMI-SAN?
HEY, SAKURA-KUN.
WHAT'S UP?
WELL, WE'VE ALL DECIDED TO GO OUT TOGETHER TOMORROW FOR LUNCH, AND...
...I THOUGHT I WOULD INVITE YOU, TOO.
AHHH... TOO BAD. I HAVE WORK ALREADY.
I HAVE TO GO FETCH THE NEXT SCRIPT FROM MUKOJIMA-SENSEI, THE PLAYWRIGHT.
I SEE.
I GUESS IF YOU HAVE TO WORK...
OH, BY THE WAY.
WHAT DO YOU THINK OF THIS, SAKURA-KUN?
DESTROYER OF WOLVES ...?
WHAT IS IT?

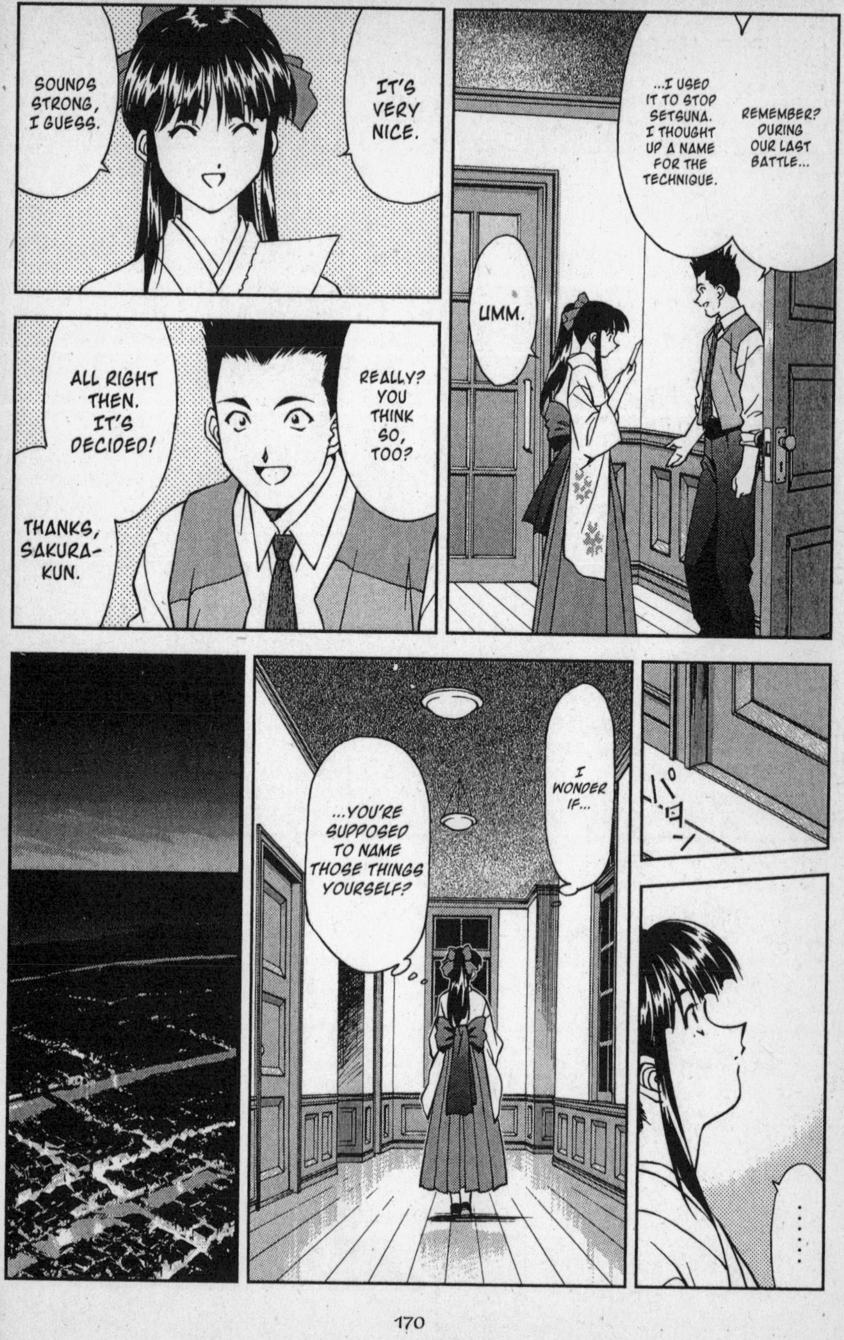
REMEMBER? DURING OUR LAST BATTLE...
...I USED IT TO STOP SETSUNA. I THOUGHT UP A NAME FOR THE TECHNIQUE.
UMM.
IT'S VERY NICE.
SOUNDS STRONG, I GUESS.
REALLY? YOU THINK SO, TOO?
ALL RIGHT THEN. IT'S DECIDED!
THANKS, SAKURA-KUN.
......
I WONDER IF...
...YOU'RE SUPPOSED TO NAME THOSE THINGS YOURSELF?

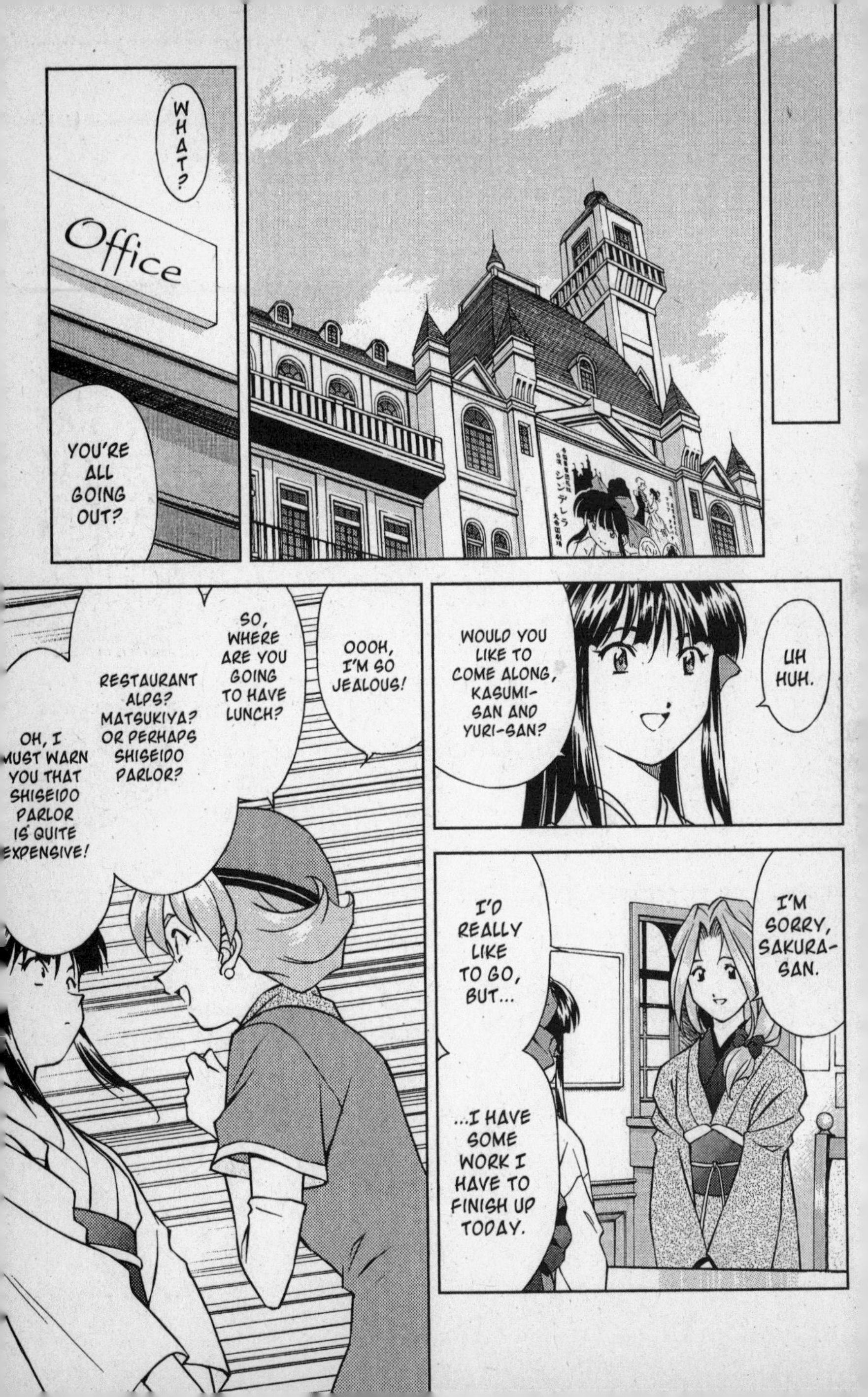

WHAT?
Office
YOU'RE ALL GOING OUT?
UH HUH.
WOULD YOU LIKE TO COME ALONG, KASUMI-SAN AND YURI-SAN?
I'M SORRY, SAKURA-SAN.
I'D REALLY LIKE TO GO, BUT...
...I HAVE SOME WORK I HAVE TO FINISH UP TODAY.
OOOH, I'M SO JEALOUS!
SO, WHERE ARE YOU GOING TO HAVE LUNCH?
RESTAURANT ALPS? MATSUKIYA? OR PERHAPS SHISEIDO PARLOR?
OH, I MUST WARN YOU THAT SHISEIDO PARLOR IS QUITE EXPENSIVE!

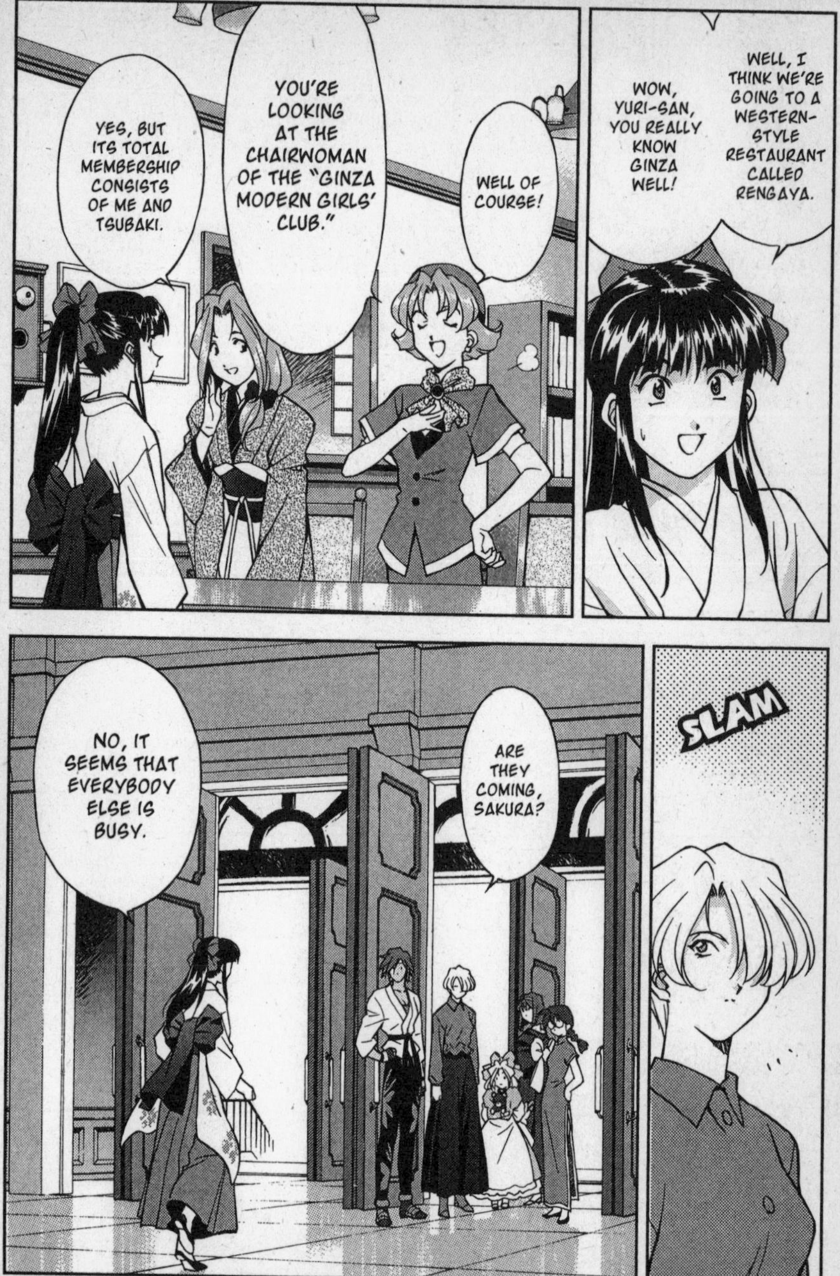
WELL, I THINK WE'RE GOING TO A WESTERN-STYLE RESTAURANT CALLED RENGAYA.
WOW, YURI-SAN, YOU REALLY KNOW GINZA WELL!
WELL OF COURSE!
YOU'RE LOOKING AT THE CHAIRWOMAN OF THE "GINZA MODERN GIRLS' CLUB."
YES, BUT ITS TOTAL MEMBERSHIP CONSISTS OF ME AND TSUBAKI.
SLAM
ARE THEY COMING, SAKURA?
NO, IT SEEMS THAT EVERYBODY ELSE IS BUSY.

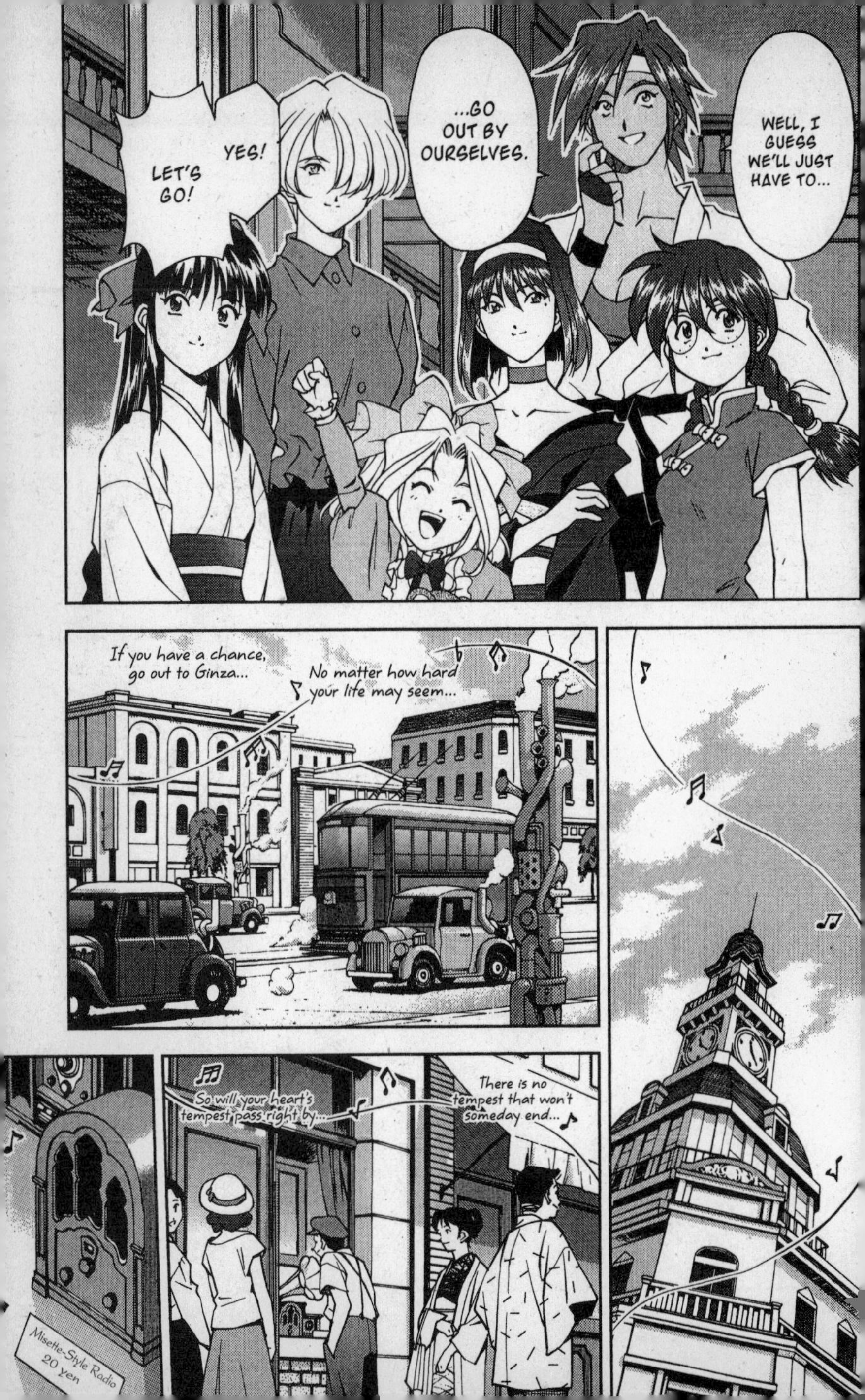
WELL, I GUESS WE'LL JUST HAVE TO...
...GO OUT BY OURSELVES.
YES!
LET'S GO!
No matter how hard your life may seem...
If you have a chance, go out to Ginza...
There is no tempest that won't someday end...
So will your heart's tempest pass right by...
Misette-Style Radio 20 yen

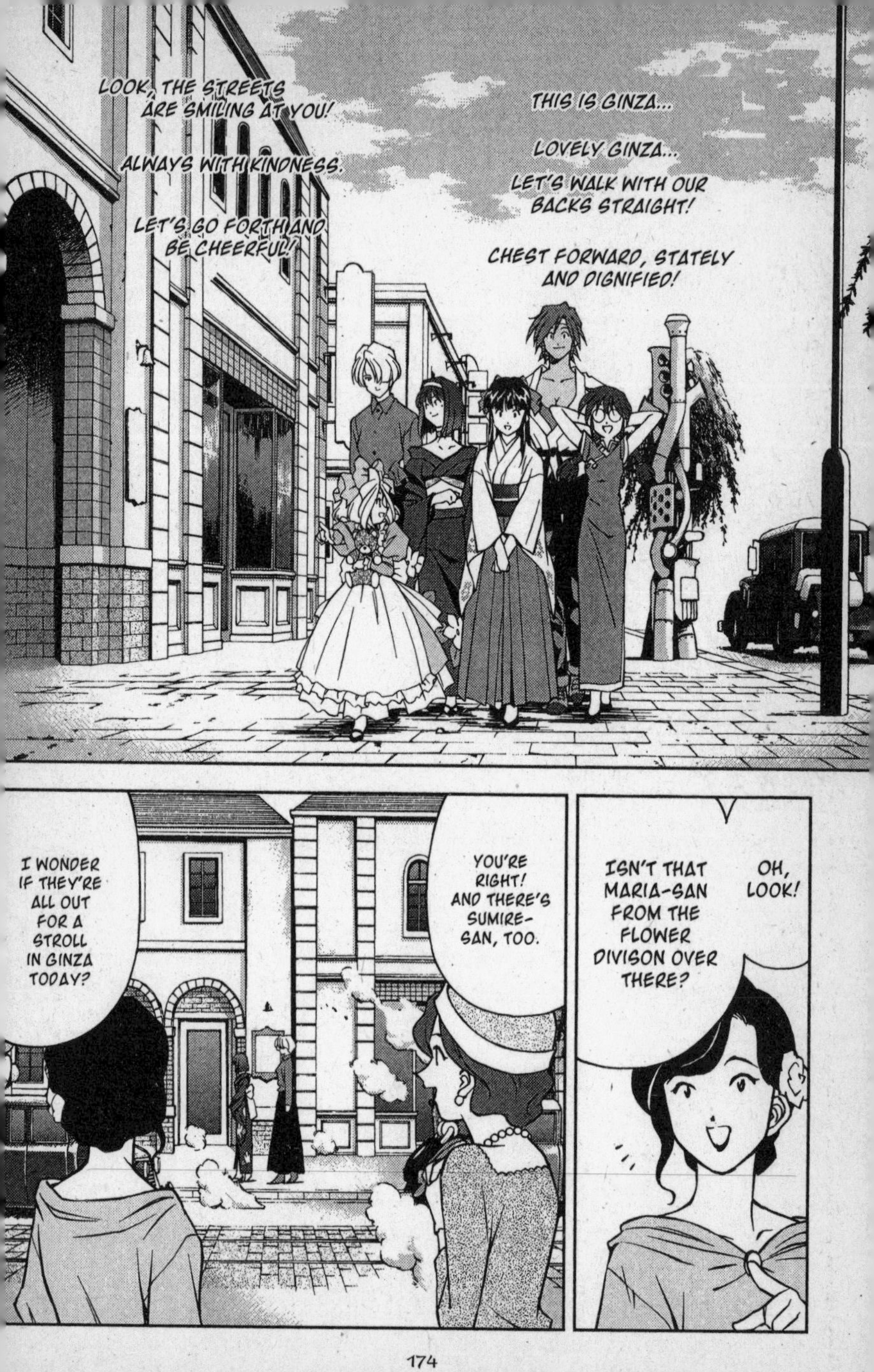
THIS IS GINZA...
LOVELY GINZA...
LET'S WALK WITH OUR BACKS STRAIGHT!
CHEST FORWARD, STATELY AND DIGNIFIED!
LOOK, THE STREETS ARE SMILING AT YOU!
ALWAYS WITH KINDNESS.
LET'S GO FORTH AND BE CHEERFUL!
OH, LOOK!
ISN'T THAT MARIA-SAN FROM THE FLOWER DIVISON OVER THERE?
YOU'RE RIGHT! AND THERE'S SUMIRE-SAN, TOO.
I WONDER IF THEY'RE ALL OUT FOR A STROLL IN GINZA TODAY?

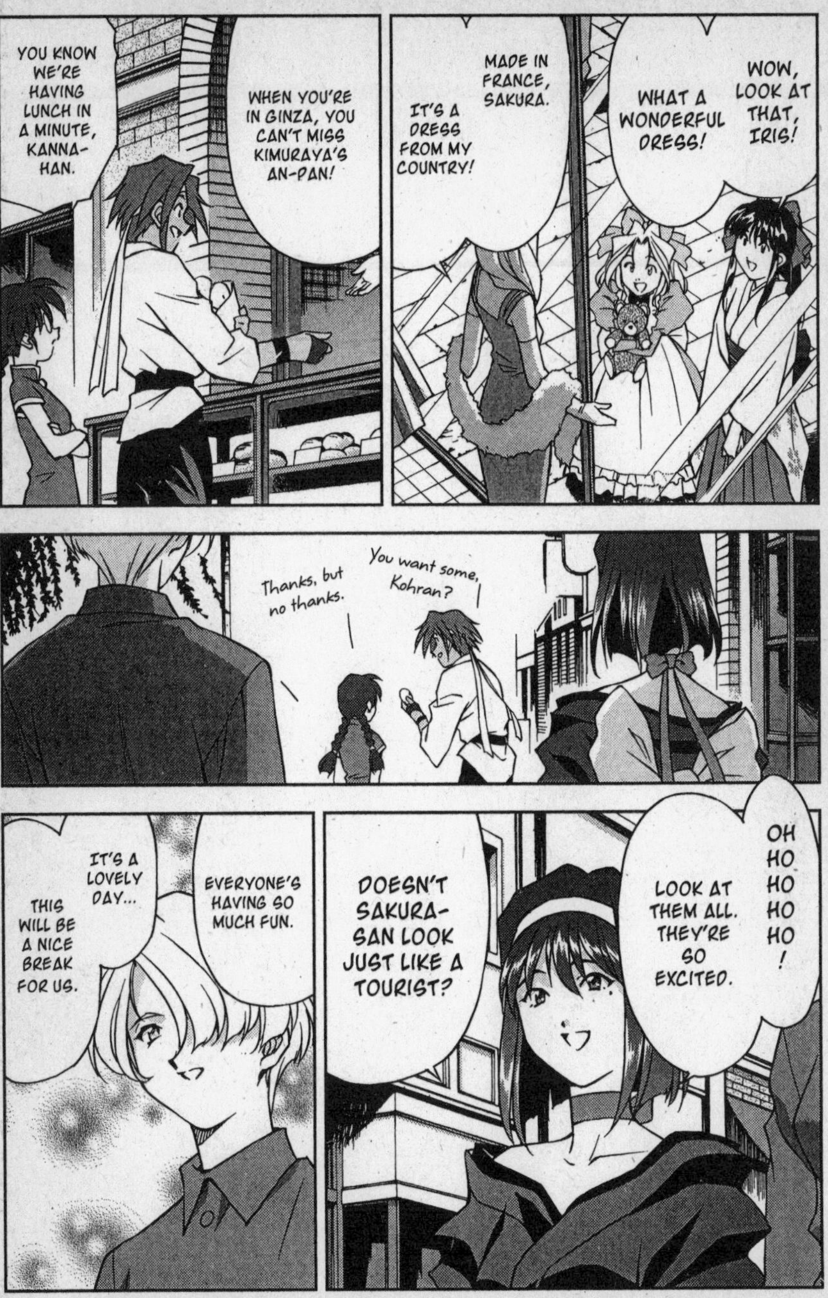
WOW, LOOK AT THAT, IRIS!
WHAT A WONDERFUL DRESS!
MADE IN FRANCE, SAKURA.
IT'S A DRESS FROM MY COUNTRY!
WHEN YOU'RE IN GINZA, YOU CAN'T MISS KIMURAYA'S AN-PAN!
YOU KNOW WE'RE HAVING LUNCH IN A MINUTE, KANNA-HAN.
You want some, Kohran?
Thanks, but no thanks.
OH HO HO HO HO!
LOOK AT THEM ALL. THEY'RE SO EXCITED.
DOESN'T SAKURA-SAN LOOK JUST LIKE A TOURIST?
EVERYONE'S HAVING SO MUCH FUN.
IT'S A LOVELY DAY...
THIS WILL BE A NICE BREAK FOR US.

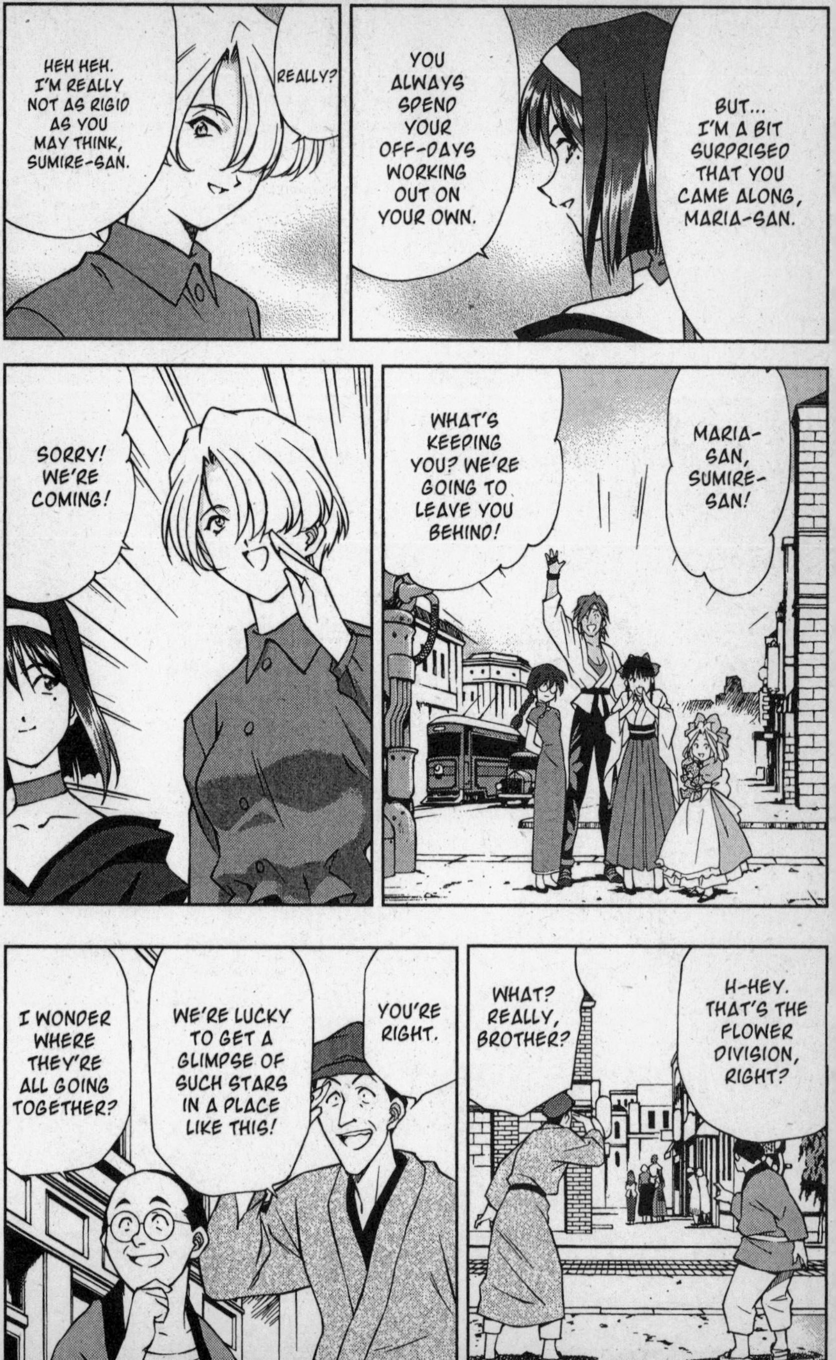
BUT... I'M A BIT SURPRISED THAT YOU CAME ALONG, MARIA-SAN.
YOU ALWAYS SPEND YOUR OFF-DAYS WORKING OUT ON YOUR OWN.
REALLY?
HEH HEH. I'M REALLY NOT AS RIGID AS YOU MAY THINK, SUMIRE-SAN.
MARIA-SAN, SUMIRE-SAN!
WHAT'S KEEPING YOU? WE'RE GOING TO LEAVE YOU BEHIND!
SORRY! WE'RE COMING!
H-HEY. THAT'S THE FLOWER DIVISION, RIGHT?
WHAT? REALLY, BROTHER?
YOU'RE RIGHT.
WE'RE LUCKY TO GET A GLIMPSE OF SUCH STARS IN A PLACE LIKE THIS!
I WONDER WHERE THEY'RE ALL GOING TOGETHER?

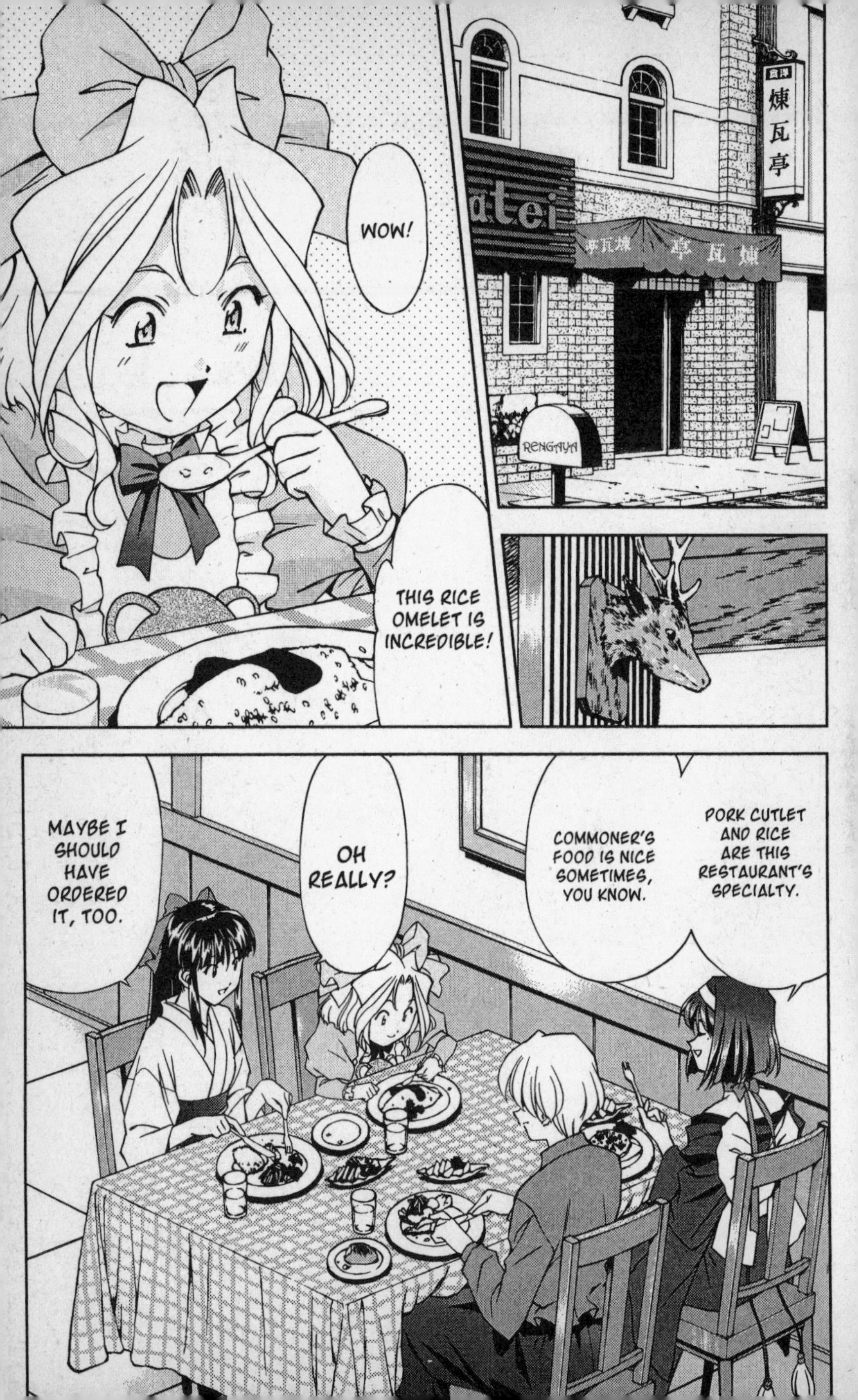
煉瓦亭
atei
RENGAYA
WOW!
THIS RICE OMELET IS INCREDIBLE!
PORK CUTLET AND RICE ARE THIS RESTAURANT'S SPECIALTY.
COMMONER'S FOOD IS NICE SOMETIMES, YOU KNOW.
OH REALLY?
MAYBE I SHOULD HAVE ORDERED IT, TOO.

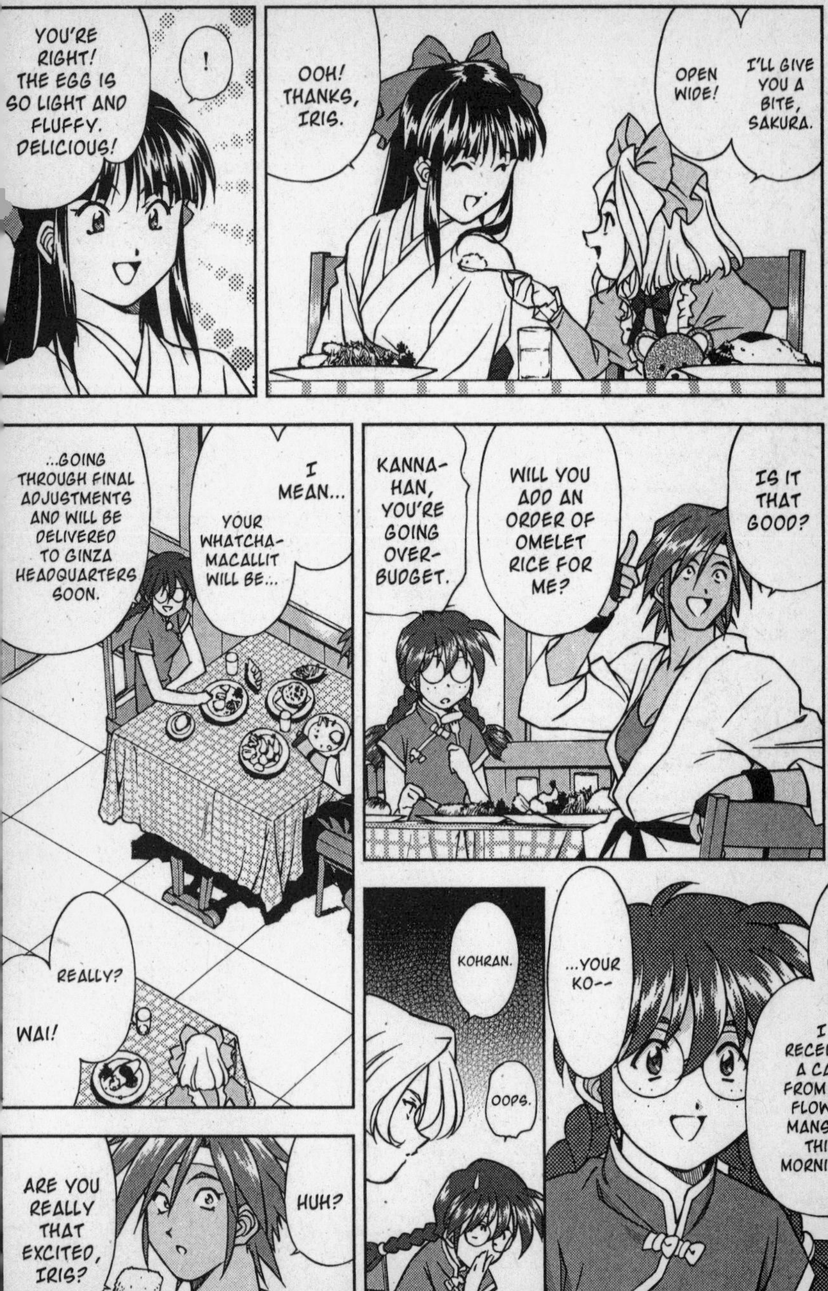

I'LL GIVE YOU A BITE, SAKURA.
OPEN WIDE!
OOH! THANKS, IRIS.
!
YOU'RE RIGHT! THE EGG IS SO LIGHT AND FLUFFY. DELICIOUS!
IS IT THAT GOOD?
WILL YOU ADD AN ORDER OF OMELET RICE FOR ME?
KANNA-HAN, YOU'RE GOING OVER-BUDGET.
BY THE WAY, IRIS.
I RECEIVED A CALL FROM THE FLOWER MANSION THIS MORNING...
...YOUR KO--
KOHRAN.
OOPS.
I MEAN...
YOUR WHATCHAMACALLIT WILL BE...
...GOING THROUGH FINAL ADJUSTMENTS AND WILL BE DELIVERED TO GINZA HEADQUARTERS SOON.
REALLY?
WAI!
HUH?
ARE YOU REALLY THAT EXCITED, IRIS?

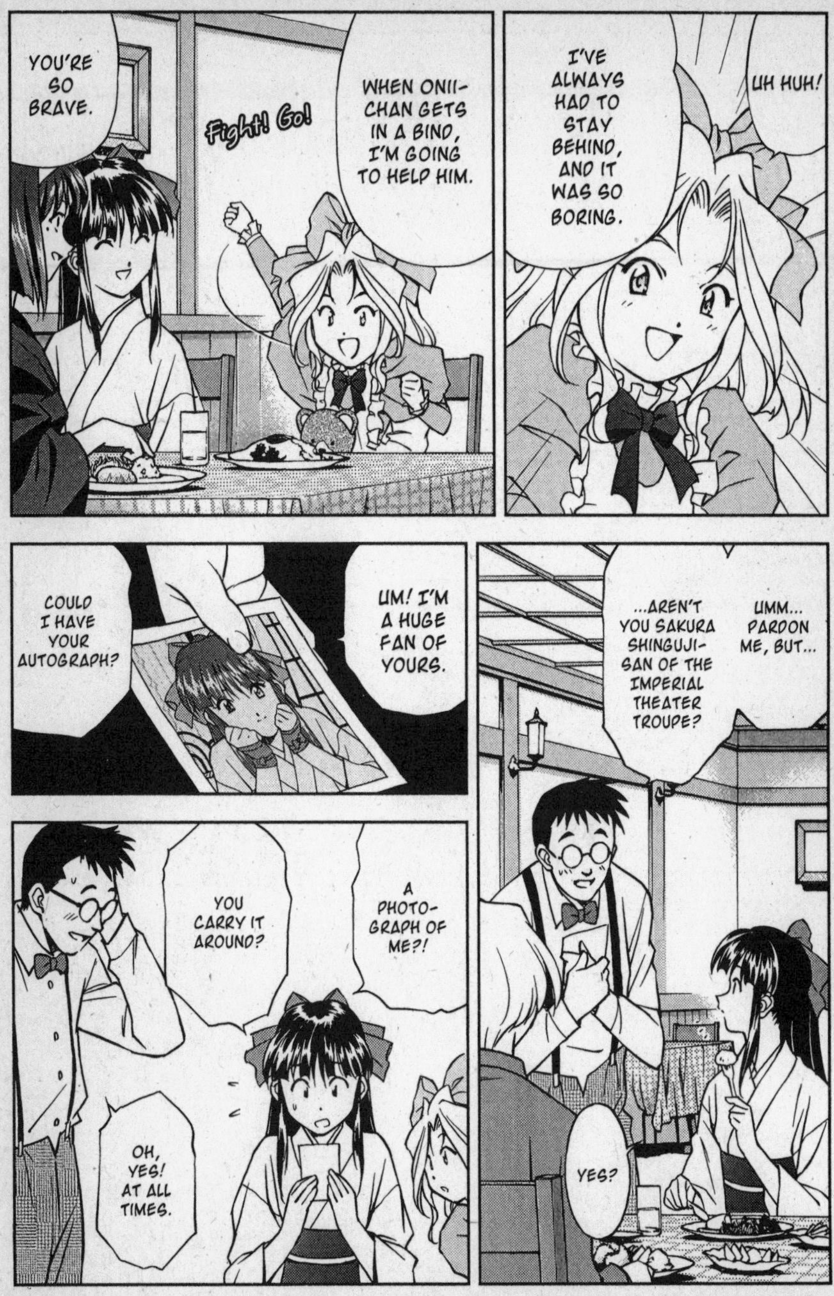
UH HUH!
I'VE ALWAYS HAD TO STAY BEHIND, AND IT WAS SO BORING.
WHEN ONII-CHAN GETS IN A BIND, I'M GOING TO HELP HIM.
Fight! Go!
YOU'RE SO BRAVE.
UMM... PARDON ME, BUT...
...AREN'T YOU SAKURA SHINGUJI-SAN OF THE IMPERIAL THEATER TROUPE?
YES?
UM! I'M A HUGE FAN OF YOURS.
COULD I HAVE YOUR AUTOGRAPH?
A PHOTOGRAPH OF ME?!
YOU CARRY IT AROUND?
OH, YES! AT ALL TIMES.

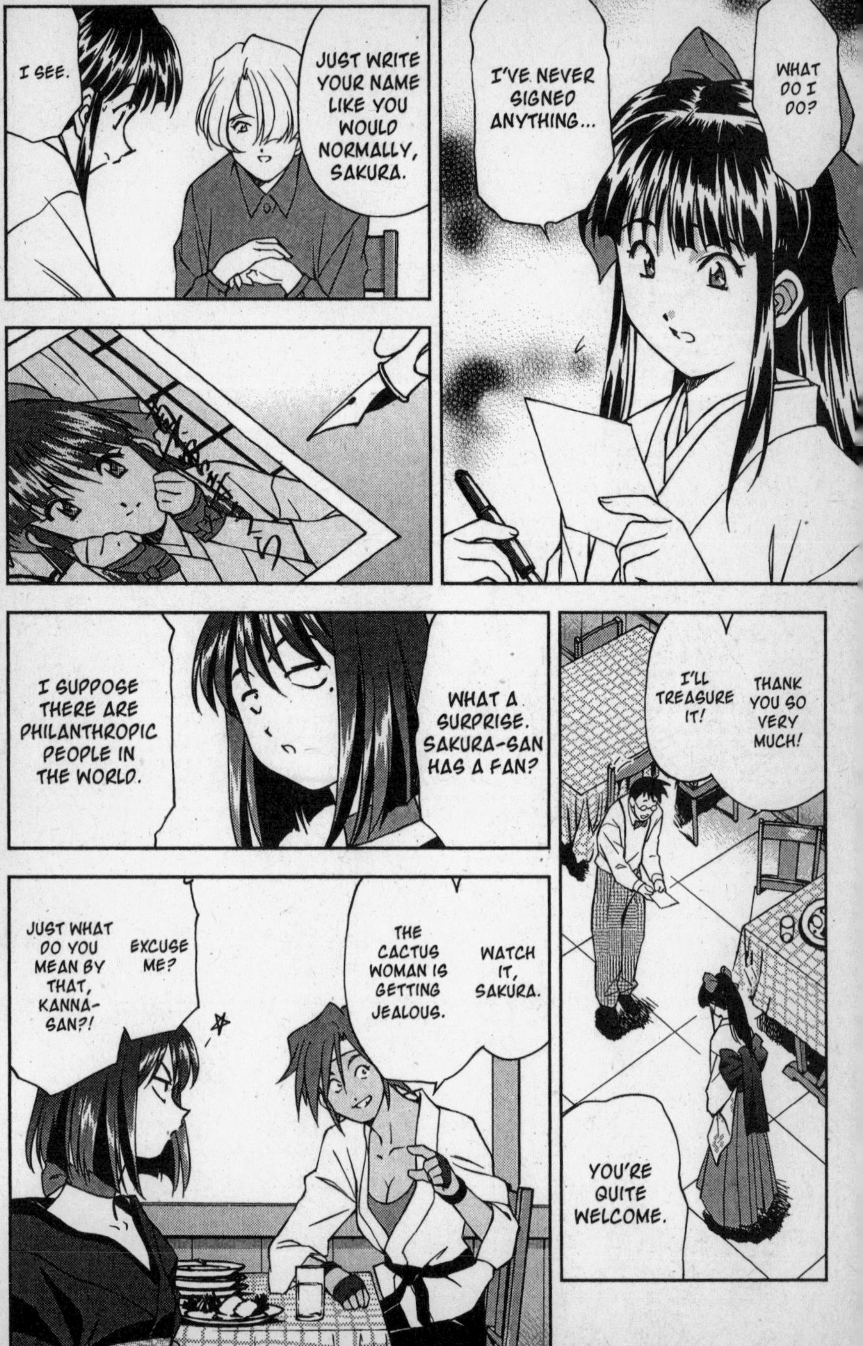
WHAT DO I DO?
I'VE NEVER SIGNED ANYTHING...
JUST WRITE YOUR NAME LIKE YOU WOULD NORMALLY, SAKURA.
I SEE.
THANK YOU SO VERY MUCH!
I'LL TREASURE IT!
YOU'RE QUITE WELCOME.
WHAT A SURPRISE. SAKURA-SAN HAS A FAN?
I SUPPOSE THERE ARE PHILANTHROPIC PEOPLE IN THE WORLD.
WATCH IT, SAKURA.
THE CACTUS WOMAN IS GETTING JEALOUS.
EXCUSE ME?
JUST WHAT DO YOU MEAN BY THAT, KANNA-SAN?!

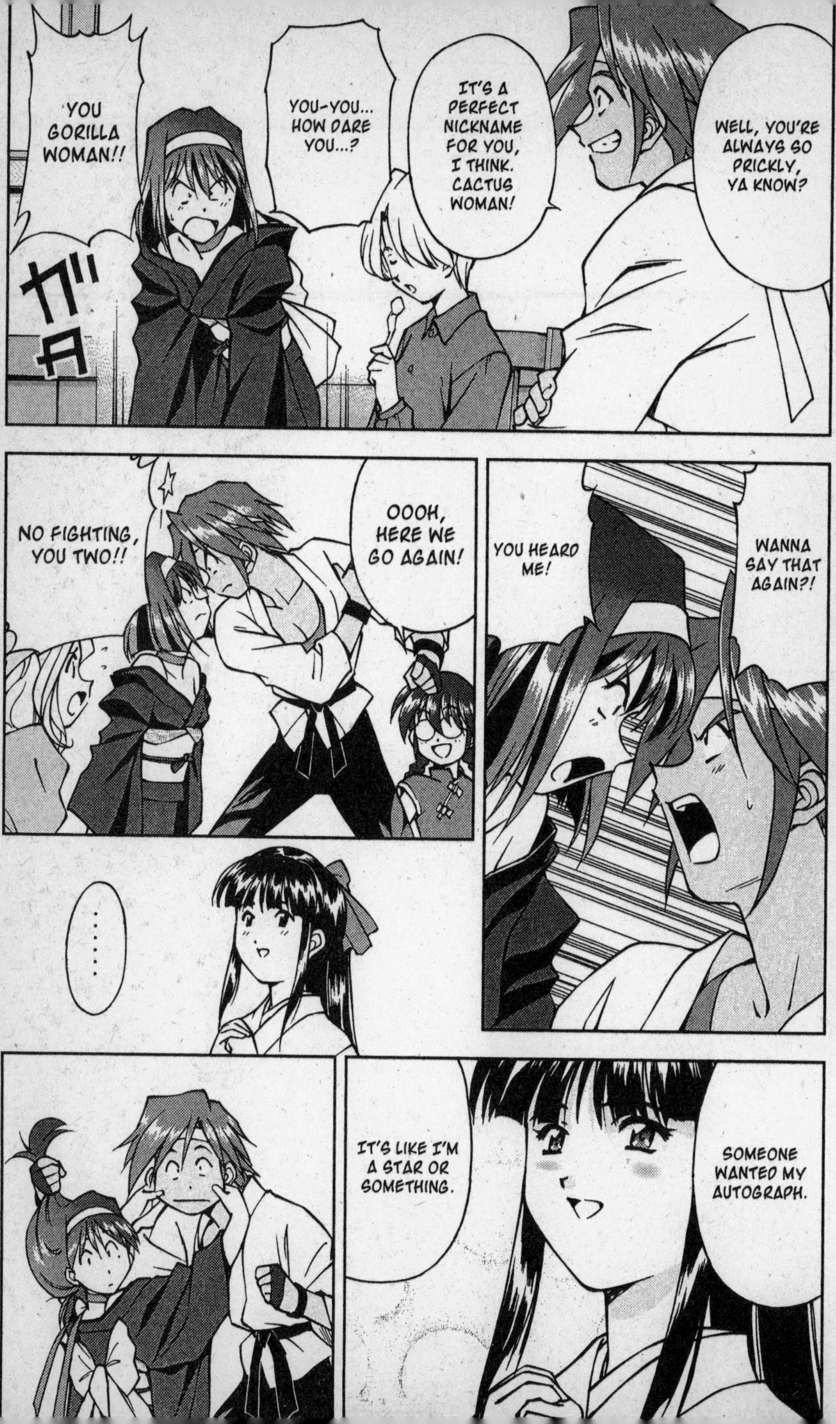
WELL, YOU'RE ALWAYS SO PRICKLY, YA KNOW?
IT'S A PERFECT NICKNAME FOR YOU, I THINK. CACTUS WOMAN!
YOU-YOU... HOW DARE YOU...?
YOU GORILLA WOMAN!!
ガタ
WANNA SAY THAT AGAIN?!
YOU HEARD ME!
OOOH, HERE WE GO AGAIN!
NO FIGHTING, YOU TWO!!
......
SOMEONE WANTED MY AUTOGRAPH.
IT'S LIKE I'M A STAR OR SOMETHING.

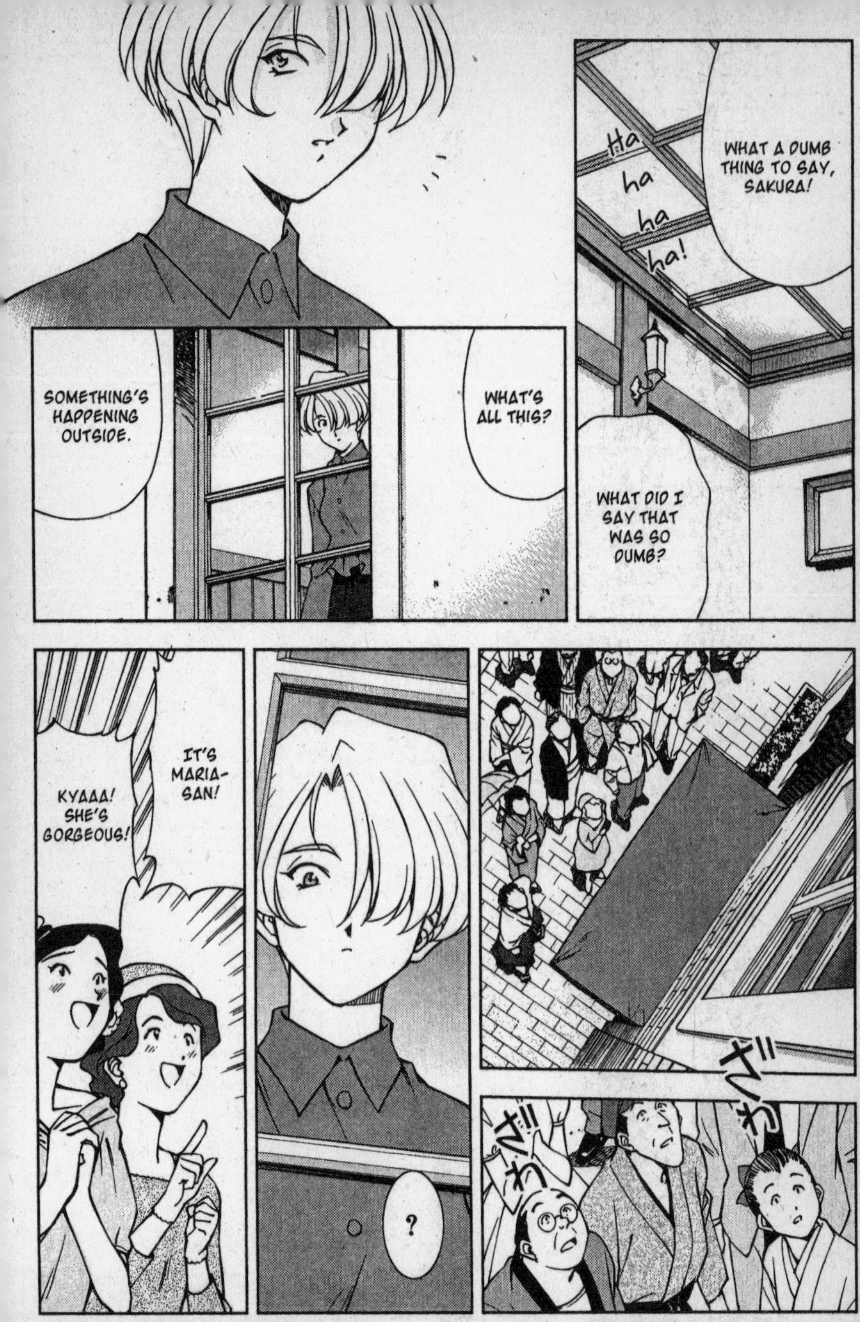
Ha ha ha ha!
WHAT A DUMB THING TO SAY, SAKURA!
WHAT DID I SAY THAT WAS SO DUMB?
WHAT'S ALL THIS?
SOMETHING'S HAPPENING OUTSIDE.
ざわ
ざわ!!
?
IT'S MARIA-SAN!
KYAAA! SHE'S GORGEOUS!

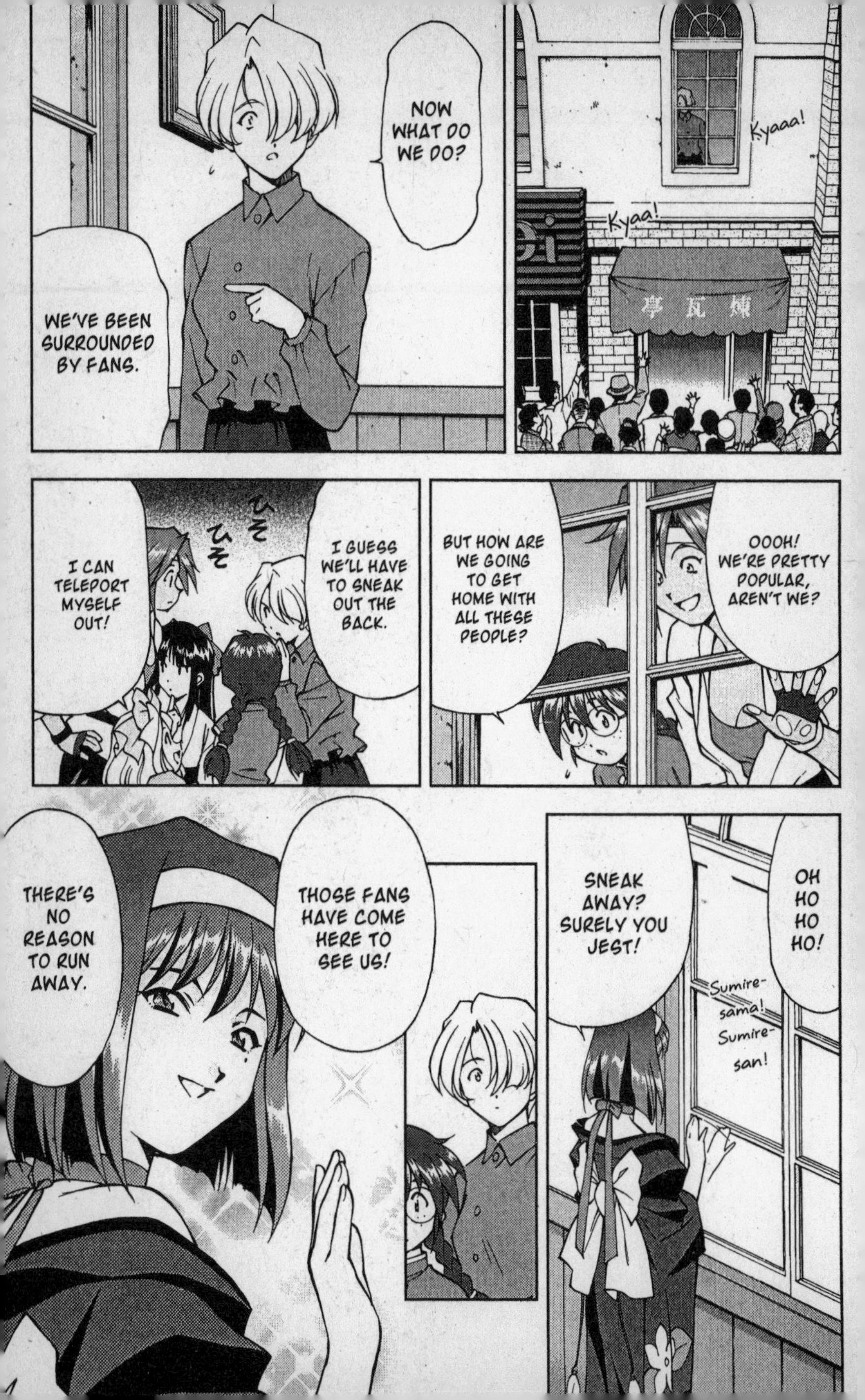
Kyaaa!
Kyaa!
NOW WHAT DO WE DO?
WE'VE BEEN SURROUNDED BY FANS.
OOOH! WE'RE PRETTY POPULAR, AREN'T WE?
BUT HOW ARE WE GOING TO GET HOME WITH ALL THESE PEOPLE?
I GUESS WE'LL HAVE TO SNEAK OUT THE BACK.
I CAN TELEPORT MYSELF OUT!
OH HO HO HO!
Sumire-sama! Sumire-san!
SNEAK AWAY? SURELY YOU JEST!
THOSE FANS HAVE COME HERE TO SEE US!
THERE'S NO REASON TO RUN AWAY.

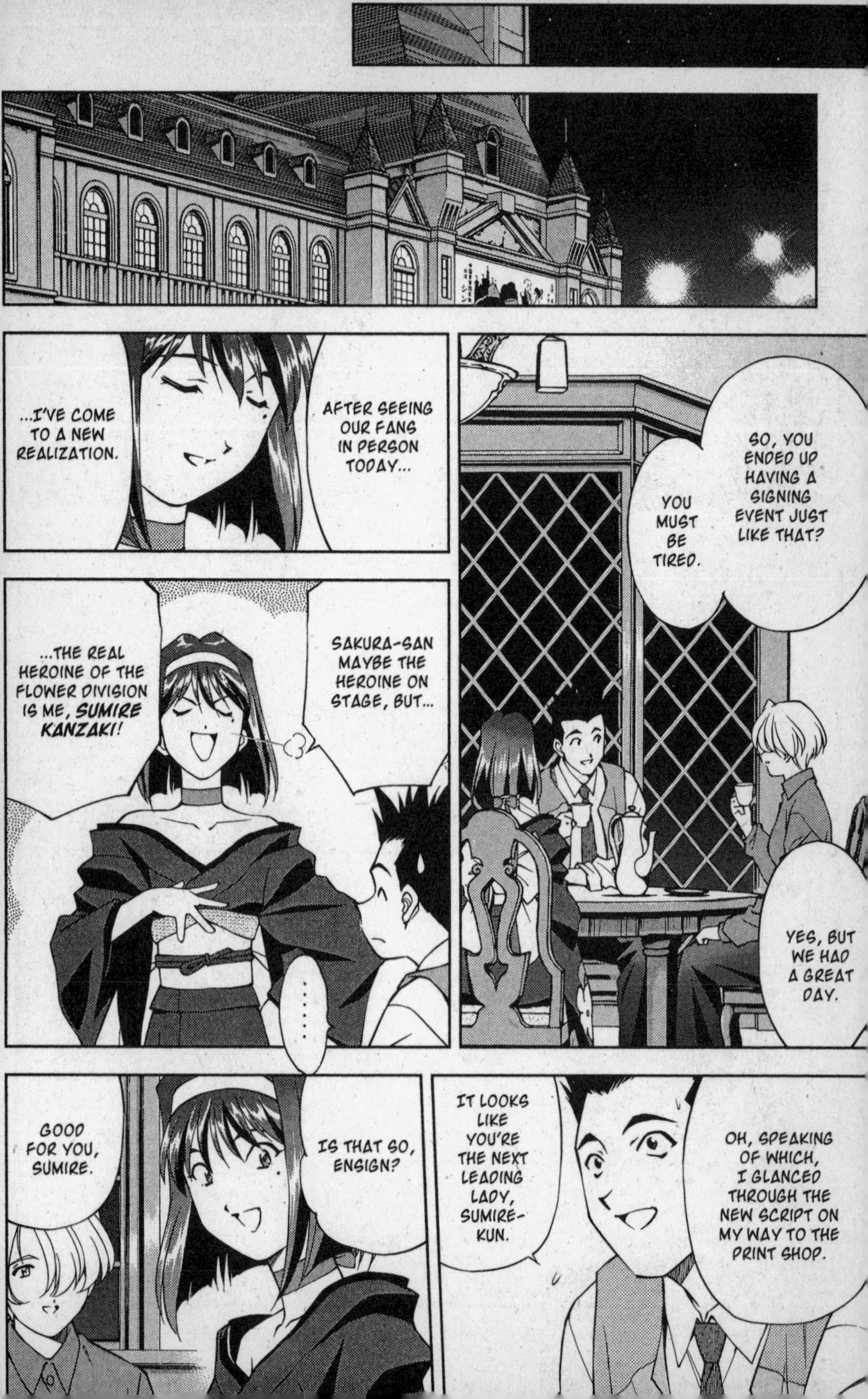
SO, YOU ENDED UP HAVING A SIGNING EVENT JUST LIKE THAT?
YOU MUST BE TIRED.
YES, BUT WE HAD A GREAT DAY.
AFTER SEEING OUR FANS IN PERSON TODAY...
...I'VE COME TO A NEW REALIZATION.
SAKURA-SAN MAYBE THE HEROINE ON STAGE, BUT...
...THE REAL HEROINE OF THE FLOWER DIVISION IS ME, **SUMIRE KANZAKI!**
......
OH, SPEAKING OF WHICH, I GLANCED THROUGH THE NEW SCRIPT ON MY WAY TO THE PRINT SHOP.
IT LOOKS LIKE YOU'RE THE NEXT LEADING LADY, SUMIRE-KUN.
IS THAT SO, ENSIGN?
GOOD FOR YOU, SUMIRE.

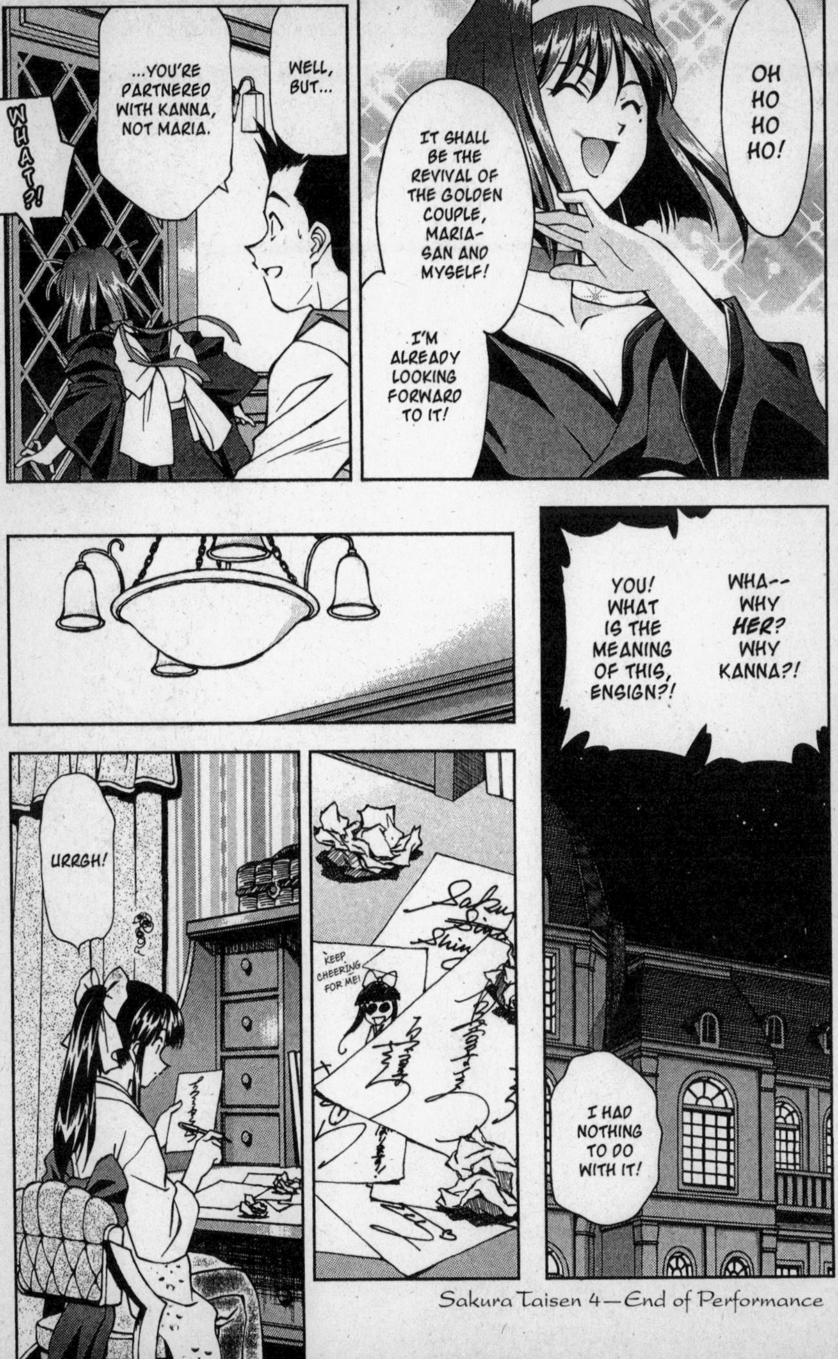
OH HO HO HO!
IT SHALL BE THE REVIVAL OF THE GOLDEN COUPLE, MARIA-SAN AND MYSELF!
I'M ALREADY LOOKING FORWARD TO IT!
WELL, BUT...
...YOU'RE PARTNERED WITH KANNA, NOT MARIA.
WHAT?!
WHA-- WHY *HER*? WHY KANNA?!
YOU! WHAT IS THE MEANING OF THIS, ENSIGN?!
I HAD NOTHING TO DO WITH IT!
KEEP CHEERING FOR ME!
URRGH!

Sakura Taisen 4—End of Performance

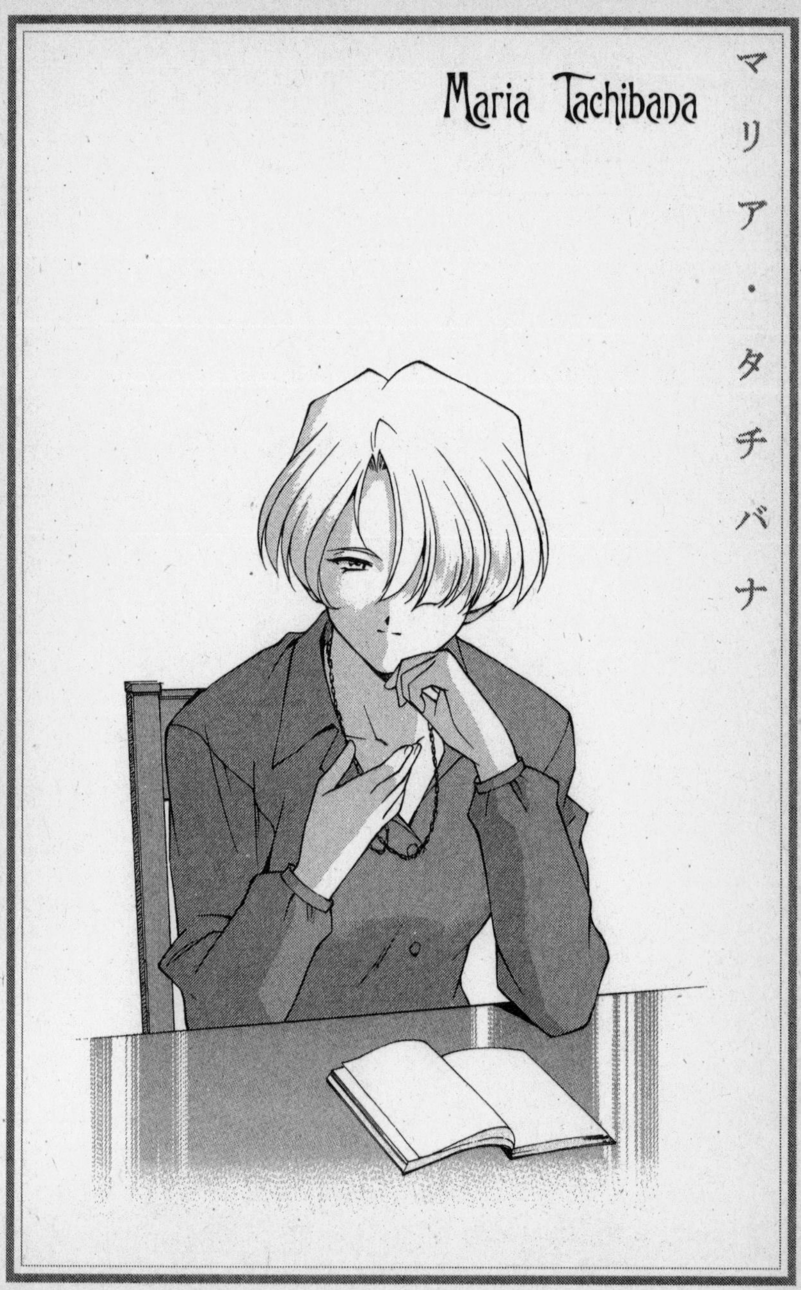
マリア・タチバナ
Maria Tachibana

Imperial Fighting Troupe

Bonus Section

Fourth Installment

The staff was arguing over whether or not to put sugar in buckwheat tea.
"Of course you add sugar!"
That's how I drank it, ever since I was a child. At least around Mukojima, in the old part of Tokyo where I grew up.
As she put sugar in the tea, the beautiful secretary Kanako said, "How nice it was that you were released."
"You know, you shouldn't be glad that I was released from Siberia, but that I was able to submit Sakura's original manga manuscript!" I slapped her with my slipper.
"I'm sorry. I'm sorry," Kanako apologized repeatedly as she spilled sugar all over the floor.
"If apologies were enough, we wouldn't need the police!" I wanted to tell her, but I restrained myself. I was proud that I had grown up so much.
But what gets me mad is that Editor-In-Charge Nomura, who sent in Kodansha's Siberian Special Correspondent. No matter how blocked a writer is, is there really a need to lock them up in Siberia? I do want to see that Reiko Isomura again, however.
While confined in snowy Siberia, I managed to write three chapters of Sakura Taisen's original manga story. While I was sharpening my trusty Mitsubishi pencil to start writing the fourth chapter, I smelled that sweet scent and lost consciousness.
It was just a short while, or maybe it was long, but when I came to, I was back in my bed at home.

I had been released from Siberia.

When I looked at my cell phone, the date showed it was June. I had been in Siberia for a month and a half.
It took one week to get back into the daily routine.
"How about a giant panel for the poster this time?" the dinosaur-brained Okumura came running with the poster and fell, unable to endure the weight of the paper.

Cherry Blossoms Flourish in Otowa

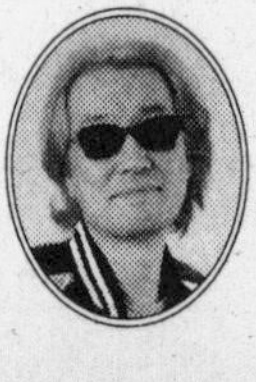

By
Ohji Hiroi

At the same time, the celebrity wanna-be Ueda yelled, "I want
to hold the next release exhibit on top of Tokyo Tower!"as he
danced around. "Mars Fighting Troupe! This is the next big thing!"
Akahori showed up pedaling his Mercedes Benz tricycle.
Behind him, the bottom feeders of RED [his company] are
playing around with cherry blossoms flakes for the stage.
They're all idiots.
But this is my daily life.
"Nomura-san is here." Kanako, the secretary came flying in. She really flies.
Apparently she was born in India and did yoga all her life, and she actually
flies about 20 cm off the ground. Whether this is actually useful is unclear.
"Show him in."
"Okay."
By the time Kanako answered, Nomura had
already made his way into the room.
"Hey, Hiroi-sensei! This is really good! This beginning
right here!" He swings the manuscript excitedly.
Whether it's good or bad, it's just following the game plot, idiot.
"I'd like you to continue in the same way, and do ten chapters this month!"
You think it's so easy, you idiot?!
As I the thought crossed my head, I said coolly, "Is
that so? But I can't. I have other work to do."
"So, you haven't had enough, huh?"
Nomura said with a grin. It was an eerie smile. His
eyes behind his glasses weren't smiling.
"What the hell do you mean?!"
The tone was a bit strong.
"Look at this." He took out some raw manuscripts
from the envelope he had been holding.
The drawings were beautiful.
"What? Already?"
I was lost for words. The manga was ready only one
week after I submitted the original story script?
"See this is Chapter One, and here is the draft of Chapter Two. These
is the lines for Chapter Three. Quick, don't you think? Masa-sensei is
great, right? That's why we need Hiroi-sensei's original story quickly."
"But isn't Magazine Z a monthly?"
"It's a monthly made at the pace of a weekly."
What the hell is that?!
"I can't write at that kind of pace!"
"Oh, oooh! You shouldn't talk to the Editor-in-Charge
at Kodansha like that. No you shouldn't!"
"Shut up, you idiot. You're a weirdo!"
"Y-you... You called me a weirdo, didn't you!?"
Nomura's face was bright red.
Crap. I called a true weirdo a weirdo.

There are things that shouldn't be uttered in this world. There are many instances in which truth should not be said.
"I'll remember this! Y-you...This is war!"
"Huh?"
So now he's talking "war"? He's way past weirdo; he's a true moron.
"Not 'huh?' It's definitely war. It's Kodansha V.S. RED."
"It's not V.S.; it's versus."
"Who cares! It's war. It's war! Ah ha ha ha!."
Nomura left, excited.
I was exhausted.
I wanted very much to see Reiko. I wanted to be confined in Siberia.

Two hours later...
Accounting Department Manager Yoshida came running in. "It's terrible!"she said.
Yoshida says that she is related to the former Japanese Prime Minister Yoshida, but that's a lie. She has a tendency to lie. Sometime ago, she said, "I'm going to marry into an Arab Royal Family,"but we never heard her mention A for Arab since. Her lies are always a transitory thing.
"The bank has ceased all transactions with us! We can't pay our workers!"
What is the fun in saying such lies? I sighed.
"It's true! What shall I do?"
"There is no way that the banks would stop all transaction."
My uncle had been the Chairman of the Board of a credit association. He was the one that referred me to my bank, and we've had a good relationship for 25 years. There is no way that they would stop all transactions on me. It's not that kind of a relationship.
"Please call the president of the bank."
"For sure?"
"How can I kid about something like this?! Transactions have been ceased! RED will be destroyed!"
I called the bank immediately. President "Nukakugi"was out. The section chief in charge of RED is out, too. I tried to ask what had happened, but the banker on the phone is not talking clearly. It's as if he's got something stuck in the back of his teeth.
"We've done some investigations on RED-sama's latest performances, and well, upper management has decided that for the time being we would like to stop all dealings..."
"What the...That's nonsense! Get me the president!"
Though normally mild-mannered, I was yelling.
The bank hung up the phone.
At that very moment I remembered Nomura's voice: "It's war. It's war~!"
"Call Kodansha NOW!!"
I was screaming with all my might.

To be continued in the next volume.

Iris and I

"I'm still a kid." I used to say. When I was a little girl, people often thought I was older than I actually was. Perhaps it was because in addition to being an honor student, I was big for my age. I was mistaken for a junior-high student when I was in second grade! I had always yearned to be the small, cute, innocent little girl. So, yes! Iris-chan, after she arrives in the Capital, is the ideal image I had as a child!! To play the ideal person, not only in the world of audio, but on stage with my entire body is my childhood dreams come true. I feel very, very lucky.

But on stage, I feel so full of gaps between me and Iris! There are so many hurdles that I simply cannot overcome!! The face, nationality, age, and above all the height! The only things we share are the voice and blood type. For that reason, I want our souls to be close together. If that happens, I believe there will be magic on stage. The magic of imagination! By reading this manga, I think Iris and I have become a little closer in spirit. And this summer in our music show, the magic will be even greater.

Kumiko Nishihara
playing
Iris

Iris, the smallest and bubbliest of the Flower Troupe finally gets her spot in the limelight, when she goes on a date with captain Ogami. A perfect date in the city goes awry when the memories of her scarred childhood rise to the surface, and she unleashes her awesome power -- almost bringing Ogami into the turmoil, as well! But with little time to set things right, Lord Satan and his minion Rasetsu storm onstage once again, ready for a fight of the century!

All this and more in Sakura Taisen, Vol. 5!

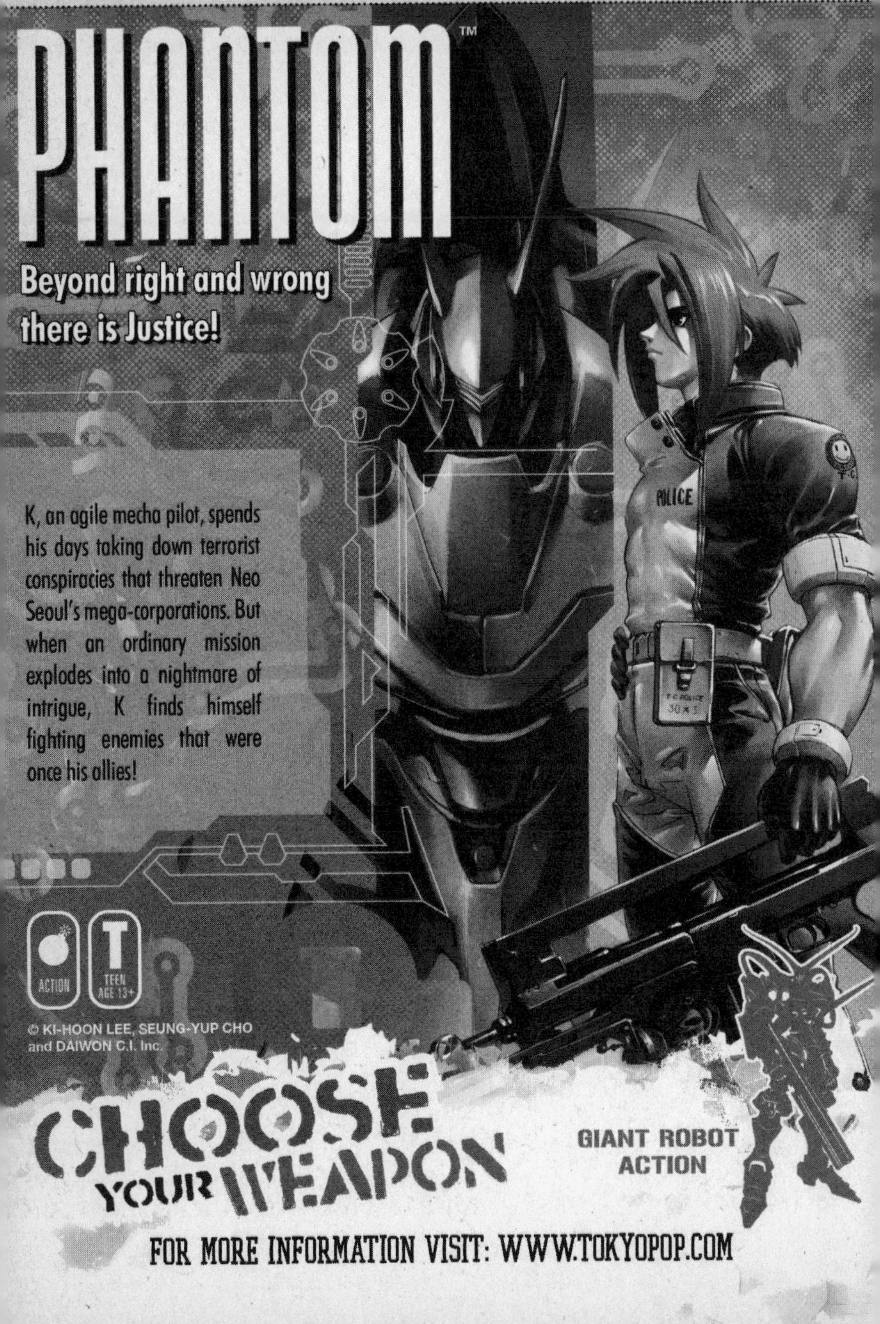
PHANTOM™
Beyond right and wrong there is Justice!
K, an agile mecha pilot, spends his days taking down terrorist conspiracies that threaten Neo Seoul's mega-corporations. But when an ordinary mission explodes into a nightmare of intrigue, K finds himself fighting enemies that were once his allies!
POLICE
ACTION
T
TEEN AGE 13+
© KI-HOON LEE, SEUNG-YUP CHO and DAIWON C.I. Inc.
CHOOSE YOUR WEAPON
GIANT ROBOT ACTION
FOR MORE INFORMATION VISIT: WWW.TOKYOPOP.COM

STOP!

This is the back of the book. You wouldn't want to spoil a great ending!

This book is printed "manga-style," in the authentic Japanese right-to-left format. Since none of the artwork has been flipped or altered, readers get to experience the story just as the creator intended. You've been asking for it, so TOKYOPOP® delivered: authentic, hot-off-the-press, and far more fun!

DIRECTIONS

If this is your first time reading manga-style, here's a quick guide to help you understand how it works.

It's easy... just start in the top right panel and follow the numbers. Have fun, and look for more 100% authentic manga from TOKYOPOP®!

1
2
3
4
5
6
7
8
9
10

漫画革命

THE MANGA REVOLUTION · LEADING · THE MANGA REVOLUTION · LEADING

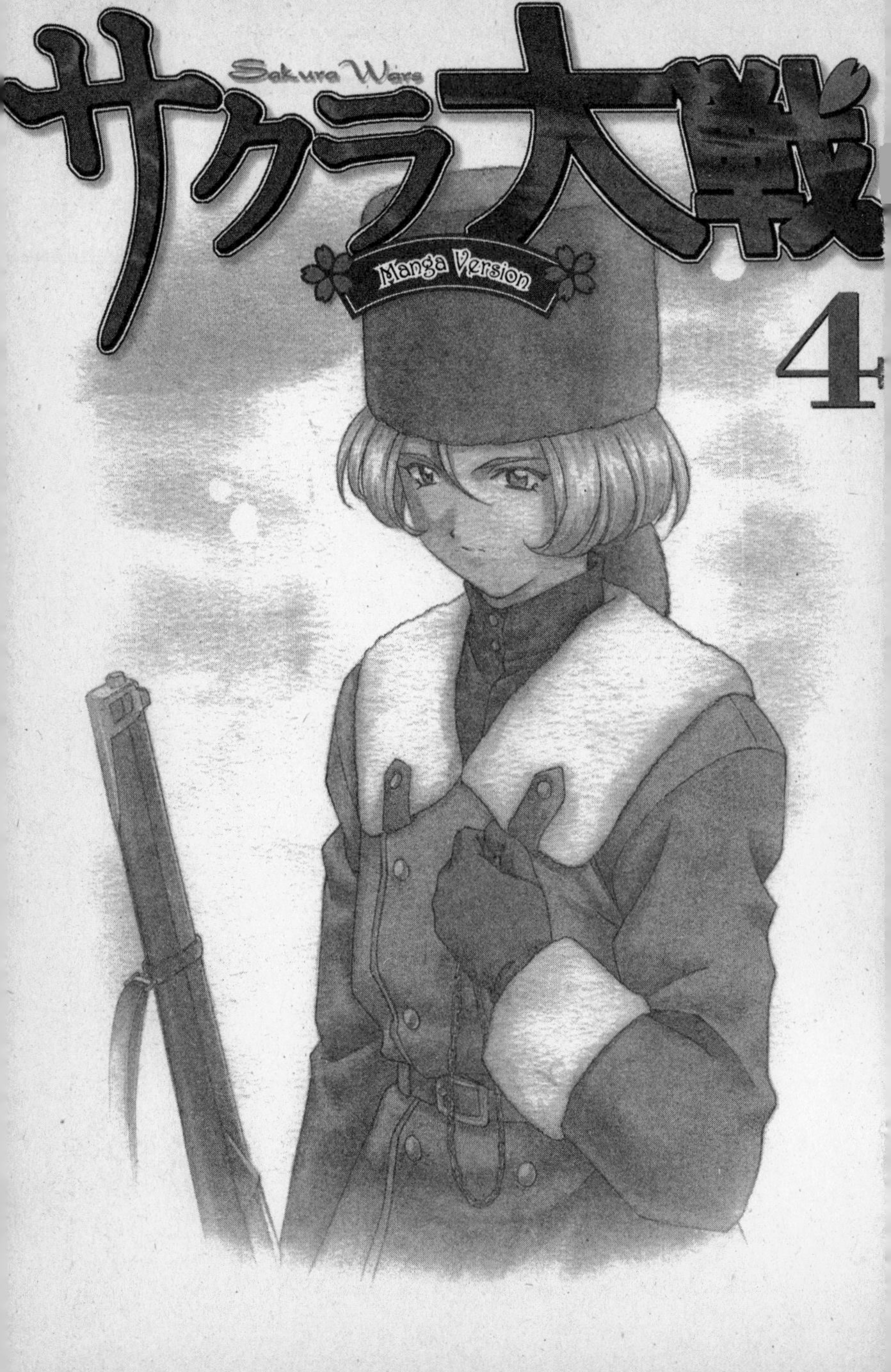
サクラ大戦
Sakura Wars
Manga Version
4

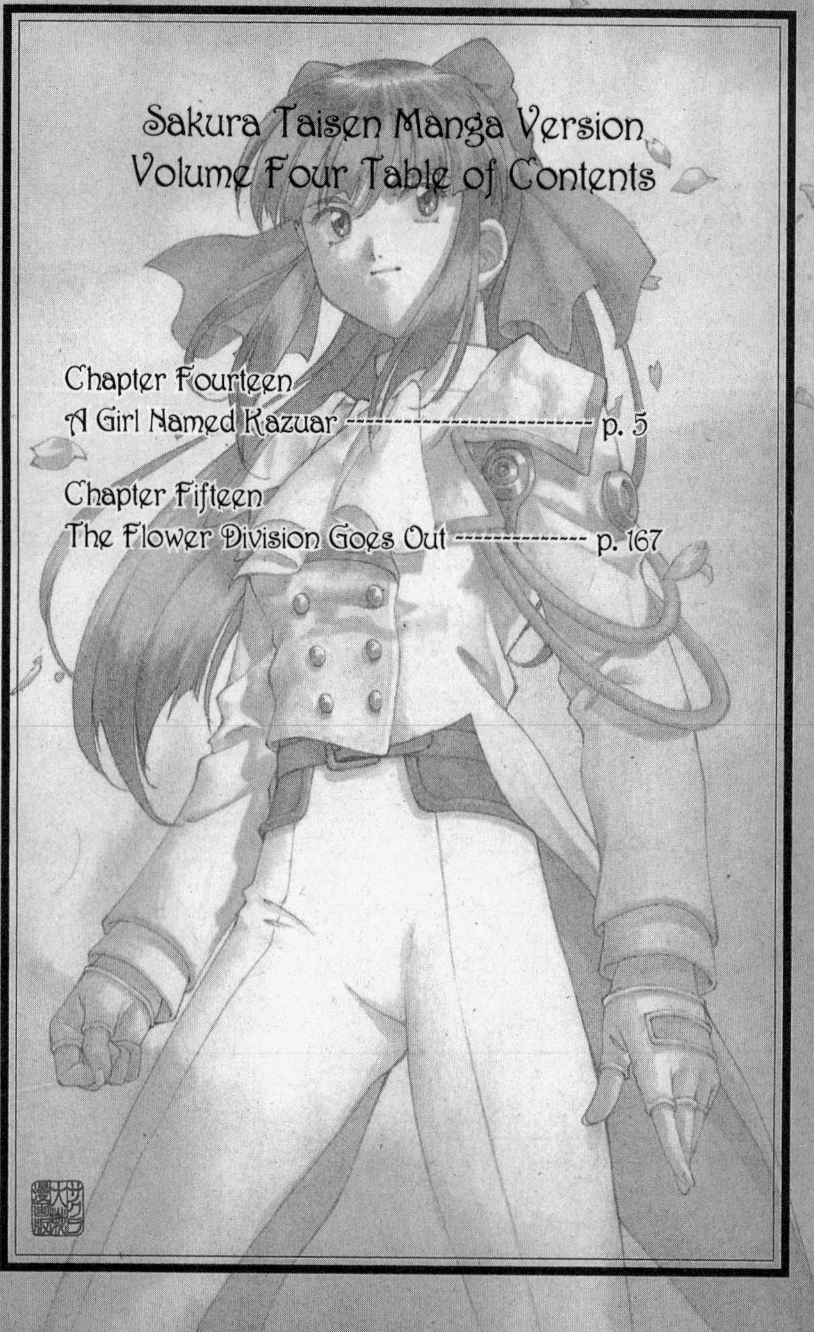

Sakura Taisen Manga Version Volume Four Table of Contents